CONIECTANEA BIBLICA · NEW TESTAMENT SERIES 7:1

Editors: Birger Gerhardsson, Lund,
Lars Hartman and Harald Riesenfeld, Uppsala

Hans Clemens Caesarius Cavallin

Life After Death

Paul's Argument
for the Resurrection of the Dead
in I Cor 15

Part I
An Enquiry into the Jewish Background

CWK GLEERUP LUND SWEDEN

Doctoral thesis at Uppsala University 1974
ISBN 91-40-03523-9

236.1
C314

188664

Parentibus
Resurrectionem Mortuorum
Et Vitam Venturi Saeculi
Expectantibus

CONTENTS

Preface

This volume forms the first part of a larger investigation concerning the Pauline argument for the resurrection of the dead in I Cor 15 and its background in Judaism, the Hellenistic culture, the Gospel tradition (above all the controversy with the Sadducees in Mk 12:18-27 parr) the *kerygma* and *didache* of the Primitive Church and Paul's first sketch of a resurrection teaching in I Th 4:13-18. For practical reasons this study of the Jewish background is published separately as my doctoral dissertation; yet I want to stress my intention to see this part of my work as a preparation for the study of I Cor 15. So the dialogue with the Jewish texts is carried on by questions formulated in a preliminary examination of I Cor 15. This is sometimes developed into an explicit comparison between the Jewish texts. But applying the results of this investigation to the study of Paul will mainly be reserved for the second volume.

Some remarks on the quotations and references used in this work may be added:

Shorter references are enclosed in the contents by parenthesis. Literature and editions of texts are listed by the author's or editor's name, (followed by the *sigla* of the periodical, dictionary, etc.), the year of publication of the edition which was used, and page numbers. The titles of the works and editions and all necessary information can be found in the bibliography. Cross-references are indicated by numbers of the chapters and subdivisions, such as 4.3.7.1.

As a rule, literature is quoted from the latest available edition in the *original* language, but in some cases, especially for works in Scandinavian languages, an English translation is used.

The latest available English translations are used as much as possible for the frequent quotations of the texts, while checking the original text, or any other text on which the English translation may be based. (This does not concern the texts preserved in the Ethiopian or Slavonic languages, for which I had to rely on Western translations and the assistance of friends.)

The preparation for the English text of this book has been read and corrected by the generous American students, who share in the life and work at *Koinonia*. The Syriac has been transliterated by the Hebrew-Aramaic alphabet, for various technical reasons.

Koinonia, Uppsala, March 5, 1974

H. C. C. Cavallin

Abbreviations of names of periodicals, dictionaries, commentaries and handbooks

AmJTh = American Journal of Theology

AnglThR = Anglican Theological Review

AP = Apocrypha and Pseudepigrapha

BASOR = Bulletin of the American School of Oriental Research

Bibl = Biblica

BiLe = Bibel und Leben

Bill = H. Strack-P. Billerbeck, Kommentar zum NT aus Talmud und Midrasch

BJRL = Bulletin of John Ryland's Library

BM = Beth Miqra

BO = Bibliotheca Orientalis

BTh = Biblical Theology

BZ = Biblische Zeitschrift

CB = Coniectanea Biblica

CBQ = Catholic Biblical Quarterly

CIJ = Corpus Inscriptionum Judaicarum, ed. J. B. Frey

Conc = Concilium

Cong Quart = Congregational Quarterly

DJD = Discoveries in the Judaean Desert

DkP = Der kleine Pauly

DTT = Dansk Teologisk Tidskrift

EncJud = Encyclopaedia Judaica

EThL = Ephemerides Theologicae Lovanienses

EThRel = Etudes Théologiques et Religieuses

EuA = Erbe und Auftrag

EvTh = Evangelische Theologie

ExpT = Expository Times

FRLANT = Forschungen zur Religion und Literatur des Alten und Neuen Testaments

GCS = Griechische Christliche Schriftsteller

GerefTT = Gereformeerde Teologische Tijdschrift

HAT = Handbuch zum Alten Testament

HistRel = Historia Religionum

HS = Hennecke, E.—Schneemelcher, W., Neutestamentliche Apokryphen

HTR = Harvard Theological Review

HUCA = Hebrew Union College Annual
IDB = Interpreter's Dictionary of the Bible
IEJ = Israel Exploration Journal
Interpr = Interpretation
Jahrb.f.jüd.Volkskunde = Jahrbuch für jüdische Volkskunde
JBL = Journal of Biblical Literature
JeBiCo = Jerome Biblical Commentary
JewEnc = Jewish Encyclopaedia
JJS = Journal of Jewish Studies
JQR = Jewish Quarterly Review
JSS = Journal of Semitic Studies
JSJud = Journal for Studies in Judaism
JThS = Journal of Theological Studies
Jud = Judaica
JüdLex = Jüdisches Lexikon
KuD = Kerygma und Dogma
KuM = Kerygma und Mythos
LondQuart = London and Holborn Quarterly
LS = Liddell, H. G—Scott, R.—Jones, H. S., A Greek-English Lexicon (1968).
LThK = Lexikon für Theologie und Kirche
NewCathEnc = New Catholic Encyclopedia
NKZ = Neue Kirchliche Zeitschrift
NovTest = Novum Testamentum
NTS = New Testament Studies
NTT = Norsk Teologisk Tidskrift
OxfClassDict = Oxford Classical Dictionary
PG = Patrologiae Cursus Completus, Series Graeca, ed. J. P. Migne.
PL = Patrologiae Cursus Completus, Series Latina, ed. J. P. Migne.
RAC = Reallexikon für Antike und Christentum
RB = Revue Biblique
REG = Revue des Etudes Grecques
REJ = Revue des Etudes Juives
RevThom = Revue Thomiste
RFIC = Rivista di Filologia e d'Istruzione Classica
RGG = Religion in Geschichte und Gegenwart
RheinMus = Rheinisches Museum
RHPR = Revue d'Histoire et de Philosophie Religieuses
RivArchCrist = Rivista di Archeologia Cristiana

RQ = Revue de Qumran

RSPT = Revue des Sciences Philosophiques et Théologiques

RSR = Recherches de Science Religieuse

RThPh = Revue de Théologie et de Philosophie

SacrMundi = Sacramentum Mundi

SBL = Society of Biblical Literature

ScJTh = Scottish Journal of Theology

SCS = Septuagint and Cognate Studies

SDB = Dictionnaire de la Bible. Supplément

SEÅ = Svensk Exegetisk Årsbok

Sem =Semitica

SemBiblEsp = Semana Biblica Espanola

SoOr = Sources Orientales

StEv = Studia Evangelica

StHRel = Studies in the History of Religions

StTh = Studia Theologica

SupplVT = Supplements to Vetus Testamentum

TBNT = Theologisches Begriffslexikon zum Neuen Testament

TdschrTeol = Tijdschrift voor Teologie

ThLZ = Theologische Literaturzeitung

ThQ = Theologische Quartalschrift

ThRu = Theologische Rundschau

ThZ = Theologische Zeitschrift

TU = Texte und Untersuchungen

TWNT = Theologisches Wörterbuch zum Neuen Testament

VD = Verbum Domini

VigChrist = Vigiliae Christianae

VT = Vetus Testamentum

WKTNJb = Werkgemeenschap van Katholieke Theologen en Nederland
    Jaarboek

WZKM = Wiener Zeitschrift für die Kunde des Morgenlandes

ZAW = Zeitschrift für die Alttestamentliche Wissenschaft

ZkTh = Zeitschrift für katholische Theologie

ZNW = Zeitschrift für die Neutestamentliche Wissenschaft

ZThK = Zeitschrift für Theologie und Kirche

ZWissTh = Zeitschrift für Wissenschaftliche Theologie

Other abbreviations

Beside those which are supposed to be understood by every reader, and the *sigla* of the texts, which are given in the Index of passages, the following may be listed:

AT = Altes Testament, Ancien Testament
cj = conjecture
comm. = commentary
diss. = dissertation
ed. = edition, edited by, editor
ET = English Translation
Eth. = Ethiopian (version)
Gr. = Greek (version)
In hon. = Publication in honour of . . . .(*Festschrift*)
In mem. = Publication in memory of . . .
j = jerushalmi, for tractate in the Palestinian Talmud
LXX = Septuagint
M = Mishnah, for tractate in Mishnah
midr = midrash
MS(S) = Manuscript(s)
n = foot-note
NEB = New English Bible
NT = New Testament, Neues Testament, Nouveau Testament etc.
OT = Old Testament
ref. = reference
s.v. = *sub voce,* an article in a dictionary on the term which is discussed
T = Tosefta, for tractate in Tosefta
Tg = Targum

1. Introductory remarks

Rudolph Bultmann says:

> [Paul] holds fast to the traditional Jewish-Christian teaching of *the resurrection of the dead* (Bultmann's italics) and in so doing he also retains the apocalyptic expectation of the last judgment and of the cosmic drama which will end the old world ... (NT Theology. ET 1955, 346).

Apart from the fact that it is a judgment on Pauline exegesis, this statement is apparently built upon several presuppositions, namely that

1) there is a *primitive Christian* (Hellenistic or Palestinian) tradition on the resurrection of the dead (German original,[5] 1965, 347, says "*urchristliche ...*"),

2) "the traditional *Jewish* teaching of the resurrection of the dead" existed at the time of Paul,

3) such a tradition would surely be combined with ideas about the last judgment and the final cosmic drama.

It is hardly a daring assertion to say that all of these suppositions can be questioned and need to be questioned. Precisely the fact that Bultmann, as well as many others, does not seem to do so is the chief argument for the need of a critical re-examination of the grounds and sources of the suppositions. The first supposition will be dealt with in the second volume of this work (cf. the Preface), the second is treated in this present volume, whereas the third is to be examined in the study of both the Jewish and the Christian sources, i.e., throughout the pages of both volumes.

1.1 Background

The contrast between "the Hellenistic" or "Greek doctrine of the immortality of the soul" and "the Jewish teaching about the resurrection of the body"[1] is a common point of departure for modern treatises on the Christian view of life after death. This is often found in various types of theological dictionaries[2] and more or less popular theological books and articles which address this theme[3]. Sometimes this contrast is complemented with another which distinguishes the attitudes of Palestinian Judaism (denoting that which is really meant by "Jewish") from those of "Hellenistic Judaism" (i.e. representatives of the Greek-speaking diaspora). The genuine Jewish teaching is based on Palestinian attitudes, whereas the Hellenistic Jewish writings tend to accept the Greek doctrine about the immortality of the soul[4]. These distinctions can be used in various ways by different schools of thought and in changing contexts. In works of Biblical theology, where the hermeneutic problems are more or less left aside, the "Hebrew", "Biblical" or "Jewish" anthropology of "the whole man", as opposed to the "Greek" body-soul dichotomy, forms the means of interpreting Pauline teaching on the resurrection of the dead. It is held that Paul or the other Early Christian writers could not possibly have accepted or even understood any other idea of life after death than that which included the whole man, body and soul, i.e., the resurrection of the body, simply because they were Jews. This resurrection faith, based on Hebrew anthropology, will then be stated as *the* NT doctrine, and *the* genuine Christian approach to the question of after-life, as opposed to the Greek idea of the immortality of the soul. The name of O. Cullmann would perhaps be the first one mentioned among the representatives of this attitude[5].

1.1.1

Basically, the same assumption of a Jewish doctrine of the resurrection may be used in quite a different manner among scholars, where the hermeneutic problem, classically formulated in R. Bultmann's programm of "demythologizing" the NT[6], stands in the centre of interest. This doctrine is considered to be part of a mythological image of the world (*Weltanschauung*) which formed a frame of reference within which the Gospel about the liberation from death was first proclaimed. Accordingly, the early Christians expressed the idea of a defeat of death with the help of the Jewish eschatological myth of the resurrection of the body. But, it is the task of the exegete to go beyond the external mythological forms of expression in order to uncover the central motifs and intentions themselves and therefore understand that which the original author(s) intended to say in his (their) mythological formulations[7]. The statement of the resurrection of Jesus must be interpreted in the same way[8].

1.1.2

Yet, there is another way of using the concept of "the Jewish doctrine of the resurrection": Paul's teaching, especially in I Cor 15[9], is opposed to a materialistic and naive view of the resurrection, which would have been represented by the Jews[10]. Undoubtedly there are Jewish descriptions of the eschatological meal or the overwhelming fruitfulness of the life to come[11]. The argument of Mk 12:18-27 parr and I Cor 15:35 ff. might seem to be directed against such materialistic ideas about post-resurrection life.

1.1.3

K. Schubert (BZ 6, 1962, 177-214) espouses a different view on the relation between Jewish and Hellenistic anthropology and eschatology which forms the background of Paul. Greek terminology and anthropology influenced Jewish ideas about life after death in the transitional period from the second century BC until the first century AD in such a way that a synthesis was created. This combined elements of the old Oriental (including OT) traditions with those of a Greek origin. This evolution corresponds to the general pattern of Hellenistic religion syncretism. The growing assimilation between Jewish and Greek is the background and presupposition of both Christianity and Rabbinic Judaism, here as elsewhere[12].

16

1.2 Earlier research

Thus, the pre-supposed Jewish doctrine of the resurrection plays a rather important role in the interpretation of central NT texts and themes. Yet it has long been said here and there that there is no such "Jewish doctrine", since the variations of eschatological ideas in all forms of Judaism of the considered period are much more comprehensive than the simple distinction of Hellenistic and Palestinian Judaism[13]. This pluralism is already clearly seen by several earlier descriptions of Jewish eschatology. Among these I could mention the text-books of W. Bousset-H. Gressmann[14], G. F. Moore[15], J. Bonsirven[16], K. Schubert[17] and others[18], the relevant excurses in the commentary of P. Billerbeck[19], as well as a number of monographs, e.g., by R. H. Charles (1913), P. Volz (1934), J. B. Frey[20], C. V. Pilcher (1940), A. T. Nikolainen (1944-46), K. Schubert[21], P. Hoffmann (1966), and recently G. W. E. Nickelsburg (1972) and G. Stemberger (1972).

Recent discussions of the theme "resurrection of Jesus" also include a section on Jewish beliefs about the resurrection of the dead, such as the books of U. Wilckens (1970, 101-144), B. Rigaux (1973, 3-22), and others[22]. These and other scholars have analyzed and synthetized almost all the texts and facts that might be of any importance. Thus, there is no lack of surveys of Jewish eschatology and ideas about resurrection and immortality. Yet, especially from the angle of approach in this work, the existing literature could be criticized or completed with the following points:

1.2.1

The danger of generalization and harmonization in order to find some doctrinal system has not always been avoided. For example, in the recent book by Stemberger (1972), where the Hellenization of Palestinian Judaism is rightly stressed with M. Hengel and others[24], the Biblical/Jewish anthropology of "the whole man" is used as the point of departure and the focus of the investigation in a way that threatens a careful analysis of each text and a consciousness of the variations and the vagueness of all these images used to convey the concept of continued or renewed life after death[25].

1.2.2

Some of the older books (e.g., Volz, 1934), where the authors rightly try to present all the material in its variety, end up with such an overwhelming richness of information that the readers may feel completely lost.

1.2.3

Several (and especially more recent) monographs, which try to treat the individual texts very carefully, limit themselves to certain types of texts and to questions of form analysis in a way which does not serve the present purpose, namely to elucidate the background of Pauline thinking. It seems to the present author that Nickelsburg's thesis (1972) and the work of Stemberger (1972), to some extent, are cases in point.

1.2.4

There is a need to relate the results which have been achieved in earlier research to Paul's argument on the resurrection of the dead more directly than in previous works.

1.3 Method

In order to meet these needs and complete the literature for the special purpose of this present investigation (cf. the preface), I shall try to apply the following methods in my work with the material:

1.3.1

Each text is treated in its own context without systematization, if the different passages do not clearly permit comparisons and the establishment of relations with each other. Before each discussion the ET of the actual text is given so that the argument can adhere to the text as strictly as possible. In this way it should be easier to follow the application of the other methods used.

1.3.2

A survey is given in the form of a quasi-statistical table in order to summarize the results (with all their possible vagueness) and to make them easily available to the readers. This is done with all reservation for the dangers of using statistics in such a context as this.

1.3.3

A wide selection of texts is offered for analysis, texts that belong to all the types of Judaism in the period between circa 167 BC (when Dn 12 was written) and AD 90-110, i.e., when the separation between Church and Synagogue was definite, with the re-establishment of Judaism under the leadership of the Academy of Jabneh. There may be older ideas in traditions and texts later than this date, but their relevance as background material for the theology of Paul can hardly be proved.

1.3.4

Provoked by the previous pre-examination of I Cor 15 and other Pauline and NT texts, the following questions are formulated and are individually addressed to each of the Jewish passages. **(A)** Does the text speak about life after death, and if so **(B)** about the resurrection of the body, immortality of the soul or other alternatives, as **(C)** a return to earthly life or a glorified heavenly existence? **(D)** When does new life after death begin and how is it related to final judgment? The following paragraphs (1.3.4.1-4) should explain the formulation of these questions:

1.3.4.1

(A) The problem which Paul tries to solve in I Th 4 and I Cor 15 concerns the life *after death* of those in the congregations who have died, but not eternal life in general[26]. The following discussion of the different texts will show the necessity for this distinction. Thus the Deuteronomic promise of "life" to all who keep the commandments of Yahweh does not mean "life after death" (cf. 2.1.2). Likewise, it is not clear whether the Qumran texts, which explicitly promised eternal life to the righteous, included a consciousness of life after death (3.5). The Corinthian Christians (or some of them), 53-54 AD, seem to have believed in eternal life for the Christians without any intervening death. So the first question will obviously be: Does the passage under investigation really speak about *life after death?*

1.3.4.2

(B) Both I Th 4 and I Cor 15 speak about life after death, as if there were no other ways of conceiving this new existence than life in a resurrected body. This must be related to Jewish ideas about the mode of *post mortem* life. Would they explain why there is no alternative to the resurrection of the body given or considered by Paul? If the first question is answered affirmatively, our second question addressed to the passages is as follows: Does the text describe the *resurrection* of the body *or* rather the *immortality* of the soul—or yet offer another possibility?

1.3.4.3

(C) Whatever the answer would be, a further question will throw light on the background of Pauline thinking: When the righteous and their fate after death are considered, are they pictured in any way as being glorified in heavenly or angelic splendour? Moreover, if the answer to the preceding question **(B)** is "resurrection of the body", is this seen as a mere return to earthly life, or will the resurrected body be transformed (as according to I Cor 15:35 ff.)?

1.3.4.4

(D) In I Th 4 and I Cor 15 the resurrection occurs immediately at the *parousia* of the Lord. Of course, anything quite corresponding to the *parousia* is lacking in any Jewish text. Yet the resurrection may often be closely knit to the Last Judgment, as a theophany or generally to the great universal revolution between this present age and the Age to Come. Sometimes, however, judgment is rendered immediately upon death—and then the idea of a resurrection may fade away, being replaced by some spiritualized notion about an incorporeal existence after death.

1.3.4.4

So, closely connected with question **(B)** our fourth theme of consideration is: *When* does resurrection occur and/or the immortal life begin? How is this "date" related to ideas about a final judgment?

1.3.4.5

I am fully aware of the fact that these questions represent only a small section of all the problems which are uncovered through the study of Jewish ideas about after-life in the period under consideration. For example, one might ask about the universality of the resurrection or the immortality which is mentioned. Does it concern all men, both righteous and wicked, or only the righteous, or maybe only the righteous Israelites or only the members of the elected remnant? It can further be asked: Who is the agent of the resurrection? How is the argument for the introduction of these ideas developed? I hope to be able to return to such an analysis, since I have already collected some material and have done some preparatory work. But a study of that kind would not be possible within the framework of this present book—and would not aid in clarifying Pauline thinking and argumentation in the texts under consideration.

[1] For the conviction that the Jews in NT times were completely dominated by the resurrection faith cf e.g. the following formulations:
Der Wiederkunftsgedanke war wie für alle aus dem Judentum hervorgegangenen Christen so auch für Paulus eine psychologische Notwendigkeit. Dasselbe wird man von der Auferstehung sagen dürfen. (E. Teichmann, 1896, 33.)

As a Jew, Paul was unable to imagine personal existence except in terms of a body . . . (H. M Shires, 1966, 98.)

For similar expressions about "*the* Jewish doctrine" on the resurrection cf. e.g. U. Wilckens (1966) 54 f.; G. Kegel (1970) 19, 119 (resurrection of the dead is part of the "Weltanschauung" of Jews in the days of Jesus and Paul); F. Mussner, Conc 6 (1970) 693; B.v. Iersel, *ibid.* 701; X. Léon-Dufour (1971 44, 47-49; G. Stemberger (1972) 2, 115.

[2] E.g. E. Lohse, RGG I (1957) 694 f.; L. L. Morris, New Bible Dictionary (1962) 1086; J. Schmid SacrMundi V (ET 1970) 333-340; S. B. Marrow, NewCathEnc XII (1968) 419 f.; H. M. McElwain. *ibid.* 425 ("the then Jewish doctrine on the resurrection").

[3] E.g. among probably innumerable others: O. Cullmann, EThRel 18 (1943) 3; *id.* (1954, 1965) 9-53 *id.* ThZ 12 (1956) 126-156; *id.* Immortality and Resurrection (1965) 20-25; A. T. Nikolainen I (1944 164 (speaking about "Old Testament" rather than of "Jewish" when he labels the resurrection doctrine—cf. 63-77 for the immortality of the soul among the Greeks); E. Stauffer (ET 1955) 217 Bultmann (1965) 80 (cf. 77 on the Jewish apocalyptic background), 347, where he prefers the term "Gnostic myth" to "the Hellenistic idea of immortality"—cf. also *id.* in KuM I (1941, 1967) 26, 30; X Léon-Dufour (1969) 161 f.; Conc 6 (1970) 733-735 (with a survey of some important contributions to the recent discussion); H. A. Williams (1972) 21-25. Cf. also A. Ahlbrecht (1964) 44-61 (for somewhat earlier Protestant exegetes).

[4] Thus, e.g. Lohse, RGG I, 694 f.; *id.* (1971) 142-144; Schmid, SacrMundi V, 335-337; surprisingly also M. Hengel, ThQ 153 (1973) 268: "In Palästina war 'Auferstehung' nur als leibliche Auferstehung denkbar"—cf. *id.* (²1973) 364.

[5] Beside the works by Cullmann mentioned in n.3, see also in Cullmann (1966) 403-413, esp. 403. On the same line, basically, though with some criticism of C:s acceptance of the intermediate state for NT e.g. J. W. Doeve, NovTest 2 (1958) 157-161, and C. Masson, RThPh 8 (1958) 250-267. Further Léon Dufour (1969) 162. A similar approach is represented by Nikolainen II (1946) 240-245 (summary). In his work the Hellenistic mysteries function as the contrast of Biblical resurrection faith more than the philosophical idea of the immortality of the soul. See also dogmatic works as O. C. Quick (1938 267 f.; A. R. Vidler (1950) 111-113; P. Tillich (1963) 412.

[6] Bultmann (1941), published in KuM I (⁵1967) 17-48.

[7] Cf. Bultmann, KuM I, 26 f., further e.g. Kegel (1970) 119 f.

[8] See e.g. W. Marxsen (1966) 33 f.; Kegel (1970) 120. Cf. also v. Iersel, Conc 6, 701.

[9] With the same basic structure as that found already in I Th 4:13 f.: The dead will rise as Christ died and rose, repeated in short formulas such as I Cor 6:14; II Cor 4:14; Rm 8:11.

[10]Cf. e.g. H. Odeberg (1944) 302; Nikolainen II (1946) 243 ("Pharisaic materialism"); H. D. Wendland (1968) 159. On the other hand, cf. the works which stress the transformed nature of the resurrection body in certain Jewish apocalyptic texts, e.g. Wilckens (1970) 130 f.; W. Pannenberg (1964) 76; Grelot (1971) 37; Léon-Dufour (1971) 50.

[11]See e.g. Jub 23:26-29 (3.1.1 and 4); II Bar 29:4-8 (3.10.1 and 3.10.2.2); 50:2-4 (3.10.2.1); 73:7 (3.10.2.2—n.35); Sanh 90b; Keth 111b; Shab 30b; AbRN rec B 60b. Cf. e.g. R. Mach (1957) 205-209.

[12]See also e.g. R. Meyer (1937); T. F. Glasson (1961).

[13]Cf. e.g. C. K. Barrett, LondQuart 34 (1965) 91-102; J. Barr (1966) 52-54; K. Hanhart (1966) 238, summarizing; P. Hoffmann (1966) 172-174; G. Greshake (1969) 232 f.; B. Rigaux (1973) 9-15.

[14]1926, 202-301, especially from 269.

[15]II (1927) 280-395.

[16]I (1934) 307-541.

[17]1955, 34 ff.

[18]E.g. F. Weber ([2]1897) 390 ff.; D. S. Russell (1964) 353-389 (also on anthropology 140-157).

[19]IV (1928) 799-1212, especially 1016-1198.

[20]Bibl 13 (1932) 129-168.

[21]WZKM 56 (1960) 154-167; BZ 6 (1962) 177-214.

[22]Kegel (1970) 17-20; P. Grelot (1969) 17-53.

[23]E.g. S. Spira (1889); F. Schwally (1892); W. Haller, ZThK 2 (1892) 274-342; J. Lindblom (1914) 1-77; A. Löwinger, Jahrb.f.jüd. Volkskunde 25 (1923) 23-122; G. Molin, Jud 9 (1953) 225-239; G. Wied (1965); Hanhart (1966) 10-104; Hoffmann (1966) 58-174; W. S. P. Boyd, StEv 5 (1968) 39-56; Grelot (1971); A. J. Beresford (1971).

[24]Stemberger 3 n.7; Hengel (1973), further the works referred to in Stemberger 3 n. 7 and n. 12 *supra.*

[25]See Stemberger 2 f., 115, and the review by G. W. E. Nickelsburg, CBQ 35 (1973) 555 f.

[26]These and other statements on the interpretation of I Th 4:13-18 and I Cor 15 will be grounded in the second part of this work. I refer to the analysis there.

2 The Hebrew Bible

2.1

It is a well-known fact that belief in the resurrection of the dead appears only on the fringe of the Hebrew Bible[1]. Modern critics must join the denial of the Sadducees. "The resurrection of the dead cannot be derived from the Torah" (MSanh 10:1)[2]. The "Torah" may denote the Pentateuch, which was the most important authority for the dominating groups of Judaism, especially for the Sadducees (6.2.4). But even though the term would here also include the Prophets and the Hagiographa[3], the statement of the Sadducees would still hold true in the eyes of modern OT research, with one or possibly two exceptions in the latest parts of the Palestinian canon[4].

2.1.1

However, after-life was not altogether denied in ancient Israel. Although there are testimonies of some vague notions about some kind of a personal survival after death in Sheol[5], this existence in the form of ghosts and shadows could not really be called "life"[6], since it implies the separation from Yahweh and his cult[7]. Neither rewards nor punishments are distributed after death to the individual person. When "life" is promised to those who keep the commandments, e.g. in Dt[8], long life on this earth is that which is likely intended[9]. This is seen in the case of the patriarchs[10]. Or "life" is "the seed", children and grandchildren etc. That is the only type of "eternal life" known to ancient Israel[11], according to its normative traditions, at least[12]. So any contact with the world of the dead is strictly condemned as idolatrous[13], though it is not considered as being impossible[14].

2.1.2

Even though ancient Israel did not know of the concept of personal life beyond death, they were conscious of Yahweh's power over life and death. This is expressed in the old proclamation:

> Yahweh kills and he gives life, he sends down to Sheol, he can bring the dead up again.[15]

The assumptions of Enoch (Gn 5:24) and Elijah (II Ki 2:11), as well as the miraculous resurrections reported by the Elijah- and Elishatraditions[16] are concrete examples of this power. The consciousness of this in pre-exilic or early post-exilic Israel may be an important foundation for the later development towards an emergence of the belief in the resurrection of the dead at the end of time.[17]

2.1.3

This development was probably due to both internal Israelite factors and the external influence of the surrounding nations and cultures. Thus, *within Israel* there was a detachment of the individual person from the collective—the people, the clan, the family—already in late preexilic time[18] and during the exile (Ez 18).

As long as the collective functions as a real unity, a certain balance between success and failure in the lives of the individual members of the collective may be kept. The Divine justice is vindicated by the history of the generations. But when the individual stands alone, *retribution* becomes a real problem: Why do the righteous suffer and even die an early death, perhaps childless, whereas the ungodly flourish in a long life, with riches, sons and daughters?[19] The promise of life to those who keep the commandments of Yahweh would in such a new context make these questions burning. On the more positive side, the intense feeling of *communion with God* as the source of life is expressed in some of the Psalms[20] in a way that has until recently been and still could easily be interpreted as a proclamation of the belief in immortality[21].

2.1.4

Most scholars would admit that *external influences,* above all[22] Canaanite[23] and Iranian[24], have contributed to the formulation of the belief in immortality and resurrection, but there is no consent as to the extent of this influence and how it worked[25].

2.1.5

The decisive moment, when a clear assertion of an eschatological resurrection of individuals from the dead appears, is the persecution of Antiochus IV Epiphanes. Members of those pious circles, which form the *Sitz im Leben* of e.g. Dn, are martyred for their loyalty to the Law. The new article of faith can solve the problem of retribution[26]. How far this solution was influenced by Greek thought already in these days of Greek persecution, we do not know, but the paradox of such a relation is quite credible.[27]

---

[1]Cf. e.g. W. Eichrodt II-III (1961) 143-152, 346-367; G. v.Rad I (1957) 405; II (1962) 362; Wilckens (1970) 103.

[2]Even a modern Jewish theologian like S. S. Cohon (1971) 363. Cf. on MSanh 10:1 *infra* 5.2, and on the resurrection denial of the Sadducees *infra* 6.2.

[3]For this looser use of the term, cf. the references in e.g. N. Schmidt, Jew Enc 3 (1903) 141; L. I. Rabinowitz, EncJud XV, (1971) 1236.

[4]Dn 12 (*infra* 2.2-3), and possibly Is 26:19 (*infra* 4.1.5).

[5]1 Sm 28:8-19; Is 8:19. Cf. e.g. Schwally (1892) 7 f.; J. Pedersen I-II (1926) 180, 462; C. Barth (1947) 54-66; R. Martin-Achard (1956) 22; Eichrodt II (1961) 145-147; Hoffmann (1966) 60; N. J. Tromp (1969) 194-196.

[6]Cf. e.g. Is 38:10-20, and Pedersen I-II (1926) 153; Barth (1947) 54-56; Schubert BZ 6, 183-187; Hoffmann (1966) 60; Tromp (1969) 187-195; J. B. Burns, ScJTh 26 (1973) 339.

[7]Ps 6:5; 88:5, 10-12; Is 38:11, 18; Jonah 2:4. Cf. e.g. Martin-Achard (1956) 40; Tromp (1969) 208-210.

[8]5:16; 30:6, 9, 19 f.

[9]Cf. Ex 20:12 and see further Lindblom (1914) 4-6; Barth (1947) 23; Mussner (1952) 3.

[10]They are satisfied $\left(\text{שׂבע}\right)$ with life. See e.g. Gn 25:8; 35:29; I Chr 29:28. Cf. e.g. Gn 15:15; Jg 8:32; Ps 21:5; 91:16; 119:17, 37, 88, 116, 149 etc.; 143:11; Prv 3:2; 4:10; 5:6; 8:35 ff.; 9:11; 11:30, and e.g. Mussner (1952) 3.

[11]Background of the legislation on levirate marriage—Gn 38:8-26; Dt 25:5-10; Rt 4:10,14. Cf. Mk 12:19 parr, and e.g. Martin-Achard (1956) 25-27. Closely related to the "seed" is the "name" or "memorial"—cf. Dt 25:5-10; Rt 4:10, 14 and e.g. S. B. Frost, Interpr 26 (1972) 437-450.

[12]In Canaanite-Israelite syncretism popular beliefs may have been rather different on this point, too—cf. *infra* n. 23.

[13]Dt 18:11; I Sm 28:3, 9, 13; Is 8:19. Cf. Ex 22:18; Lv 19:31; 20:27, and also e.g. v.Rad II (1962) 361 f. Death and everything dead is considered as unclean (Lv 11:24-40; 21:1-11).

[14]Cf. e.g. I Sm 28:7 ff.

[15]I Sm 2:6 (ET:NEB). Cf. Dt 32:39, and Tromp (1969) 197-204, further e.g. G. v.Rad (1964) *ad loc.* for Dt 32:39 in its context, and H. J. Stoebe (1973) *ad loc.* for I Sm 2:6: The canticle of Hannah is a secondary composition of different older motifs. J. Mauchline (1971) *ad loc.* believes that "Sheol" here stands for extreme danger.

[16]I Ki 17:17-24; II Ki 4:31-37; 13:21. Of course, these were not resurrections to eternal life, only returns to the temporal life on earth. Cf. e.g. F. Nötscher (1926) 129-133; Nikolainen I (1944) 119 f.; Martin-Achard (1956) 51-53.

[17]Thus e.g. Nikolainen I (1944) 113-121; O. Schilling (1951) 32-41; Martin-Achard (1956) 47-51; H. Ringgren (1957) 117 f.; G. Stemberger, Kairos 14 (1972) 285.

[18]E.g. in the lonely figure of Jeremiah (Jr 1:4-10; 16:2). Cf. E. Sellin, NKZ 30 (1919) 239 ff.; F. König (1964) 212.

[19]The problem of Job and several psalms as 37, 73 and 88. See e.g. Nötscher (1926) 215-218; Nikolainen I (1944) 128-133; Martin-Achard (1956) 165-170; König (1964) 281 f.; Wilckens (1970) 110 f.; Cohon (1971) 356-363.

[20]E.g. 16:8-11; 36:9; 73:23-26. Cf. Nötscher (1926) 223-237; Nikolainen I (1944) 122-125; Martin-Achard (1956) 170-172.

[21]For immortality interpretation of *Ps 16* (with different nuances), see e.g. Sellin, NKZ 30, 281 f.; Schilling (1951) 49-51; Mussner (1952) 9; Molin, Jud 9, 233; J. Coppens (1957) 40 (in the French summary); König (1964) 211 f.; Wied (1965) 18; the following comm. *ad loc.*: A Weiser (1950); A. Maillot-A. Lelievre (1961); M. Dahood (1966). For a more sceptical or absolutely negative view concerning this exegesis of Ps 16, see e.g. Charles (1913) 72; E. W. Sutcliffe (1946) 76-81; Barth (1947) 153-155; G. Fohrer, KuD 14 (1968) 260; the following comm. *ad loc.*: H. J. Kraus (1960); N. H. Ridderbos (1962). Concerning *Ps 73* similarly *pro*: Sellin, NKZ 30, 285; Schilling (1951) 28-31; Mussner (1952) 8; M. Dahood (1966) *ad* 16:10; Cohon (1971) 362 f.; B. Vawter, JBL 91 (1972) 162. *Contra*: Barth (1947) 161-63; E. Jenni, ZAW 65 (1953) 20; L. Wächter (1964) 196 f.; Fohrer, KuD 14, 260; Rigaux (1973) 7. Cf. also on *Ps 49 infra* 4.1.2.

[22]Beside the following sources mentioned we may think also of Egypt (cf. Nikolainen I, 1944, 1-21; H. Kees, 1926; H. Bonnet, 1952, 341-355; Schubert, BZ 6, 178 f.) or Mesopotamia (cf. Nikolainen I, 1944, 39-50; G. Widengren, 1951, 33, 47; Schubert, BZ 6, 179-182; R. Stola, Kairos 14, 1972, 258-272, esp. 270 f.).

[23]Stressed by, among others, W. Baudissin (1911) 403-406; H. Riesenfeld (1948) 4-7; T. H. Robinson (1954) *ad* Hos 6:2; Martin-Achard (1956) 64-73, esp. 70-73. Cf. also Nikolainen I (1944) 50-60.

[24]Stressed by e.g. E. Böklen (1902); A. Causse (1908), esp. 24-30; P. L. Suarez, XV SemBiblEsp 1954 (1955) 1-20; Löwinger, Jahrb.f.jüd. Volkskunde 25, 24; Nikolainen I (1944) 143-147 (stressing decisive differences); H. J. Kraus, RGG I (1957) 692 f.; König (1964) 267-285; Wächter (1964) 194 f.; Barrett, LondQuart 34 (1965) 94 ("Persian influence served as a catalyst"); R. Mayer, Kairos 7 (1965) 200 ff. For a survey of Iranian views on after-life, see e.g. Nikolainen I (1944) 22-38; König (1964) 121-165; Mayer, Kairos 7, 194-207.

[25]For a criticism of theories about Canaanite influence, see e.g. H. Birkeland, StTh 3 (1949) 60-78, and about Iranian inspiration e.g. Schilling (1951) 102-106; Eichrodt II-III (1961) 360 f. Summarizing and synthetizing this discussion: Wilckens (1970) 114 f.

[26]Cf. Nikolainen I (1944) 132 f.; Martin-Achard (1956) 173 f.; H. Cazelles SO 4 (1961) 121; Wilckens (1970) 112 f.; Rigaux (1973) 9-11.

[27]Cf. T. F. Glasson (1961) esp. 26-32, 82.

2.2 Daniel 12:2-3

The height of the persecution of Antiochus IV Epiphanes, 167 BC, is the exact date of the formulation of the only universally accepted statement of an eschatological resurrection from the dead within the Hebrew Bible, Dn 12:2-3[1] Including 12:1, these verses form the climax of the revelation beginning in 11:2b[2] This revelation is introduced by the description of the vision in 10:1-11:2a, and it is concluded by returning to the dialogue between Daniel and "the man clothed in linen" (10:5; 12:6, 7) in 12:4-13. The revelation surveys the history of the Persian empire (11:2b), Alexander (11:3), the Diadochs (11:4), their relations and wars (11:5-9), Antiochus III (11:10-19), Seleucus IV and Heliodorus (11:20), and finally Antiochus IV Epiphanes (11:21-45)[3]. On the latter's return from the Egyptian campaign, the End suddenly breaks into history (11:45b) with the appearance of Michael, the great distress (12:1) and the deliverance of the people *(12:2-3)*.

(2) Many of those who sleep in the (land[4] of)[5] dust, will wake[6], some to everlasting life and some (to reproach[7]) to everlasting abhorrence. (3) The wise leaders[8] shall shine like the brightness of the firmament and those who have turned many[9] to righteousness like the stars for ever and ever.

2.2.1

(A) Hardly anybody doubts that this passage does describe a real resurrection of the dead (cf. n.l) or, at least, some of the dead, if "many of" is taken literally[10] Some would find the dogma of the universal resurrection of both the good and the wicked here[11]. Some would restrict the resurrection in this passage to Israel,[12] while others would include outstanding good or evil non-Israelites[13]. Still others limit the resurrection to the exceptionally wicked or righteous,[14] or even to only the righteous in Israel[15]. So the meaning of v. 2 is not at all clear, and there is no consent among the scholars as to its interpretation in detail.

26

2.2.2

(B) The terminology (sleep-wake) indicates the idea of a final resurrection rather than a post-death spiritual immortality. The body is not mentioned, but the reference to the dust and the term דראון, which refers to corpses in decay in Is 66:24, probably imply a resurrection of the body. Is 26:19 seems to have inspired the author of this verse, too (הקיץ , עפר) . Whatever the original meaning of Is 26:19 may have been (4.1.5 n.29), the author of Dn 12 is likely to have read the passage as a statement of the resurrection—of the corpse (נבלתי)[16].

2.2.3

(C) Some would hold that the resurrection of the righteous is nothing but a return to earthly life, though everlasting[17]. We shall not consider the question about the possible resurrection of the wicked mentioned in v.2[18]. But for at least the leading *élite*[19] future life seems to be of a heavenly, transcendent character (v.3). Some scholars emphasize that what is said about "the wise leaders" and their future glorification is nothing but sheer comparison, telling us nothing more concrete about the heavenly state of those outstanding righteous people[20]. But the comparison with the stars could hardly only be an *ad hoc* similitude from nature. They are very often cited together with angels as sharing the transcendent glory of heaven, and sometimes they are more or less identified with them[21]. So it seems difficult to deny that the stars symbolize or denote the heavenly glory to be given to the wise leaders in the eschatological change of the order of the world. This would happen after their resurrection, if they had already died.

Moreover, Dn 12:3 seems to "democratize" the statements on the high exaltation of the Servant of Is 52:13b, of him who shall see light, according to Is 53:11 (following lQIsa and LXX), after his death (53:10), and "make many righteous" (53:11)[22]: the group of משכלים receives the promises given to the Servant in Is 53.

Thus, the least one might say is that the resurrection statement of Dn 12:2 does not describe a mere return to physical life. On the contrary, by the addition of v.3, it is open to the idea of transformation into heavenly existence, glory and light.

2.2.4

(D) The resurrection occurs, according to v.1, in the final time of distress, when Michael appears, i.e., at "the end" (v.4) immediately after the defeat of the tyrant (11:45). So the resurrection is one of those events which accompany that decisive change of the ages, which is one of the most important characteristics of Jewish apocalyptic[23]. The appearance of Michael corresponds to the *parousia* of Jesus, being the signal of resurrection[24]. As usually connected with the eschatological trumpet of summons and resurrection,[25] Michael appears to be closely related to the raising of the dead in later Jewish and Christian texts[26]. This may be more or less inspired by Dn 12.

[1] As far as I have been able to find, only Löwinger, Jahrb.f.jüd. Volkskunde 25, 25, and perhaps W. Brueggemann, ZAW 84 (1972) 11 f. (since "dust" is associated with kingship as its negative counterpart, maybe with some cultic *Sitz im Leben*, he draws the conclusion that what is really meant in Dn 12:2 and Is 26:19—is no "departure from the graves" but enthronement of Israel among the nations, the great reversal of history, "when the lowly are exalted, and the lofty are brought low . . ."). According to Sutcliffe (1946) 145, Polychronius of Apamea thought that the resurrection of the dead in Dn 12:2 was figurative for national restoration. Other passages, sometimes mentioned as testimonies to the belief in the resurrection, are: Is 26:19 (4.1.5 n.29); Ez 37:1-14 (4.1.6 n.35); Hos 6:2 (5.8.4 n.63); Job 19:25-27 (4.1.4 n.23). On Pss 16:9-11; 49:16, and 73:23-26 *v.supra* 2.1.3 nn.20-21 and *infra* 4.1.2 n.9-10.

[2] Cf. e.g. O. Plöger (1965) 143; N. W. Porteous (1965) 170; M. Delcor (1971) 215 f.; Nickelsburg (1972) 27.

[3] For the identification of the historical events, cf. comm. *ad loc.*, e.g. A. Bentzen (1952); Porteous (1965); Delcor (1971). For the date of the present passage, reached by this identification, cf. comm. *ad loc.*

[4] Many translations, from LXX ($\grave{\epsilon}\nu \, \tau\varphi \, \pi\lambda\alpha\tau\epsilon\iota \, \tau\eta\varsigma \, \gamma\eta\varsigma$) and Theodotion ($\grave{\epsilon}\nu \, \gamma\eta\varsigma \, \chi\omega\mu\alpha\tau\iota$), render the phrase אדמת–עפר as if the states of cstr. and abs. had been inverted. The common combination of the cstr. אדמת with the name of a country, e.g. Egypt (Gn 47:20) or Israel (Ez 37:12), makes a translation closer to the original perfectly possible. Cf. R. H. Charles (1929), who prefers the reading of LXX, but thinks that the Hebrew text as it stands must be translated as here—and holds it acceptable. For this translation, see also Nickelsburg (1972) 17.

[5] The fluidity of the ancient versions may suggest that this may be an example of secondary conflation of variant readings—*v.* S. Talmon, Textus 1 (1960) 167 f.; Nickelsburg (1972) 17 n.

[6] The LXX $\grave{\alpha}\nu\alpha\sigma\tau\eta\sigma\sigma\nu\tau\alpha\iota$ suggests that the original reading was יקומו rather than יקיצו (followed by Theodotion), but that is, of course, no decisive argument against the Masoretic text (cf. B. Lindars, 1961, 66n, who argues too rapidly for LXX here).

[7] The more common word (ל) חרפות looks very much like a gloss to the rare (ל) דראון—only in Is 66:24 beside here. Cf. Nickelsburg (1972) 19n, summarizing the arguments of various scholars on this question for a shorter reading: the parallel is broken, there is no copula before the following word, a rare word like דראון would easily get the gloss חרפה, a much more common expression. Cf. also Charles (1929) and Delcor (1971) *ad loc.*

[8] This translation of המשכלים from NEB suggests the causative form, parallel to מצדיקי (ם) in the second half of the verse. Cf. Plöger (1965) 171 f.; A. Mertens (1971) 63 f., referring to 1QS III, 13 ff.; IX, 12, 21—in spite of the judgment of H. S. Nyberg, SEÅ 7 (1942) 41, who says that the hifil of שכל seldom means "to bring saekael to someone".

[9] The Hebrew has the definite article here—unlike v.2—but a literal rendering would be impossible in English. Beside v.2 and here רבים appears many times in the context (11:33, 34, 39, 44; 12:4), its special, almost technical use here alluding probably to Is 52:13-53:12, cf. H. L. Ginsberg, VT 3, 1953, 402 f.; R. Tournay, RB 69 (1962) 488n; Wied (1965) 33; Mertens (1971) 70.

[10] Sutcliffe (1946) 139, suggests an explanatory rather than partitive interpretation of מן. The translation would then be "many, i.e. those. . ."—and we would be closer to the universal resurrection of both righteous and wicked. The text seems to be used as support for that doctrine both in Judaism and Christianity (TestBenj 10:8; II Bar 50-51; IV Ezr 7:32; Jn 5:28 f.; Acts 24:15, are likely to allude to Dn 12:2). So Paul may have read it in this way. Still, there is evidence to show us that Jewish theologians later on were perfectly aware of the vagueness of רבים —e.g. in the dispute between the Houses of Shammai and Hillel quoted *infra* 5.1.2: the Shammaites quote Dn 12:2 for the existence of an intermediate group, which is not included in "many of those who sleep . . ."Dn 12:2 did

not refer to a 1 1, then. Cf. W. Bacher I (1884) 18. See also e.g. I En 91:10; 92:3-5; TestJud 25; PsSol 3:10-12; II Bar 30:2-5, and other passages with allusions to Dn 12:2, which do not teach the universal resurrecttion.

[11]J. A. Montgomery (1927) *ad loc.*; Sutcliffe (1946) 139; Schubert (1955) 50 n. 75 and WZKM 56, 158—he retracts this judgment in BZ 6, 189 f.; v.Rad I (1957) 405; König (1964) 241-243; M. A. Beek, GerefTT 68 (1968) A. J. Beresford (1971) 146 f. Cf. J. Jeremias, TWNT VI (1959) 536-540 on the meaning of

[12]O. Plöger (1959) 28 f.; *id.* (1965) *ad loc.*; H. Schmid, Jud 27 (1971) 213 ("alle Toten des Jerusalemer Tempelstaates"); Wilckens (1970) 13; Rigaux (1973) 10 f.

[13]E.g. Volz (1934) 14.

[14]E.g. Charles (1899) 132; Bousset-Gressmann (1926) 270; Montgomery (1927) and Bentzen (1952) *ad loc.*

[15]S. P. Tregelles (1852) 162-169, refers to Saadiah Hagaon and Ibn Ezra for interpreting the second אֵלֶּה in v.2 as pointing back to the renegades according to 11:32, 39, and not to רַבִּים in 12:2a. The translation would then be: Many among those who sleep in the land of dust will wake. These will have eternal life, but those (formerly mentioned) reproach . . . On the same line B. Alfrink, Bibl 40 (1959) 355-371; F. F. Bruce, ScJTh 24 (1971) 458.

[16]Cf. Nickelsburg (1972) 22 f., further Nötscher (1926) 165 f.; Ginsberg, VT 3, 403 f.; Alfrink, Bibl 40, 366; Russell (1964) 188; Wied (1965) 34.

[17]E.g. T. W. Manson, CongQuart 32 (1954) 12; (1964) 376; Fohrer, KuD 14, 261 f.; Beresford (1971) 17.

[18]Cf. n.15. The deformation of their bodies after their possible resurrection (as in II Bar 51—*infra* 3.10.2) is not mentioned in the Pauline texts. They are completely under the horizon in I Th 4 and I Cor 15.

[19]The מַשְׂכִּלִים —cf. n.8.

[20]Thus e.g., Bentzen (1952) *ad loc.*; Nötscher (1926) 164 f. Also Nickelsburg (1972) 36, 171, emphasizes that Dn 12:3 uses the language of simile, but suggests that "the light imagery is intended to describe the theophanic glory that will envelope the new Jerusalem . . . There . . . the wise teachers will shine with particular brilliance." He avoids the hermeneutic question: what is the symbolic function of this shining in starlike brilliance?

[21]*V.infra* 7.2.1-7.2.1.9 with further references and cf. also Volz (1934) 400; Hengel (1973) 359, and e.g. I En 80:1, 6 f.; 86:3 f.

[22]On the relation between Dn 12:3 and Is 52:13-53:12, cf. e.g. G. Dalman (1887) 6, with references to older works; W. Staerk (1933) 39; G. Wiencke (1939) 163 f. n; Nyberg, SEÅ 7, 33; I. Engnell, BJRL 31 (1948) 77; H. W. Wolff (1952) 38 f.; W. H. Brownlee, BASOR 132 (1953) 12 f.; Ginsberg, VT 3, 402 f.; A. Feuillet, RB 60 (1953) 336; Tournay, RB 69, 488n, quoting also A. Gelin, Lumiere et Vie 7 (1958) 127; Russell (1964) 188; F. F. Bruce, *In hon.* M. Black (1969) 228n; H. C. Cavallin, SEÅ 37-38 (1972-3) 49-56. For the term "democratize" in this connection, cf. e.g. H. Riesenfeld (1947) 69 f., 83. And the comm. *ad loc.* by Bentzen (1952), Porteous (1965) and Delcor (1971). Finally Schmid, Jud 27, 213n, 220. And see *infra* 7.2.1.

[23]Cf. e.g. v.Rad II (1962) 314; M. Rist, IDB I (1962) 157; Russell (1964) 223 f.; Schreiner (1969) 117-121.

[24]Cf. e.g. I Th 4:16; I Cor 15:23.

[25]*Infra* 5.8.3 on TgIs 27:12-13.

26 Cf. the texts quoted in nn.55-58 to 5.8.3, and further e.g. W. Lueken (1898) e.g. 50; J. Michl, RAC V (1962) 244 f.; *id.* LThK VII (1962) 393 f.; E. Lohse, RGG IV (1960) 932, all with plenty of references to both Jewish and Christian texts, especially *DescMariae* 3, where Mary says to Michael:

χαιρε, Μιχαηλ ἀρχιστρατηγε, ὁ μελλων σαλπιζειν και

ἐξυπνιζειν τους ἀπ'αἰωνος κεκοιμημενους.

The document was written in the 8th or 9th century, but is likely to represent older traditions about the role of Michael—cf. H. Pernot, REG 13 (1900) 239.

Without any specific connection with the trumpet, Michael is associated with the final gathering of the righteous (immediately after death or at the final gathering of the righteous (immediately after death or at the final resurrection) in ParJer 9:4 (on its date and origin cf. e.g. A. M. Denis, 1970, 70). He functions as the psychopomp, especially of the righteous—cf. Jud 9. This is more fully developed in the description of the death of Moses in DtR 11:10 (cf. Lueken, 1898, 44) and the death of Abraham according to TestAbr (*infra* 3.12) ch. 15-22.

2.3   Daniel 12:13

The concluding words of the final dialogue between Daniel and the *angelus interpres,* and of the entire book as it is found in the Hebrew Bible, probably contain a promise to Daniel about his own future resurrection:

But go your way till the end comes $\left(\gamma\bar{p}\,\bar{\triangleright}\right)$. You shall rest $\left(\Pi\,1\,\mathtt{1}\,\Pi\right)$ and you shall rise $\left(\intercal\,\mathtt{n}\,\mathtt{y}\,\Pi\right)$ for your lot $\left(\intercal\,\bar{\triangleright}\,\mathtt{1}\,\mathtt{1}\right)$

(A) As one of "the wise leaders" $\left(\mathtt{D}\,^{\flat}\,\bar{\triangleright}\,\mathfrak{v}\,\mathtt{n}\right)$ Daniel is himself promised a share in the resurrection for eternal life. This is the most reasonable interpretation of the verb $\intercal\,\mathtt{n}\,\mathtt{y}\,\Pi$ though $\intercal\,\mathtt{n}\,\mathfrak{y}$ is not so common in this sense as $\mathtt{D}\,\bar{\triangleright}$ or $\gamma\,^{\flat}\,\bar{\triangleright}\,\Pi$ We shall later return to the archaeological evidence for this meaning of $\intercal\,\mathtt{n}\,\mathfrak{y}$ (3.14.3). LXX obviously understands the saying in this way[1], as well as Theodotion[2]. This is also the Rabbinic interpretation[3]. A number of modern scholars accept it[4]. **(B, C)** Nothing more precisely is said about the form of the resurrection predicted for Daniel. The "lot" mentioned here reminds us of Qumran terminology, and there $\bar{\triangleright}\,\intercal\,\mathtt{1}\,\mathtt{1}$ is associated with "the holy ones" in 1QS XI, 7 (3.5.1) and 1QH XI, 11 (3.5.4), i.e., with the angels or the community in its association with the angels (7.2.1.8). So we cannot exclude that the "lot" referred to the glory that is described in Dn 12:3, i.e., an angelic state. **(D)** The date of Daniel's resurrection is clearly defined: "the end of days", the end of history and the old age, just as in the case of the general resurrection of Dn 12:2 (2.2.4 and n.23).

[1]With an addition in the beginning of the verse, which may reflect the "Parusieverzögerung" (*sit venia verbo*), according to some scholars also behind the changing "dates" for "the end" given in the preceding verses (e.g. L. F. Hartman, JeBiCo, 1968, 459—but cf. also for a sceptical view towards this explanation, Porteous, 1965, *ad loc.*), and partly found in Theodotion, too, cf. *infra* n.2:

και συ βαδισον αναπαυου · ετι γαρ εισιν ημεραι και ωραι εις αναπληρωσιν συντελειας. και αναπαυσῃ και αναστησῃ επι την δοξαν σου εις συντελειαν ημερων.

Thus גרלך is rendered την δοξαν σου which makes it very clear that the translator thought of Daniel's final resurrection "for glory", as the other συνιεντες the κατισχυοντες τους λογους μου in 12:3, contrasted with the resurrection of the wicked according to LXX Dn 12:2b εις ονειδισμον ... εις διασποραν και αισχυνην αιωνιον.

[2] και συ δευρο και αναπαυου· ετι γαρ ημεραι εις αναπληρωσιν συντελειας, και αναστησῃ εις τον κληρον σου εις συντελειαν ημερων.
On the addition cf. the preceding note. The more literal κληρος has replaced LXX δοξα but αναστησῃ in such a context (cf. also LXX Dn 12:2 αναστησουνται) would necessarily have to be interpreted as "rise" for the final resurrection.

[3]See PRK צי ור תאמר a quotation from R. Azariah and R. Abbahu in the name of Resh Laqish: There the saying is broken up into a dialogue:

The Lord says: Daniel, go to your end. Daniel asks: To make דיך ובשנ ור The Lord replies: You shall rest. He asks: For ever? The Lord replies: You shall rise (תעמד). Daniel: with whom—the righteous or the wicked? The Eternal: לגרלך for your lot, with the righteous. Daniel: When? God: At the end of days.

Further Sanh 92a (a proof for the resurrection of the dead in the Torah, according to R. Ashi); LamR II, 3 § 6 (R. Azariah, in the name of R. Judah b. R. Simeon, interpreting ימין as "right hand", which = Israel: The resurrection of Daniel will occur at the end of the slavery of Israel). Cf. also PRE 33 (ET Friedlander 246) R. Jochanan combining Dn 12:13 with I Sm 28:19.

[4]E.g. Schilling (1951) 64 f., against Nötscher (1926); Wied (1965) 24-35; Porteous (1965) *ad loc.*; Delcor (1971) *ad loc.*; Hartman, JeBiCo, 459.

3 Palestinian apocalyptic texts

Before we enter the study of the various texts presented under the above heading, some of the terminology to be used shall first be defined. The exclusion of some writings and the inclusion of others will then be related to these definitions.

3.0.1

The etymology of the term *apocalyptic* serves as a definition following H. Ringgren, who defines apocalyptic as a kind of literature, which communicates the revelation of various secrets. These secrets may first of all be concerned with the future and the end of the world, or the heavenly world beyond, the state of the blessed or of the damned after death (*eschatology*), but furthermore, it is also concerned with the stars, the order of the universe, the angels, the meaning of events in history etc.[1] Thus apocalyptic denotes above all the *form* of communicating certain ideas, the method of transmitting the message (in D. S. Russell's terms, 1964). The phenomenon of pseudepigraphy is a dominating feature of this form of literature. The secrets are revealed through a prophet or a man of God of a distant past, such as Enoch, Daniel, Abraham, Job, the sons of Jacob, etc. The pseudonymous author receives himself the revelations through angels or dreams[4], according to the accounts given in the apocalyptic books. But a great deal of the mysteries which are disclosed to him is recognized by the scholars as reinterpreted prophecy[3]. In the revelations of the apocalyptic writings there is, also however a common message, a theology and a way of thinking, which is a characteristic for the whole *genre,* and at the same time it is found in Rabbinic and Christian traditions. This concerns e.g. the radical opposition between the two ages and the expectation of the change of the ages, when eternity succeeds time[4]. In a similar way ideas about life after death came into Judaism via the apocalyptic groups and were accepted by writers in the Greek-speaking diaspora[5], the Rabbis and Jesus and his followers. An *eschatology* similar to that found in the apocalyptic writings can then be transmitted in a different form, such as by exegesis of Scriptural texts in Rabbinic traditions, long speeches in Josephus' books, or simple assertions with or without argument.

3.0.2

The term *eschatology* has been used here, and it will be used many times in this work. It should be noted that the special theological significance which the term has obtained in certain schools of thought[6] shall not be considered in this work. The more general meaning, used e.g. by C. M. Edsman in his article for RGG[7], is chosen as the definition of the term, again based on the etymology of the word: teaching concerning "the last things" of the world or the individual, death and what comes beyond death, the end time events. The difference between eschatology and apocalyptic is that whereas eschatology concerns the *matter,,* the contents of a revelation e.g., *what* is said about life after death or the end of the world, apocalyptic is both a special *form* of communicating this matter, i.e., *how* information is given about life after death or the end of the world, and a definite spirituality, by which specific consistent ideas are conveyed in this form. The following little illustration may summarize these two definitions:

3.0.3

		Eschatology	Apocalyptic
Matter:	Statements concerning	end time events	cosmology
		death and beyond death	angelology
Form:	in an argument from	reinterpretation	
	reason, Scripture etc.	of Scripture themes	
		and motifs	
		revelation of secrets	

So it is the middle column which is of interest: Eschatology in the form of apocalyptic.

3.0.4

"Palestinian" is not primarily a geographical but is instead a linguistic and consequently a cultural concept. The criterion for the use of this label is the (supposed) original language of a text: Hebrew or Aramaic. This definition is better than the strictly geographical, since the geographical origin of the writings is often very difficult or impossible to ascertain. Even though it can be decided in some cases, this ascertainment does not determine the definition of the cultural setting of the documents, since large parts of Palestine were as much hellenized as cities in Egypt or Asia Minor were[8]. The problem of distinguishing the original language of a text is normally easier to solve, and the language does tell us more about the cultural background. Cf. e.g. Philo and Ps-Philo (LAB)[9].

3.0.5

"Hellenistic" is used as a designation of the entire cultural environment marked by the Greek language and Greek thinking after the conquest of Alexander,[10] including *all* types of Judaism[11]. Therefore, the term "Hellenistic Judaism" is *not* used to distinguish the Greek-speaking Jews of the diaspora (or Palestine) from "Palestinian Judaism". Such a use of the term would be perfectly plausible, as long as we do not leave the Jewish frame of reference. Keeping this wider cultural context in mind, however, it seems better to speak of "Judaism of the Greek-speaking diaspora" than of "Hellenistic Judaism".

3.0.6

Using these definitions, the *lines of demarcation* between the three groups of Jewish texts which shall be investigated ought to be clearly drawn, i.e., between Palestinian apocalyptic, Greek-speaking diaspora and Rabbinic traditions. The original *language* forms the criterion for the distinction between the two former groups, the *form* of communicating eschatology separates the apocalyptic literature from the Rabbinic.[12] These writings which are called apocalyptic were historically often transmitted in a Christian environment by being translated into the languages of the mediaeval Eastern and Western Churches. The Rabbinic sources, on the other hand, represent the tradition of the synagogues.

3.0.7

"The first of the apocalyptic writings is the Book of *Daniel*" (italics are mine), writes D. S. Russell (1964, 48). Dn undoubtedly suits the above definition of apocalyptic perfectly. Yet the conventional borderline which was drawn by the canonization process between Dn and the rest of the apocalyptic literature is accepted in our disposition of the material[13]. Thus, the fundamental importance of this apocalyptic book is stressed. Again and again we shall meet allusions to Dn 12:2 f. throughout the material. The fact of its canonization and its use in NT show its unique importance among the other apocalyptic writings[14].

3.0.8

The *Qumran* scrolls are included in the section on Palestinian apocalyptic texts, though they are generally quite different in *form* from the other texts in the section. Fragments of some of the apocalyptic writings have, however, been found in Qumran[15]. This indicates that the beliefs and thoughts of the Dead Sea community were not too far from those of the authors of that apocalyptic literature known before the discoveries in 1947. This external evidence is partly supported by the exegetical work on the Scrolls, though undeniable and important differences remain[16].

3.0.9

The archaeological evidence for Palestinian Jewish beliefs in the centuries around the rise of Christianity contains also *the tomb inscriptions* (3.14). Since the geographical definition of "Palestinian" can be followed strictly in this case, it is given priority before the language criterion. But the language used on a sepulchral inscription does not tell us very much about the language normally used by its authors, whether it is Hebrew in the Greek-speaking diaspora or Greek among the Rabbis, whose tombs are found in Beth-Shearim[17]—or Latin in inscriptions of 20th century Europe! The main reason for listing the Palestinian Jewish inscriptions among the "Palestinian apocalyptic texts" is simply practical: By excluding Dn and including Qumran and the inscriptions of Palestine, this chapter gathers all the non-Rabbinic Palestinian Jewish sources.

---

[1] Ringgren, RGG I (1957) 464. Similarly e.g. Russell (1964) 37; Schreiner (1969) 80-82; D. Flusser, EncJud III (1971) 179. For recent discussion on apocalyptic, see e.g. P.v.d. Osten-Sacken (1969); Schreiner (1969) 165-198; J. C. H. Lebram, VT 20 (1970) 519; K. Koch (1970, ET 1972)—for "a preliminary definition" esp. 18-35.

[2] See e.g. P. Vielhauer, HS II, (1964) 408; Russell (1964) 109-118, 127-139; Schreiner (1969) 74-79, 86-90; Flusser, EncJud III, 179, referring to the ceasing of the spirit of prophecy as the explanation; Koch (1972) 26.

[3] Cf. Russell (1964) 178-202; L. Hartman (1966) 71-141.

[4] Cf. 2.2.4 and n.23.

[5]Concerning the Greek influence in this matter, cf. however 2.1.5 and n.27. Also Russell (1964) 387-390, with a questionmark for his generalization of the opposition between "the Hebrew mentality" and the Greek.

[6]Cf. e.g. Bultmann, KuM I, 47: "Im Erklingen des Wortes . . . ereignet sich das eschatologische Jetzt"; Shires (1966) 12-14; A. Strobel (1967) 1-35, 188-198; R. Pesch (1969) 313; Koch (1972) 98-101 (and also 101-111 for a general survey of the discussion on eschatology and apocalyptic in 20th century systematic theology).

[7]II (1958) 650 f., using "Jenseitsvorstellungen" as a synonym.

[8]See e.g. M. Hengel (1973) 108-195; B. Salomonsen, DTT 36 (1973) 173.

[9]On LAB, cf. infra 3.8, and on Philo 4.5.

[10]Cf. e.g. H. Volkmann, DkP II (1967) 1009, for this definition of "Hellenistic" and its background.

[11]Cf. e.g. Hengel (1973) 567; Salomonsen, DTT 36, 173.

[12]Cf. K. Schubert (1970) 23-32, on the Pharisaic opposition against the apocalyptic Asidaeans and their "Naherwartung", and then the return of apocalyptic among the Rabbis of the second century AD. The difference in form corresponds to a difference in spirituality during the period investigated in this work.

[13]Unlike e.g. Nickelsburg (1972, 11), who calls Dn 12:2 "our earliest datable intertestamental reference to a resurrection from the dead" (italics are mine).

[14]Cf. the observations on possible allusions to Dn 12:2 f. infra 3.2.3.1, 2, 6; 3.3.2; 3.4.1; 3.9.1 . 2; 3.10.2 (II Bar 51); 4.3.7; 4.4.3.3; 4.5.6 (?); 5.1.2; Further, in the concluding survey, 7.3, on the importance of Dn. In NT, see Mt 25:46; Jn 5:29; Acts 24:15 for Dn 12:2; Mt 13:43 and Eph 5:14 for Dn 12:3.

[15]Cf. 3.1 n.1; 3.2 n.4; 3.3 n.1; Russell (1964) 38 f.

[16]Cf. Russell (1964) 39 f. The forms of the Qumran literature are often quite different from the apocalyptic pseud-epigrapha. In Qumran we find commentaries (of the special pesher-type), hymns, books of rules, liturgies etc., and very few pseudepigrapha, besides the fragments of those already known before the discoveries in the Judaean desert.

[17]Cf. 4.12.4 and nn.6, 17 and 29 to 4.12, concerning the use of Hebrew in sepulchral inscriptions outside Palestine. Concerning the use of Greek on Palestinian Jewish tombs, cf. 3.14 and 3.14.2.

3.1 Jubilees

The discovery of a few Hebrew fragments in the first cave of Qumran[1] of this midrash on Gn[2], or rather rewritten, Gn proved that the original language of Jub was Hebrew[4]. The book is often dated toward the end of the reign of John Hyrcanus, before his conflict with the Pharisees, i.e., between 110 and 105 BC[5]. It may contain secondary additions, however, and M. Testuz, in his book on the religious ideas of Jub (1960, 39-42), suggests that the only clear statement on after-life which may be found in the book, 23:31, belongs to one of those secondary sections[6]. This conclusion depends upon the interpretation of the apocalypse in Jub 23:11 ff. as a description of history. But with the same method Nickelsburg (1972, 46 f.) is able to date the apocalypse before the writing of Dn 11-12, i.e., between 168 and 152 BC. However, one might ask whether such a method is at all applicable to a piece of literature, preserving so many traces of the traditional apocalyptic pattern, since this includes times of abnormal calamities as well as final salvation and peace (cf. Hartman 1966, 28 ff.). Anyhow, it seems rather clear that the book as a whole is older than any other of the writings quoted in the following section.[7] Some scholars have suggested a member of the Dead Sea Community as author, referring e.g. to the fragments of 1Q and to the Calendar proposed in Jub[8]. But the discovered fragments prove nothing more than the fact that this book was used by the Qumran sect. Further, the fact that similar ideas were shared by the people behind Jub and the Qumranites, with some qualifications, justify the designation of Jub as Essene (Testuz, 1961, 197, 199). At the present stage nothing more can be established by the considered evidence[9].

3.1.1

In the context of the above mentioned passage, 23:26 describes a conversion to the study of the Law and the way of righteousness among children[10]. This is followed by a fantastic lengthening of the days of "the children of men" (v.27) "to a greater number of years than was the number of days before" (G. L. Davenport's translation, 1971, 98). Nobody will be old any more, everybody is to be a boy or a child (v.28). All their days and their end will be of peace and joy without the destruction by Satan or anything evil, days of blessing and healing (v.29) and v.30 continues:

At that time, the Lord will heal his servants, and they shall rise up and be made whole, and drive out their adversaries. The faithful shall see and be thankful, and rejoice with joy forever, and shall see all their judgments and all their curses on their enemies. (31) Then their bones shall rest in the earth, and their spirits shall have much joy; and they shall know that it is the Lord who executes judgment, and shows mercy to hundreds and thousands, and to all that love him. (Davenport, 1971, 99, for ET.)

3.1.2

(A) In a recent monograph on Jub (1971, 40 n) G. L. Davenport has argued for an understanding of this passage which, unlike the interpretation of most other scholars[11], does not allow a reference to life after death: "The real point is not the rejoicing of the dead, but that which they celebrate. This is a more lively existence of the dead than that in the general OT view, but it is not so far in the direction of resurrection." The dead remain in the graves, but they are restless until they have been avenged. Man is a unity, even at death.

Although Davenport may be right in telling us where the accent of the passage is placed, his efforts to avoid an interpretation implying real life after death for that group, called "the righteous"[12], are not convincing. It is, after all, easier to accept the terminology "life after death" with all due reservations for the lack of clarity about its precise meaning here than to speak about "a more lively existence of the dead than that in the general OT view".

3.1.3

(B) The resurrection of the physical body was evidently excluded by v.31: "Their bones shall rest in the earth." (Testuz, 1960, 171) speaks with some reluctance about the resurrection of the souls of the righteous with reference to v.30, "rise up". But "the righteous" in v.30b do not seem to be the same people as the "servants" of the Lord in v.30a. "The righteous" seem to be spectators in relation to the "servants" of the Lord, who fight the battle and win it (Volz, 1934, 29; Hoffmann, 1966, 100 f.). So "rise up" should probably be interpreted as generally referring to the victory over the enemies with prolonged life and happiness for the people of God, described in the preceding context. So nothing is said here about any resurrection. On the contrary, there is an undeniable dichotomy between the "bones" and the "spirits" of the righteous[13]. We are not so far from the idea of a blessed immortality of the spirits or souls of the righteous—whether the background of the expressions of Jub may be Greek influence or rather the result of an inner Jewish development, which was already in process in the formulation of some of the Psalms[14].

3.1.4

(C) The blessed life of the end time is described in very earthly terms in the preceding context. This is puzzling when it is compared with the statement of the spiritual and heavenly, transcendent life of the righteous according to v.31 (cf. Nickelsburg, 1972, 32 f.). No harmonization between concepts, which were just simply juxtaposed, can be discerned in the context, e.g. suggestions about an intermediate state of the souls between death and final resurrection[15].

3.1.5

(D) Although the final salvation of the righteous, including the joyful life given to their spirits[16], seems to be part of an eschatological future where judgment is also executed (v.30), the concept of the Last Day and final universal judgment is absent. On the other hand, this idea is evidently found in Jub 5:13-16[17] and probably also in 36:9 f.[18]—but there nothing is said about a resurrection from the dead (against Volz, 1934, 29 f.), nor about any life after death.

3.1.6

Thus, Jub 23:31 is an interesting early testimony of a totally spiritual concept of life after death in a Palestinian Jewish apocalyptic milieu. The suggested Essene background of this writing would be confirmed by such an idea about after-life, if the testimony of Josephus (3.6.1) can be trusted. Inasmuch as we lack real parallels from the Qumran texts (3.5), it is for the time being impossible to reach any certainty in this question. There is no relation between the statements on a future final judgment in the book and the belief in a blessed immortality of the righteous according to 23:30 f.

[1]From Cave 1 Jub 27:19-21; 35:8-10; 36:12, and two other pieces which have not been identified. Cf. DJD I (1955) 82-84; III (1962) 77-79 (cave 2); J. T. Milik, RB 63 (1956) 60 (cave 4).

[2]Russell (1964) 54: "a midrashic Targum". Noack (1958) 178: "a precursor of the midrashic literature".

[3]"Little Genesis"—e.g. Russell (1964) 53. Schreiner (1969) 34. Cf. also M. Testuz (1960) 16 f. Parts of Exodus (1-14) are incorporated as well.

[4]Cf. B. Noack (1958) 182; Testuz (1960) 12. This was already the conclusion of R. H. Charles, AP II (1913) 4, on other grounds. Russell (1964) 54, says that Aramaic was the original language without any references—a sheer mistake? The book is completely preserved only in the Ethiopic version, about a quarter in Latin.

[5]Cf. e.g. Charles, AP II, I; Cazelles, SoOr 4, 123-125; Noack (1958) 179 f.; Testuz (1960) 34-39; Volz (1934) 28 merely states that the date is uncertain. Russell (1964) 54, suggests the middle of the second century. Nickelsburg (1972) 46 f. prefers a pre-Danielic date, around 167 BC. Davenport (1971) 10-18 finds three redactors at work. The second of these, working under the Maccabaean struggles, 166-160 BC (15) was responsible for the addition of 23:14-31 (46).

[6]Suggesting for this addition a date between the arrival of the Romans in Palestine 65 BC and the beginning of the reign of Herod the Great in 38 BC, pp. 39-42. Also Volz (1934) 29, believes that v.30 f. is secondary, likewise Davenport about the whole section (cf. the preceding note).

[7]For the first edition Davenport (1971) 14 gives a date of late third-early second century BC, where 5:13-16 and 36:9 f. may possibly belong. An even earlier date suggested by S. Zeitlin—see Davenport (1971) 18.

[8]Cf. e.g. A. Jaubert, VT 3 (1953) 250-264; J. Morgenstern, VT 5 (1955) 34-76; A. Jaubert, VT 7 (1957) 35-61; Noack (1958) 180.

[9]Cf. Noack (1958) 180; Russell (1964) 54; Davenport (1971) 17 f.

[10]According to v. 25 "the heads of the children will be white with grey hear, and a child of three weeks will appear old like a man of one hundred years". The relation between these children and those of v. 26 is unclear.

[11]E.g. Charles, AP II, and Noach (1958) ad loc. Further Volz (1934) 29; Molin, Jud 9, 236; Schubert WZKM 56, 159; id. BZ 6, 193-196; Testuz (1960) 171; Hoffmann (1966) 100-104; Beresford (1971) 35 f.

[12]Cf. 3.1.3 for the relation between "the righteous" and "the servants" Volz (1934) 29 believes that "the righteous" are the martyrs, recently killed in the persecutions described in the preceding context.

[13]In spite of Davenport (1971) 40n., Hoffmann (1966) 102-104 speaks of a transitional stage between the old Hebrew anthropology and Hellenistic dichotomy, and employs the term "pre-dichotomic"—which requires some pattern of development. I prefer to state only that which the text says, without applying now any diachronic aspects. Cf. also Wilckens (1970) 117, against Schubert, BZ 6, 193, on the question of the resurrection faith of the author/redactor, which the latter affirms and the former denies.

[14]Thus according to Hoffmann (1966) 103. Cf. supra 2.1.3 and nn.20-21.

[15]With e.g. Volz (1934) 29, 238; Hoffmann (1966) 101, against Molin, Jud 9, 236.

[16]22:22, and above all 24:31 f., may suggest that the wicked are punished in Sheol immediately after death—cf. Volz (1934) 29. But there is no need to interpret these statements on judgment in Sheol as literal punishment after death—cf. e.g. Hoffmann (1966) 98 f.; Davenport (1971) 54-56.

[17]This future judgment replaces the Flood in this new Gn. Cf. also v. 10: "the day of the great condemnation, when judgment will be executed . . ." Cf. Davenport (1971) 47-49.

[18]A man who devises evil against his brother ". . . shall depart into eternal execration . . . in torment and in indignation and in plagues and in disease forever." Cf. Davenport (1971) 66-68.

3.2. I Enoch

In form and content, the final redaction of the collection of Enoch traditions gathered in the present Ethiopian book of Enoch is a rather typical apocalypse. The ante-diluvian patriarch, mentioned briefly in Gn 5:21-24, is the spokesman of the author(s) in pietistic Jewish circles in the centuries around the beginning of CE[1]. His assumption, according to Gn 5:24, enables him to be a suitable revealer of heavenly mysteries[2]. The Ethiopian version was translated from the Greek, now preserved only in some sections of the book.[3] Originally it was written in Hebrew and/or Aramaic. The Qumran fragments of the book represent both languages[4]. The five main parts of I En[5] contain apocalyptic material, visions and dreams, describing the world above or beneath, the age to come and the final history of the world, astronomic speculations and an interpretation of contemporary Jewish history. All of this with great variety of age and type. Ch. 37-71 the second part, the so-called Similitudes or Parables, with the Son of Man as a central figure presents a special problem. Fragments of this part have not as yet been found in the Dead Sea caves, and thus their pre-Christian origin has not been decisively proven[6]. In spite of this, we shall treat the Similitudes as a part of the Palestinian Enoch literature without any reservation, basing our decision on the finds of more competent authorities in this field[7]. My discussion of the texts relevant to this investigation will be arranged in an order which more or less agrees with the general opinions about the age of the different parts of I En.

3.2.1

"The Book of Visions" (ch. 83-90) contains one possible reference to the resurrection, 90:33. It is located in the context of the vision of the sheep being attacked by the wild beasts, the eagles and the ravens (ch. 90). This vision is an allegory of contemporary Jewish history, Hellenistic oppression and Maccabaean revolution (cf. comm. *ad loc.*):

> All those who were exterminated and spread all around, and all the beasts of the earth, and all the birds of the sky gathered in the house . . .

The house represents the new Jerusalem, the place of gathering for those Jews who had died before the day of salvation[8], the exiled Jews[9] and the Gentile nations[10]. **(D)** The resurrection of the dead is one of final salvation events. As in other Jewish descriptions of the resurrection[11], it is closely associated with the restoration of the people of Israel. **(A, B)** The fact of a reference to the resurrection of the dead can hardly be doubted, **(C)** but it is obvious that this brief allusion does not tell us the manner in which this resurrection was conceived[12].

40

3.2.2.1

The so-called *Noachic fragments*, I En 6-11[13], contain **(A)** references to souls of the dead: the righteous (9:3, 10) who cry for vengeance and justice (cf. Rev. 6:9 f.); the wicked (10:15[14]) who are punished with the children of the "Watchers" (perhaps being identified with them?). **(B)** The idea of a separation between body and soul at death seems to lie underneath the formulations (cf. P. Grelot, RQ 1, 1958, 117), but they do not, however, tell us anything about a future resurrection. **(D)** The soul obviously continues some kind of a personal existence after death, but the expressions about the souls of the righteous would seem to presuppose a future final administration of justice.[15]

3.2.2.2

What is more important in the first section of I En is *ch.* 22 with its description of the waiting-places of the souls between death and final judgment, four (or three[16]) hollow places in a high mountain where Enoch is said to have arrived during his journeys described in ch. 17-36. One room is for the spirits πνευματα of the righteous (v.9); another is for the sinners (v.10). The description of the third cave is not quite clear, but with the analogy from the clear verses 9-10 it seems more likely to me that (in the Greek version, at least) *four* caves in the mind of the author:

v.9 και ούτως εχωρισθη	v.12 και ούτως εχωρισθη
εις τα πνευματα των	τοις πνευμασιν
δικαιων ...	των εντυγχανοντων ...
και ούτως εχωρισθη	v.13 και ούτως εκτισθη
	τοις πνευμασιν των ανθρωπων
των άμαρτωλων ...	όσοι ούκ έσονται όσιοι άλλα άμαρτωλοι ...

Then the third cave would be a separate room of the slain righteous who accuse the sinners of their being slain (cf. 9:3, 10 and 3.2.2.1), and the fourth hollow place apparently is occupied by sinners who, because they were already punished (θλιβεντες) while living, will be punished somewhat more mercifully than those sinners who were not judged during their lifetime (v. 10 f.). Thus it is expressed in v.13b:

> They shall not be punished on the day of judgment and they shall not be raised (μετεγερθωσιν) hence.

(A) In this probably rather early part of I En[17] there is a clear affirmation of individual existence after death, meaning *post-mortem* retribution of both righteous and wicked. **(B)** The immortality (i.e., indestructibility or non-ceasing of existence) of all souls/spirits[18] seems to be presupposed (cf. "all" in v.3), which does not exclude a resurrection of some or even most of the souls. Consequently, this text seems to contain the concept of an intermediate state[19]. This does not imply any reunion between body and soul at the resurrection, but rather indicates a "resurrection of the spirit or soul", however strange such an idea might seem to us[20]. In any case, in this description of the compartments of the souls between death and final judgment, resurrection is not central. **(C)** Although the mentioning of the resurrection seems to be closely related to the day of judgment, the immediate situation after death implies some kind of judgment following the death of the individual.

Here a further reflection may be added: To what extent was this description of the world of souls after death intended to be symbolical? Or did the author[22] really imagine the souls in the intermediate state to be preserved in hollow places in a mountain located somewhere in the world? The *genre* of pseudepigraphy should itself denote a rather high degree of consciousness of using symbolic language or myth[23]. If the author feels free to create his story about Enoch, he ought to be capable of producing the vision of the mountain as an image of *post-mortem* existence. And what really matters to him is the conviction that justice will prevail at last. That is the point of the story of the four caves[24].

In the *Book of Exhortations* (I En 91-104)[25] there are two references to the resurrection of the righteous, which seem to make allusions to Dn 12:2 f. (2.2), namely *91:10* and 92:3-4. (I have underlined the words which may constitute a connection with Dn 12:2 f. in the following quotations.)

3.2.3.1
But the *righteous* one shall arise (jetnasa) from his *sleep*, and wisdom shall arise (jetnasa) and shall be given to them.

(A) "Sleep" probably refers to death[26], and "the righteous (91:10) one" should be interpreted corporately. **(B)** A resurrection for the righteous is maintained[27], but **(C)** there is no mention as to how this resurrection was conceived[28]. **(D)** The resurrection is located in a context of an apocalyptic pattern: After the culmination of wickedness, the Lord himself shall come to judge and punish all idolaters (vv. 7-9)[29]. Then the resurrection of the righteous shall occur.

3.2.3.2
Very similar formulations appear in the somewhat longer statement of 92:3-4:

And the righteous one[30]shall arise (jetnasa) from *sleep* and walk in the paths of righteousness. And all his path and conversation shall be in *eternal* goodness and grace. He will be gracious to the righteous and give him *eternal* uprightness. And He will give him power so that he shall be (endowed) with goodness and righteousness. And he shall walk in *eternal light*.

(A, B) Again there is a resurrection,[31] but only of the rightous. **(C)** There is something more specific in this passage. The resurrection life is presented as being glorified ("eternal light"), eternal, and also transformed into moral perfection. **(B)** There is no way of deciding whether the author was thinking of a

42

resurrection of the body or of the spirit, as may be indicated later in the same section of I En (ch. 102-104). **(D)** V.5, concerning the disappearance of sin "from that day on", suggests that the resurrection in v.3 shall take place on a Last Day.

3.2.3.3

There is another allusion to the "sleep" of the righteous in 100:5, which may refer to their death, and thus, **(A, B)** it possibly also alludes to their coming resurrection. As in the preceding passages, this is doubted by Stemberger (1972, 40 f.). But the contrast to v.4 seems to be intentional. In this verse the angels are related as gathering all of those who are responsible for the existence of sin, and the angels apparently descend into Sheol for this action. So it seems probable that the righteous mentioned in v.5 are those who have died and that their "sleep" refers to death. **(D)** According to v.4, the day of judgment is the "date" of the sinners' punishment. So it is likely that the same day is implied in the next verse as the date of the resurrection of the dead. Yet each of these three texts' testimony to the resurrection must be viewed with some reservation, and should therefore be treated with precaution. The situation is clearer in the latter part of the Book of Exhortations, e.g. in 102:4 f.:

3.2.3.4

Be of good cheer, souls of the righteous, who have died . . .[32] do not grieve because your souls have descended in grief into Sheol and the body of your flesh has not fared in your life according to your piety . . . (ET Nickelsburg, 1972, 115).

The theme of ch. 102-104 can thus be described: Although the righteous are persecuted, and perhaps slain, and their evil oppressors who lead a comfortable life triumphantly declare that they are not at all rewarded for their being righteous (since there is no difference in the state of death—102:6-11; 103:6-15; 104:6-9), God shall finally vindicate the souls of the righteous (103:3-4; 104:6-9) and punish the souls of the wicked (103:7-8; 104:3b)[33]. **(A)** This conviction, together with the following sayings on the glorious state of the righteous souls after death, is a presupposition of the statements exhorting good cheer. **(B)** Only the righteous souls are addressed. Nothing is said about a resurrection of the body[34] nor **(C)** anything more precise about the righteous souls after death. **(D)** No "date" is given for the realization of these promises.

3.2.3.5

A similar text is found in 103:3-7:

(3) Good things and joy and honour are prepared and written down for the souls of the pious who have died[35] (4) and their spirits will rejoice and will not perish[36] nor the remembrance (of them) before the face of the Great One for all eternal generations . . . (5) And you, dead, who belong to the sinners . . . (7) you know yourselves[37] that they will bring your souls down to Hades (8) and there they will be in great distress, and in darkness and in chains and in a burning flame, and your souls will enter the great judgment for all the generations of eternity . . .[38]

(A) Following their death, a just retribution of both the righteous and the wicked will take place. **(B)** Nothing is said about the resurrection of the body as it is only the souls (or spirits) which are mentioned. **(C)** The souls of the righteous shall have an eternal life of joy, whereas the sinners are to be punished in Hades for ever. **(D)** The formulations could indicate that the sinners are punished in Hades immediately after death, whereas the reward of the righteous is given some time later ("the souls of the pious who have died, των ἀποθανοντων εὐσεβων ... will rejoice, χαιρησονται ..."). However, it seems unlikely that a difference between the righteous and the sinners is intended in this respect[39].

3.2.3.6
And finally 104:2:

> Be of good cheer then, you who were formerly in misfortune and distress, you will *shine and be radiant as the lights of heaven,* the portals[40] of heaven will be opened for you ...

The Ethiopian version adds in v.4:

> Be hopeful ... for you will have great joy as the angels in heaven (ET Nickelsburg, 1972, 120).

(A, B) This passage does not say anything about death or new life after death, but it is located in a context which does so, (cf. Nickelsburg, 1972, 121), as we have seen. **(C)** It describes the righteous' change of condition in a way strikingly similar to Dn 12:3, and thus, it may contain a direct allusion to this text which is preceded by a clearly expressed hope in the resurrection[41]. So, considering the context and this probable allusion to Dn 12:3, it can rather safely be assumed that the glorification promised to the righteous also concerns those who had died. The transcendence of this future glory is expressed in symbolic language by the opening of the portals of heaven. The addition of the Ethiopian version compares the future glory of the righteous with that of the angels. This may be a later interpolation, having been influenced by Mk 12:25 parr or perhaps II Bar 51:10 (3.9), as Stemberger (1972, 43) suggests. But the association between the blessed righteous, the "lights of heaven" and the angels is a motif which returns in different combinations in Jewish, Christian and even pagan texts concerning resurrection and immortality (see 7.2.1).

(D) The transformation of the life of the righteous seems to be related to "the day of the great judgment" (v.5, which immediately follows this passage).

3.2.4
The most distinctive part of I En would probably be the Parables or the *Similitudes of Enoch,* ch. 37-71 (cf. nn.6-7 *supra*). Statements about resurrection and after-life are rather different from those in other parts of I En, too. This is the only section of I En which clearly expresses a belief in the resurrection of the body on the Last Day. The most important passage is 51:1:

> And in those days shall the earth also give back that which has been entrusted to it, and Sheol also shall give back that which it has received, and Hell shall give back that which it owes ... (ET:Charles, 1912).

44

(A) The bodies of the dead (of Israel or of all men?) is certainly that which has been entrusted to the earth and will be given back by the earth. Then that which is given back by Sheol and Hell ought to be the souls, maybe the souls of the righteous by Sheol and those of the wicked by Hell (*haguel* in Eth.—cf. e.g. Hammershaimb, 1956 *ad loc.*). But it is naturally difficult to determine whether Sheol and Hell are anything other than expressions for death used in the old Israelite way (2.1.1). It is also perfectly plausible that all the three expressions (that which has been entrusted to the earth, that which Sheol has received, and that which Hell owes) are synonymous parallels. Then there would be no clear distinction at all between the three groups in the mind of the author. On the foundation of the earlier Israelite anthropology such a vagueness would be very natural.

(B) P. Grelot (RQ 1, 1958, 122) qualifies the resurrection, evidently described here, as the resurrection of the spirit, found, according to his interpretation, in the rest of I En, rather than as the resurrection of the body. But the fact that the earth is mentioned definitely strengthens the more usual interpretation (e.g. by Charles, AP II; Hammershaimb, 1956, *ad loc.*): a resurrection of the body conceived in a very concrete way[42]. But the continuation of the text assures us that this is intended to be more than a mere return to earthly life, 51:4:

3.2.4.1
All shall be angels in heaven; their faces shall be radiant with joy (ET:Charles, 1893; Hammershaimb, 1956, in Danish).

This can also quite possibly be translated:

And the faces of (all) the angels in heaven shall be lighted up with joy (ET:Charles 1912; Hammershaimb, 1956, Danish in a foot-note).

(C) We have already seen the comparison of the resurrection glory of the righteous with that of the angels (3.2.3.6), and we shall meet it again (further references in 7.2.1). This is an argument for the older interpretation of Charles, though it is not decisive[43]. However, if it would be deleted from the passage, the context tells us that resurrection implies more than a new, happy life on earth: that the conditions of the righteous would be radically changed. 50:1 explicitly states a transformation of light and glory. The mountains shall jump and the earth rejoice according to 51:4 f. On the other hand, 51:5 directly says that the righteous shall live "on earth" and that the elect shall "walk on it". So the concept of a post-resurrection existence of the righteous might here be described as "a transformed life on a transformed earth"[44] without any further precise thoughts about the implications of this transformation (cf. Grelot, RQ 1, 122 f.).

(D) The transformation and resurrection will take place "in these days", "on the day of distress" and the day of judgment when the Elect One has risen (51:5) and is enthroned in glory (49:2; 51:3).

3.2.4.2
Another resurrection text in EnSim, though somewhat obscure, is 61:5:

And these measures[45] shall reveal all the secrets in the depths of the earth and those who have been destroyed by the desert, and those who have been devoured by the beasts and those who have been devoured by the fish of the sea, that they may return and stay themselves on the day of the Elect One, for none shall be destroyed before the Lord of the Spirits, and none can be destroyed (ET:Charles, 1912).

(A, B) The passage in all probability speaks of the resurrection of all the righteous[46], whose deaths have various causes[47]. Since it refers to the places where these people died and their bodies were destroyed, buried etc., a resurrection of the body is probably in the mind of the author (cf. Grelot, RQ 1, 121 f.). **(C)** V.6 should probably be understood as referring to the angels (in light of Hammershaimb, 1956,, *ad loc.*). Therefore, nothing is said about any transformation of the bodies of the righteous who are to rise. **(D)** The enthronement of the Elect One and the judgment are mentioned in the context of the saying about the resurrection (v.8); and the events are dated "in these days" (v.1).

3.2.4.3
46:6 seems to presuppose the resurrection of the righteous when it denies the hope of resurrection for the tyrants **(A, B)**.

3.2.4.4
A number of passages mentions "the eternal life" without describing any resurrection. Beside two short allusions (37:4; 40:9), 58:3 is worth quoting here:

And the righteous will be in the light of the sun and the elect in the light of eternal life, and the days of their life shall be unending and the days of the saints without number (ET Charles, 1912).

(C) The image of light symbolizes the transformed character of the eternal life to come, but nothing more precise can be said about the nature of this transformation. (Cf. also 39:7!)

3.2.4.5
This **(C)** transformation, **(D)** on the Last Day, of the righteous into a state of glory and immortality is symbolized in 62:15-16 by the image of the apparel of glory incapable of being worn out:

And they shall have been clothed with garments of glory (v.1: of life). And these shall be the garments of life from the Lord of the Spirits and your garments shall not grow old, nor your glory pass away before the Lord of the Spirits (ET Charles 1912).

The Deuteronomistic description of one of the miracles of the forty years in the desert (Dt 8:4; 29:5) has been transposed to an eschatological level: now those garments, incapable of being worn out, symbolize the eternal life of glory (cf. I Cor 15:36, 49, 53 f.).

3.2.4.6

(D) According to 63:10, the kings of the earth shall descend into the flames of Sheol[48] on the *day of judgment* (cf. 62 and 63:1).

3.2.4.7

Enoch's adoration, which takes place at the coming of the Lord of the Spirits, is described in 71:11:

> I fell down on my face and the whole of my body was dissolved and my spirit was transformed, and I cried in a loud voice in the spirit of power (ET Charles 1912)

Although this may merely be metaphorical language expressing the overwhelming impression that the theophany made upon Enoch (cf. 60:3), **(C)** it could also say something about the character of the new life which resurrection would bring to the righteous. Then this new life seems to be conceived as something rather spiritual, even as being without a body. The passage would thus describe the assumption of Enoch as the pattern and model of what happens to all the righteous in death[49]. If this is true, the third "parable" of Enoch, with special problems as to origin and date[50], would give another image of *post-mortem* life: one more similar to the image seen in the other sections of I En[51] than what is seen in the rest of EnSim.

3.2.5

I En 108:11-15 is part of a late addition to this collection of Enoch traditions. This says nothing about the date of its composition, however[52], and so it shall not be excluded here:

> And now I will summon the spirits of the good who belong to the generation of light, and I will transform those who were born in darkness, who in the flesh were not recompensed with such honor as their faithfulness deserved. And I will bring forth in shining light those who have loved my holy name, and I will seat each one on the throne of his glory. There they will shine in unending times . . . And the sinners will cry out and see them resplendent, and they will depart . . . (108:11 ff., 15 in ET by Nickelsburg, 1972, *ad loc.*)

(A) This text speaks rather clearly about a *post-mortem* retribution of both the righteous and the wicked. **(B)** The *spirits* of the righteous experience a sort of resurrection, being brought out from darkness (Sheol?) into dazzling light, whereas the sinners remain in darkness, being painfully conscious of the glory of the righteous. **(C)** The righteous are glorified and transformed in the highest possible manner: being placed on thrones of glory just as the Son of Man is placed on his throne of glory[53]. **(D)** This will happen at some not determined time in the eschatological future: perhaps at the last judgment (cf. v.13: "Justice is the judgment of God").

3.2.6 *Summary*

By complementing those texts which mention resurrection with those which merely mention life for the souls after death it can be calculated that a doctrine of an intermediate state, followed by a final resurrection on a "Last Day" of judgment was known by the authors. Three passages would logically presuppose some kind of intermediate existence, since they mention both the soul/spirit after death and some kind of resurrection, but this is not explicitly stated. S. Aalen is one who maintains that I En, as well as Palestinian Jewish literature in general (and NT), contains the doctrine of the intermediate state on such grounds. But are such a secondary combination of texts and logical deductions from these texts at all permissible?

It seems quite evident (Cf. index III *ad* I En) that the resurrection of the body is explicitly proclaimed only by Sim, the latest section (except, maybe, the epilogue of ch. 108). There is a remarkable difference between Sim and the rest of I En (cf. Grelot, RQ 1, 122 f., and *supra* 2.3.4). It is hardly possible to avoid this conclusion of P. Volz (1934, 16 ff.): there are different eschatologies in the various strata of the traditions behind I En. They were simply and easily juxtaposed both in the final redaction and probably also in earlier stages of the process of redaction (see Charles, AP II, 280; 1912, 269). This shows us that the redactors did not feel any real opposition between the concept of a resurrection of the body and the concept of an eternal life for the righteous souls. These concepts appear as alternative valid descriptions of after-life which cannot be harmonized in the doctrine of the intermediate state of the souls between death and resurrection.

Another result of this investigation is that eternal life is consistently described in all of these Enoch traditions as a glorified life in light, being radically transformed as compared to earthly life. The same is also true about the concept of the last day, the "date" on which new life is given to the dead. It is often combined with references to the judgment, even in texts which only speak about the immortality of the soul. The views about the end of history, the decisive transition of the earth and the status of the dead seem to be more important in all of these texts than their anthropological views (whether the essential unity or the dichotomy of body and soul in man be stressed).

[1]Cf. A. M. Denis (1970) 16 f., 26 ff., with a survey on the discussion on the date and origin of the different parts and final redaction of I En. Also e.g. O. Eissfeldt ([3]1964) 838 ff. The basic facts may be summarized here: Jub 4:17-19 seems to pre-suppose I En 12-36 and 72-82. That would date these parts of I En before the last quarter of the second century BC or even around 170 BC (cf. *supra* 3.1 for the date of Jub). The Apocalypse of Ten Weeks (93 + 91: 12-17) seems to be pre-Maccabean as well, whereas the apocalypse with the animal symbols (85-90) may be dated between 170 and 100 BC. 94-104 could be placed in the first quarter of the last century BC. I En 37-71, the Similitudes, constitute a special problem, to which I shall briefly return (*infra* and n.7).

[2]For a presentation on pseudepigraphy as a characteristic feature of apocalyptic literature, esp. the use of the name of an ancient patriarch or hero in the faith, and the role of journeys to heaven, see e.g. Russell (1964) 127-139; Schreiner (1969) 74-86; Hengel (1973) 371-378. Cf. *supra* 3.0.1.

[3]1-32:6; 97:6-104; 106-107—cf. for the first part J. Flemming and L. Rademacher (1901)—with a German translation of the Ethiopian text—and R. H. Charles (1906)—with the Ethiopian text, for the last two pieces C. Bonner (1937)—and for the whole of the Greek text now M. Black (1970).

⁴Cf. e.g. E. Hammershaimb (1956) 75 f.; Black (1970) 6 f.; DJD I, 84-86; 152 (IQ 19, 20,19 bis—fragments that seem to correspond to pieces of I En 8:4-9:4; 106.

⁵I: ch. 1-36: angelological part; II: ch. 37-71: Similitudines; III: ch. 72-82: astronomical part; IV: ch. 83-90: Visions; V: ch. 91-105: Exhortations. Ch. 106-108 are an addition. Smaller, originally independent units can be discerned within these main parts. Cf. e.g. Charles (1912) 1, 67, 180, 222; Hammershaimb (1956) 69 f.; Denis (1970) 26; Black (1970) 5.

⁶It is denied by e.g. P. Vielhauer, ZThK 60 (1963) 169 f.; J. T. Milik acc. to e.g. Eissfeldt (1964) 840; J. C. Hindley, NTS 14 (1967/8) 551-565, who suggests a date "during or soon after the Parthian campaign of Trajan" (564).

⁷E.g. E. Sjöberg (1946) 1 ff., 38 f. (rather late date: the beginning of the first pro-curacy); Hammershaimb (1956) 75; Eissfeldt (1964) 839 f.

⁸"Those who were exterminated"—cf. e.g. Hammershaimb ad loc.

⁹Those who were "spread all around"—cf. e.g. Hammershaimb ad loc.

¹⁰"All the beasts of the earth and all the birds of the sky"—89:10-27, 42-43, 49, 55-58, 65-68; 90:2-19 and Hammershaimb (e.g.) ad loc.

¹¹Cf. Ez 37:1-14 in Jewish interpretation (infra 4.1.6 and n.32) and the Tg of Is 27:12 f. (infra 5.8.3). See also Schubert, BZ 6, 192, on this passage.

¹²Cf. e.g. Wied (1965) 91; P. Grelot, RQ 1 (1958) 120, who stresses the opinion that it is not possible to learn anything about the mode of resurrection (of the body or of the soul/spirit) from this passage. Stemberger (1972) 38 refers to 10:17-22; 25:4-6, which would prove that the resurrection of I En 22 would be only to life on this earth—cf. his own criticism of the harmonization danger, p. 38, and n.18 infra!

¹³Concerning this designation I En 6-11 + 54:7-55:2; 60; 65:1-69:25; 106-107, cf. e.g. Charles, AP II, 168; Grelot, RQ 1, 117; Denis (1970) 17.

¹⁴In the context this seems to be a description of the punishment of the "souls" (Eth.) or "spirits" (Gr.) after death.

¹⁵Cf. Schubert, BZ 6, 192n: 10:17 and 25:4 refer to the risen righteous. Otherwise ch. 6-36 speak about souls with the qualities of bodies.

¹⁶V.2 speaks of four hollow places, three of which are dark, whereas the fourth is bright and contains a fountain of water. V.9 says that this hollow place is occupied by the spirits of the righteous—but mentions only three places. That would suit an image of two places for the sinners, one for the righteous, but there seems to be two places for the righteous as well in vv.9 and 12—cf. infra and Glasson (1961) 14-17, considering the possibility that only one class of the righteous is raised, those who died a violent death; Wilckens (1970) 118 f.; Grelot (1971) 210. Nickelsburg (1972) 137, with a good survey and discussion of the possibilities, including textual corruption, suggests interpolations in vv.2 and 12, so that the text originally would have only spoken of three compartments.

¹⁷Cf. Charles (1912) 2: Pre-Maccabaean, referring to Jub 4:17-19 and I En 83-90, which seem to presuppose ch. 12-36 and 72-82—cf. n.1 supra. See also Nickelsburg (1972) 134 n.15: they "need not presuppose the totality of En 6-36 in its present written form". More important facts are the Qumran MSS, which contain ch. 30-32, 4QHen^b and 4QHen^d—cf. J. T. Milik, RB 65 (1958) 70-77.

¹⁸In v.3 both the Greek and the Ethiopian version combines the two terms, whereas in v.11 (bis) and 13 (bis) Gr. has πνευματα and Eth. manfas ("souls"). For the fluctuation of these terms throughout this passage, cf. Nickelsburg (1972) 135 n.17. Hengel (1973) 361 f., finds a Greek

49

anthropology expressed here (body-soul dualism), whereas Grelot, RQ 1, 118, still finds the biblical idea of man as one whole being: the soul/spirit denotes the whole person. Thus the retribution, as described in I En 22, is incomplete until the spirits arise on the Day of Judgment ($\pi\nu\epsilon\upsilon\mu\alpha\tau\alpha$ is the subject of $\mu\epsilon\tau\epsilon\gamma\epsilon\rho\vartheta\omega\sigma\iota\nu$) —cf. Nickelsburg, 1972, 136. Stemberger (1972) 38 (with n.45) asserts that if I En 22 teaches a resurrection it is a resurrection of the righteous to new, long and happy life on earth, which is not eternal or transcendent. His argument is based on the context of I En 22 being in I En 1-36—in spite of the warning (p. 38): "Äusserste Vorsicht ist hier am Platz: ein zusammenhängendes Bild der Endzeit ist Hen 1-36 nicht zu entnehmen." Wilckens (1970) 119, believes that only those who have not been rewarded or punished in this life "need" the resurrection, the others have already received the retribution in this life (as in old Israelite thinking—2.1.1).

[19]Cf. Grelot, RQ 1, 118 ("lieu transitoire"); Hoffmann (1966) 110, who limits the intermediate state to the righteous, since he finds that in v.13 $\tau\iota\mu\omega\rho\eta\vartheta\eta\sigma\sigma\nu\tau\alpha\iota$ and $\mu\epsilon\tau\epsilon\gamma\epsilon\rho\vartheta\omega\sigma\iota\nu$ function as mutually exclusive possibilities (but is that a necessary interpretation of v.13?). On the other hand, if the verse is interpreted as referring to the medium class of sinners (Hoffmann, 109), then Hoffmann's interpretation of the relation between $\tau\iota\mu\omega\rho\eta\vartheta\eta\sigma\sigma\nu\tau\alpha\iota$ and $\mu\epsilon\tau\epsilon\gamma\epsilon\rho\vartheta\omega\sigma\iota\nu$ is natural: this medium class of sinners are not $\acute{o}\sigma\iota\sigma\iota$ and thus they have no right to share in the resurrection (then only a salvation event), nor are they the worst type of sinners and so they shall not be punished on the day of judgment, as those of v.11, who neither rise, according to Hoffmann, 110.—A Rabbinic parallel concerning the medium class of sinners or those who are neither sinners nor righteous is treated infra 5.1.2. Cf. also Bill IV, 1183-1192, and Sanh 108a. The "exclusion formulas" of MSanh 10:3, which I intend to discuss in a separate article, also contain the idea of special group of sinners, who are not raised even for judgment. Cf. Glasson (1961) 18, with reference to a parallel idea in Plato.

[20]Cf. Grelot, RQ 1, 121; Nickelsburg (1972) 136—about the sinners, at least. Glasson (1961) 18, thinks that "the Messianic period in Enoch 1-36 is not eternal life; men still die, though there is now no early or untimely death. Presumably the resurrected righteous also die in the course of time." But the final state of the righteous (ibid. n.13) would be conceived as spiritual, and he refers to Jub 23:30-31 as a parallel (3.1.1 supra). The present author cannot find any statements at all concerning a special Messianic kingdom in I En 1-36. The conclusions of Glasson are then quite uncertain. For Stemberger and a criticism of his position, see n.18 supra.

[21]We find an allusion to the resurrection only in v.13—and then by inference from the negative statement. Cf. e.g. H. H. Rowley (1947); Schubert, WZKM 56, 159.

[22]With the term "author" I include the possibilities of an individual person, a transmitting community with several authors, a final redactor, etc.

[23]Cf. Plato's use of the term $\mu\upsilon\vartheta\sigma\varsigma$ in Gorgias 523A-527A: Phaedrus 237A; Phaedo 60B; 61B (Aesopus!); Republic I, 330D; III, 414B-415D. Further, on Philo's allegorical interpretation as an example of such a consciousness, U. Früchtel (1968) 81-106.

[24]Cf. infra 7.1.3, 8, 11.—In 20:8, according to the MS Gg[2] (the verse is lacking in Gg[1] and the Eth. version, but is original according to Charles, 1912 and Hammershaimb, 1956 ad loc.; Nickelsburg, 1972, 136 n.21, since Gg[1] mentions seven archangels, and without Remiel, there would be only six; Black, 1970, gives the text of Gg[1] as the main text, but registers Gg[2] underneath with our description of the seventh archangel, without any comments): "Remiel, one of the holy angels, whom God put over those who rise." (A, B) This brief allusion to the resurrection does not tell us (C) anything about the mode of the resurrection stated here, nor does it (D) give us any "date" for the resurrection of the dead. Cf. here e.g. Glasson (1961) 16; Nickelsburg (1972) 136 f.; Stemberger (1972) 36.

[25]The relation of ch. 105 to the preceding chapters is somewhat uncertain—cf. e.g. Charles (1912) 262; Hammershaimb (1956) 71. On the treatment of immortality and resurrection here, see e.g. Grelot, RQ 1, 118-120; Wied (1965) 56-72; Hoffmann (1966) 120-127; S. Aalen, NTS 13 (1966/7) 1-13; Nickelsburg (1972) 112-130 (only on ch. 94-104); Stemberger (1972) 40-44.

[26]Stemberger (1972) 40, doubts that this is a reference to resurrection on the ground that "wisdom" is used with the same verb as a parallel to "the righteous". Then the statement is interpreted as a general proclamation of the victory of the righteous—as well as of wisdom—in the end time. But the possible allusions to Dn 12:2 f. would strengthen the assumption of most scholars (A. Dillmann, 1853; G. Beer, 1900; Charles, 1912; Hammershaimb, 1956, ad loc. G. Wied, 1965, 73-77, e.g.) that "sleep" refers to death and "rise" to resurrection. See also Wilckens (1970) 123, but the direct combination with I En 51 is doubtful ("wie man sich das vorzustellen hat, schildert I En 51").

[27]For the collective interpretation of the singular "the righteous", cf. e.g. Hammershaimb (1956) ad loc. See further Beer, Kautzsch AP II (1900) ad loc.

[28]Cf. Schubert, BZ 6, 1960198, on the Book of Exhortations generally: though no resurrection of the "flesh-body" (Fleischleib) is maintained here, a future resurrection is stated. However, the retribution is the central motif.

[29]A common apocalyptic pattern described in Hartman (1966) 28 ff.

[30]Cf. n.28 on the collective interpretation, and Dn 12:3.

[31]Stemberger (1972) 41, concedes the possibility that this passage does refer to a resurrection but, making reference to the work of C. Barth (1947), stresses that the differences between death and life and maybe heaven and earth are not at all sharply distinguished in "Hebrew thought" (n.55, with H. W. Kuhn, 1966, 55). Above all he underlines the textual uncertainty of this verse. Codex G reads: "Wisdom shall rise from sleep, she will rise and righteousness will walk . . ." As lectio difficilior this is preferred by Wied (1965) 56. But Stemberger's final conclusion seems to be the concession that this is a situation where death is abolished, 42, n.56.

[32]Eth.:
Do not be afraid, you souls of the righteous,
and be of good hope, you who have died in righteousness
(ET Charles 1912).

[33]Wilckens (1970) 122, recognizes the same four groups here as in ch. 22, which is not very obvious. But he agrees that nothing is said about the resurrection in these chapters.

[34]According to the Gr.text and some Eth. MSS a reference to the resurrection is found indirectly in 102:7 f., the scornful talk of the sinners against the righteous:
They died just as we do. See then how they die with sorrow and darkness, and what more did they get? From now on let them rise (ἀναστητωσαν) and let them be saved (σωϑητωσαν) , and may they see for ever, how we eat and drink (cf. e.g. I Cor 15:32). Cf. here Stemberger (1972) 43 f., and edd. with comm. ad loc.

[35]Eth.: the spirits of those who died in righteousness, Nickelsburg, 1972, 118 and n.26.

[36]Eth. vv. 3b-4a:
3b And much good will be given to you in place of your toils
c And your lot exceeds that of the living.
4a And the spirits of you who have died in righteousness will live and rejoice and your spirits will not perish (Nickelsburg, 1972, 118 and n.26).

[37]Concerning Eth. cf. Nickelsburg (1972) 118 n.26, 127 n.59.

[38]Eth.: And darkness, chains and burning flame, where the great judgment takes place, will your spirit enter, and the great judgment will occur to all the generations of the world. See Charles (1912) *ad loc.* and cf. Nickelsburg (1972) 118.

[39]Cf. e.g. Hoffmann (1966) 124-127; Nickelsburg (1972) 117 f.; Stemberger (1972) 42 f., who again tries rather unsuccessfully to throw doubts on an interpretation implying life after death. In the end he does not give any alternative interpretation.

[40]The Gr. word $\vartheta\upsilon\rho\iota\varsigma$ usually means "window", and is rendered thus by e.g. Stemberger (1972) 43—rather unnaturally. G. W. H. Lampe, (1961) s.v., gives several examples of the meaning "gate" or "door", however, which is already used by the Eth. version. Nickelsburg's suggestion, "portal", has been chosen here.

[41]Cf. *supra* 2.2 and e.g. Nickelsburg (1972) 121 f. He prefers to think of a parallel tradition rather than of direct influence, though he concedes the possibility of the latter. However, since we have no earlier testimonies to the tradition postulated by Nickelsburg apart from Dn 12:3, it would seem more safe to think of this as a direct allusion or at least an influence from Dn 12:3.

[42]Cf. this with Stemberger (1972) 46-48, who does not think that there is any difference in meaning between earth, Sheol and Hell: they all signify "the land of dust", the kingdom of death. So he interprets 51:1 as an affirmation of the resurrection of the whole man, body and soul in unity and not as the reunion of body and soul. This is, however, applied only to the righteous. But the reference to the thought of "Biblical man" (47) is not very convincing: "Zerfällt der Leib in der Erde, so denkt der biblische Mensch nicht mehr an seine Wiederbelebung." Is "the Biblical man" the author of I En? Does I En belong to the Bible?

[43]Stemberger (1972) 48, uses the same facts in an opposing argument: an Ethiopian scribe has changed the original meaning of the texts, which was the second alternative, since he did change it in 104:4, 6 by making secondary additions.

[44]Cf. also 45:4 f. and Stemberger (1972) 48.

[45]The measures which the angels use to measure the dwelling-place of the blessed—cf. vv. 1-4, and Hammershaimb (1956) *ad loc.*

[46]The wicked are not at all mentioned here. The resurrection is obviously an act of salvation. Cf. also for the same conclusion on 51:1 Stemberger (1972) 47 f.

[47]"The secrets of the depth of the earth" would refer to those who died and were buried in more usual ways, whereas "those who were destroyed by the desert . . . eaten by wild beasts and . . . by the fish of the sea" are examples of extremely difficult cases: even here resurrection will occur; therefore, "nobody . . . will be exterminated".

[48]The difference between Sheol and Hell is not very clear—cf. 56:8 and 51:1 with the comm. *supra* and n.42.

[49]Cf. here e.g. Volz (1934) 187; Sjöberg (1946) 147-159, 164-189; Strobel (1967) 50 f.; F. H. Borsch (1967) 146-152; H. R. Balz (1967) 64-67, 96-107.

[50]Cf. e.g. Charles (1912) XIII, XLIX; Sjöberg (1946) 147, 159-167; Hammershaimb (1956) *ad loc.*

[51]Cf. also 71:1: "My *spirit* was taken away . . ." and on the passage in general Wilckens (1970) 134-137.

[52]Cf. e.g. Charles, AP II, 280; *id.* (1912) 269; Hammershaimb (1956) 70; Nickelsburg (1972) 86 f., esp. n. 145.

[53]Cf. here Russell (1964) 377 f.; Stemberger (1972) 44 f., with references to parallels in Rabbinic literature and NT. For "the throne of glory" as the glory of the Son of Man see esp. 45:3; 55:4; 62:3, 5; 69:27, 29 and Mt 19:28; 25:31.

3.3 The Testaments of the Twelve Patriarchs

Based on the judgment of a relatively large number of scholars[1] I accept Test XII Patr as a collection of Palestinian Jewish texts, probably pre-Christian and certainly independent of Christianity, with the exception of the self-evident interpolations made by a later Christian scribe[2].—These do not, however, affect the essential contents of the statements on the resurrection of the dead[3]. According to the opinion of J. Becker (1970, 325 f.) these may be later than the basic original document, but their authorship is dated not later than the first century AD and is definitely Jewish (*ibid.* 373-376, and cf. Stemberger, 1972, 65). Thus, the resurrection statements can be used for our purpose as testimonies of ideas expressed by a Palestinian apocalyptic group[4].

3.3.1

One group of resurrection sayings in TestXIIPatr especially concerns the patriarchs and other great heroes of old. In TestSim 6:7[5] the patriarch is presented asserting his own future resurrection:

> Then I shall rise in joy and I shall bless the Most High for His wonders.

(A, B) There is a *post mortem* resurrection of at least some of the ancient elected persons **(D)** at the end of time (cf. the preceding verses). **C)** But there are no details given about the resurrected body or about the soul between death and resurrection. TestJud 25:1[6] records a promise of a resurrection "to life" for Abraham, Isaac, Jacob and the twelve sons of Jacob who are to be the leaders of the tribes of the future Israel. The addition εἰς ζωην may establish an allusion to Dn 12:2. TestZeb 10:2[7] is the third example of this type of resurrection predictions. Here, as in TestJud 25:1, the rising patriarch will be the leader of his tribe in the eschatological people of God. Finally we may quote *Test Benj 10:6 f.*[8]

> And then you shall see Enoch, Noah and Shem[9] and Abraham and Isaac and Jacob rising on His right hand in joy. Then shall we also rise, each at his tribe[10] and adore the King of Heaven

(C) The exaltation of the ancient heroes and patriarchs to the right hand of God expresses the heavenly and transcendent character of this resurrection. However, for some reason Stemberger (1972, 66) thinks that TestZeb 10:2 univocally (*eindeutig*) locates the resurrected life on earth. The argument is based on Zebulun's stating that he shall rise in the midst of his tribe with the presupposition that the tribe will be living on earth. But this is not said anywhere. The φυλη may just as well refer to all of the generations of the tribe of Zebulun, who will be with their patriarch on the day of resurrection. The φυλη is most probably not meant to denote a geographical location.

TestLevi 18:14[11] represents a similar way of expression, though death and resurrection are not explicitly mentioned (cf. Stemberger, 1972, 66 ff.).

3.3.2

There are two clear statements on a general resurrection in Test XIIPatr, Jud 25:4 and Benj 10:8, both containing possible allusions to Dn 12:2, underlined in the following quotations: *Jud 25:4:*

> And those who have finished in sorrow will *rise* (ἀναστησονται) in joy[12] and those poor for the sake of the Lord will be made rich ... and[13] those who die for the sake of the Lord will *wake up* (ἐξυπνισθησονται) *to life* (εἰς ζωην)[14].

(A, B) The resurrection predicted here[15] is obviously an act of salvation for the righteous who were not rewarded while living[16]. **(D)** The perspective of a future judgment after the resurrection is not expressed. The context "dates" the resurrection to take place after the appearance of the Messiah (24:1-25:1), and the general resurrection to take place after that of the patriarchs[17]. **(C)** Stemberger (1972, 67) declares: "Auch hier ist die Auferstehung als eine Rückkehr auf Erden gedacht." Nothing in the text supports his statement, neither does he make any effort to find support for it. The text does not actually give any information at all about the mode of resurrection.

TestBenj 10:8 teaches a universal resurrection of both good and evil men, being inspired by Dn 12:2[18]:

> And all shall *rise* (ἀναστησονται) [19], *some for glory, others for dishonour,* and the Lord will judge Israel, first of all, for their unrighteousness.

(A, B) The resurrection **(C)** leads to a transformation of the conditions of all those who rise, for better or for worse, without precisely relating what is meant by δοξα or ἀτιμια. **(D)** The resurrection seems to be the presupposition for the final judgment of Israel and all the nations (v.9).

3.3.3

Though *Test Levi 18:9-14* and Dan 5:12 f. do not explicitly mention death or resurrection, they are cited by Stemberger (1972) 67. The first passage describes the future salvation of the righteous by the appearance of the Messianic "priest-saviour" (for this term see Hultgård, 1971, 125, 130, 133-135 *passim*): The gates of paradise will be opened to the righteous (v.10), they will eat of the tree of life (v.11) etc., and the patriarchs

> will rejoice and all the saints be clothed in righteousness[20].

(A) In the case of the patriarchs this eschatological joy is realized after death (3.3.1). This would probably apply to the righteous in general. **(D)** The new situation for the righteous (and wicked!) will be brought about by the appearance of the New Priest.

Test Dan 5:11 ff. (according to Becker, 1970, 353 f., originally an independent apocalypse) is a description of the future salvation of Israel, but it does not explicitly say anything about this salvation as an event *post mortem*, though this might be presupposed. The fact that "the captivity" of v.11[21] is defined as "the souls of the saints" is, however, likely to indicate that at least some of those who are saved (according to these verses) are conceived to be dead. The life to come is described as "rest" and "eternal peace" (v.11) and as the definite liberation of Jerusalem and Israel. None of this allows further definite conclusions **(B)** about the nature of the souls and/or bodies of those **(C)** who share in this glorified existence. The Eden to be established for the saints seems to be more or less identified with a new Jerusalem and a new Israel, in whose midst the Lord himself will reign, "living together with men" (τοις ἀνϑρωποις συναναστρεφομενος). If the alternative "earthly" or "heavenly" salvation would be applied to this text (which may altogether be a false alternative), perhaps one should speak about a "transformed, earthly" salvation. That which is of importance is the presence of the Lord himself on this earth, in the new Israel and Jerusalem. **(D)** This will be realized in an indefinite eschatological future.

3.3.4

The preceding texts do not give particular mention to the body or the soul. However, one of the Testaments, *TestAsher,* seems to regard afterlife as the soul's continued existence rather than a resurrection. Nickelsburg has already pointed out the importance of TestAsher 6:5-6 for an examination of current theories on the distinction between Greek and Jewish concepts of resurrection and immortality (1972, 161 f., 165, 179). He finds this to be an example of a "two-way-theology", also represented in the Qumran texts[22], in Wi 1-5[23], and in Early Christian documents[24]. In this context, where the fate of the righteous is sharply contrasted with that of the sinners, **(D)** it is death that is described as leading to an immediate judgment of the *soul,* bringing salvation to the righteous and punishment to the wicked. No resurrection is mentioned. A good example is Test Asher 1:3-6:6. The final consequences of the two ways are described in *6:5-6:*

When the evil soul departs (ἀπερχεται) it is tortured by the evil spirit, which it served, too, in lusts and evil deads, But if it is tranquil in joy, it recognizes the angel of peace, and it brings him into[25] *eternal life* (cf. Dn 12:2).

(A) Both types of souls "survive" death[26]. **(B)** Nothing is said about the body. **(D)** The judgment, either torture or eternal life, seems to be executed immediately after death.

3.5 *Summary*

It is conceded that the concept of resurrection with its terminology dominates the impression which TextXIIPatr give about life after death, but Stemberger's attempt (1972, 65-71, esp. 69) to harmonize TestAsher with the rest of TestXIIPatr cannot be accepted. He refers to a presupposed, clearly defined anthropology, which never separates the body from the soul—but all his quotations in the section on anthropology refer to other Testaments than that of Asher (with one exception, Asher 2:7, where a possible opposition between body and soul is asserted). Even a direct Greek influence cannot be excluded, e.g., in the doctrine of the two spirits[27]. But, above all, neither TestXIIPatr nor any other apocalyptic texts must be treated as textbooks of dogmatic theology containing teaching and doctrine on eschatological matters or anthropology. Rather, the different forms of eschatological teaching should be isolated and analyzed. Then the function of the eschatological symbols and statements will be seen, each in its context, and in this way an easy harmonization can be avoided. Thus, the form of "two-way theology" has been isolated by Nickelsburg (1972, 156-164). Another "form" appears to be the resurrection prediction[28], which is followed by the statements on the general resurrection, the only clear resurrection sayings in TestXIIPatr.

[1]Above all on the basis of Qumran fragments of TestLevi in Aramaic (DJD I, no 21, 87-91; J. T. Milik, RB 62, 1955, 398-406, 4Q) and TestNapht in Hebrew (Milik, RB 63, 1956, 407 n.1) which prove a Semitic original, probably Hebrew (Russell, 1964, 55; Denis, 1970, 57). J. Becker (1970) 374, suggests a non-Palestinian origin, probably in Egypt. He rightly stresses the fact that the Hellenistic Judaism of the diaspora was by no means free from apocalyptic (*ibid.* 4 f.)—but that is hardly a weighty argument against the Palestinian origin of TestXIIPatr. Cf. Russell (1964) 55-57; Denis (1970) 57-59; Stemberger (1972) 63-65, with further references there. M. De Jonge has been forced to change his opinion, in his work of 1953, that TestXIIPatr was a Christian writing from around AD 200 using Jewish material, originally written in Greek—cf. *id.*, StEv 1 (1959), 546-556; NovTest 4 (1960) 182-235; NovTest 5 (1962) 311-319, further also A. Hultgård (1971) 181-184.

[2]The refusal of M. Philonenko, RHPR 38 (1958) 309-343, to accept any Christian interpolations in TestXIIPatr, is generally regarded as untenable. Cf. e.g. Denis (1970) 55, further R. H. Charles (1908) xlvii-li; AP II, 291; Hultgård (1971) 180; Stemberger (1972) 64 f. Though some Christian interpolations are self-evident, it is very hard to draw the border-line between that which belonged to Jewish original texts or redactions and the Christian influence. For all the manifold and complicated problems of the integrity, text, origin and date, of each single testament and the collection as a whole, I refer to the introductions of the edd. (Charles, 1908; M. R. James, JThS 28, 1927, 337-348; M. De Jonge, 1970) and translations (Charles, 1908; AP II, 282 f., 289 f.), as well as to recent monographs (C. Burchard, NTS 12, 1966, 245-258; *id.* 1969, 1-29; J. Thomas 1969, 62-72, 80-88, 147 f.; Becker 1970, 128, 373-377; Hultgård, 1971, 1-37).

[3]Cf. Becker (1970) 326, 403 f.; Stemberger (1972) 64 f., correcting De Jonge (1953) 96.

[4]The contents of the Testaments as well as the fact that fragments have been found in Qumran causes one to believe that the origin was in the milieu of such a group—cf. Hultgård (1971) 184.

[5]An addition of the Jewish redactor according to Becker (1970) 332.

[6]Cf. n.5 for Becker's view, which concerns this passage, too, and Becker (1970) 404.

[7]See nn.5 and 7.

[8]See nn.5 and 7 and Becker (1970) 255-257.

[9]For the variant readings of the names here, *v.* Charles (1908) *ad loc.*

[10]The resurrection seems to be associated with the gathering of the people of Israel. Cf. *supra* 3.2.1 on I En 90:33 and n.11 there.

[11]According to Becker (1970) 299 f., another example of later Jewish redactional material.

[12]The words ἐν χαρᾳ may be secondary—they are left out in the Armenian version—cf. Charles (1908) *ad loc.*

[13]The corresponding words in Gr. πτωχοι and πλουτισθησονται are not found in the Armenian version according to Charles (1908) *ad loc.*

[14]Cf. the image of "sleep" for death in Dn 12:2, though LXX uses ἀναστησουσται and Theodotion ἐξεγερϑησουσται "wake up".—De Jonge (1970) has ἐν ζωῇ instead of εἰς ζωην.

[15]Cf. e.g. Sutcliffe (1946) 168-170; Volz (1934) 31; Nickelsburg (1972) 35 f.

[16]Cf. Schubert, WZKM 56, 160.

[17]The order of those who rise may remind us of I Cor 15:23 ff., as Stemberger (1972) 65, suggests in his comment on TestBenj 10:6-10.

[18]Cf. e.g. Cazelles, SoOr 4, 130; Philonenko, RHPR 38, 340; Stemberger (1972) 65. On the contents of Dn 12:2 and the question whether a resurrection of the evil is really in the mind of the author, see, however, *supra* 2.2.1.

[19]The Armenian version seems to presuppose a Gr. text, modelled on I Cor 15:51—cf. Charles (1908) *ad loc.*

[20]Instead of δικαιοσυνην (as in the text of Charles, 1908, in spite of his preference in a foot-note for εὐφρωσυνην) both De Jonge (1970) *ad loc.* and Hultgård (1971) 112, read εὐφρωσυνην, which seems more credible to the context, as the parallel of the reaction of the patriarchs.

[21]Bracketed as a Christian interpolation by Charles (1908) 139. But cf. Hultgård (1971) 105, 107, who accepts it without discussion.

[22]1QS III, 13-IV, 26—cf. *infra* 3.5.1 and Nickelsburg (1972) 156-159. Cf. also Becker (1970) 368, who distinguishes between the cosmic, apocalyptic eschatology of 1QS and the individual eschatology of TestAsher. TestAsher has taken up the "Hellenistic-Neoplatonic doctrine of the immortality" of the soul, though it is not explicitly asserted, "weil offenbar die alttestamentlich-jüdische ganzheitliche Vorstellung vom Menschen noch traditionellerweise einwirkte". That is an over-simplification! Cf. on this contrast between "Jewish" and "Greek" *supra* 1.1.—Becker (1970) 371 f., thinks that the whole of the section 1:3-6:6 is a secondary addition of an originally independent source.

[23]*Infra* 4.4.1-7, and Nickelsburg (1972) 162-164.

[24]Did 1-6; Barn 18-20; Hermas, Mand—cf. Nickelsburg (1972) 159-161.

[25]The text is unclear—cf. the edd. of Charles (1908) and De Jonge (1970) for the different readings; according to De Jonge the meaning "console" (παρακαλειν or maybe παραμυϑειν) should be preferred; according to Charles εἰσφερειν εἰς. In this context the difference is not that important.

[26]"The soul leaves the body in death" is the most probable interpretation, in spite of Stemberger's opinion (1972, 69n—cf. *infra* 3.3.5).

[27]Cf. Nickelsburg (1972) 164n, referring to Hesiod, Works 287-292; Xenophon, Mem. II, 1:20-34. Also Becker (1970) 368.

[28]Cf. Cavallin, SEÅ 37-38, 56 f., for this "form".

3.4 The Psalms of Solomon

This collection of hymns, composed around 50 BC[1], was originally written in Hebrew, and probably in Palestine[2]. It has been described to be representative of Pharisaic piety[3]. The Qumran discoveries have added some doubts to this qualification, and today there is a tendency to regard PsSol as representing a type of Judaism which had a more general eschatological orientation[4]. PsSol contains one clear reference to the resurrection (of the righteous only), which we quote in its immediate context, *3:10-12:*

3.4.1

(10) He added sins to sins in his life; he fell, for his fall was very grievous, and he shall not rise (ἀναστησεται) (11) The destruction of the sinner is for ever, and he shall not be remembered when He (God) visits the righteous. (12) This is the lot of the sinners for ever. But those who fear the Lord will *rise to eternal life* and their life will be in the *light* of the Lord and will no longer come to an end (ET inspired by Nickelsburg, 1972, 131).

(A, B) The sinners appear to be annihilated, whereas those who fear the Lord will have eternal life. Probably the verb ἀναστηναι refers to resurrection after death, though Stemberger (1972, 56-59) tries to interpret it as rising again after a fall of sin. The use of the expression, "to eternal life", used also in Dn 12:2, makes such a suggestion highly improbable (cf. also Nickelsburg, 1972, 131 f.). The words underlined in the text may be allusions to Dn 12:2 f. They connect the resurrection of the righteous (v. 12b) with the "theophanic glory" (Nickelsburg, 1972, 132). "The light of the Lord" is more likely to be a symbol of heavenly transcendence than to be an expression of new earthly life, as Stemberger postulates, based on the background of general anthropology, the "Hebrew" view of the unity of body and soul, which he found in PsSol. **(D)** The dating of the resurrection, the "visitation" of the Lord, is made indirectly by the negation in v. 11. In our discussion of Wi we shall meet this term again (*infra* 4.4.1). It denotes the theophany at the end of time which saves the righteous and leaves the sinners in their death and destruction. *PsSol 15:12* defines it as a day of judgment. We may next quote this passage:

3.4.2

And sinners will perish on the day of the judgment of the Lord for ever, when God visits the earth with his judgment. But those who fear the Lord will find mercy in that day and they will live by the mercy of their God, and sinners will perish for all time (ET inspired by Nickelsburg, 1972, 133).

The context in this psalm of thanksgiving for salvation in times of distress (vv. 1-3) describes the salvation of the righteous as occurring in the time of punishment for the sinners (vv. 4-9). This punishment is first described as a series of catastrophes in the order of the world: Famine, sword, death (v.7), the annihilation of house and family (v. 11), but v.10 states that

the inheritance of the sinners is destruction and darkness and their misdeed will persecute them until Hades.

A *post-mortem*-punishment of sinners (cf. the "flame of fire" in v.4) is not clear in the context. Perhaps final destruction in death is all that is meant, as it seemed to be in Ps Sol 3. **(A)** It is neither possible to decide whether ζησονται means resurrection and new life after death or merely continued life (the death of the righteous is not mentioned at all in this psalm[5]). **(D)** Both the judgment of the sinners and the "visitation" of the righteous take place on "the day of visitation", which in itself and in the immediate context of this psalm might denote a temporal visitation and judgment of the Lord. The close similarity with 3:10-12 makes the interpretation of a judgment on the Last Day much more probable (cf. Nickelsburg, 1972, 133).

3.4.3

PsSol 13:11 is more clear:

> For the life of the righteous is forever.

This statement on the righteous is again contrasted with the destruction of the sinner (v.11b), apparently as a complete annihilation. **(A)** Though only the παιδεια (v.9—cf. Nickelsburg, 1972, 132) is mentioned, not the death of the righteous, their eternal life is undoubtedly asserted here. As in 15:13, this is closely connected with "the mercy of the Lord" (13:12). **(B, C, D)** Nothing more is said about the future life of the righteous.

3.4.4.

PsSol 14 treats the same theme, with allusions to Ps 1:

> (3) The pious of the Lord (ὁσιοι κυριου) shall live by it[6] for ever. The Lord's paradise, the trees of Life, are his pious ones. (4) Their plant is rooted for ever, they shall not be plucked up all the days of heaven. (5) For the portion and the inheritance of God is Israel . . . (9, about the sinners) Therefore their inheritance is Hades (Sheol) and darkness and destruction, and they shall not be found in the day when the righteous obtain mercy. (10) But the pious of the Lord shall inherit life in gladness.

(A) Whereas the sinners perish, the righteous will have new life. The term "inherit" may indicate that this is a life which is not yet possessed, though nothing is said about the death of the righteous (cf. Nickelsburg, 1972, 133). **(B)** Nothing more precise is said about this new life—about the resurrection or the immortality of the soul, **(C)** nor about a transformation or return to an earthly, though joyful, everlasting life. **(D)** But the "date" is again given as "the day of mercy for the righteous", when the sinners will be exterminated, thus as the day of judgment (cf. Nickelsburg, 1972, 133).

3.4.5 *Summary*

The theme of the destruction of the sinneras and the everlasting life of the righteous given by the mercy of the Lord on the "Day", apparently the day of judgment, is quite frequent in PsSol. Only one passage mentions the resurrection, that of the righteous alone, without any words about the body and with the imagery of Divine light, transformation to a heavenly existence. No relations have been observed between any anthropology and ideas about new life after death.

---

[1]For the date, cf. e.g. J. Lindblom (1909) 41-51; J. Viteau (1911) 38-45; G. B. Gray, Charles, AP II (1913) 627-630; Volz (1934) 26 f.; Russell (1964) 37, 57 f.; Denis (1970) 64; Nickelsburg (1972) 131; Stemberger (1972) 53.

[2]Cf. e.g. R. Kittel, Kautzsch, AP II (1900) 128, 130; Viteau (1911) 105-125; Russell (1964) 57; Denis (1970) 63 f.; Stemberger (1972) 53.

[3]E.g. Kittel, Kautzsch, AP II (1900) 128 f.; Viteau (1911) 63, 87; Grelot, RQ 1, 123n, and cf. Denis (1979) 64; Stemberger (1972) 53, with further references.

[4]Thus already Lindblom (1909) 57 f., 184-195, further, more recently: Eissfeldt (1964) 830; Hoffmann (1966) 127; Stemberger (1972) 53 (with references there; he speaks of "Chasidim" more in general than of Pharisees); R. Wright, SCS 2 (1972) 136-154. Volz (1934) 26 f., thinks that these Psalms, as well as those of the canonical Psalter, come from different groups with varying eschatologies.

[5]Cf. Nickelsburg (1972) 133: "The author need not explicitly mention resurrection, because the death of the righteous is not in focus." Stemberger (1972) 58 f., thinks that PsSol represent a concept of a "realized eschatology", in which death is not considered. But PsSol 3:10-12 is likely to treat the resurrection of the righteous *after death.*

[6]"It" refers to νομος in v.2.

3.5 Qumran

Did the Essenes of Qumran[1] believe in the resurrection of the dead and/or eternal life after death? This question has indeed received varying answers. Some scholars assert that the sectarians shared what they consider to be the Palestinian Jewish apocalyptic belief in the resurrection of the body[2]. Others deny that any form of belief in life after death existed among the Qumran people[3]. Some recognize in the Scrolls the description of Essene doctrines given by Josephus (3.6.1)[4]. A fresh and fruitful approach to this question has been suggested by Nickelsburg (1972): An analysis of the form and function of the texts which have been cited in this connection should precede their actual interpretation. He applies his method to 1 QS III, 13-IV, 26 (156-160) and to some of the Hymns of thanksgiving (146-156). His results will be cited in our treatment of the different passages.[5]

3.5.1
1QS IV, 6b-8, 11b-14

(6b) And as for the visitation of all who walk in this (spirit)[8], it consists of healing (7) and abundance of bliss, with length of days and fruitfulness and all blessings *without end* (ע ד) and *eternal* (ע ו ל מ י ם) joy in *perpetual life* (ח י י נ צ ח) and the glorious crown (8) and garment of honour in *everlasting light* (א ו ר   ע ו ל מ י ם) ... (11b) And as for the visitation (12) of all who walk in this (spirit), it consists of an abundance of blows administered by all the angels of destruction, in the *everlasting pit* (ש ח ת   ע ו ל מ י ם) by the furious wrath of the God of vengeance, of *unending dread* (ז ע ו ת   נ צ ח) and *shame* (13) *without end* (ע ד   ח ר פ ת) and of the disgrace of destruction by the fire of the regions of darkness. And all *their times from age to age* (כ ו ל   ק צ י ה ם   ל ד ו ר ו ת ם) are in the most sorrowful chagrin and bitterest misfortune, in the calamities of darkness till (14) they are destroyed with none of them surviving or escaping[9].

The quotations are found in the section about the two spirits, III, 13-IV, 26, with several parallels in the "two-way documents" of Judaism and early Christianity[10]. "It is a kind of catechism to be used by the מ ש כ י ל in the instruction of the community" (Nickelsburg, 1972, 157—cf. III, 13). The two ways of life and the struggle between the two spirits in the hearts of men are described (IV, 23). In this context the ultimate consequences of the two ways are described in the quotations above.

3.5.1.1
(A) The expressions for eternity abound in both sections[11]. But their meaning is not immediately evident, at least when the bliss of the righteous is described as "length of days" (אורך ימים) and "fruitfulness" (פרות זרע). The description of the punishment of the wicked may point more decisively towards a transcendent eternity, "eternal damnation", though the expressions for an unceasing torture are juxtaposed with phrases which resemble annihilation (14). From this parallel we may conclude that the first section is also intended to describe eternity (cf. Nickelsburg, 1972, 157), although death is not mentioned. 13b-14 could also be interpreted as a description of calamities within history.

3.5.1.2
(B) A literal interpretation requires the eternity of the bodies of both the righteous and the wicked, since the states of blessedness and damnation seem to be physical: "fruitfulness" (7) and "abundance of blows" (12). We do not know, however, whether the expressions refer to situations before or after death.

3.5.1.3
(C) Thus life after death would be quite physical, if "fruitfulness" and "abundance of blows" are to be interpreted literally. Yet we find a symbol of transformation to heavenly existence in this passage, too, namely "the garment of honour in everlasting light" (8).

3.5.1.4
(D) The administration of immortal bliss and eternal punishment is expressed by the term "visitation"[12]. The context following IV, 11-14, connects this "visitation" (18-19) with the judgment (20). Nothing is said about death or that which follows immediately after death.

3.5.1.5
This passage is a typical representative of the "two-way theology" (Nickelsburg): life or death are the two alternative ends of the two ways. But these ends are described in quite general and vague terms, for the statements are not primarily intended to describe future life or future damnation. Rather, the ethical instruction is the point of the contrast between the two ways. So no precise information on the beliefs about future life can be expected in a text of this type.

3.5.1.6
1QS XI, 7b-9a

God gave them[13] for eternal possession to those whom God had chosen and he made them inherit a share in the lot גורל (8) of the holy ones, and with the sons of heaven did he associate their community for a common council and a congregation סוד of a holy building for an eternal plantation for all (9) the time to come.

The words are part of the prayer which concludes 1QS, X, 8b-XI, 22. In the above passage God is praised for his gifts of understanding and knowledge to the one who prays and for the glorification which is a present reality to the one who has made entrance into the community.

3.5.1.7

(A) This passage has been used to prove that the Qumranites believed in eternal life[14]. However, the eternity is primarily a quality of the congregation according to these lines. The eternal life of the individual members might be implied, but nothing is explicitly stated.

3.5.1.8

(B) The association of the community with the angels (7.2.1.6 and 8) does not help us to answer the question whether the sectarians believed in the resurrection of the body or in a more spiritual type of life after death, but (C) it does express the conviction that the eternal life was not, according to Qumran, an ideal physical and material life after death, or which is not intervened by death. Rather it must be of an angelic, i.e. heavenly, transcendent, glorified kind[15]. (D) It does not only seem to be a future hope, but it also appears to be a present reality for those who have entered the community and who have thus been cleansed from their sin and iniquity.

3.5.2

CD[16] III, 20

Those who stick to it (i.e. the Law[17]) are (destined) for eternal life $\left(\; ח\, י\, י\quad נ\, צ\, ח\;\right)$ and all glory of man $\left(\; א\, ד\, ם\;\right)$ belongs to them.

This sentence forms a conclusion of the first general parenetical introduction of the document. The community is later described more exactly as the true priests, Levites and sons of Zadok (III, 21 ff.). (A) Again, those who obey the Law will have eternal life, but nothing is said about death and resurrection[18].

CD VII, 6a

... that they may live for a thousand generations.

This promise comes in the context of the exhortations to keep the Law and follow the commandments (VI, 20-VII, 5). (A) $\;ל\, ח\, י\, ו\, ת\, ם\;$ can be determined not only to be qal, as presupposed by the above translation (e.g. in Lohse, 1964, *ad loc.*), but also to be either pi'el or hif'il. In the latter case it would mean either "to revive them"—then the resurrection would be mentioned here—or "to keep them alive"[19]. Without any parallels in the rest of the document the resurrection should not be read into this expression. The phrase "for a thousand generations" can hardly be combined with a verb meaning "to revive".

62

3.5.3 *1QSb III, 4-6*

(4) in(perpetual g)lory (and may He) sanctify your seed with eternal glory. May He lif(t His face) (5) (Peac)e eternal may He give to you and a kingdom (6) . . . from flesh(מבשר)[20] and with holy angels.

This blessing, as well as several other *berakhot* in the context, is an expanded and interpreted version of the Aaronite blessing (Nm 6:24-26). The text is too fragmentary to permit any important conclusions. However, in **(B)** line 6 the מבשר might be interpreted as referring to a noncorporeal state in the company of the angels[21]. **(C)** This would then be a glorified, heavenly existence, but what is then the meaning of the seed (4) to be sanctified[22]?

3.5.4.1 *1QH[23] IV, 21b-22a*

(21b) Those who are after your mind, will stand before you for ever, and those who walk in the way of your heart (22a) will be steadfast for evermore.

This *hodayah* (IV, 5-V, 4) sets the ways of the wicked and the righteous in opposition to each other—an example of the "two-way theology" with the usual promise of eternal life to the righteous[24] in its usual vagueness[25].

3.5.4.2 *1QH VI, 29b-30a, 34-35a*

All the children of his truth will awake to (destroy the children) (30) of wickedness and all the children of guilt will be no more . . . (34) and those who sleep in the dust will raise an ensign and the worm of the dead will lift a banner . . . (35) in wars with insolent men.

This thanksgiving hymn seems to begin in V, 20 and continue until VII, 6. The immediate, preceding context introduces the theme of the final battle between the wicked and the sons of God. **(A)** Does this quotation say that the righteous who had died awake for this eschatological warfare? That is affirmed by some scholars[26]. The terminology used here is similar to that of the two passages on the resurrection in the Hebrew Bible, Is 26:19[27] and Dn 12:2[28]. The Qumran text may indeed contain conscious allusions to these two OT passages[29]. Although that does not imply, however, that the verses have to be interpreted as statements on the resurrection of the dead, it seems quite likely that the author of the *hodayah* knew the concept of the resurrection, at least from these two Bible passages.[30] But the context rather suggests that the verbs for "wake" and "rise" may merely mean: Be ready for (war)—cf. Is 52:1[31]. And "those who sleep in the dust" and "the worm of the dead"[32] may be used as expressions of lowliness rather than as descriptions of dead people[33]. **(B)** If the passages are to be interpreted as referring to the resurrection, the terminology would probably denote an involvement of the body. **(D)** It would take place in the end-time.

3.5.4.3. *1QH VIII, 31*

. . . in order to destroy the flesh for many times (עד מועדים . . .)

The context, a lamentation[34], describes the distress of the speaker (VIII, 27b-IX, 7a). (A) As in some canonical Psalms, belonging to this *Gattung*, the deep distress of the speaker is described as death[35]. That is the most probable interpretation, more likely than Rabin's (1957) suggestion (cf. also Beresford, 1971, 89) that the line refers to the coming resurrection of the flesh which is to occur after a long time ("many times").

3.5.4.4. *1QH XI, 10-14*

(10) For your glory's sake you have purified man from sin that he may be sanctified (11) before you from all impure abominations and the guilt of transgression that he may be united with the sons of your truth and in a lot with (12) your holy ones, to raise the worm of the dead from the dust to (eternal) council and from a crooked spirit to (your) insight (13) that he may stand in a place of standing before you with an eternal army and spirits (of knowledge) to renew himself with all (14) that there is and with those who know in common exultation.

These lines form the conclusion of a short hymn of thanksgiving for the revelation of Divine truth and for the secret council of God to the author (XI, 3-14). (A) Resurrection terminology similar to what we have previously encountered in 1QH[36] is used on line 12. This most probably refers to the revelation of spiritual truth, which is given by entrance into the community[37]. (D) Thus, this is described as a present, realized resurrection[38]. The comparison with early Christian thinking about baptism is close at hand[39]. (C) Of most importance is the association between the community and the angels: the members of the community live with the angels, which entails a present, transcendent spiritual life.

3.5.5. *4Q Amram*

(And all the children of light will walk) towards light, towards joy (everlasting) and towards happiness, whereas all the sons of darkness will go towards dark(ness and deatn- - -) for the People light and one will revive- - -[40]

This fragment seems to represent the "two-way theology" (Milik, RB 79, 89 f.). The last verb, the af'el אתחיו could be interpreted either "keep alive" or "revive", figuratively or literally. (A) In the last case it would imply resurrection after death, but that is most uncertain, evidently.

3.5.6. *4QPsDn 38-40*

(38) These will stray in blindness-
(39) (Tho)se, they will arise
(40) (the) ho(l)y ones, and will return - - -[42]

The "two-way theology" is again exhibited. The contrast between the wicked, who stray in blindness, and the righteous, (A) who will share in the resurrection, is very explicit in this passage. Both the idea of the resurrection and the contrast of "these"—"those" are probably allusions to Dn 12:2,[42] (B) implying, perhaps, a resurrection of the body. (C) The "return" might be the return of the exiled to the

Land of Israel, denoting a physical type of resurrection faith. **(D)** The "context" (lines 37 and 41—see n.41), containing the contrast between the two ways, presupposes some type of judgment.

3.5.7. *4Q181 1 II, 3-6*

(3) In God's mercy his goodness and wonderful glory he will bring some of the children of the earthly round (- - -) to be counted with him in the com(munity) (4) (of g)ods as a holy congregation in the *resurrection for eternal life* (עולם לחיי במעמד) and in a *lot* (בגורל) with his saints (- - -) (5) (- - -) every man according to his *lot* (גורל) which he has assigned for (- - -) (6) (- - -) *for et(er)n(al) life* (לחיי ע(ו)ל(ם))ֿ [43].

This fragment clearly describes the eternal life of the chosen congregation as opposed to the damnation of the congregation of Belial in the preceding context. The statement that some of the children of תבל will be counted with God "in the community of gods" (בי(חד) אלים) might be inspired by Ps 82:1 (עדת-אל) The above words in italics indicate the possible influence of Dn 12:2, 13.

(B) The word מעמד has been rendered "resurrection" on the basis of the use of the verb עמד in Dn 12:13 and some other places with the same connotation (2.3 and 3.14.3). J. T. Milik (JJS 23, 1972, 114) suggests "permanence" as the translation. According to Dalman's dictionary (1922) s.v., one of the connotations of מעמד is, however, "rising" (*Aufstehen*), which in this context might be understood as "resurrection".

(C) The members of the congregation are joined with "the saints", i.e., primarily angels and heavenly beings (cf. *supra* 3.5.1.8 and 3.5.4.4, *infra* 7.2.1.8). The expression reminds us of Dn 7:18, 21, 22, 25, 27. It is hard to state that this is a conscious allusion. If this is the case, then the Qumran author(s) has(have) worked with the Dn text in an interesting way, combining Dn 7 and Dn 12.

(A, D) However, the resurrection possibly mentioned here may be another expression of realized eschatology. There is nothing which says, beyond a doubt, that the writer thought of a resurrection after death.

3.5.8 *Summary*

Of all the passages in the Qumran scrolls (including CD) which may testify to a belief in the resurrection of the dead or life after death in general, only one text, or possibly two, proved to represent a sure, supporting testimony. The rest was found to be most doubtful as statements supporting after-life.[44] Assertions of the eternal life of the elect, the members of the congregation, are not so rare, but nothing is said about their death. The "two-way theology" type of texts do not inform us much of anything other than generalizations about a blessed life for the righteous and a punitive death for the sinners. The available texts themselves do not tell us more. So I shall proceed to the external testimonies, assuming that the Essenes described by Josephus and Hippolytus are at least closely akin to the community of Qumran (if not identified with them, cf. n.1, *supra*).

¹For this identification cf. most text-books, e.g. M. Burrows (1955) 273-298, who is, however, rather cautious: the Dead Sea Community was not exactly identical with the Essenes described by Philo and Josephus, but "it is clear that the sect of Qumran was more closely related to the Essenes than to any other group known to us" (298); *id.* (1958) 263-274, more confidently; further, Schubert (1970) 50, and E. Lohse (1971) 78 (straight identification); J. Maier (1972) 61-63 (a little more cautious). Among the later contributions to the discussion on the identification of the Qumran sect, see e.g. R. de Vaux, RB 73 (1966) 212-235, against G. R. Driver (1965), who suggested the identification of the Qumranites with a 1st century AD Zealot group rather than with the Essenes, and further E. J. Pryke, NovTest 10 (1968) 43-61: Can the sectarians be described as a Jewish apocalyptic group with Essene origins?

²E.g. F. Nötscher (1956) 151-158; *id.* BZ 2 (1958) 132 f., rather cautiously; M. Mansoor, JBL 76 (1957) 146 n.64; C. Rabin (1957) 73; K. Schubert, WZKM 56, 154-167, though the resurrection body may not be a "body of the flesh"; *id.* BZ 6, 202-204 (the resurrection is pre-supposed rather than explicitly stated); *id.* (1970) 59 f. (the fact that the Qumran texts tell us very little about their belief in the resurrection may be a result of their stress on the realized eschatology, but we must not doubt the existence of such a hope in Qumran, because the resurrection doctrine did become more and more clear and massive in Judaism); J. Buitkamp (1965) 109 f., though the vagueness of the testimonies is stressed (91 f.). Cf. also M. Black (1961) and his description of the tombs.

³E.g. J. Licht (1957) 119, 163; R. B. Laurin, JSS 3 (1958) 344-355; H. Braun II (1966) 282; R. Meyer, TWNT VII, 40: practically, though not theoretically, the resurrection was denied in Qumran. Without any definite judgment in the question the following scholars are sceptical towards the acceptance of a resurrection or even immortality faith in Qumran: Cazelles, SoOr 4, 125 f.; C. F. Evans (1970) 27-30; A. Mertens (1971) 154-158: the silence of the texts (with the exception of 4QPsDn) is striking, and we must acknowledge a deliberate though silent repudiation of the doctrine, which could hardly be unknown at this time. Was the future hope, rather, a blessed, continued (eternal) life in this world for the members of the community? Further: J. Le Moyne (1972) 167 f., who finds nothing but an earthly eschatology in Qumran, no hope beyond death. Bruce, ScJTh 24, 459 f., stresses the fact that the Qumran texts "speak plainly enough of eternal life for the righteous and annihilation for the wicked, but throw no clear light on the question of the resurrection". Beresford (1971), repudiating the efforts to find the faith in the resurrection of the dead in the Scrolls, suggests that the sectarians believed in a blessed life after death for the deceased righteous, who in the end would be joined by the surviving, transformed to a spiritual mode of existence: the accent lies on the present eternal life already lived by the members of the community. Burrows (1955) 270 f., and *id.* (1958) 344-346, gives a survey of the early discussion on the matter, without a definite personal judgment.

⁴J. v.d. Ploeg, VT 2 (1952) 171-175; *id.* BO 18 (1961) 118-124; H. H. Rowley (1957) 17-19; J. Carmignac, RQ 1 (1958) 235-248; E. Vogt, Bibl 38 (1957) 466; J. O'Dell, RQ 3 (1961/2) 257; Coppens (1957) 41; M. Mansoor (1961) 86 f. - cf. *id.* JBL 76, 146 n.64, and *supra* n.2. - Tournay, RB 69, 489; E. J. Pryke, StEv 5 (1968) 301 f.: "at the most, 'immortality of the soul'". R. Mayer-J. Reuss (1959) 67-70, assert that the Hymns (1QH) express belief in the resurrection, whereas only testimonies for the doctrine of immortality are found in the rest of the documents thus far studied. H. Ringgren (1963) 148-151, tries to balance the silence of the Qumran Scrolls with the testimony of Josephus on the Essenes and arrives at something very near John's Gospel: the eternal life already here and yet it "belongs to another world in its consummation" (151). The immortality of the soul "must be ascribed to Josephus' Hellenizing tendency"—cf. *infra* 3.6.

⁵Nn. 5-7 moved with the corresponding text to 3.0.8.

⁸Cf. the preceding context for the addition of "spirit", and E. Lohse (1964) n.27 *ad loc.*

⁹ET: Nickelsburg (1972) 156 f.

¹⁰Cf. 3.3.4 on TestAsher 6:5-6 and further references there (nn.23-24).

¹¹They are underlined in the above translated text with the words of the Hebrew original in the parentheses.

[12]Hebrew: פ ק ו ד ה . Cf. Wi 3:7 ἐπισκοπη and *infra* 4.4.3.4. Cf. Ringgren (1963) 152 f.

[13]Referring to the Divine gifts of the preceding context: intelligence, understanding, righteousness, new powers etc.

[14]E.g. by Bruce, ScJTh 24, 459 f.

[15]Cf. *infra* 7.2.1.4 and 8.

[16]CD is placed here as closely related to 1QS in its final redaction, being, however, probably younger than 1QS. Cf. e.g. Lohse (1964) 63 f.

[17] ב ל refers to the general description of the way of righteousness according to the Law in the preceding context (cf. 12-19).

[18]Rabin (1957) 73, associates "eternal life" here too readily with life after death, though he does not use the text as a proof for anything but the belief in eternal life for the righteous.

[19]Cf. C. Rabin (1954) *ad loc.* (pi'el or hif'il); *id.* (1957) 73 n.1: "If read as Hiph'il (with *h* omitted) this could mean 'to resurrect them'".

[20]Cf. 1QH XV, 17 and Ringgren (1963) 144.

[21]Cf. the translation in DJD I (1955) 124: "hors de la chair", and Job 19:26 f.

[22]Similar in 1QSb IV, 24-26:

And may (25) you be as an angel of the Presence in the holy dwelling (in the service) of the glory of the God of host(s for ever. And may) you be a servant round about in the temple (26) of the Kingdom and throw the lot with the angels of Presence. And joint council (with the saints) for eternity and for all times for ever . . .

[23]1QH III, 19-23 is similar to 1QH XI, 10-14 and is treated in a note there *infra*.

[24]Cf. *supra* 3.3.4 and 3.5.1.5.

[25]Similar is 1QH XVIII, 28 f:

. . to bring into a covenant with you and to stand (29) - - - in an eternal place, to perfect life for ever . . .

The text around and within these lines is quite fragmentary. The meaning seems to be, however, that the man who is the "I" of this *hodayah* is brought to eternal life and glory with God—but we are not told if this concerns life after death.

[26]As G. Vermes, Cahiers Sioniens 9 (1955) 46; Nötscher, BZ 2, 132; Mansoor, JBL 76, 146 n.64; Rabin (1957) 73; Schubert, WZKM 56, 156; *id.* BZ 6, 203 (at least a possibility; the expressions, which may be used only in a metaphorical way, presuppose the existence of the belief in the resurrection of the dead); H. Bardtke (1958) 243.

[27]Is 26:19 ע פ ר י שכנ י 1QH VI, 34 ע פ ר שו כ ב י .Cf. Nötscher, BZ 2, 132.

[28]Dn 12:2:"sleep in the land of dust"—"wake" (צ ר י ק י /ע פ ר-ע ד מ ת י שנ י)—1QH VI, 29: "rise" (ר ר ו ע י)—"those who lie in the dust" (34). Cf. also Nötscher, BZ 2, 132.

[29]Cf. Rabin (1957) 73; Nötscher, BZ 2, 132.

[30]Cf. Schubert, BZ 6, 202 f.

[31]Cf. Carmignac, RQ 1, 236 f.; S. Holm-Nielsen (1960) 120 n; Vogt, Bibl 38, 466; Beresford (1971) 86 f.

[32] מ ת י ם ת ו ל ע ת —cf. Is 41:14 and e.g. Carmignac, RQ 1, 236; Mansoor JBL 76, 146 n.64; v.d. Ploeg, BO 18, 123; Rabin (1957) 73; Mertens (1971) 156.

[33]Cf. again Is 41:14 and Carmignac, RQ 1, 237, comparing with similar expressions in 1QH II, 13; 1QM XI, 13; Licht (1957) 119; G. Jeremias (1963) 237 f. n.17; v.d. Ploeg, BO 18, 123; Mertens (1971) 156.

[34]The *hodayah* begins in VIII, 4 and ends in IX, 36. Cf. Holm-Nielsen (1960) 142, 169 f. ("Psalm 14").

[35]Cf. Barth (1947) 92-166, and e.g. Ps 88; 141:7; 143:3-4, 7; Jonah 2; Lam 3:53-55.

[36]VI, 29, 34. Cf. also III, 19-23, where God is praised for redemption from Sheol to an eternal hope in fellowship with the angels. By A. Dupont-Sommer (1950) 89; M. Delcor, RSR 26 (1952) 375; A.-M. Dubarle, RSPT 37 (1953) 439 f.; v.d. Ploeg, BO 18, 122, the *hodayah* of III, 19-23, is seen as affirming resurrection or immortality after death. More likely it refers to the entrance into the community—cf. the following foot-note and H. W. Kuhn (1966) 44-78.

[37]Cf. Carmignac, RQ 1, 237 f.; Vogt, Bibl 38, 466; Schubert, WZKM 56, 157; Holm-Nielsen (1960) 187 n.23; Jeremias (1963) 238 n.17; Mertens (1971) 156.

[38]Cf. Kuhn (1966) 80, 83-88, 113 f., 161, 168, 175, 185.

[39]See Rm 6:3-11; Col 2:12 f.; Eph 2:5 f.; 5:14. Cf. also JA and *infra* 4.9.1-3.

[40]For the text (Aramaic) and a French translation see J. T. Milik, RB 79 (1972) 90. It "could be another copy of the Testament of Amram" (*ibid.*), but this is not ascertained.—The title of the writing to which this fragment may belong is given in a fragment, quoted and discussed *ibid.* 77 f.: "Visions of Amram." Amram is the father of Moses. The fragment 4Q Amram[b] describes a struggle between מלכי-רשע and (probably) מלכי-צדק (Melchizedek/Michael), which may concern the soul or body (or the whole man) of Amram after death. Milik suggests a direct literary relation between the Testament of Amram and Jud 9 as well (*ibid.* 95) as with Origen (Hom XXXV in Luc, *ibid.* 86 f.). Cf. also *id.*, JJS 23 (1972) 95-144. K. Berger, JSJud 4 (1973) 1-18, questions the direct literary relation and points to a broad tradition, where the motif of the dispute between the two spirits, Michael and Satan (or equivalents), is found. The text of 4Q Amram would be the first testimony to this tradition. According to these scholars 4Q Amram would represent some kind of *post-mortem* situation **(A)**. But the text is too fragmentary to allow any ascertained conclusions.

[41]The Aramaic text quoted in J. T. Milik RB 63 (1956) 414; R. Meyer (1962) 92; Mertens (1971) 44:

$$(37) \quad (ל)מסף ר(ש)עֲאֹ$$
$$(38) \quad \text{---} \quad \text{אלו} ן בעור יטער$$
$$(39) \quad (א)ל ך אנֹוֹ ן יקומו ן$$
$$(40) \quad (ק)דיש(יְ)א ר ייֹלבו ן$$
$$(41) \quad \text{רשעא} \quad \text{-----}$$

[42]Cf. Mertens (1971) 49, also stressing that whereas both righteous and wicked share in the resurrection in Dn 12:2 (according to his interpretation—cf. *supra* 2.2.1), only the righteous arise in this passage.

[43]The text can be found in Milik, JJS 23, 114, and in DJD V (1968) 79 f.

[44]There are several other quotations of a similar type (or even more vague) which might be discussed here. The following may be just mentioned: 1QM XII, 1-5 (cf. Mertens, 1971, 156 f.); 1Q19bis (praying dead souls it seems); 1Q34, 3, II:7; 1Q35, 2; 1Q36, I, 2-3; 4Q171, 9-11 (seems to be a grossly materialistic description of the joys of the future world, "all the delights of the flesh"); 4Q185, 1-2, 1, 89 (man changed to a flame like the angels before God); 4QpPs 37: 14-15 (cf. J. M. Allegro, JBL 75, 1956, 89-95); 4QPsfVII-X, in J. Starcky, RB 73 (1966) 366, about the eschatological judgment and salvation.

3.6 Essene beliefs about immortality

Several ancient authors describe the Essenes, more or less independently of each other (cf. A. Adam's collection of testimonies, 1961). Only Josephus and Hippolytus (among the sources of the first two centuries CE) refer to their beliefs about after-life[1].

3.6.1 *Josephus concerning Essene views on after-life*

In the context of the description of the different Jewish parties (cf. *infra* 4.6.1 and 2; 6.2) in BJ II and Ant XVIII, Josephus gives a very sympathetic picture of the Essenes. Concerning their beliefs about after-life, he says *(BJ II, 154-157)*:

> For this opinion is strong among them, that bodies are corruptible, and their material impermanent, but that souls will endure immortal forever. Emanating from the finest ether, these souls become entangled, as it were, in the prison-house of the body, to which they are dragged down by a sort of natural spell; but when once they are released from the bonds of the flesh, then, as though liberated from a long servitude, they rejoice and are borne aloft. Sharing the belief of the sons of Greece, they maintain that for virtuous souls there is reserved an abode beyond the ocean, a place which is not oppressed by rain or snow or heat, but is refreshed by the ever gentle breath of the west wind coming in from ocean; while they relegate base souls to the murky and tempestuous dungeon, big with neverending punishments...[2] Their aim[3] was first to establish the doctrine of the immortality of the soul[4], and secondly to promote virtue and to deter from vice; for the good are made better in their lifetime by the hope of a reward after death, and the passions of the wicked are restrained by the fear that, even though they escape detection while alive, they will undergo never-ending punishment after their decease. Such are the theological views of the Essenes concerning the soul, whereby they irresistibly attract all who have once tasted their philosophy (H. St. J. Thackeray's ET, 1926, *ad loc.*).

And *(Ant XVIII, 18)*:

> They regard wouls as immortal (ἀθανατιζουσι δε τας ψυχας)

To what extent is Josephus, more or less conciously, hellenizing the views of the Essenes, regarding the interests of his own taste or of his readers? The question, quite naturally, is often raised[5]. We have not found in the Qumran documents any traces of such an elaborate anthropological dualism as the one which Josephus attributed to the Essenes. There may be some historical truth in the distinction he makes between the Essene views on afterlife and the Pharisaic doctrine of the resurrection, (BJ II, 163—*infra* 4.6.1), or revival (Ant XVIII, 14—*infra* 4.6.2) of the dead, but since we have hardly any primary sources of Essene teaching about life after death, this is very difficult to prove[6]. Jub 23:31 would fit the description of Josephus (cf. 3.1.1-3 *supra*) and has indeed been described as "Essene" (Testuz, 1960, 179-199, and *supra* 3.1.—this has been supported by the fragments found in Qumran—cf. *supra* 3.1). But the gap between the description of Essene eschatology, given by Josephus, and that found in the Qumran Scrolls remains. Only one thing can be stated as a common feature in this area: the resurrection of the body was not so important for the Essenes as it was for the Pharisees[7].

3.6.2 *Hippolytus concerning Essene views on after-life*

In the description of the Essenes, found in Hippolytus, Ref IX, 27, which seems to be based on Josephus or a source, common to both of them[8], Hippolytus deviates from Josephus precisely in the question of after-life beliefs:

> Also the doctrine of resurrection is strongly held among them, For they confess that the flesh also will rise, and that it will be immortal, just as the soul is already immortal. When the soul has left the body it is now to rest in one place with a gentle wind and light. When the Greeks heard of this place, they called it "the isles of the blessed".

Hippolytus' text is rather obviously the result of a secondary change of a source, either Josephus, BJ II, 154-157, or a common *Vorlage*[9]. Beside the convincing arguments of Nickelsburg (1972, 168 f.) against M. Black (*In hon.* C. H. Dodd, 1956, 175; *id.* 1961, 190) we may add that the description of the place of the blessed souls hardly gives any room for a future resurrection. The order of Josephus' text is also followed; first come two assertions on the body,[10] and then one concerning the soul. The introductions of the pericopes are identical (cf. the synopsis in n.10). So the testimony of Hippolytus has no independent value regarding Essene belief in the immortality of the soul and does not prove anything concerning their hope of a future resurrection of the body.[11]

3.6.3 *Essene celibacy as a testimony to Essene eschatology*

On the basis of the ancient authors'[12] descriptions of the Essenes, the celibacy of the full members of the Qumran community is normally assumed as a fact[13]. There is no clear evidence of this in the Qumran texts or excavations[14]. Perhaps there were different groups within the community with different attitudes toward marriage, as Josephus (BJ II, 160 f.) suggests, too. There is, anyhow, no valid reason why the unanimous testimony of the ancient authors should be questioned. Now, in the old Israelite view "the seed" represented "eternal life" (2.1.1). But if eternal life will be given after death to the individual person, "the seed" and the obligation of marriage lose this existential function. It is no mere coincidence that the Sadducees confront the legislation on Levirate marriage (Dt 25:5-10) with the belief in the resurrection (Mk 12:18-27 parr); neither is it surprising that the question whether marriage is allowed at all appears in a community which appears to be filled with the sense of a realized eschatology, an already present resurrection, as the young Corinthian Church (I Cor 7:1 ff.). So two possible interpretations of the assumed fact of Essene celibacy may be suggested from the eschatological point of view[15]:

3.6.3.1

(1) Since they expected eternal life after death, the idea of celibate life appeared at least as a possible and even preferable alternative to normal married life.

3.6.3.2

(2) If entrance into the community and membership were conceived of in terms of resurrection and eternal life with the angels, as we saw[16], marriage would be irrelevant or even inappropriate[17].

70

3.6.3.3

If the former interpretation is accepted, Essene celibacy could **(A)** testify to the Essene belief in a life after death, **(C)** which was probably understood in a spiritualized way.

[1] Philo describes the attitude of the Therapeutae concerning the eternal life (Vita cont 13, 4.5.2 *infra*), but in his treatment of the Essenes (Quod omnis probus liber sit 72-91; Hypothetica 1-18—in Adam, 1961, 1-7) he has nothing to say about their belief in after-life.

[2] The beliefs of the Greeks are described, the isles of the blessed and the punishment of the impious in Hades.

[3] The aim of the Greeks but also of the Essenes:

[4] Gr: ἀιδίους ὑφιστάμενοι τὰς ψυχὰς ...

[5] *Affirming* the question e.g.: M. Black, *In hon.* C. H. Dodd (1956) 175; *id.* (1961) 190; Ringgren (1963) 151; Hoffmann (1966) 79 f.
Relative *trust* in Josephus: S. Zeitlin, JQR 49 (1958) 292-300 (denying any relation between the Scrolls and the Essenes); Beresford (1971) 94-96.
Only the *terminology* was *hellenized* by Josephus, not the actual theology: R. Meyer (1937) 69 ff., esp. 72; P. Grelot, RQ 1 (1958) 113-131; M. Smith, HUCA 29 (1958) 273-293; J. Strugnell, JBL 77 (1958) 106-115.

[6] We found no evidence for a belief in the immortality of the soul as distinct from the resurrection of the body—and very little to prove the existence of faith in the resurrection (3.5-3.5.7).

[7] Cf. 4.6.1 and 2, and Nickelsburg (1972) 168 f.

[8] Cf. Smith, HUCA 29, 273-293; Nickelsburg (1972) 167-169.

[9] Possibly more similar to the Slavonic Josephus—cf. Adam (1961) 41 f. (and 42-51, with a parallel German translation of the corresponding section in the Slavonic Josephus).

[10] Though with directly contrary opinions. Cf. the following synopsis:

BJ II, 154-156	Ref IX, 27
Καὶ γὰρ ἔρρωται παρ᾽ αὐτοῖς ἥδ᾽ ἡ δόξα, φθαρτὰ μὲν εἶναι τὰ σώματα	Ἔρρωται δὲ παρ᾽ αὐτοῖς ὁ τῆς ἀναστάσεως λόγος· ὁμολογοῦσι γὰρ καὶ τὴν σάρκα ἀναστήσεσθαι
καὶ τὴν ὕλην οὐ μόνιμον αὐτῶν, τὰς δὲ ψυχὰς ἀθανάτους ἀεὶ διαμένειν ...	καὶ ἔσεσθαι ἀθάνατον, ὃν τρόπον ἤδη ἀθάνατος ἐστιν ἡ ψυχη· .
... ἀνεθῶσι τῶν κατὰ σάρκα δεσμῶν ... καὶ ταῖς μὲν ἀγαθαῖς, ὁμοδοξοῦντες παισὶν Ἑλλήνων, ...	ἣν χωρισθεῖσαν νῦν ἐστιν (ἕτερα τούτων δόγματα πολλοὶ τῶν Ἑλλήνων σφετερισάμενοι ἰδίας δόξας συνεστήσαντο.)
χῶρον ... ὁ ... πραὺς ἀεὶ ζεφυρος ἐπιπνέων ἀναψύχει	εἰς ἕνα χῶρον εὔπνουν καὶ φωτεινὸν ἀναπαύεσθαι ἕως κρίσεως, ὃν χῶρον Ἕλληνες ἀκούσαντες
μακάρων νήσους	μακάρων νήσους ὠνόμασαν. ἀλλὰ καὶ κτλ.

71

11Black's question why Hippolytus, or a tradition before him, made the Essene "heresy" the spokesman for Catholic orthodoxy without any actual foundation in history, may possibly be answered in this way: The ancient authors who describe the Essenes, normally do so very sympathetically. See Adam (1961) 1-7 for Philo (cf. n.1), 26-32 for Josephus, BJ II, 119-161, 36 f. for Ant XVIII, 18-22, 38 for Pliny, Nat. hist. V, 17, 38 f. for Dio Chrysostomus (a fragment in Synesius, PG 66, 1859, 1120c). Hippolytus himself is not negative (cf. Ref. IX, 18-28—Adam, 1961, 42-51). So why would he be unable to use this outstanding group of Jews as witnesses for orthodoxy?

12Philo, Hypothetica 11:14; Pliny, Nat.hist. V, 17; Josephus, BJ II, 160; Ant XVIII, 21; Hippolytus, Ref IX, 18.

13Cf. e.g. C. Daniel, RQ 6 (1968) 353-390; A. Guillaumont, In hon. A. Dupont-Sommer (1971) 395-404; A. Steiner, BZ 15 (1971) 1-28. On Qumran and Essenes cf. n.1 to 3.5.

14Cf. Ringgren (1963) 140: 1QS seems to presuppose a community without women, but 1QSa I, 4, 8 f. and CD VII, 6; XIX, 3 give instructions concerning marriage. Female skeletons have also been found at Qumran.

15The OT precepts on ritual purity are the most important factor behind Essene celibacy according to Guillaumont, In hon. A. Dupont-Sommer, 395-404, and Steiner, BZ 15, 1-28. J. Massingberd Ford (1967) 52-57, makes a distinction between a more philosophically oriented celibacy among the Essenes according to Josephus and Philo, and the more sacerdotal type in the Qumran documents, perhaps representing a Zealot group.

16Supra 3.5.1.6 and 3.5.4.4. Cf. also Philo on the Therapeutae infra 4.5.2.

17Cf. Clement of Alexandria, Strom III, 47, 3-48, 1, on the Encratites: they abstain from marriage on the ground of Christ's saying that after the resurrection there would be no marriage (implying that they have already passed the resurrection). G. Quispel, VigChrist 19 (1965) 69 f., observes a similar relation between an already realized resurrection and abstention from marriage in EvThom 22; 38; 79; 114. Cf. here the judgment of U. Bianchi, StHRel 12 (1957) 742 f.

3.7 Vita Adae et Evae (with the Apocalypse of Moses)

The questions about the origin and development of the two old versions of the Adam traditions, preserved now in the Greek Apocalypse of Moses[1] and the Latin Vita Adae et Evae[2], are extremely complicated. The work is probably of Jewish origin[3]. The original author may have been an Alexandrian Jew writing in Greek[4]. But it is just as possible that the original language was Hebrew (Eissfeldt, 1964, 863) or Aramaic (Russell, 1964, 59). The probable date of authorship is estimated to be during the period between the construction and destruction of Herod's temple (20 BC-AD 70)[5]. Since its contents may be described as apocalyptic (cf. *supra* 3.0.1), it was decided to include VAE (ApcMos) in this section of the present investigation.

3.7.1

There are several references to the resurrection, especially in the Greek version (ApcMos). They all seem to contain the same rather classical image of a universal resurrection of all mankind[6] on the last day[7] after the intermediate state of those who have died[8]. It is sufficient to quote *13:3b-6*, which gives the most complete description:

Then shall all flesh be raised up from Adam till that great day—all that shall be of the holy people. Then shall the delights of paradise be given to them and God shall be in their midst. And they shall no longer sin before his face, for the evil heart shall be taken from them and there shall be given them a heart understanding the good and to serve God only.—But do you go back to your father . . . when his soul is departing, you will behold the awful (scene of) his passing.

(A, B) The idea of a universal resurrection seems to be somewhat modified by the addition: "All that shall be of the holy people." Is this a later interpolation[9]? A resurrection of the body is probably implied by the phrase "all flesh", though it does not, of course, say anything other than "all mankind" (cf. e.g. Joel 3:1; Zch 2:17; Is 40:5). (C) A transformation, at least an ethical kind, will coincide with the resurrection: no more sin; a change of the heart. The paradise and the immediate presence of God is restored to Adam and those descendants who are "of the holy people". (D) "That great day" is the day of the resurrection at the end of all times. Death itself means a separation between the body and the soul.

Since most of the texts mention an end time resurrection and 13:6 suggests an intermediate state, we may suppose that this is also implied in *32:4*, where Eve is told by an angel:

Adam, your husband, has gone out of his body. Rise up and behold his spirit borne aloft to his Maker[10].

(B) It is only the separation between the body and the soul (D) at death and possibly a spiritual immortality with God that is mentioned in this verse.

3.7.2
A special seventh day eschatology is found in the Latin parallel version of *Vita Adae et Evae*. It is first seen in *43:1*, which is similar to the above quoted passage:

Six days hence[11] his soul shall go off his body and when it shall have gone out, you shall see great marvels in heaven and in the earth and the luminaries of heaven.

(A, B) The soul's spiritual type of *post mortem* life, (D) starting some time after death, seems to be described. But 51:2 adapts the speculation about the seventh day to a (A, B) resurrection message:

Man of God, mourn not for your good[12] more than six days, for on the seventh day is the sign of the resurrection and the rest of the age to come; on the seventh day the Lord rested from all his works.

The only counterpart in the Gr. version of this seventh day eschatology is found in ApcMos 43:2. At the burial of his mother, Eve, Seth is ordered by the archangel Michael not to mourn more than six days, since the seventh day is a day of joy for God and the angels "with the righteous soul, who has passed away from the earth" (ἐν τῇ μεταστασει ἀπο γης δικαια ψυχη).

(C) Finally, a transformation and glorification is promised to Adam in *39:2*.

I will transform you to your former glory and set you on the throne of your deceiver.[13]

The glorification implies both a return to the pre-fallen state of Adam and an inthronization of man, fallen and saved, on the throne of the fallen archangel.[14]

[1]The Greek text in C. v.Tischendorf (1866) X-XI, 1-23; A. M. Ceriani(1868) 19, 21-24. The diss. of M. Nagel, Strasbourg 1972, has not been at my disposal.

[2]I have used the texts of W. Meyer (1878) 185-250, and J. H. Mozley, JThS 30 (1929) 128-148.

[3]Cf. e.g. L. S. A. Wells in Charles, AP II, 126, accepting the possibility of some Christian interpolations; Eissfeldt (1964) 863; Russell (1964) 366; Denis (1970) 6—with references to the theories about a Christian author as well.

[4]Wells in Charles, AP II, 127; Denis (1970) 6f.—accepting Hebrew or Aramaic sources.

[5]Cf. Wells in Charles, AP II, 127; Eissfeldt (1964) 863; Russell (1964) 37, 366; Denis (1970) 6f.

[6]Implied in 10:2: the sinners are to rise with Eve (who is a little uncertain, it seems, about her own resurrection: "if") and she fears their accusations, since her sin was the origin of theirs; 13:3b; 41:3; 43:2. Only 28 seems to speak of the resurrection as a salvation event: God speaks to Adam, who had requested the permission to eat of the tree of life:

> Yet when you are gone out of paradise, if you should keep yourself from all evil, as one about to die, when again the Resurrection has come to pass, I will raise you up and then the Tree of Life shall be given to you (Wells' translation, slightly modernized, like all the translations given here).

[7]10:2: "The day of the Resurrection"; 43:2 (d:o); 13:3b; 41:3.

[8]32:4 (which does not mention the resurrection, however, and so I shall come back to that passage *infra*) and 13:6. (41:3 presupposes some type of intermediate state, though nothing is said about a personal survival at death.)

[9]On the universalist tendency in the book, manifested in the choice of Adam, the father of all mankind, as its "hero", cf. e.g. Volz (1934) 49.

[10]In Gr. the last words are: ἀναφερομενον εἰς τον ποιησαντα αὐτο ἀπαντησαι αὐτῳ. According to Mozley's ed. 47, God gives the following command to Michael, the archangel, about Adam's soul:

> Sit haec anima in custodia tua in suppliciis usque ad diem dispensationis in novissimis diebus, in quibus convertam luctum eius in gaudium. Tunc vero sedebit in throno illius qui eum supplantavit.

For the last statement cf. VAE 39:2, *infra*. This text gives us a very clear example of belief in an intermediate state.

[11]These words are missing in Mozley's text.

[12]Mozley: dead.

[13]For the text of Mozley v. *supra* n. 10.

[14]Cf. also, on VAE, Beresford (1971) 109f., and J. L. Sharpe, CBQ 35 (1973) 35-46.

3.8 Liber Antiquitatum Biblicarum (Pseudo-Philo)

Preserved only in Latin under the name of Philo, the Liber Antiquitatum Biblicarum (LAB) is actually a midrashic re-telling of Biblical history prior to the death of Saul[1]. The original language is Hebrew[2]. It is closely related to IV Ez and II Bar[3] and belongs probably to the early part of the same period, between AD 70 and 135[4]. Its spiritual milieu is that of a Palestinian apocalyptic Judaism, which is much closer to Rabbinism[5] than to Philo. Quite a few statements on resurrection from the dead are found in this writing. A couple of the most important will be quoted and discussed.

3.8.1 *LAB 3:10:*

When the years of the world (*seculi*) shall be fulfilled, then shall the light cease (*quiescet*) and the darkness be quenched (*extinguuntur*), and I will quicken the dead and raise up from the earth them that sleep. And Hell (*infernus*) shall pay back its debt, and destruction give back that which was committed unto him,[6] that I may render unto every man according to his works, and according to the fruit of their imaginations (*adinventionum*), even until (*quousque*)[7] I judge between the soul and the flesh. And the world (*seculum*) shall rest (*requiescet*) and death shall be quenched, and Hell shall shut its mouth. And the earth shall not be without birth, neither barren for them that dwell therein; and none shall be polluted that has been justified in me. And there shall be another earth, and another heaven, even an everlasting habitation (ET: M. R. James, 1917, here and in the following quotations).

(A, B) This passage seems to speak of a universal resurrection of both the righteous and the wicked dead. The formulation of the belief in resurrection is similar to that of I En 51:1[8] and other passages in IV Ezr[9] and II Bar[10]. The raising of those who sleep from the earth implies the resurrection of the body, though the expression *quousque iudicem inter animam et carnem* is quite unclear[11]. It somehow seems to allude to a certain dichotomy between the body and the soul[12].

(C) The last sentence refers to a new creation of the heavens and the earth. This saying is juxtaposed with the preceding one on the fruitfulness of "the earth", either a new earth or the old one, being radically transformed. The preceding sentence pronounces the end of death and of *seculum*—time, generations of mankind[13], as the first statement in the passage declares a fundamental change in the order of the world. But from these statements we are not able to ascertain any information regarding the state of the risen bodies. We shall soon return to a few other passages, which speak of glorification in terms of the star imagery (cf. *infra* 7.2.1-7.2.1.3). **(D)** The resurrection is clearly "dated" at the end of the world—*seculum* (Hebrew: עוֹלָם?) . This means a total reversal of the order of the world. Light and darkness cease and another earth and another heaven are created. A judgment somehow takes place in the same context but, as we have found, the reference *quousque iudicem . . .* is quite vague and difficult to interpret.

3.8.2

LAB 4:11 states, concerning Abraham:

He shall set his dwelling on high (*super excelsa*) . . .

This is said in a context which treats Abraham's earthly happiness and his place in salvation history. The statement refers to some sort of glorification (A) after death (C) in a heavenly, transcendent existence. We have already found that Abraham and the other patriarchs have a special position among those who are to receive the blessed life after death (TestJud 25:1; Benj 10:6 f.—*supra* 3.3.1). The image of heavenly exaltation is also well known to us.[14] This is the idea which also seems to inspire the exhortation of Deborah in *LAB 33:5*. The people are told to imitate their fathers:

3.8.3

Then your likeness shall be seen as the stars of the heaven, which have been manifested unto you at this time.

As is described in 32:11, Deborah refers to the stars as fighting for the people of Israel (following Jg 5:20). The stars are (as usual—cf. *infra* 7.2.1.4) more or less identified with angels—cf. 10:5, concerning the giving of the Law, when the stars gathered and the angels rushed forward (*procurrebant*).

3.8.4

According to the Deborah of *LAB 30:5,* Israel is already now exalted:

He led you unto the height of the clouds and subdued angels under your feet.

3.8.5

The context of the above mentioned exhortation of Deborah is interesting, too. In 32:3 ff. Deborah is preaching: Turn to the Lord in this life, for after your death that will not be possible. After death everything is sealed and the years render their deposit. It is not even possible to live wickedly in hell (*in inferno*) after death, because passion and desire have ceased. Hell will not give back that which was entrusted to it. When hearing Deborah's exhortation, the people start crying and asking Deborah to pray for them both in the present time and even after death[15]. Deborah, however, declines this request, because one can only pray for one another in the temporal life[16].

Thus, there is no real life after death; it is just a shadowy Sheol, wholly in agreement with early Hebrew thought (2.1.1). This impression is confirmed by the prayer of Jeftah's daughter in LAB 40:5-7. The earlier notions are preserved side by side with the hope of the resurrection of the righteous (cf. Hoffmann, 1966, 135-137).

3.8.6

The souls of the righteous rest in peace in their store-houses after death[17]. But existence in "Sheol" or "hell", without subsequent resurrection, is the eternal punishment for the wicked,[18] especially for certain extremely wicked groups, the generation of the Flood, the Egyptians and the sons of Korah (16:3)[19].

76

3.8.7

On the other hand, some outstanding heroes of faith are promised an exaltation and glorification immediately after death, similar to that of Abraham. This is the case of Moses (32:9) and of Phinees (48:1). Apparently the latter is not to die at all. Instead, he is brought to a distant mountain and receives food from an eagle of God until the appointed time of return to the people. Thereafter he is able to open or close the heavens just by his word. These statements cause us to believe that he is identified with Elijah. After this appearance he is elevated to join the others who had been previously elevated, until the end of time (*quousque memorabor seculi*). He will then be brought out with the others, and they will "taste what is death"[20].

3.8.8

According to 44:10 death is separation between body and soul (cf. Hoffmann, 1966, 141). But the soul is not purely a spiritual entity, when Jonathan says to David in *62:9:*

Even though death may separate us, I know that our souls will recognize each other.

This statement presupposes some consciousness after death, but the soul of Samuel is asleep (as in I Sm 28:15) according to 64:6, when he is called back to life by the witch of En-Dor: When he is first awakened, Samuel thinks that the hour of resurrection has come. The description of death and the intermediate state as sleep is, of course, very common both to LAB[21] and to other comparable texts[22].

3.8.9

This is true also of *LAB 19:12,* about the death and resurrection of Moses:

You shall rest in that place, until I visit the world (*seculum*). And I shall wake you and your fathers from the land (of Egypt[23]) where you sleep, and you shall find at the same time also an immortal habitation which is not occupied (*tenetur*) in time.

The context continues to describe the events of the last days, when the heavens will disappear and times and days shall be shortened:

Because I shall hasten to awake you who sleep, so that all who can live may dwell in that sacred place which I showed to you (v.13).

(A) A clear belief in life after death is expressed here, as well as probably, (B) a belief in a resurrection of the body, since the resurrected life is to be lived in a special "habitation", i.e., the land of Israel (cf. 19:7 relating that Moses sees the land but is not permitted to enter it "in this age"). (C) The land is "sacred" and "immortal", i.e. transformed, glorified, whether these qualifications concern the Holy Land only after the resurrection or already during the present age. Otherwise nothing is said about a transformation and glorification at the resurrection. But at the *death* of Moses his face was changed into glory and he died in glory, being preceded by lightnings etc. (*fulgura et lampades et sagitte omnes unanimes*).

Notwithstanding the assertions about future life in what is probably meant to be the Land of Israel, *LAB 19:4* states:

God has revealed the end of the world, that he might covenant upon his high places, and has kindled an everlasting lamp among you.

This description of heavenly glory and exaltation is easily juxtaposed with the traditional expectation of the final gathering of the people in the land of Israel[24]. Therefore, we should not interpret the various statements too literally. Their primary function is not to serve as doctrine about the final blessed state of the righteous but instead as encouragement and consolation in present tribulations, assuring the righteous of a glorious future.

(D) As usual, the resurrection according to LAB 19, takes place at the end of apocalyptic events, when the Lord "visits" the earth.

3.8.10
Other passages in LAB which refer to faith in the resurrection[25] or a blessed after-life[26] do not offer any further information for our investigation.

3.8.11. *Summary*

LAB presents a rather consistent faith in the resurrection of the dead. The resurrection takes place at the end of this world. There are allusions to the heavenly glorification of the righteous as well as to their dwelling in the Promised Land. Some passages do not seem to know of any consciousness in the state between death and final judgment, whereas other texts describe the glorification of some righteous immediately after death. Therefore I conclude that the contents of the different statements are not meant to be information about facts, but instead are meant to be motifs for exhortations, reassurances of final rewards. Death, as a separation between body and soul, and some vague idea of an intermediate state, seem to be expressed more clearly in this text than in most of the passages thus far analyzed.

---

[1]Cf. e.g. L. Cohn, JQR 10 (1898) 314, 322; M. Delcor, SDB VII (1966) 1364-1367; A. G. Wright (1967) 87-89; L. Sabourin, BTh 2 (1972) 211 f.; Stemberger (1972) 97; W. S. Towner, JJS 24 (1973) 114.

[2]Cf. e.g. G. Kisch (1949) 92; D. J. Harrington, HTR 63 (1970) 503-514.

[3]Cf. M. R. James, JThS 16 (1915) 403-405; *id.* (1917) 46-58; B. Violet (1924) XLVII-XLIX; Eissfeldt (1964) 853; P. Bogaert I (1969) 242-258; Stemberger (1972) 97 f.

[4]For varying judgments on the date of LAB within this period cf. e.g. Cohn, JQR 10, 327; James (1917) 29-33; Kisch (1949) 92; Delcor, SDB VII, 1370 f.; O. Eissfeldt, NTT 56 (1953) 53; Bogaert I (1969) 252-258; D. J. Harrington, CBQ 33 (1971) 1-17; Towner, JJS 24, 114. Harrington even suggests the possibility of a date before AD 70 and does not accept the argument for a later date (CBQ 33, 17).

[5]Cohn (1898) 324; Kisch (1949) 16 f.

[6]For the reading *paratecen* cf. e.g. Stemberger (1972) 106 f.

[7]Cf. for this translation P. Riessler (1928) *ad loc.;* Stemberger (1972) 108.

[8]Cf. Stemberger (1972) 46-48, 107, 119 (*supra* 3.2.4).

[9]7:32—cf. Stemberger (1972) 74-84, 106, 119 (*infra* 3.9.1).

[10]21:23 f.; 42:7; 50:2—cf. Stemberger (1972) 87, 91 f., 95 f., 107, 119 f. (*infra* 3.10.1 n.7; 3.10.2; 3.10.3).

[11]Cf. *supra* n.7. For alternative interpretations, see Stemberger (1972) 108, who despairs about a satisfactory explanation.

[12]Stemberger (1972) 104, refuses to accept any body-soul dichotomy in LAB in light of the background of its general anthropology, discussed 99-104. Only as a corpse is the body distinguished from the soul. The soul is equated with the living person, according to this author. Hoffmann (1966) 141-143, on the other hand, holds that there is indeed a certain tendency towards a dichotomic anthropology, though the soul is not at all considered immortal; neither is the body regarded as impure, or as the prison of the soul in any sense. Hoffmann refers to LAB 23:13; 28:3; 32:13; 33:4; 43:7; 44:10; 54:6; 62:9; 64:5-7, passages which speak of death as the separation between body and soul or as the reception of the souls after death.—It seems rather difficult to avoid Hoffmann's conclusion. The dichotomy is there even though "body" with equivalents does actually mean "corpse". It is a secondary question whether or not this is due to influence from "Greek" anthropology.

[13]For the translation of *seculum*, see e.g. C. T. Lewis-C. Short (1879, 1969) 1614 C *s.v.*, "like the Biblical עולם αἰων.

[14]Cf. *supra* 2.2.3 on Dn 12:3; 3.2.3.6 on I En 104:2; 3.2.4.1 on I En 51:4; 3.2.4.7 on I En 71:11; 3.3.1 on TestBenj 10:6. Further *infra* 3.8.7 on LAB 32:9 (Moses entered heaven); 3.10.2.2 on II Bar 51:10, and 7.2.3-7.2.3.3 for a survey.

[15]*Post recessum tuum erit anima tua memor nostri in sempiternum* (33:4).

[16]*Post finem suum non poterit orare sed nec memor esse alicuius. Propterea nolite sperare in patribus vestris. Non enim vobis proderunt, nisi similes inveniamini eis* (33:5).

[17]23:13; 32:13. Cf. Hoffmann (1966) 137 f., further IV Ezr 7:32, 78-101 (*infra* 3.9.4) and II Bar 30:2 (*infra* 3.10.1). See also Schubert, BZ 6, 207.

[18]Thus 51:5, rendering the canticle of Hannah, I Sm 2:6—cf. Hoffmann (1966) 135, 139 f.

[19]Cf. MSanh 10:3 and TSanh 13:6-12. These texts will be discussed in a paper on the formulas of exclusion from the Age to Come, which I hope to publish rather soon.

[20]ET: James (1917) *ad loc*—cf. the Latin original: *Gustabitis quod est mortis*—addressed to those who have been elevated. Cf. Hoffmann (1966) 139.

[21]3:10; 19:10 ff.; 28:10; 51:5.

[22] Is 26:19; Dn 12:2; I En 91:10; 92:3; 100:5.

[23](Of Egypt) is a secondary intrusion, according to James (1917) *ad loc.*

[24]*V. infra* 4.1.6 and 5.8.3 on Ez 37:1-14 and Is 27:13 f. in this context.

[25]25:7: *Si modo moriamini miserebitur tamen vobis Deus cum vivificabit mortuos.* We notice the terminology. *Vivificare,* corresponds to Hebrew pi'el חיה, the standard term for "resurrect" in Rabbinic texts. Cf. also 22:10; 23:13; 52:10; Hoffmann (1966) 135 f.; Beresford (1971) 111 f.

[26]28:10: *Si sic est requies iustorum posteaquam defuncti fuerint oportet eos mori corruptibili seculo, ut non videant peccata.*
51:5: *Nam iustis conservat lumen suum . . . Nam cum dormierint iusti, tunc liberabuntur.* Cf. also 32:13; 40:3; 44:10; 62:9, and Hoffmann (1966) 138-143.

3.9 I V Ezra

In that group of writings which consists of LAB, IV Ezr and II Bar (cf. 3.8 n.3), the ideas about after-life are obviously more developed, more complicated, reflected, harmonized and systematized than what we found in the apocalyptic writings treated so far[1]. IV Ezr and II Bar are especially closely related, but the manner in which they are related is disputed: Is IV Ezr older than II Bar and has the latter been influenced by the former or should we rather assume the opposite relation?[2] The relation of LAB to both IV Ezr and II Bar is also unclear and disputed[3]. This question may be of some interest when comparing the particular statements on the resurrection of the dead, but is, otherwise, of rather less importance to the present investigation.

3.9.1

In IV Ezr the most outspoken, and thus most important text for my purpose, is *7:26-38:*

26 Listen! The time shall come when the signs I have foretold will be seen; the city which is now
27 invisible shall appear and the country now concealed be made visible. Everyone who has been
28 delivered from the evils I have foretold shall see for himself my marvellous acts. My son the Messiah shall appear with his companions and bring four hundred years of happiness to all
29 who survive. At the end of that time, my son the Messiah, shall die, and so shall all mankind
30 who draw breath. The the world shall return to its original silence for seven days as at the
31 beginning of creation, and no one shall be left alive. After seven days the age which is not yet
32 awake shall be roused and the age which is corruptible shall die. The earth shall give up those who sleep in it, and the dust those who rest there in silence; and the storehouses shall give back
33 the souls entrusted to them. Then the Most High shall be seen on the judgment-seat, and there
34 shall be an end of all pity and patience. Judgment alone shall remain; truth shall stand firm
35 and faithfulness be strong; requital shall at once begin and open payment be made; good deeds
36 shall awake and wicked deeds shall not be allowed to sleep. Then the place of torment shall appear and over against it the place of rest; the furnace of hell shall be displayed, and on the opposite side the paradise of delight.
37 Then the Most High shall say to the nations that have been raised from the dead: "Look and understand who it is you have denied and refused to serve, and whose commandment you have
38 despised. Look on this side, then on that: here are rest and delight, there fire and torments." That is what he will say to them on the day of judgment (ET:NEB).

3.9.1

(A) The ideas of after-life found in this passage are well developed and rather complicated: the Messianic kingdom between two separate resurrections and some hint of the soul's continued life after death.

3.9.2

(B) The resurrection of the dead most likely implies the raising of the bodies—cf. the wording v.32, which alludes to Dn 12:2[4]. That would be presupposed by the description of hell in v.36 as well.

3.9.3

(C) The corporeal aspect is not stressed; neither is anything said about the bodies being transformed into a state of glory. But the statement that "the age which is corruptible" shall die (v.31) seems to imply that all conditions of life at the resurrection are radically transformed. In terms similar to Dn 12:3 and other earlier texts on the blessed state of the righteous (cf. *infra* 7.2.1), this transformation is clearly expressed in *7:97*, which describes "the sixth degree" of the happiness of the departed righteous souls (7:78):

> Their sixth joy will be the revelation that they are to shine like stars, never to fade or die, with faces radiant as the sun[5]

Again *vv. 113-114* assert that

> the day of judgment will be the end of the present world and the beginning of the eternal world to come, a world in which corruption will be over, all excess abolished, and unbelief uprooted, in which justice will be full-grown, and truth will have risen like the sun.

Cf. also *v.125*a, where Ezra, confessing his own sins, declares that:

> Those who have practiced self-discipline shall shine with faces brighter than the stars.

Also *8:52-54:*

> For all of you, paradise lies open,
> the tree of life is planted,
> the age to come is made ready,
> and rich abundance[6] is in store;
> the city is already built,
> rest from toil is assured,
> goodness and wisdom are brought to perfection.
> The root of evil has been sealed off from you;
> for you there is no more illness,
> death[7] is abolished,
> hell has fled,
> and decay is quite forgotten.
> All sorrows are at an end,
> and the treasure of immortality[8] has been finally revealed.

All these texts express the idea that the post -judgment and -resurrection world shall be totally transformed and glorified. this also includes the bodies of the righteous; there is no consideration given to the resurrection of the wicked.

3.9.4

(D) The question of the "date" of the resurrection is a bit more difficult. It seems quite clear at first glance that the resurrection occurs at the end of history, combined with the Last Judgment (7:31-38, 113-114). But two ideas complicate the picture. First, the intermediate state describes the soul as being separated from the body (7:78, 100) and experiencing a preliminary judgment (7:78-101). Secondly, the ideas of "the first resurrection" and the Messianic kingdom seem to appear in 7:28 f.

3.9.4.1

Death is conceived of as the body being separated from the soul (7:78, 100). It is never explicitly stated that they are reunited at the resurrection, but it is probably implied in the description of the resurrection (7:32), i.e., those who are "given back" can not be divided into three different categories, since the two first groups are evidently synonymous, perhaps denoting primarily the bodies, which are distinguished from the third group, the souls in the "store-houses".

3.9.4.1.1

It might be preferable, however, not to make any clear distinction between the three categories, allowing the souls to represent the whole man, as in OT anthropology[9]. Therefore, these passages which describe the resurrection on the last day, make no clear distinction between the body and the soul. Only vague allusions to the intermediate state are found there.

3.9.4.1.2

But when the intermediate state is in the centre of interest, as in 7:78-101, the resurrection of the body is always presupposed, but at the same time is seen as fading away in the background. In this passage the anticipated vision of the post-resurrection state, hell and heaven, is given to both the wicked and the righteous souls immediately after death as a preliminary judgment. The wicked souls never enter the "store-houses", since part of their punishment is that of perpetual wandering. The righteous souls are allowed to be outside "the store houses" seven days in order to see their future joys, before they are gathered in these abodes (vv.100-101). These seven days and the final resurrection tend to overlap and join to form one blessed state, and the stay in the "store-houses" is apparently an auxiliary concept, which is needed for the combination of the idea of an immediate retribution after death with the belief in a final resurrection from the dead. But the auxiliary concept may easily be forgotten, as e.g. in *v.98*:

> Their seventh joy, the greatest joy of all, will be the confident and exultant assurance which will be theirs, free from all fear and shame, as they press forward to see face to face the One whom they served in their lifetime, and from whom they are now to receive their reward in glory.

The movement towards "the beatific vision", as related in this verse, does not indicate any resurrection.

3.9.4.1.3

On the other hand, most of the seven stages of joy, given to the righteous souls after death (v.91), are indeed anticipatory (vv.93, 95-98). The fulfiment has yet to come, and so the joy of anticipation immediately after death and the final glory of the resurrection are not completely overlapped.

3.9.4.1.4

The descriptions of the resurrection on the last day and the beatitude or torment immediately after death are quite loosely connected. But they can be adapted to a unified pattern which includes death as separation between body and soul, an intermediate state which anticipates future joy or damnation, and a final resurrection. This is the classical harmonization, found both in Jewish and Christian eschatology of two originally independent ideas about after-life and rewards in the future *post mortem*[10].

3.9.4.1.5

The storehouses of the souls in the intermediate state are compared to pregnant wombs in 4:40-42. Ezra asks (*v.33*):

> But when? How long have we to wait?

And Uriel, the *angelus interpres* (4:1), replies (*inter alia, vv. 35-37*):

> Are not these the very questions which were asked by the righteous in the storehouse of souls: "How long must we stay here? When will the harvest begin, the time when we get our reward?" And the archangel Jeremiel gave them this answer: "As soon as the number of those like yourselves is complete. For the Lord has weighed the world in a balance, he has measured and numbered the ages; he will move nothing, alter nothing, until the appointed number is achieved."

Ezra continues to ask why the reward of the just is delayed (v.39). He receives the reply (*vv.41-42a*):

> The storehouses of souls in the world below are like the womb. As a woman in travail is impatient to see the end of her labour, so they are impatient to give back all the souls committed to them since time began.

3.9.4.1.5

The souls of the righteous in the intermediate state have some consciousness, since they are able to ask their questions according to 4:35[11]. The comparison between child-birth and resurrection reappears here and there in the Rabbinic literature[12]. The description of the impatience of the righteous souls in the storehouses implies that this is an unsatisfactory situation and that only the resurrection is full salvation, since it is the time when the righteous receive their reward.

3.9.4.2

The second problem in the context of IV Ezr 7:32 is the idea of the Messianic kingdom. This concept is found in *7:28,* and is possibly combined with that of a first resurrection:

> My son the Messiah shall appear with his companions and bring four hundred[13] years of happiness to all who survive.

Evidently this takes place before the universal resurrection (7:31 ff.). The "companions"[14] are probably, above all, the patriarchs and other heroes of sacred history (cf. 3.3.1 and TestBenj 10:6). It is not explicitly stated that they rise, but the parallel idea of the millennium, preceded by the first resurrection, in Rev 20:3, might be used to interpret this text (Noack, 1953, *ad loc.*, e.g.). However, the difficulties to understand Rev 20:3 are well-known. II Bar 29-30 (3.10.1), which is obviously more important and relevant to the interpretation of IV Ezr, has been interpreted as presenting both a Messianic millennium and a first resurrection. But, as we shall see, this text is extremely obscure and allows a number of possible interpretations (3.10.1). Therefore, the statement of IV Ezr 7:28 appears to be very isolated. Its relation to the immediate context is very loose, too. The fact that all die after the four hundred years, including the Messiah, who then totally disappears in IV Ezr 7, plainly reveals that the idea of the Messianic *interregnum* is an appendix without any real function.

3.9.4.2.1

There seems to be a tendency in IV Ezr to try to combine and harmonize different eschatological ideas, inasmuch as it describes the intermediate state, harmonizing the end time resurrection with the immediate retribution after death. We may suspect that 7:28 is an attempt to adapt the expectation of the Messiah and the earthly Messianic kingdom to an image of eschatology, which is otherwise dominated by the idea of a universal resurrection and followed by a subsequent judgment of God himself, without any place for the Messiah. The Messiah was expected to appear at the end of the Messianic woes in order to save the surviving people, the righteous remnant[16]. But in order to assure a universal resurrection he also dies with all of the survivors. This is an interesting effort to combine the expectation that the Messiah will come during the lifetime of a generation of mankind with the belief in the universal resurrection[17]. His death and subsequent total disappearance in the eschatological drama clears the way for the description of the Last Judgment, where God alone will preside.

3.9.5

A concentrated description of the resurrection and Last Judgment is found in *14:35:*

> For after death will come the judgment; we shall be restored to life,[18] and then the names of the just will be known and the deeds of the godless exposed.[19]

(A) New life is evidently given to both the righteous and the wicked after death. **(B)** The expression "restored to life" (Latin: *iterum reviviscemus,* Syriac: ן ג ח ך י י ח ב ר ת) implies a resurrection, though nothing is said about the body (*vs.* Box, Charles AP II, 1913, *ad loc.*). **(D)** The purpose of the resurrection is clear: universal judgment. The question when this will happen is comparably unimportant, as compared to the fact of future universal judgment.

3.9.6. *Summary*

The last quotation concentrates that which is important in IV Ezr concerning death and resurrection: a universal judgment and retribution *post mortem*. This central motif is developed on the basis of earlier traditional material concerning the resurrection of the righteous after the appearance of the Messiah; or a universal resurrection for judgment; but also an immediate retribution of the souls after death, of reward or punishment; and the restful, yet impatient expectation until the day of resurrection, the final vindication of God's justice. The details of the earlier traditions are combined and harmonized. The tensions between the different traditions are quite visible, but IV Ezr represents the first clear example of an effort to synthesize the different elements in its statements on the Messianic kingdom and an intermediate state.

[1]On the original Semitic text (Hebrew or Aramaic), cf. e.g. W. Harnisch (1969) 15n.; Denis (1970) 199, with further references, on the Greek fragments, the Latin, Syriac and other versions *ibid.* 195-198. See also Russell (1964) 62 f.; Stemberger (1972) 73 (mentioning the possibility of a Hebrew original translated into Aramaic). In spite of the Semitic original language, the book may have been written outside Palestine, e.g. in Egypt or Rome, *circa* AD 100 (Denis, 1970, 200).

[2]Cf. e.g. Denis (1970) 185, for a fairly recent orientation on the different judgments. Ante-dating II Bar among more recent authors e.g. P. Bogaert I (1969) 118 f.; C. Thoma, Kairos 11 (1969) 134 f. (II Bar AD 70-80, IV Ezr 81-96), ante-dating IV Ezr e.g. Russell (1964) 64; Harnisch (1969) 11 n.1; Denis (1970) 186, and A. C. B. Kolenkow (1971) 4. The unanimous opinion is that no matter which one is prior, it quite certainly influenced the other. Cf. also Stemberger (1972) 73, who leans towards the priority of IV Ezr.

[3]Cf. *supra* 2.2.2 and e.g. Nickelsburg (1972) 139. For a more exhaustive treatment of 7:32, see e.g. Stemberger (1972) 74-84.

[5]ET: NEB, as in all of the other quotations from IV Ezr. Cf. *infra* 7.2.1-7.2.1.2 with further references there, and also e.g. H. Gunkel in Kautzsch, AP II (1900) *ad loc.*, 375 f., where, however, conclusions about the relations between the different ideas of the blessed sharing the glory of angels and/or stars and about questions of the origins of these ideas are drawn too quickly.

[6]Latin: *habundantia, sc. beatitudinis* or similar expression, cf. Syriac פ ד נ ק א. Violet (1924); Noack (1953) *ad loc.* suggest the translation *Wonne, salighed,* blessedness, on this basis.

[7]"Death" is missing in the Latin version, but is inserted here by the Syriac and accepted by e.g. Violet (1910, 1924) Noack (1953); NEB. The verse may allude to Is 25:8—cf. Noack (1953) *ad loc.*

[8]*Immortalitatis* in the Latin (and Armenian, Noack, 1953, *ad loc.*) version. The Syriac version says ד ח י ן and a corresponding expression is used in the Ethiopian (according to Violet, 1910, 1924; Noack, 1953, *ad loc.*, who choose "of life" for their translation).—The whole passage describes future salvation as a return to the lost paradise (Noack, 1953, *ad loc.*).

[9]Cf. Hoffmann (1966) 144, against J. Keulers (1922) 150-153. But Stemberger (1972) 79-82, finds an undeniable anthropological dichotomy here, with an independent soul after death.

[10]Cf. Schubert WZKM 56, 162; id. BZ 6, 207: Stemberger (1972) 84.

[11]Cf. I En 9:3, 10; Rev 6:9 f., and *supra* 3.2.2.1, further e.g. Noack (1953) *ad loc.* See Stemberger (1972) 77 f., against Violet (1924) 20, for the view that the souls mentioned here are the souls of the dead, not the unborn souls.

[12]Cf. *infra* 5.1.1—the opinion of the Hillelites; 5.4.3, Sanh 90b-91a (implication of the argument of Gamaliel's daughter) and Sanh 91a (implication of Gebiha's argument); Sanh 92a-b (R. Tabi in the name of R. Joshiah).

[13]This number of years is probably calculated via a combination of Ps 90:15 and Gn 15:13—cf. Gunkel (1900) and Noack (1953) *ad loc.*

[14]Latin: *cum his qui cum eo* Syriac: ד ע מ ה ן ד י ל א ע ם. Cf. also I Th 3:13; 4:14; II Th 1:7 (angels); Noack (1953) *ad loc.*

[15]On the Messianic kingdom in Rev and Jewish apocalyptic, cf. e.g. H. A. Wilcke (1957) 21-47, on IV Ezr 44 f.

[16]Cf. e.g. PsSol 17:21 ff.; TestLevi 18; Judah 24 (cf. Hultgård, 1971, 111-162, on these passages); II Bar 28-29.

[17]The death of the Messiah seems to be a strange idea, having, of course, nothing to do with the gospel accounts of the death and resurrection of Jesus—nothing is actually said about the *resurrection* of the Messiah in IV Ezr; we are not even told that he is with the others who rise from the dead. Cf. Harnisch (1969) 256 n.8 against the view that the statement of the death of the Messiah would be a Christian interpolation (P. Grelot).—On the combination of the different conceptions here cf. e.g. Wilckens (1970) 133.

[18]Box, Charles AP II (1913) *ad loc.*, relates the view of Kabisch that this clause is a gloss. This would explain his own difficulty why it does not suit the theology of the apocalypse of Salathiel, the supposed source of IV Ezr (*ibid.* 549). Obviously these scholars expect to find a systematic eschatological doctrine in a Jewish apocalypse...

[19]Cf. also the preceding verse (v.34) about mercy after death, for the righteous.

3.10 II Baruch

The present Syriac Apocalypse of Baruch (II Bar) is based on a Greek version probably of a Hebrew or Aramaic original[1]. We have already referred to the question on the date of this work, which is obviously closely related to IV Ezr (3.9). No matter if it is earlier or later than IV Ezr, *terminus post quem* would be the destruction of Jerusalem (AD 70) and *terminus ante quem* would be the writing of Barn (not later than AD 140)[2]. Therefore, we would expect to find an eschatology and a teaching on the resurrection rather similar to IV Ezr (and to LAB, 3.8). The first relevant text is *30:1-5:*

3.10.1

(1)   And it shall come to pass after these things, when the time of the advent[3] of the Messiah is
(2)   fulfilled, that he shall return in glory. Then all who have fallen asleep in hope of Him shall rise again. And it shall come to pass at that time that the treasuries will be opened in which is preserved the number of the souls of the righteous, and a multitude of souls shall be seen together in one assemblage of one thought, and the first shall rejoice and the last shall not be
(3)   grieved. For they know[4] that the time has come of which it is said, that it is the consummation
(4)   of the times. But the souls of the wicked, when they behold all these things, shall then waste
(5)   away the more. For they know that their torment has come and their perdition has arrived.

The central problem in the interpretation of this text is the statement on the Messiah, "that he shall return in glory". Does it refer to the return from heaven—as the Christian *parousia,* or to the return *to* heaven from the earthly task? There are not any known Jewish parallels to the former. The context, especially 29:5, supports the latter. When the Messiah is said to be "revealed" in 29:5 and then is not mentioned until 30:1, it is apparently implied that the time between the two statements on the Messiah is to be regarded as his reign on earth. A close parallel is found in IV Ezr 7:28 f. (3.9.4.2). Its description of the end of the Messianic reign may have been consciously corrected by II Bar 30:1 (cf. n.28 *infra,* the reference to A. C. B. Kolenkow): Instead of dying, the Messiah returns *to* heaven in glory[5].

3.10.1.1

(A, B) A resurrection of "all who have fallen asleep in hope of him" is predicted. On the other hand, the souls of both the righteous and the wicked seem to survive death. At least those of the righteous are preserved in the "treasuries". We found the same concept in I En 22 (3.2.2.2) and IV Ezr 7[6], and it is also recognized in II Bar 21:23[7]. The resurrection is described (30:2) as the appearance of the souls of the righteous, preserved in the treasuries, while the souls of the wicked waste away. An intermediate state of the souls between death and the resurrection of the body would seem to be the natural consequence of this description of after-life. On the other hand, death is not stressed as the separation of the body and soul. Neither is resurrection stressed as a resurrection of the body. We might even maintain that this passage only teaches a resurrection of the soul without the body. The comparison with ch. 50-51, however, makes it more probable that the author of ch. 30 was speaking of the resurrection of the body.

3.10.1.2

(C) As we have seen, the physical aspect is not especially stressed. If the return of the Messiah is interpreted as a return to heaven, it would then imply a fairly spiritualized view of the resurrected body, similar to the one expounded in ch. 50-51, describing the glorification and transformation of the righteous.[8]

3.10.1.3

(D) The eschatological time-table is more complicated here than in the previous texts (except IV Ezr). The probable meaning of the text is that those who hoped in Messiah are raised when the Messiah returns to glory. But the various end-time events seem to be rather loosely related to each other. These ideas from different origins are combined: the Messiah and his reign of abundant fruitfulness and riches and the resurrection of the dead for a final judgment. Although nothing explicit is said about the resurrection of the wicked, as in ch. 50-51, their fate at the end time resembles annihilation[9], which in fact implies a judgment.

3.10.2

The second important text of II Bar, previously mentioned several times, is ch. 49-51. This is one of the very few passages, if not the only one, which explicitly treats the question of what the resurrected bodies will look like:[10]

49:1 Nevertheless, I will again ask from Thee, O Mighty One, yea, I will ask mercy from Him who
2 made all things. "In what shape will those live who live in Thy day? Or how will the splendour
3 of those who (are) after that time continue? Will they then resume this form of the present. And put on these entramelling members, which are now involved in evils, and in which evils are consummated, or wilt Thou perchance change these things which have been in the world as also the world?"

50:1 And He answered and said unto me: "Hear, Baruch, this word, and write in the remembrance
2 of thy heart all that thou shalt learn. For the earth shall then assuredly restore the dead (which it now receives, in order to preserve them)[11]. It shall make no change in their form, but as it has
3 received, so shall it restore them, and as I delivered them unto it, so also shall it raise them. For then it will be necessary to show to the living that the dead have come to life again, and that
4 those who had departed have returned (again). And it shall come to pass, when they have severally recognized those whom they now know, then judgment shall grow strong, and those things which before were spoken of shall come.

51:1 And it shall come to pass, when that appointed day has gone by, that then shall the aspect of
2 those who are condemned be afterwards changed, and the glory of those who are justified. For the aspect of those who now act wickedly shall become worse than it is, as they shall suffer
3 torment. Also (as for) the glory of those who have now been justified in My law, who have had understanding in their life, and who have planted in their heart the root of wisdom, then their splendour shall be glorified in changes, and the form of their face shall be turned into the light of their beauty, that they may be able to acquite and receive the world which does not die,
5 which is then promised to them . . . When therefore they (i.e. the wicked) see those, over whom they are now exalted, (but) who shall then be exalted and glorified more than they, they shall respectively be transformed, the latter into the splendour of angels, and the former shall yet
6 more waste away in wonder at the visions and in the beholding of the forms. For they shall first behold and afterwards depart to be tormented.
7 8 But those who have been saved by their works . . . shall behold the world which is now invisible
9 to them, and they shall behold the time which is new hidden from them: And time shall no
10 longer age them. For in the heights of that world shall they dwell, and they shall be made like unto the angels, and be made equal to the stars, and they shall be changed into every form they
12 desire, from beauty into loveliness, and from light into the splendour of glory . . . Moreover, there shall then be excellency in the righteous surpassing that in the angels . . .

52:7 (Exhortation to the righteous:) Make ready your soul for that which is reserved for you, and prepare your souls for the reward which is laid up for you[12].

3.10.2.1

(A) The fate of the dead is clearly treated, and (B) their resurrection is described. This is implied by the question of 49:3[12 bis]. When "the soul" is mentioned (52:7), it is used in the old Israelite sense of the whole man, which excludes the concept of the spiritual part of man being distinct from the body. Faith in the resurrection of the whole man, including the body, is presupposed by the author.

3.10.2.2

(C) Two rather different types of resurrection belief are skilfully combined. The first is the idea that the body is restored to its pre-existing state. This is one of the most extreme expressions of literal faith in the resurrection of the body[13]. The second is the hope for a transcendent glorification of the righteous into an angelic state.—This is the most explicit expression concerning a spiritually resurrected body which can be found in the Jewish literature investigated in this work.[14] The problem of identifying those who rise again leads to this combining of the two types of resurrection belief (50:3-4), or even to the necessity of proving the reality of resurrection.

3.10.2.2.1

It seems that a denial or a doubt of the resurrection is presupposed, which calls for an apology and a deepened reflection on the nature of the resurrection body[15]. This obvious and special similarity with Paul's teaching on the resurrection of the dead in I Cor 15 justifies a detailed comparison between these two passages.

There are four important *similarities* between II Bar 49-51 and I Cor 15:

(1) the general background of apology for belief in the resurrection,
(2) the reflection on the nature of the resurrection body,
(3) the survival of some until the day of resurrection (II Bar 50:3 and I Cor 15:51 f.), and
(4) the idea of a transformation and heavenly glorification of the righteous at the resurrection.

Of course, this comparison cannot lead us to any theories about literary dependance, i.e. II Bar upon I Cor, which must be at least fifteen years older[16]. But it does show how the denial of the resurrection provoked similar reflections on the nature of the resurrected body, though conditioned by somewhat different questions. This is actually the first of five *dissimilarities* between the two texts, which are worth noting for our purposes:

3.10.2.2.1.1

(1) Although the questions in II Bar 49 are similar to those in I Cor 15:35, those in II Bar are actually more precise: (a) In II Bar the problem of the belief in the resurrection of the body is partly the concept that the body is closely linked with sin[17]. This is not explicit in I Cor 15, whatever the attitude towards the body may have been among those who denied the resurrection of the body in the Corinthian Church. (b) The questions of ch. 49 require a radical change of the shape of the resurrected bodies, partly related to the fact that the resurrected life will be lived in a totally changed new world[18], beyond human sensation[19] and time[20]. Consequently, a problem of identification arises, which seems to be the background of the formulation in II Bar 50:3 f. I Cor 15 does not treat the question: How shall we be able to recognize the risen dead? The reflection of the author of II Bar proves to be more refined and nuanced in this respect.

3.10.2.2.1.2

(2) But II Bar probably does not say anything about a transformation of the survivors on the last day (cf. 3.10.2.1), as I Cor 15:51 f. The expectation of survival until the Last Day was probably not so central in the minds of the Jewish circles which produced II Bar as it was in the first Christian generation (cf. also I Th 4:13-18).

3.10.2.2.1.3

(3) I Cor 15 has nothing to say about the fate of the wicked. They are not even considered.

3.10.2.2.1.4

(4) The original idea of II Bar about the exact restoration of the bodies is not found in I Cor 15, where the dead rise incorruptible simultaneously as the living are changed (15:52). This idea gives a solution to the problem of identification according to II Bar - (b) *supra.*

3.10.2.2.1.5

(5) Whereas death in I Cor 15 implies the possibility and necessity of change and transformation (v.36 ff.) with the death of Christ as the pattern and model, it has no positive role whatsoever in II Bar 49-51. Here it is nothing but a parenthesis. Resurrection implies a recontinuance of the life which ended at physical death. Consequently, in II Bar, the transformation follows some time *after* the resurrection.

3.10.2.2.2

The comparison between the risen state (of the righteous) and the glory of stars and angels, more or less identified with each other (7.2.1.1), is a *topos* of apocalyptic tradition[21]. Keeping the comparison with I Cor 15 in mind, it is, of course, especially interesting to note that the stars are used as images of the state of the risen bodies in I Cor 15:40-41—though the point of comparison in I Cor 15 is different from the point found in this and the other apocalyptic passages. It is not the radiant glory of the stars which is compared, but is instead the pluralism of bodies and "glories" among the different stars and heavenly bodies.

3.10.2.2.3

What is perhaps more startling is the assertion in II Bar 51:12 that the glory of the righteous will surpass that of the angels. This thought has a number of parallels in Rabbinic writings[22] and analogous statements in the NT[23].

3.10.2.2.4

The statements on the angelic "glory of those who have been justified in . . . (the) Law" (51:3a) are well suited to the localization of their risen life: "the heights of that world" (51:10). This idea is often found in the texts, as has been and shall be seen[24]. Here it is clearly expressing the transcendence of the new postresurrection world beyond time and human sensation[25]. This description of the world to come is very much unlike the image of the Messianic age given in ch. 29 with its supernatural abundance of food and drink[26]. A similar picture is found again, however, in ch. 72-74[27]. Although there is a distinction made in ch. 30 between the Messianic age and the final fulfilment, the age after the Messianic days is hardly described at all. Only the fact that the resurrection is mentioned as an event towards the end of the Messianic reign with the return of the Messiah to his heavenly glory (3.10.1.3) leads us to the conclusion that the Messianic age is not the final age of happiness and bliss. In ch. 72-74 there is nothing in the context which contradicts the assumption that the period which is pictured is indeed the final age to come. Some of the scholars who comment on II Bar try to systematize the different eschatological statements, such as Messianic reign and final post-resurrection glory (or damnation), into one coherent image. The author imagines a Messianic age, which is concluded by the general resurrection and the return of the Messiah to his glory, and this is followed by the judgment and the transcendent age to come[28]. To me, this interpretation seems to go beyond that which is permitted by the pure testimony of the texts. Different ideas are quite loosely juxtaposed without making any great effort to either harmonize or systematize them[29]. When the two different eschatologies, the Messianic age on earth and the resurrection of the dead to a heavenly existence, are combined in ch. 30, their inter-relationship remains very unclear. Elsewhere they are not combined at all, since they appear in different contexts[30]. So the consequences of the author's own sharp reflection on the resurrection in ch. 49-52 have not been followed elsewhere in his work.

3.10.2.3

(D) In the preceding section we already touched the question of the date of the resurrection in II Bar. In ch. 49-52 the date given is defined as "Thy day" (49:2, Syriac יומך) or "when that appointed day has gone by" (51:1, מן בתר דעברהי יומא דקים. It is obviously "the Last Day", the decisive turn of events which border this present age and the Age to Come. The preceding context (48:50) distinguishes "this corruptible world"(עלמא דעבד הנא) from "that world without end" (עלמא הו דסוף לית לה) and also mentions "Thy day" (48:47) as the day of the punishment of the sinners. This is the day when "judgment shall grow strong" (50:4). Ch. 51 describes the rewards of both the righteous and the sinners, i.e., the results of a divine judgment, which, however, is not described itself.

3.10.3

One more text in II Bar may be mentioned here, 42:7:

> Destruction takes that which belongs to it and life that which belongs to it, and the dust is summoned and it is said to it: "Give back that which is not yours and let everything arise that you have preserved for its time."

In the context of this statement the theme is final justice and compensation for all. (D) Thus, resurrection is closely linked with judgment. (A-C) The image of resurrection is very similar to that of ch. 49-52, at least in so far as those who rise come from the earth, "the dust". This expression (עפרא) recalls Dn 12:2 (2.2), and it is likely that it presupposes a resurrection of the body. Treasuries of the souls are not mentioned, in comparison to 30:2.

3.10.4. *Summary*

II Bar is quite interesting as a document containing reflections parallel to those of the early Christians on the subject of the resurrection of the dead. Above all, the comparison between II Bar 49-52 and I Cor 15 is fruitful for our purpose (cf. 1.2.4). In a similar way, earlier traditions are transmitted in secondary combinations or in a stage of further reflection without any inter-dependence between the two writings. In II Bar 51 the transformation of the resurrection body is described, but there is no pattern, no εἰκων nor any ἀπαρχη των κεκοιμημενων (I Cor 15:49, 20).

[1]Cf. e.g. Russell (1964) 64, mentioning only Aramaic as the original language, and Harnisch (1969) 15n.; Denis (1970) 184, with references to authors who suggest Hebrew, too. On the Greek fragments, see Denis (1970) 183 f.; Bogaert I (1969) 363-370. Bogaert, *ibid.* 353-380, questions the proofs by earlier authors for a Semitic original. Only the fact that the Syriac version is translated from Greek can be proved.

[2]Cf. Bogaert (1969), referring to what seems to be quotations in Barn for the *terminus ante quem*, 272-280, and concluding, after a discussion of other theories and arguments, for the plausibility of a date of AD 96, 281-294; further, Thoma, Kairos 11, 134 f.; Denis (1970) 184 f.

[3]Syriac: מ א ת ת י ה א (ד) . For the meaning of the statement, cf. *infra* in my commentary.

[4]Following the emendation of Charles, AP II (1913) *ad loc.,* whose ET is generally followed, and Bogaert (1969) *ad loc.* V. Ryssel, Kautzsch AP II (1900) *ad loc.,* suggests *es weiss ein jeder.*

[5]Cf. e.g. Charles, Ryssel, Riessler (1928) and Bogaert *ad loc.;* Wilcke (1967) 42; Stemberger (1972) 92 f. B. Violet (1924) *ad loc.,* defends the interpretation of a return from heaven.—According to Wilcke, 44 n.151, the verse is possibly an interpolation. He questions the interpretation implying the concept of a Messianic reign in this passage.

[6]Cf. *supra* 3.9.4.1 and 3.9.4.1.5; Stemberger (1972) 91 f.

[7]The hope of eternal life and resurrection of some kind is expressed here, too, though rather vaguely:

> Bring to an end therefore henceforth mortality. And reprove accordingly the angel of death, and let your glory appear, and let the might of your beauty be known, and let Sheol be sealed so that from this time forward it may not receive the dead, and let the treasuries of souls restore those which are enclosed in them.

(A, B) "The restoration" of the souls in the "treasuries" may denote both only a spiritual resurrection and the same belief in the resurrection of the body that is found elsewhere in this book. Cf. e.g. Stemberger (1972) 91 f.

[8]With Stemberger (1972) 94 f., who holds that II Bar 30 represents a simplified version in relation to 49-51, undisturbed by apologetic aims, such as those which appear in the latter text (answering the questions of identity and identification of the resurrection bodies).

[9]They shall "waste away" (v.4)—but on the other hand, the text speaks about "their torment . . . and their perdition". Actually this functions only as the background of the glorification of the righteous—cf. Stemberger (1972) 95. Volz (1934) 46 f., senses a doctrine of a continued existence of the wicked in pains—contrasted with the return of the righteous from the "treasuries", but asks whether this passage is not a Christian interpolation. But the vagueness and relative inconsistency of the descriptions of the fate of the wicked suit very well the general impression of most similar descriptions in Jewish apocalyptic literature.

[10]Cf. e.g. Wilckens (1970) 126 f., but his assertion that salvation and judgment "selbstverständlich . . . als leibhaftig-konkret aufgefasst und ernst genommen wird" is questionable in the light of the material gathered in this volume.

[11]According to Charles, AP II, *ad loc.,* this is an interpolation (he brackets it without any commentary)—cf. II Bar 4:2-7. Ryssel, Kautzsch, AP II, *ad loc.,* and Bogaert (1969) *ad loc.,* keep the words without any commentaries.

[12]Again Charles, AP II,*ad loc.,* has bracketed 52:4-7 as an interpolation. But cf. Bogaert (1969) 98, against this assumption.

[12bis] Although the question of 49:2, concerning "those who live in Thy day", is ambiguous: those who survive or those who rise from the dead?

[13]Cf., however, II Mcc 7:11 (4.2.1.2); 14:46 (4.2.1.3); OrSib IV, 181 f. (4.7.1); PsPhoc 103 (4.8.1); GnR 14:5⫽LvR 14:9 (5.1).

[14]Cf. the survey in the table of 7, the column TH, for other writings, where the thoughts about transformation and glorification of the righteous after death appear in various forms, further 7.1.5 and 7.2.1. But nowhere do we find the thoughts of the body being spiritualized and transformed, which are here explicitly formulated.

[15]Concerning this apologetic tendency, cf. also n.8 *supra* and Stemberger (1972) 87 f.

[16]For the date of II Bar, cf. *supra* 3.10 (70-140); likewise of I Cor (including ch. 15), cf. e.g. H. Conzelmann (1969) 16n (circa 55).

[17]"These entramelling members, which are now involved in evils etc.". (49:3a). Cf. however Rm 7:23 f., where Paul expresses himself in a similar dualistic way.

[18]Vv. 49:3b and 51:3b—cf. also the quotations in the following foot-notes, and Stemberger (1972) 90.

[19]51:8-10: "The world which is now invisible to them . . . in the heights of that world shall they dwell . . ."

[20]51:8-9: "The time which is now hidden from them: And time shall no longer age them . . ."

[21]Cf. 7.2.1-7.2.1.2 with notes for further references and a survey, and see also Bogaert II (1969) *ad loc.*

[22]See Bogaert II (1969) *ad loc.,* and the passages to which he refers: SNm § 103 (ed. of Friedmann 27b-28a); GnR 78:1; Sanh 92b-93a.

[23]I Cor 6:1-4; I Pt 1:12; Hbr 2:16—cf. also 1:4-14; 2:5 ff.

[24]Cf. the survey of 7.2.3-7.2.3.3 *infra*!

[25]Cf. *supra* 3.10.2.2.1.1 with foot-notes 18-20.

[26] *29:4-8:* Behemoth . . . and Leviathan . . . shall be for food for all that are left. The earth also shall yield its fruit ten thousandfold and on each (?) vine there shall be a thousand branches, and each branch shall produce a thousand clusters, and each cluster produce a thousand grapes, and each grape produce a cor of wine. And those who have hungered shall rejoice:moreover, also, they shall behold marvels every day. For winds shall go forth from before Me to bring every morning the fragrance of aromatic fruits, and at the close of the day clouds distilling the dew of health. And it shall come to pass at that self-same time that the treasury of manna shall again descend from on high, and they will eat of it in those years, because these are they who have come to the consummation of time.

Cf. also *supra* 3.10.1.

[27]The following statements may be quoted (*73:1-74:3*):

And it shall come to pass, when [the Messiah] has brought low everything that is in the world, and has sat down in peace for the age on the throne of His kingdom, that joy shall then be revealed, and rest shall appear. And then healing shall descend in dew, and disease shall withdraw, and anxiety and anguish and lamentation pass from amongst men, and gladness proceed throught the whole earth. And no one shall again die untimely, nor shall any adversity suddenly befall, And judgments, and revilings, and contentions, and revenges, and blood, and passions, and envy, and hatred, and whatsoever things are like these shall go into condemnation when they are removed . . . And wild beasts shall come from the forest and minister unto men, and asps and dragons shall come forth from their holes to submit themselves to a little child. And women shall no longer then have pain when they bear, nor shall they suffer torment when they yield the fruit of the womb.
And it shall come to pass in those days that the reapers shall not grow weary, nor those that build be toilworn; For the works shall of themselves speedily advance together with those who do them in much tranquillity. For that time is the consummation of that which is corruptible, and the beginning of that which is not corruptible . . . Therefore it is far away from evils, and near to those thing which die not.

Cf. the discussion in Stemberger (1972) 93 f., on the question whether the text here does express belief in immortality or merely something which comes close to immortality. Bogaert (1969) *ad loc.*, and Violet, (1924) *ad loc.*, find immortality, and the latter even finds resurrection of the dead mentioned here. The present author joins Stemberger in the view that the text does not carry the burden of proof for that interpretation (1972, 94).

[28]Thus e.g. Stemberger (1972) 96, and maybe also A. F. J. Klijn, JSJud 1 (1970) 75 f.: By a study of the final redaction of the source material, it is possible to state that the redactor corrects an apocalyptic tradition, the expectation of a restoration of the temple, nation and country. He stresses "a break in the history of this world. At this break a resurrection of the dead will take place"—the most important idea of the Apocalypse (against the work of W. Harnisch, 1969, 259 f. n, who thinks, however, that in 30: (1) 2-5 the author of II Bar is consciously correcting the tradition of 29:1-8 by stressing his opinion that the period of earthly salvation described there is not yet the end). Further: According to A. C. B. Kolenkow (1971) 60-90: II Bar 70-71 corrects the description of the return to primaeval silence and the death of the Messiah found in IV Ezr 7:26 ff. In II Bar a peaceful transition from corruption to incorruption is found to take place during the reign of the Messiah.

[29]This is also the judgment of Hoffmann (1966) 150-155; Wilcke (1967) 42-44 (when the Messianic age is described, it is seen as the end).

[30]Except for ch. 28-30 we find the Messianic age in ch. 72-74 and the transcendent eschatology in ch. 49-52. The resurrection statement in 42:7 belongs in the context of the restoration of the true people of Israel as also 75:7 f. (cf. the comm. *ad loc.* by Charles and Bogaert; Hoffmann, 1966, 151)—i.e. closer to the eschatology of the Messianic age. On 42:7 *v. infra* 3.10.4.

3.11 Apocalypse of Abraham

The origins of the present Slavonic Apocalypse of Abraham may be traced back to a Greek translation of a Semitic original which was probably composed between 70 and 110-120 AD[1]. The book is "important as one more interesting example of the apocalyptic ideas of late Judaism" (Box, 1918,xxxii), which form part of the background of early Christianity. Thus, e.g., Satan is the prince of this world, called here Azazel (ch. 13-14, 20, 22, 23, 29) and described as a fallen archangel[2]. The *angelus interpres,* who accompanies Abraham, exorcizes the demon appearing in the shape of a bird (ch. 13):

> Disgrace upon you, Azazel! For Abraham's lot is in heaven, but yours upon the earth . . . for God . . . has not permitted that the bodies of the righteous should be in your hand, in order that thereby the life of the righteous and the destruction of the unclean may be assured . . . For it has not been given to you to play the tempter in regard to all the righteous. Depart from this man! . . . For, behold, the vesture which in heaven was formerly yours has been set aside for him, and the mortality which was his, has been transferred to you[3].

3.11.1

We recognize here the motif of the patriarch's share in eternal life[4], close at hand with Abraham as the central figure. **(A)** Nothing is said, however, about the death of Abraham in ApcAbr, as distinguished from Test Abr, which treats the death of the patriarch and his reception into paradise (3.12). Only the description of the Garden of Eden in ApcAbr 21 may indicate a belief in life *after* death, when the blessed state and happiness of "those who behaved righteously" is pictured in contrast to the perdition of the ungodly in the Abyss. We may by inference believe that Abraham's exaltation to the former throne of the fallen archangel took place after his death, according to the author(s) of ApcAbr (who must have read Gn 25:8), as Box-Landsman (1918, xxviii) do in the analogous case of the righteous dead, when they comment upon the paradise picture of ApcAbr 21. Without including the concept of death, ApcAbr looks forward to the final salvation and the gathering of the elect people when the Elect One is sent and the eschatological trumpet is sounded, (ch. 31)[5].

3.11.2

(B) Thus, ApcAbr tells us nothing about a resurrection and nothing about the immortality of the soul. The expression about the bodies of the righteous in the above quotation may be interpreted differently. The comm. *ad loc.* by Box-Landsman thinks that it concerns a special protection against temptation and sin. This is suggested by the context, but the final clause of the quotation might tell us that the reason for Abraham's perseverance, when confronted with the temptations of Azazel, is his reception of the heavenly vesture of immortality[6]. Then the saying about the bodies of the righteous being protected against Azazel may also suggest their resurrection or assumption.

3.11.3

(C) What is clear, however, is the promise of Abraham's heavenly glorification and transformation. The former "vesture" of the fallen archangel is given to Abraham with a "lot in heaven"[7]. The motif of the angelic glory of the righteous in future life is recognized,[8] as well as the symbol of the garments of glory[9]. In ApcAbr 21, however, the glory of Paradise is described in rather earthly terms, and Paradise is explicitly located on the earth[10]. Thus, no consistent "doctrine" about the nature of eternal life can be discerned.

3.11.4

(D) "The life of the righteous and the destruction of the unclean" is an allusion to a future judgment. Ch. 31, following the summoning of the chosen people at the sound of the trumpet, gives a broader description of the punishment of the wicked in "the fire of Hades". A scene of judgment is, however, neither found here nor in ApcAbr as a whole. The perspective is clearly that of a future history, culminating in eschatological plagues near the "twelfth hour of the earth" (ch. 30) and the sound of the trumpet (ch. 31).

3.11.5

A final remark may be added: The conversion of Abraham from his father's idolatry—and even commercialized idol making—is described in the first part of ApcAbr (1-8). This theme binds ApcAbr to Hellenistic Jewish documents to be discussed later: JA and TestJob. Abraham is a proselyte in the same respect as Asenath or Job. By his conversion to the worship of the one true God, he receives the promise of eternal life in glory in the same respect as Asenath or Job (4.9.2 and 4.10). Is this part of the story originally from the diaspora situation—Babylonian just as Deutero-Isaiah, evidently alluded to in the story of ApcAbr 5 (cf Is 44:14-20)—or Greek, as Wi 13:11-19, JA and TestJob? This image of Abraham the proselyte[11] resembles that in the midrash of Paul on the Genesis story in Gal 3:6-9 and Rm 4, where Abraham is the prototype of the Gentile believer, who receives the Gospel without circumcision.[12]

[1]Cf. e.g. G. H. Box-J. I. Landsman (1918) xvi; R. Meyer, RGG I (1957) 72 (early second century); Russell (1964) 60; Denis (1970) 37 f. (midrashic agada, first century); J. Licht, EncJud II (1971) 125-127 (second century). On the Semitic original-suggesting Hebrew-see A. Rubinstein, JJS 4 (1953) 108-115; 5 (1954) 132-135. According to N. Bonwetsch (1897) 55, the author was a Christian of the first century.

[2]Cf. Lv 16:8-10, the notes 5 and 6 on p. 52 in Box-Landsman (1918), and A. Rubinstein, JJS 8 (1957) 45-50.

[3]ET: Box-Landsman, slightly modernized, pp. 52 f.

[4]Cf. *infra* 7.2.2.2 and further references there.

[5]Cf. Box-Landsman (1918) xxxi, who suggest that the eschatology of TestAbr should be regarded as complementary to that of ApcAbr, the former individual, from an "Essene" standpoint, the latter the "national" eschatology.—On the eschatological trumpet see *infra* 5.8.6 on Is 27:12 f.—Volz (1934) 28 f., states that men go either to paradise or to Azazel after death, a little too much of an effort to systematize what is said in ApcAbr.

[6]The former vesture of Azazel as an archangel and the mortality of Abraham, before the change, obviously forms parallels in the final clause. Thus we are justified in interpreting the vesture of Azazel as immortality—cf. the following section! For the image of the garments for the body, cf. Box-Landsman (1918) *ad loc.* and *infra* n.10.

[7]Cf. *supra* 2.3 on Dn 12:13 for the term "lot" and further references there.

[8]Cf. *infra* 7.2.1, esp. 4-8, with further references there.

[9]Cf. I En 62:15 f. (*supra* 3.2.4.5); II En 22:8 f.; AscIs 4:16 f.; 8:14; 9:1-2, 17 f., 24-26; I Cor 15:37 f., 49, 53 f.; II Cor 5:2-4; Rev 3:4 f., 18; 6:11; 7:9.

[10]Cf. Box-Landsman (1918) 67 n.5.

[11]On later Jewish tradition about Abraham as both the ideal proselyte—this is why each proselyte is given the name of – בן or האברהם – בת at the conversion to Judaism—and the first proselyte maker, cf. M. Grunwald, JüdLex I (1927) 38, with reference to GnR to 12:5.

[12]Cf. already Philo, Abrah 15; Josephus, Ant I 155, further also e.g. N. Bonwetsch (1897).

3.12 The Testament of Abraham

There is hardly any consensus about the origin and date of TestAbr. It is either Jewish, more or less overworked, interpolated and re-edited by the Christian tradition[1], or is originally Christian[2]. Whereas the final two Greek recensions (A and B) can be dated with some certainty[3], the possible Hebrew[4] original is placed within a very wide framework, between the second century BC[5] and the second century AD[6]. In spite of all this uncertainty, it has been decided to include a short section on this remarkable description of Abraham's death, which is one of the clearest examples of a dichotomic view of man.

3.12.1

(A, B) The soul alone survives death and (D) is confronted with the final decisive judgment immediately after death. This is first of all described in relation to Abraham himself: Michael, the ἀρχιστρατηγος and death are sent to "take his soul" away from him (rec. A, 7; B, 13). Abraham's death signifies his soul leaving the body (rec. A, 1; rec. B, 4) and being assumed into heaven (rec. B, 14). While still in the body (rec. A, 9), Abraham makes a tour of the universe (rec. A,

10-14) and is brought to the first gate of heaven (rec. A, 11) or to the river Oceanus (rec. B, 8), where he sees many souls entering "the wide gate leading to destruction" and a few souls being brought into heaven through "the narrow gate to life". The allusions to the Jesus logion of Mt 7:13-14//Lk 13:23-24 (in the Matthaean version) are obvious[7]. On the other hand, the scene with the two angels, Dokiel and Pyrouel, before Abel the judge, with their books (rec. A, 12-13—cf. B, 9) is probably not of Christian origin. The names of the actors in the scene are Jewish, but this picture of a *post-mortem* judgment is very similar to popular Greek[8] and Egyptian[9] thought. The souls are weighed by their deeds, and the records of the books are checked (rec. A, 12-13; B, 9-11). We recognize, however, the "two-way theology". Neither the future blessed state nor the punishments after death are described in elaborate detail[10].

3.12.2

The only resurrection mentioned in TestAbr is a miracle worked by Abraham prior to his death, according to rec. B, 14: the resurrection of Abraham's servants ($\pi\alpha\iota\delta\epsilon\varsigma$) who had died in horror of death.

3.12.3

(A, B) We find in TestAbr a consistent teaching of the immortality of each soul, (D) implying immediate judgment after death, and (C) a heavenly assumption for the holy men of God, e.g. Abraham (rec. A, 20; B, 14—cf. also the *post-mortem* roles of Abel and Enoch, rec. A, 13; B, 11).

---

[1] Thus e.g. K. Kohler, JQR 7 (1895) 581, 591-606; H. Fuchs, JüdLex I (1927) 48; Riessler (1928) 1332 f. (no Christian work in rec. B); N. Turner, NTS 1 (1954/5) 220 f.; R. Meyer, RGG I (1957) 73; D. Flusser, EncJud II (1971) 129; G. W. E. Nickelsburg, SCS 2 (1972) 209 f.

[2] M. R. James (1892) 23-25, 29; Cf. also Denis (1970) 36 f.

[3] Cf. e.g. James (1892) 49: language older in B, but as a whole A is older, in spite of its mediaevalized language; Riessler (1928) 1332 f., prefers B as pre-Christian; Turner, NTS 1, 221: B in the present form perhaps third century AD, A mediaeval; Nickelsburg, SCS 2, 210-266: priority to A; according to Nickelsburg the diss. of F. Schmidt (1971, unavailable to me): priority to B (SCS 2, 211).—On the Arabic version cf. James (1892) 34-49—and generally on the versions Nickelsburg, SCS 2, 224-226.

[4] Turner, NTS 1, 222 f.; Riessler (1928) 1333; Denis (1970) 36 f.

[5] Thus Turner, NTS 1, 221, for the material itself.

[6] Thus Fuchs, JüdLex I, 48; Meyer, RGG I, 72. Flusser, EncJud II, 129, finds a more exact date impossible to establish.

[7] Cf. James (1892) for a general survey of possible Christian elements in TestAbr. For Mt 7:13-14 see rec. A, 11; B, 8-9. However, the Lukan question $\epsilon\iota\ \dot{o}\lambda\iota\gamma o\iota\ o\dot{\iota}\ \sigma\omega\zeta o\mu\epsilon\nu o\iota;$ (13:23) is also echoed, it seems, in rec. A, 13, $\psi v\chi\alpha\varsigma\ \sigma\omega\zeta o\mu\epsilon\nu\alpha\varsigma$, and $\dot{o}\lambda\iota\gamma o\iota\ \delta\epsilon\ o\dot{\iota}\ \sigma\omega\zeta o\mu\epsilon\nu o\iota$ ibid.

[8] See Nickelsburg, SCS 2, 184-187, 189 f., with ref. also to G. H. Macurdy, JBL 61 (1942) 213-226.

[9] The diss. of Schmidt (1971)—cf. Nickelsburg, SCS 2, 190-194, with similar *post-mortem* judgment scenes in the Egyptian texts.

[10] Cf. *supra* 3.3.4, 3.5.1 and 4.4.1 and further references there; Nickelsburg, SCS 2, 186.

3.13 Apocryphon Ezekiel

In his argument for the resurrection of the body against the Origenists (Haer 64, 70, 5-17 = GCS 31, 516 f.), Epiphanius refers to:

> that which was said by the prophet Ezekiel in his own apocryphon concerning the resurrection . . . For in a parable he relates ($\alpha i\nu i\gamma\mu\alpha\tau\omega\delta\omega\varsigma\ \gamma\alpha\rho\ \delta i\eta\gamma o\upsilon\mu\epsilon\nu o\varsigma$) about the righteous judgment, by which soul and body are united . . .

Then follows the parable about the blind man and the lame man, who succeed in stealing fruit in the garden of their king only by collaboration, i.e., they could not do it without joint effort. The parable is also known from the Rabbinic tradition. According to Sanh 91b[1], it is told by Rabbi before the Emperor Antoninus (with some variations) in order to prove that both the body and the soul will be punished for the sins of the man after death, when body and soul are reunited. This is obviously a Palestinian Jewish story, probably of Pre-Rabbinic origin, since ApEz is likely to have been written between 62BC and AD 50[2].

3.13.1

(A, B) Here the resurrection of the body is seen as a necessary precondition of the administration of justice. Consequently, both the righteous and the wicked, especially those who are to be punished, must share in the resurrection. The fact that the body will rise is unusually stressed. (D) The function of the resurrection is merely a preparation for the judgment, i.e., the soul and the body are reunited so that both can be judged and punished. The reward of the righteous is outside the scope of this parable, as well as information about the intermediate state of the soul between death and resurrection[3].

3.13.2

The conclusion of Holl and James, to whom Denis refers (1970, 190 f.) that "the particular judgment and corporeal resurrection seem to have a great importance in this work" is a little daring, since only four fragments are preserved, and only two of them mention the judgment and only one the resurrection (cf. Fragmenta pseudepigraphorum Graeca, 1970, 120-123).

---

[1]Cf. 5.4.2. The tradition is also found in Tanch B 3:8, *Wayyiqra* 12. For a comparison between the traditions, see M. R. James, JThS 15 (1913/4) 238 f. Cf. also G. Stemberger, Kairos 15 (1973) 250-254.

[2]Cf. K. Holl II (1922, 1928) 39; L. Wallach, JBL 62 (1943) 333-339; Denis (1970) 190 f. For the Indian roots of the tradition see Holl II (1928) 37 f.; Wallach, JBL 62, 333 ff. The question of the origin of this particular tradition (C. Bonner, 1940, 185, holds it to be a late addition to the original ApEz) must be distinguished from the question of the origin of ApEz as a whole which is a "fragment of early Christian literature" according to James, JThS 15, 243. Cf. Denis (1970) 190 for the judgment: "Surely Jewish", with further references and arguments.

[3]Though Antoninus, while questioning Rabbi, describes the soul as flying freely like a bird in the air, while the body lies like a stone in the tomb. But this does not seem, to be a part of the writing quoted by Epiphanius.

3.14 Inscriptions in Palestine

The general survey of the archaeological evidence for the Jewish ideas about life after death is given *infra* in the chapter on Judaism in the Greek-speaking diaspora (4.12), since the source material is somewhat richer outside Palestine than within its borders. There is practically no difference regarding evidence for hopes about future life between these two groups of inscriptions. If the sepulchres contain anything more than the mere names of the deceased[1], this is usually a vague formula with "peace" and/or "rest". Phrases, such as ϑαρσει, οὐδεις ἀϑανατος, may be found in the most orthodox places, e.g. the necropolis of Beth Shearim. Therefore, one is not able to conclude that those who wrote them were skeptic about or denied life after death (cf. 4.12.2). A few instances, where God is designated as "helper" (CIJ 964) or is called upon for help (CIJ 874, 875[2]), apparently on behalf of the dead person must indicate some sort of belief in *post mortem* existence, perhaps even including judgment (if it is not a formula against violating the peace of the tomb—cf. 4.12.1). The same applies to the use of the phrase ὑπερ σωτηριας with the name or names of people, probably the departed who are commemorated (CIJ 965, 966 and 972[3]). **(A)** These vague allusions only affirm the *fact* of some kind of life after death. **(B, C, D)** Nothing is said about the *how or when* of that life.

3.14.1

The Hebrew inscription of prayer or pious wish, נ ו ו ה נ פ ש is found outside Palestine (CIJ 611—cf. 4.12 n.6) and in some cases in Palestine: Jaffa,[4] Nazareth[5] and the temple place[6]. The meaning of this inscription is not clear. **(A)** Does it really concern the soul's *post mortem* confrontation with the Divine judgment, or does it rather refer to the peace of the tomb[7]? **(B, D)** Even though the inscription would be a prayer for the soul after death, one cannot make any conclusive statements concerning the relation of the body and the soul after death, the intermediate state, the resurrection, etc.

3.14.2

A very fragmentary inscription, preserved in Beirut (CIJ 877), can be interpreted as the writer's assertion of his own assumption[8]. Even though the fragment cannot offer any conclusive evidence, the final phrase, "blessed is he who hopes in the Lord", may be of some interest. The epithets μακαριος and εὐμυρος (blessed and happy) are found especially in Palestinian inscriptions for the dead[9]. It is not very consistent with an older Israelite view on death and Sheol (2.1). **(A)** Some sort of blessed immortality seems to be in the mind of the people who made such formulations, but we cannot be very sure, of course, since such a term as "blessed" would tend to be worn out in a funerary context, following the law of euphemism: *De mortuis nil nisi bene!* But, at, least, the use of these designations for a dead person indicate the fact that those who started talking about the dead as μακαριοι, εὐμυροι, did consider *post mortem* existence for the righteous happy and blessed[10].

3.14.3

There is actually no distinct reference to belief in a future resurrection found in Palestine during the investigated period. It is only in Beth-Shearim that we find such testimonies, i.e., not before the second century CE[11]. Thus a fragmentary text found in the 20th catacomb of Beth Shearim might be interpreted (עמידת ר) עם הצדיקים)[12]. J. T. Milik[13] suggested that the proper name יהרעמד on a cover of an ossuary from Bethphage should be understood as a reference to the resurrection, in light of this background of the inscription in the 20th catacomb. The verb עמד would then be used as it was used in Dn 12:13.[14] He finds support for this in the proper names *Athanasii* and *Anastasii*, found in Roman inscriptions. He explains these names as Jewish *nomina sodaliciorum*, funeral societies. This is accordingly a testimony for belief in immortality or the resurrection. The theory may be ingenious, but the very fact that such theories are suggested truly confirms the scarcity of archaeological evidence on this point[15].

[1] Cf. 4.12.1 with the references there. Inscriptions in CIJ between 882 and 1414 (inclusively) belong to Palestine, 847-881 to Syria and Transjordan.

[2] Cf. also CIJ 1167, an amulet inscription with the same prayer.

[3] Cf. also CIJ 1438 in n.6 to 4.12.

[4] CIJ 892. It contains the later Jewish standard phrase זכרונו לברכה as well. The one who is buried is a son of a R. Tarfon—the great R. Tarfon, the contemporary of Akiba (cf. e.g H. Strack, 1920, 125 f.)? This is very doubtful, of course. But the title and the place would be more fitting for a date after the destruction of the Second Temple than before it. Also in Jaffa, CIJ 900.

[5] CIJ 988, undated, for Soam, son of Menahem.

[6] CIJ 1403, if the interpretation of some scholars (Dalman, Klein) is correct (cf. Frey *ad loc.*)—the inscription is fragmentary. This formula is also found in Eleutheropolis (CIJ 1195), in Berabaea (CIJ 1196) (נרח נפשה) and finally in Edessa (CIJ 1416).

[7] The peace of the tomb concerns the soul, too, according to older anthropology: the soul is related to the tomb even after death, at least some time (cf. e.g. Hoffmann, 1966, 63 f.; Grelot, 1971, 57, for the relation between Sheol and the grave). Cf. also PsPhoc 103-105, 4.8.1 *infra!*

[8] ἐλα[μβανεν] μ'[αὐτον] κυρ[ιος] [ἐν] τῇ δυνα[μει] αὐτου
[ἐγ]ω [ἐτιϑ]ην και [ἐ]τελ[ει]ωσα τοπον [αἰω]νιον
ἀναπαυσε[ω]ς. Μακαριος ὁ ἐλπιξ[ω]ν ἐπι κυριον.

[9] CIJ 870 (μακαριος) 993, 999, 1004, 1013, 1014, 1016, 1017, 1018, 1021, 1063, 1067, 1086 (εὐμυρος) Cf. also 4.12.3 and the Leontopolis inscription CIJ 1513.

[10] An Aramaic inscription on a chair in the synagogue of Chorazin (the end of the second or the beginning of the third century CE—cf. H. Kohl-C. Watzinger, 1916, 204; C. Kopp, 1959, 216, 245) commemorates the craftsman or donator, Judan, Son of Ishmael:
May he have a portion with the righteous (CIJ 981).
Similar formulations are found in the diaspora (cf. 4.12.1 n.7 and 4.12.3 on CIJ 1510 and n.14). Since this more clearly expresses a hope of *post mortem* life than most other inscriptions, it may be mentioned in spite of its late origin.

¹¹In the 13th catacomb: Ὃς ἐαν μεταϑῇ ταυτην ὁ[ς] ἐπαντιλαμενος ζωποιησε (=ζωοποιησειν) τους νεκρους κριυε (=κριυει).
and in the 20th:
εὐτυχως τῇ ὑμων ἀναστασ[ε]ι·

—cf. M. Schwabe, IEJ 4 (1954) 257; N. Avigad, IEJ 7 (1957) 247; J. T. Milik, *In hon.* A. Dupont-Sommer (1971) 87 f., further the Hebrew text quoted *infra*.

¹²Cf. Avigad, IEJ 7, 240 f., referring to a suggestion by the late president of Israel, Ben Zvi, who could support this by parallels in later Jewish inscriptions and prayers—with בשׁר י ם as an alternative of צ ד י ק י ם . Cf. also Milik, *In hon.* Dupont-Sommer, 88.

¹³*In hon.* Dupont-Sommer, 86-89.

¹⁴Cf. supra 2,3 and also 3.5.7 on the possible meaning of מעבד in a Qumran fragment.

¹⁵Concerning the efforts to interpret the various symbols found on Jewish tombs, the palms, the *menorah*, the stars, the ark etc. as expressions of after-life conceptions, cf. *infra* 4.12 and n.1.

101

4   Texts from the Greek-speaking diaspora

Without making any presuppositions about a more or less Hellenized type of Judaism and avoiding judgments from the contents of the statements on afterlife, I shall go through a number of texts which were originally written in Greek by Jews who usually lived outside Palestine. These criteria are used exclusively to distinguish this group of testimonies from the group formerly analyzed.[1] We shall commence with the Bible of the Greek synagogue.

4.1. LXX

A number of LXX renderings of the Hebrew text may be quoted as examples of the Alexandrian translators' understanding the ancient sacred texts in the light of their own developed notions about personal life after death or even resurrection.[2]

4.1.1

Dt 32:39: The Hebrew verbs אמית ומחיתי וראחיה are translated in the future: ἀποκτενω και ζην ποιησω· This might indicate that the Greek translators wanted to read the Hebrew statement on the omnipotence of Yahweh as an explicit confession of the future resurrection. The pi'el of חיה was a common verb for "resurrect" in Rabbinic terminology (cf. Kegel, 1970, 17 f.; 5.3.1 and 5.2.3 *infra*). It is interesting to find that the same interpretation of this text is found in Rabbinic traditions[3]. The wide extent of this interpretation indicates an early date. It was a common "relecture"[4] of Dt 32:39 in light of **(A, B)** the belief in resurrection (ζην ποιησω). **(D)** The revivification obviously belongs to the eschatological future.

4.1.2

Ps 1:5: δια τουτο οὐκ ἀναστησοονται ἀσεβεις ἐν κρισει
The Hebrew יקמו רשעים is translated ἀναστησοονται. Thus, the LXX translator probably denies the resurrection of the wicked[5]. This meaning is given to the Hebrew text by R. Nehemiah, a third generation *tanna* (Strack, 1920, 129), in MSanh 10:3, where he quotes the sentence to prove that neither the generation of the Flood nor the men of Sodom shall appear for the last judgment[6]. **(A, B)** The Greek text may implicitly testify to the translator's belief in the resurrection of the righteous. **(D)** This is connected with the final judgment. This connection is, however, rather strange, because no judgment would seem to be needed when only the righteous arise. The idea of a final judgment of the risen dead pertains to the context of a belief in a universal resurrection. Further reflection on the matter in light of this interpretation leads us to the consequence drawn by R. Nehemiah: the רשעים or ἀσεβεις are in this case a special group among the wicked who are punished more severely (or leniently?) than the others by not even being allowed to share in the universal resurrection for the judgment.

Ps 21(22):30: The final words in the Hebrew text, ונפשו לא חיה are rendered ἡ ψυχη μου αὐτῳ ζῃ. The translator read נפשי instead of נפשו and לי instead of לא, נפש as male, חיה as imperfect (instead of perfect). A few Hebrew MSS agree with the Gr. version on some of the points (cf. Kittel *ad loc.*). The interpretation of the LXX might mean that the translator found this text **(A, B)** to express a faith in the soul's continued life **(D)** after death.[7] S. Aalen tries to use the LXX version for proving his thesis that the belief in the intermediate state, related to faith in the resurrection, was more or less universal around the beginning of CE in those Jewish circles which accepted any kind of future life (NTS 13, 10). This thesis, of course, reads much more into these words than they could ever bear[8].

Ps 48(49):16: A number of scholars interpret the *Hebrew* text as an early assertion of a rather spiritualized sort of life after death[9]. That is regarded as very doubtful by others[10]. LXX, however, has rendered כ י by ὅταν. **(A)** This might allude to a belief in the righteous souls' future salvation from death[11]. **(B)** In such a case, the text seems to say that the soul (not distinguished from any other part of the person) is taken up from the power of Hades, perhaps immediately at death or, as in I En 102-104 (cf. *supra* 3.2.3.4-6), on the occasion of some spiritual resurrection.

Ps 65(66):1,9: In the title of the psalm most LXX MSS, with the exception of Sin, have added the word ἀναστασεως, which has no counterpart in the Hebrew text. According to a foot-note in the ed. of A. Rahlfs (1931) *ad loc.,* this is a Christian addition in the second or even first century, when the psalm was sung on the feast of the resurrection. Volz (1934, 240), however, is willing to consider this as a testimony of the traditions behind LXX. The title would be inspired from v.9, and thus the whole psalm would deal with the resurrection of the righteous.

The Gr. rendering of v.9a deviates from the Masoretic text in two instances: την ψυχην μου for נ פ ש נ ו, εἰς ζωην for ב ח י י ם **(A)** There may be a slight trend toward a belief in personal immortality in the changes of LXX, whereas the Hebrew original is more likely to speak about a preservation from death in the present life. Again, it is the ψυχη that is the death-conquering bearer of life. But "the soul" denotes the whole man and is not in any way related to any kind of anthropological dichotomy. (See 5.8.5 *infra* for the Tg interpretation.)

4.1.3

Prv 9:6: The Hebrew ו ח י ו has its counterpart in ζησεσθε in the Gr. versions (LXX, Aquila, Symmachus and Theodotion). It is replaced by εἰς τον αἰωνα βασιλευσητε in codd. Vat, Sin (first hand) and Alex, a reading which may be influenced by Wi 6:21 (cf. e.g. Bertram, TWNT II, 1935, 856; Mussner, 1952, 12 f.). The following sentence is parallel to the first and employs the verb βιωσητε , the aorist subjunctive instead of the future tense. **(A)** At least the future tense ζησεσθε may be understood eschatologically as the reward of the righteous.

Prv 10:25b: The Hebrew text, meaning literally "the righteous is an eternal foundation י ס ו ד ע ו ל ם", is rendered by δικαιος δε ἐκκλινας [12] σωζεται εἰς τον αἰωνα. Again, there is the possibility of understanding the LXX statement as a quite vague allusion to eternal life (cf. Mussner, 1952, 12 f.; Tournay, RB 69, 499). The "two-way theology" may be recognized in this verse (cf. *supra* 3.3.4).

Prv 12:28 is another, more explicit example of the "two-way theology": ἐν ὁδοις δικαιοσυνης ζωη, ὁδοι δε μνησικακων εἰς θανατον. We notice that LXX has conceived a comprehensible antithetical parallel[13] which replaces the unintelligible latter half of the verse: ‏ודרך נתיבה על מות‎ The LXX translation may actually be the rendering of a Hebrew text which is better than that of the Masoretes (cf. e.g. Kittel *ad loc.*; Tournay, RB 69, 495-97).[14]

Prv 15:24: We recognize the vague announcement of the righteous being saved and the sinners being condemned to death from the "two-way theology" in the Gr. translation:

ὁδοι ζωης διανοηματα συνετου,
ἰνα ἐκκλινας του ᾁδου σωθῃ.

This time the Hebrew text is closer to the Gr:

‏ארח חיים למעלה למשכיל למען סור משאול מטה‎

The Gr. formulation is slightly more stereotyped and resembles the pattern of the two ways more than the Hebrew. But some authors hold that this pattern is already present in the Hebrew text (e.g. Schmitt, 1954, 155, 157; König, 1964, 207 f.). This conclusion is possible, but it is hardly necessary (cf. e.g. Sutcliffe, 1946, 118-121; Wied, 1965, 111-136).

4.1.4
Job 14:14: The verse has been rendered by a statement which actually contradicts the Hebrew text[15]:
ἐαν γαρ ἀποθανῃ ανθρωπος, ζησεται
συντελεσας ἡμερας του βιου αὐτου.

The Hebrew text asks ‏אם ימות גבר היחיה‎ and continues: ‏כל ימי‎ ‏צבאי איחל‎. The meaning of this sentence pertains to its context, where vv.10-12 simply state (in ET of NEB):

But a man dies, and he disappears; man comes to an end, and where is he? As the waters of the lake dwindle, or as a river shrinks and runs dry, so mortal man lies down, never to rise until the very sky splits open. He shall never be roused from his sleep[16].

The comparison shows that the LXX translation of Job was made by someone **(A)** who probably believed in life after death. We are not able to establish further precise ideas about that life, though **(B)** the context employs resurrection theology in a negative way.

Job 19:25-27: The Masoretic text is obscure. According to Tournay (RB 69, 493), this obscurity may be caused by a later scribe's desire to amplify the words of Job with the hope of a future life. LXX speaks clearly about the resurrection in v.26a:

ἀναστησαι το δερμα μου το ἀνατλων ταυτα [17]

It seems that a very physical resurrection is expected, **(C)** if we should give a literal interpretation to what is said about the resurrection of the skin. If the present Hebrew text were to be interpreted as a statement on life after death, it would, on the contrary, indicate a non-bodily form of after-life: "Free from my flesh I shall see God.[18] Other ancient versions, including Tg (5.8.7), point more directly towards a belief in the resurrection of the body[19].

Job 42:17: In LXX there is a long addition to the Hebrew text which has no counterpart in Tg. This addition is introduced with the phrase:

γεγραπται δε αὐτον παλιν ἀναστησεσθαι μεθ᾽ὡν ὁ κυριος ἀνιστησιν.

(A) There is no doubt that this statement refers to a *post-mortem* resurrection. γεγραπται may remind the reader of 19:25-27 (cf. Fohrer, 1963, 542). Thus, Job 19: 25-27 is also interpreted from the point of view of the one who made this addition in 42:17, which perhaps was not in the first Greek version of Job[20]. **(B)** It is a resurrection and not a continued life after death that is predicted for Job, though it is obvious that **(C)** nothing more precise can be said about the type of resurrection. **(D)** The resurrection in which Job is to share is a general resurrection or, at least, a resurrection of many. On the other hand, it could hardly be a resurrection for judgment. It is promised to Job as an event of final salvation[21].

4.1.5

Is 26:19: Many scholars hold that the original Hebrew meaning of this verse involves resurrection of the dead[22], in spite of all of the problems of understanding both the Hebrew text[23] and the context[24]. Since this cannot really be proven, I did not discuss this text in connection with Dn 12 (2.2-3). **(A, B)** But it cannot be denied that the LXX version of Is 26:19 does speak about the resurrection of the dead:

ἀναστησονται οἱ νεκροι, και ἐγερθησονται οἱ ἐν τοις
μνημειοις, και εὐφρανθησονται οἱ ἐν τῃ γῃ · ἡ γαρ
δροσος ἡ παρα σου ἰαμα αὐτοις ἐστιν, ἡ δε γη των
ἀσεβων πεσειται.

Those who are to "rejoice in the land" are possibly the survivors of the last generation, or the phrase may merely be a third expression for the dead, rendering the Hebrew שכני עפר (cf. e.g. Dn 12:2 LXX). If that be the case, this verse clearly states the resurrection of the body. **(D)** The context, especially the following verses, relates this resurrection to the judgment of the Lord, though the resurrection itself seems to be a salvation event for the righteous, especially if the third sentence is a direct parallel to the two preceding ones. All that can be said about the "dew" from the Lord is that it has a healing function[25].

4.1.6

Ez 37:1-14: It is clear that the vision of the resurrection of the dry bones, in the original Hebrew and in the *Sitz im Leben* of the Babylonian exile, is a parable about the future restoration of the people of Israel in its chosen land[26]. It is obvious that such a text would easily lend itself to an interpretation indicating a real future resurrection of the dead, once the idea of resurrection had been established in the community which read Ez 37. **(A)** However, the LXX version does not contain significant changes in relation to the Hebrew text, which might support such an eschatological interpretation. One exception is perhaps found in v.7, where the two Hebrew terms קוֹל and רַעַשׁ are rendered by σεισμος· The earthquake is a *topos* in the apocalyptic descriptions of the events immediately preceding the End and the final resurrection (Hartman, 1966, 71-77). However, it is also quite possible that σεισμος is used as an attempt to describe the *commotion* of the dry bones being joined together[27]. Yet we have other testimonies which tell us that some people in the Hellenistic Jewish diaspora did interpret Ez 37 as a prophecy of the end time resurrection[28]. First, I refer to the Dura Europos paintings, which describe the resurrection of Ez 37 as a figure of the end time resurrection[29]. Further, IV Mcc 18:17 quotes Ez 37:3 in order to support a belief in the martyrs' eternal life after death (cf. *infra* 4.3.10 and 4.3.10.3 and n.4 *supra*). This presupposes that the eschatological resurrection interpretation of Ez 37:1-14 was known in the Greek-speaking diaspora at a rather early stage[30]. **(B)** Therefore, the faith in the resurrection of the body, even **(C)** a physical resurrection, would be nurtured by such a passage, if the description of the joining of bones, with the restoration of sinews, flesh and skin in vv.6-8 is read as a literal prediction of the resurrection to come (cf. *infra* 5.1 and 5.1.1), though the πνευμα is the decisive element for new life (vv.5-10)[31]. Read in the light of resurrection faith, the text combines the resurrection with the return of the exiles to the land of Israel. This is also an important characteristic of Rabbinic ideas about the resurrection, and it may have been represented by certain features in the Dura Europos frescoes[32]. **(D)** The resurrection in Ez 37 is not at all combined with judgment, but is a pure salvation event in the final eschatological turn of history.

4.1.7 *Conclusion on the LXX translations of the Hebrew text*

There are several other passages, which have been quoted to prove that the LXX translation tends to interpret the Hebrew Scriptures in light of the hopes about future life, which were developed in Judaism in the last centuries BC.[33] However, these passages either are rather unclear or they do not contribute anything substantial to our study of the questions of how this future life was conceived.

The result of this survey (cf. index III *ad* LXX) is rather clear: All of the texts which distinctly speak about future life after death, describing it more than by general reference, describe this life in terms of the resurrection of the body, partly in very physical terms. The texts from Prv are very vague and are in the context of the "two-way theology", which is not an innovation in the Greek text, but is based on the Hebrew original. The Psalm passages, with one exception, which may represent a later addition, are uncertain, but they may be interpreted as statements on a more spiritual type of immortality. However, the LXX does not deviate radically from the Hebrew original, where some Psalms may be interpreted as testimonies to a belief in a spiritual eternal life after death (cf. 2.1.3 nn.20-21). So our conclusion must be that the only type of after-life which is clearly believed by some of the LXX translators is that which is based on the resurrection of the body. This does not exclude the possibility of other spiritualized beliefs, but their existence cannot be proven.

[1] On these criteria and the terminology (avoiding "Hellenistic Judaism") *v. supra* 3.0.5-6.

[2] For similar investigations, see e.g. G. Gerleman, I-III (1946-1956), especially I (1946) 60-63.

[3] For TgJ I and II, see 5.8.1 *infra*. Cf. further MekEx Pisha 12:30; SDt § 149; Pes 68a; Sanh 91b; ExR 44:6, 7; DtR 6:15; PRE 34, and Löwinger, Jahrb.f.jüd. Volkskunde 25, 46n.

[4] Cf. R. Tournay, RB 69 (1962) 488n, for the term "relecture", used for the phenomenon of re-interpreting an older text in the light of later ideas.—See also the quotation in IV Mcc 18:18 f. and cf. *infra* 4.3.10 and 4.3.10.4. Cf. further J. F. A. Sawyer, VT 23 (1973) 218-234, concerning the re-interpretation of the *Hebrew* terms in light of belief in the resurrection.

[5] I owe this observation to an oral communication by A. Ekenberg. Cf. also Sawyer, VT 23, 232 f., concerning the re-interpretation of the Hebrew text.

[6] Cf. *infra* 5.2, 5.2.2 and 4 on MSanh 10:1-3 and TSanh 13:6-12. I hope to be able to publish a paper with some observations on this formula of exclusion from the resurrection rather soon.

[7] The interpretation of Tournay, RB 69, 499-502: Ps 21:30 in LXX is an example of a "relecture" in a time before the final establishment of the Hebrew text.

[8] Even more startling is the suggestion of Eichrodt, III (1961) 357 that the Hebrew text might speak about the return of the dead in a communion of life with God.—On the interpretation of Tg. cf. *infra* 5.8.5.

[9] E.g. Sellin, NKZ 30, 283-285; Schilling (1951) 28-31; Molin, Jud 9, 233; Mussner (1952) 8; Coppens (1957) 39 f.; Dahood, I (1966) *ad loc.*; Fohrer, KuD 14, 257 f.; A. Feuillet, RevThom 72 (1972) 539-544; Stemberger, Kairos 14, 286. Cf. also on Pss. 16 and 73 *supra* 2.1.3 nn.20-21.

[10] E.g. Wächter (1967) 195 f.; Vawter, JBL 91, 162 f. They understand the verse in the Hebrew Psalm as nothing but an expression of trust in God's saving the righteous from a sudden, premature death. Cf. also Barth (1947) 158-161.

[11] The preceding context describes how the wicked rich men are brought down to Sheol and how they cannot save their souls from death. On the interpretation in Tg cf. 5.8.5 *infra*.

[12] Probably reading יְסֹרֵךְ instead of יְסֹרֵד as Tg. Cf. here A. Kaminka, HUCA 8-9 (1931-32) 174.

[13] Cf. G. Gerleman III (1956) 17 f., 22, on antithetical parallelism *vs.* synonymous in LXX and the Hebrew text.

[14] On Tg Prv 12:28, cf. Kaminka, HUCA 8-9, 183.

[15]Unless the Gr. text, too, should be interpreted as a question—thus H. M. Orlinsky, HUCA 32 (1961) 245 f., against Gerleman I (1946) 63. Cf. also Beresford (1971) 79 f. (against Gerleman).

[16]Tournay, RB 69, 494, thinks that the Masoretes, reading בלתי instead of בלת (as the ancient versions), had already slightly changed the meaning of the text in order to include the idea of a new creation—when the resurrection would occur—cf. also Gerleman I (1946) 60, 63.—On Tg cf. 5.8.7.

[17]Cf. Riesenfeld (1948) 26n; Mussner (1952) 12 f. Even clearer are Sin (corr) and Alex: ἀναστησει δε μου το σωμα. Cf. Gerleman I (1946) 65.

[18]Following one possible rendering of the Hebrew text, given by the official Swedish Bible translation of 1917.—On the question whether immortality and/or resurrection is presupposed by the Hebrew text, see e.g. Charles (1899) 70; Molin, Jud 9, 233; Schilling (1951) 51-60; G. Hölscher (1952) ad loc., who affirm the presupposition. However, most modern scholars would probably answer negatively, cf. Sutcliffe (1946) 131-137; G. Fohrer (1963) ad loc.; id. KuD 14, 260 f.; König (1964) 245 f.; Wied (1965) 17; M. H. Pope (1965) ad loc.; E. Dhorme (1967) ad loc.; Wächter (1967) 197 f.; W. Zimmerli (1971) 24; Stemberger, Kairos 14, 281 f. Causse (1908) calls the text a "postulate" of future life. Riesenfeld (1948) 26n, and Beresford (1971) 24, declare that the interpretation is uncertain.

[19]Vg, Pesh (not so clear)—cf. Tournay RB 69, 493.

[20]Cf. S. R. Driver-G. B. Gray (1921) lxxiii; Beresford, 1971, 81 f.

[21]Volz (1934) 236, has a reference to Job 42:17 LXX, in the context of examples of statements about the resurrection of the fathers and heroes of the past.

[22]E.g. Charles (1899) 126 f.; Nötscher (1926) 126 f.; Volz (1934) 231; Riesenfeld (1948) 3 f.; Birkeland, StTh 3, 75 ff.; H. W. Wolff (1952) 40; Schilling (1951) 61-63; Edelmann (1934); L. Finkelstein I (1962) 45; Martin-Achard (1956) 106-112; O. Ludwig (1961) 123, 140 ff.; Schubert, WZKM 56, 150; id. BZ 6, 188; Russell (1964) 367 f.; Barrett, Lond Quart 34, 94; Wächter (1967) 194; E. J. Young (1969) ad loc.; Beresford (1971) 22 ff.; Nickelsburg (1972) 18. Cf. also Cazelles, SoOr 4, 115, who is very cautious. A number of exegetes, however, interpret the resurrection ideas as metaphorical expressions related to the final restoration of the people of Israel, as e.g. Löwinger, Jahrb.f.jüd.Volkskunde 25, 25; Sutcliffe (1946) 128-130; G. Fohrer (1962) ad loc.; id. KuD 14, 260; G. W. Anderson, SupplVT 9 (1963) 126; Tournay, RB 69, 487 f. (he admits a "relecture" in Maccabaean times, when נבלתי was interpreted as the corpse of the prophet Isaiah); J. T. Nelis, TdschrTeol 10 (1970) 373 f.

[23]The interpretation of the imperfect verbs יחיו and יקומון as hortative, a prayer, with O. Procksch (1930) 343 f., or as simple present, a sort of salvation oracle, with e.g. W. O. E. Oesterley (1921) 220, and M. L. Henry (1967) 112, Further: נבלתי is rather unexpected—נבלתם (NEB) or נבלתיך (Sellin, NKZ 30, 233; Procksch ad loc.) have been suggested.—The Masoretic text has הקיצו whereas 1QIsa and the Greek versions read יקיצו The Hebrew expressions טל אורת and רפאים are in some way combined in the LXX version: ἡ δροσος ἡ παρα σου ιαμα αὐτοις ἐστιν. —cf. Sellin, NKZ 30, 233; P. Humbert, ThZ 13 (1957) 491. Finally, the absolute state of ארץ in the Masoretic text is replaced by the cstr. ארץ with רשעים, which seemingly makes the sentence a little easier to understand.

[24]The wider context is the so-called Isaiah Apocalypse (see comm. and introductions and further e.g. J. Lindblom, 1938, 7, 101-110; Ludwig, 1961; Henry, 1967; G. Fohrer, CBQ 25, 1963, 34-45; Anderson, SupplVT 9, 119-126; M. A. Beek, Archiv Orientàlni 17, 1949, 31-40; J. M. Schmidt 1971, 18n 275 f.), whose composition and origin certainly presents a number of problems. The immediate context is extremely difficult to understand. V. 14 seems to create special problems, since it contains an explicit denial of the resurrection both in Hebrew and Greek. LXX, however, possibly tries to solve that difficulty by identifying οἱ νεκροι with the wicked oppressors mentioned in the context of v.14—yet the Gr. sentence, which uses ιατροι for רפאים is very hard to understand. Tg has made the meaning of v.14 quite clear: The dead who shall not rise are the false lords and heroes, whom the wicked serve and who are mentioned in the context (their punishment, according to Tg, is clearly eschatological).

109

[25]Cf. the function of the rain in Hos 6:1-3—in the context of a resurrection statement.—On Tg v. *infra* 5.8.3.—On Is 26:14, 19, in LXX, see also D. Barthélemy (1963) 83 n.140.

[26]Cf. e.g. O. Kaiser (1959) 120: "über den symbolischen character dieser Stelle dürfte heute unter den kritischen Wissenschaftlern Einmütigkeit bestehen", and see e.g. Charles (1899) 129; Bertholet, *In hon.* F. C. Andreas (1916) 55; Löwinger, Jahrb.f.jüd.Volkskunde 25, 25; Nötscher (1926) 147; R. Wischnitzer-Bernstein, JBL 60 (1941) 47; Sutcliffe (1946) 130 f.; Riesenfeld (1948) 3; Birkeland, StTh 3, 73; L. Rost, *In mem.* E. Lohmeyer (1951) 72; Martin-Achard (1956) 85; Henry (1957) 111; Fohrer, KuD 14, 159; C. Noy, BM 4, 35 (1968) 77; H. D. Preuss (1968) 38, 59, 124, 159, 167; Beresford (1971) 20; E. Haag, Trierer ThZ 82 (1973) 84 (but Ez 37 was rather important for the later development); comm. *ad loc.* by S. Fisch (1950); G. Fohrer-K. Galling (1955); W. Zimmerli (1963); W. Eichrodt (1966); D. M. G. Stalker (1968); J. B. Taylor (1969); J. W. Wevers (1969); B. Storset (Swedish translation 1970). An exception is O. Procksch, RGG I (19 27) 627; *id.* (1930) 337, who defends the interpretation of Ez 37, referring to the resurrection of earlier generations of Israel, as well as the return from the exile. He finds support in vv.21-25, which, according to Procksch, predict the resurrection of David as the eschatological king.

[27]Cf. L. S. s.v. σεισμος : shaking, shock, earthquake, commotion, vibration, are listed as possible meanings.

[28]MS Q ("Marchalianus") of the sixth century has the note νεκρων ἀναβιωσις in the margin, the Syro-hexapla has περι ἀναστασεως των νεκρων in its margin (J. Ziegler, 1952, *ad loc.*). Of course, it is not possible to prove that these notes are pre-Christian in their origin.

[29]Cf. Wischnitzer-Bernstein, JBL 60, 43-55; Riesenfeld (1948) 28-34. It is true that these paintings are rather late (AD 245-256) and that Dura Europos was situated in the outskirts of the Hellenistic world. Yet the Gr. seems to have been more familiar to the painter than any other language (cf. R. Du Mesnil du Buisson, 1939, 9, 35, 47, 93, 96 f.).

[30]Another argument for this may be the Early Christians' using Ez 37:1-14 as a resurrection text. Cf. the following NT passages:
1 Th 4:8 and Lindars (1961) 56, 59; J. Grassi, NTS 11 (1964/5) 162;
1 Cor 15:45b—and Grassi, NTS 11, 163, on the combination of Gn 2:7 with Ez 37:14 in GnR 14:8;
Mt 27:51-53—and Riesenfeld (1948) 35; Grassi, NTS 11, 163; this use seems especially clear in this passage, which the following little synopsis might show:

Mt 27:51-53	Ez 37:7, 12-13
Και ἰδου ... ἡ γη ἐσεισθη,	Και ἰδου σεισμος ...
και αἱ πετραι ἐσχισθησαν,	
και τα μνημεια ἀνεῳχθησαν	ἀνοιγω ὑμων τα μνηματα
και πολλα σωματα των κεκοιμημενων	*cf.* v. 10 – and Dn 12:2
ἁγιων ἠγερθησαν,	
και ἐξελθοντες ἐκ των μνημειων	και ἀναξω ὑμας ἐκ των μνηματων ὑμων
μετα την ἐγερσιν αὐτου	
εἰσηλθον εἰς την ἁγιαν πολιν	και εἰσαξω ὑμας εἰς την γην του Ἰ.
και ἐνεφανισθησαν πολλοις.	*cf.* Dn 12:2f in its context.
	και γνωσεσθε ὁτι ἐγω εἰμι κυριος
(v. 52)	ἐν τῳ ἀνοιξαι με τους ταφους
	ὑμων του ἀναγαγειν με ἐκ των
	ταφων τον λαον μου.

By alluding to Ez 37, the evangelist would suggest that in the death of Jesus the End is in one way realized. Cf. Riesenfeld (1948) 36; H. Zeller, ZkTh 71 (1949) 385-465; D. D. Hutton, summarized in HTR 63 (1970) 518 f.;

Mt 28:2 and Grassi, NTS 11, 162-164;
Jn 5:25, 28 and Grassi, NTS 11, 164;
Jn 11:38-44 and Riesenfeld (1948) 37 f.;
Jn 20:22 and Grassi, NTS 11, 164;
Rev 11:11 and Grassi, NTS 11, 162, and *v.13*. This use of Ez 37:1-14 presupposes an established interpretation which connects this passage with the final resurrection.
Jn 20:22 and Grassi, NTS 11, 164;
Rev 11:11 and Grassi, NTS 11, 162, and *v.13*.
This use of Ez 37:1-14 presupposes an established interpretation which connects this passage with the final resurrection.

[31]For this role of the πνευμα, cf. also I Th 4:8; I Cor 15:45b; Jn 20:22; Rev 11:11 and the commentaries referred to in the preceding foot-note. Cf. also Jn 6:63; Rm 1:4; 8:11; II Cor 3:6; I Pt 3:18 f.; 4:6.

[32]Cf. Riesenfeld (1948) 11, 30 f. and jKil 9:6; Keth 111a-b; Ginzberg V, 362 f.; JalqShimBeresh 131, 42-43. Cf. also Tgls 27:13 and *infra* 5.8.3.

[33]E.g. Prv 11:31: J. W. Wevers, ThRu 22 (1954) 183; Ps 55:14: Mussner (1952) 12 f.; Ps 70 (71):20 and Eccl 2:18: Barthélemy (1963) 83n; Eccl 3:20-22: Tournay, RB 69, 498 f.; Barthélemy 83n; Eccl 7:14; 9:3: Barthélemy *ibid.*; Ez 26:20: Beresford (1971) 82 f.; Hos 10:12: Mussner 12 f.; Joel 4:12: Tournay, RB 69, 502-504. Hos 6:1-3 might be discussed, as well as in its original Hebrew version, but is not clear enough in any of these versions. We shall return to this passage in the section on Tg—5.8.4.

4.2 II Maccabees

Having completed the discussion of the different LXX translations of the Hebrew text, we shall study those writings in the Alexandrian Jewish canon, which were originally written in Greek, in so far as they contain testimonies to a belief in life after death. The oldest of these books, II Mcc, shall be treated first.

II Mcc is actually an abbreviation of a five volume work by a certain Jason of Cyrene (II Mcc 2:23 ff.). Since the relation between II Mcc and its source cannot be clarified in each single instance, we are not able to tell when we are reading the words of Jason or when we are confronted by additions or original formulations of the "Epitomist"[1]. So it is not possible to state the origin of the texts which are of concern to this investigation, i.e. 6:18-31; 7; 12:43-45; 14:37-46; 15:12-16[2]. They may either reflect the ideas of Jason or those of the Epitomist or of both. The surname of Jason is likely to indicate his home. We cannot be sure that Cyrene was his original home or the place where he settled after leaving Palestine[3], but the former alternative appears to be more probable[4]. So it is rather likely that a Jew of the Greek-speaking diaspora is the original author of those texts which are of concern to this investigation, assuming that he is Jason of Cyrene. But if the author were instead the Epitomist, then he would probably have been a Palestinian Jew with a good Hellenistic education[5] or a Jew from Alexandria[6]. All of the scholars agree that the book was written for the Greek-speaking diaspora[7], especially that in Egypt[8].

4.2.1

One group of texts consists of the martyr stories[9]. In these narratives faith in the resurrection and/or judgment after death serves as a source of inspiration for the martyrs in their struggle to endure torments and death. The first of these, describing the martyrdom of Eleazar, *6:18-31,* makes a passing allusion to beliefs about after-life, in v.26:

4.2.1.1

I might for the present avoid man's punishment, but alive or dead, I shall never escape from the hand of the Almighty (ET:NEB, in all the quotations of II Mcc).

Eleazar, an old teacher of the Law, is speaking and defending his refusal to eat pork and even to pretend to do so[10]. **(A, D)** The sentence seems to say that there is a justice after death and this justice will effect both the righteous and the wicked. **(B)** No information is given as to how the rewards and punishments are to be administered; **(D)** neither are we told if that will take place immediately after death or at the final resurrection (cf. Stemberger, 1972, 14 f.).

4.2.1.2

The study of *II Mcc 7* is more important for our purpose. Faith in their own resurrection is expressed by the second brother in v.9b:

"Since we die for his laws, the King of the universe will raise us up (ἀναστήσει) to a life everlastingly made new (αἰώνιον ἀναβίωσιν ζωῆς)."

After him the third was tortured. When the question was put to him, he at once showed his tongue, boldly held out his hands, and said courageously: "The God of heaven gave me these. His laws mean far more to me than they do, and it is from him that I trust to receive them back" (vv. 10-11).

Further, the fourth brother says to the king in v.14:

Better to be killed by man and cherish God's promise to raise us again (ἀναστήσεσθαι) There will be no resurrection to life (ἀνάστασις εἰς ζωήν) for you.

The mother, exhorting to endurance, draws the important analogy between the creation of men in the womb and the new creation of the resurrection (vv.22 f.—cf. 5.1.2):

You appeared in my womb, I know not how; it was not I who gave you life and breath and set in order your bodily frames. It is the Creator of the universe who moulds man at his birth and plans the origin of all things. Therefore he, in his mercy, will give you back life and breath again,[11] since now you put his laws above all thought of self.

The seventh brother finally declares (v.36):

My brothers have now fallen in loyalty to God's covenant, after brief pain leading to eternal life[12].

(A, B) A, faith in the resurrection of the body is clearly expressed, at least in vv.9b-11, 14, 22 f., whereas the terminology of v.36 is more vague than that used in the rest of the verses. It can be assumed that the youngest brother also expresses belief in a life to come, which is **(C)** rather different from the present earthly life, since it is not under the judgment of death. Nothing is said **(D)** about a final judgment or about the time of the resurrection (with Bückers' interpretation of v.36—cf. n.12). But the resurrection is the event of salvation from which the tyrant will be excluded. **(C)** The resurrection faith expressed by the third brother seems to be very literal and concrete: he is to receive back the same limbs which he is now losing. However, the expression should not be overemphasized, since in the context the *function* of resurrection belief is stressed, i.e., the vindication of justice for the oppressed and tortured righteous. The second brother's statement in vv.10-11 is, above all, a drastic expression of his faith in final justice, his trust in God[13].

4.2.1.3

Although *14:37-46* describes a suicide, it really pertains to the martyr stories.[14] Razis, one of the faithful elders of Jerusalem, commits suicide instead of transgressing the Law. The violent narrative ends (v.46):

> Finally standing on a sheer rock, and now completely drained of blood, he took his entrails in both hands and flung them at the crowd. And thus, invoking the Lord of life and breath to give these entrails back to him again (ἐπικαλεσαμενος τον δεσποζοντα της ζωης και του πνευματος ταυτα αὐτῷ παλιν ἀποδουναι), he died.

(A) It is evident that the trust in the power of the Lord over life and breath (πνευμα) again functions as the source of courage and inspiration to suffer martyrdom instead of compromising the fidelity to the Law. **(B, C)** Faith in the resurrection of the body is expressed in a very concrete way: The old man hopes to get his entrails back. This may be interpreted as a gross, physical resurrection faith, but as in 7:11, the motif of vindication of justice is expressed in this way, and the literal fulfilment of the words of Razis may not be of main importance.[16] Yet, we cannot question the author's conviction that the body will be fully restored at the resurrection with all its parts, even the entrails[17]. Πνευμα, as in 7:22, is clearly breath, the principle of physical life given by God[18]. It does not refer to any personal, divine holy Spirit. **(D)** Nothing is said about "the date" of the expected resurrection.

4.2.2

Whereas the resurrection functions as vindication of justice for the righteous in the martyr stories, *12:43-45* indicates that the resurrection could imply punishment, as well as reward. Some Jewish soldiers had fallen in the battle and amulets of the idols of Jamnia were found under their tunics. Judas prepares a sin-offering in the temple of Jerusalem for these dead

> —a fit and proper act in which he took due account of the resurrection (ὑπερ ἀναστασεως). For if he had not been expecting the fallen to rise again, (ἀναστηναι), it would have been foolish and superfluous to pray for the dead. But since he had in view the wonderful reward reserved for those who die a godly death, his purpose was a holy and pious one. And this was why he offered an atoning sacrifice to free the dead from their sin (43b-45).

(A) Judas is described as one who believes in the resurrection of the dead, with an obvious polemical allusion to those who do not share his belief. Judas would probably be a weighty authority in a discussion with the Sadducees about the resurrection[19]. **(B)** The action of Judas would not logically require a particular kind of belief in life after death. However, ἀναστασις, is the single term used for after-life. The alternative of ἀναστασις is no life at all after death. But the body is not mentioned as sharing in the resurrection, **(D)** nor is any "date" of the resurrection given.[20]

4.2.2.1

There are three important similarities between this pericope and I Cor 15, which should be indicated here:

(1) Both texts defend the resurrection of the dead against those who deny it.
(2) Ἀναστασις is the only form of life after death that is considered.
(3) Both texts make reference to a liturgical, vicarious action on behalf of dead people (cf. I Cor 15:29); without faith in the resurrection of the dead, this action would have been foolish περισσον και ληρωδες ὑπερ νεκρων εὐχεσθαι —cf. I Cor 15:29 and further vv.12-19, 30-33, 58)[21].

4.2.3

(D) Life in heaven immediately after death, or at least before the End of history, is apparently presupposed by the story of Judas' dream in *15:12-16:*

> What he had seen was this: the former high priest Onias appeared to him, that great gentleman of modest bearing and mild disposition, apt speaker and exponent from childhood of the good life. With outstretched hands he was praying earnestly for the whole Jewish community. Next there appeared in the same attitude a figure of great age and dignity, whose wonderful air of authority marked him as a man of the utmost distinction. Then Onias said, "This is God's prophet Jeremiah, who loves his fellow-Jews and offers many prayers for our people and for the holy city." Jeremiah extended his right hand and delivered to Judas a golden sword, saying as he did so, "Take this holy sword, the gift of God, and with it crush your enemies."

(B) The story, told by Judas to encourage his soldiers before the last battle of II Mcc, would seem to suggest some sort of a corporeal existence after death for at least some saints of Israel, who plead the cause of their people before the heavenly Throne. It is a dream, however, and so the fact of their bodily appearance cannot be heavily stressed. We might compare, e.g., the appearance of Samuel in I Sm 28:14, which surely does not imply any thought of a real corporeal existence after death[22]. Our passage obviously belongs to the *genre* of vision stories, more precisely: stories in which a dead man (holy man) appears and brings a message which concerns the actual situation of the one who receives the vision. An element of this form is the description of the one who appears. Of course, the vision story does not emphasize this form element. Its point is the message conveyed by the one whose appearance is described. On the basis of such a form element, we can hardly make any conclusions about the narrator's opinion or "doctrine" concerning a corporeal existence immediately *post mortem*. But we may stress the importance of the fact that although II Mcc emphasizes belief in the resurrection of the dead, including the body, it is able to speak about the intercession of some saints after death in a way which is completely unrelated to beliefs about the final resurrection of the dead.

4.2.4 *Summary*

We may stress the fact that this work of the Greek-speaking diaspora clearly expresses what is considered as typical Palestinian Jewish ideas about life after death. This observation has sometimes lead the scholars to describe the book as representing Palestinian Judaism rather than the Greek diaspora[23]. Thus, the opportunity to state a serious irregularity in the classification of ideas was actually missed.

[1]Among those who have recently worked with these questions, we may mention the Bonn diss. by J. G. Bunge (1972) 273-279, 607, and also Hengel (1973) 176-183. Cf. also R. Pfeiffer (1949) 514-519; V. Tcherikover (1959) 383-388; Eissfeldt (1964) 719.

[2]Cf. Stemberger (1972) 13; Hengel (1973) 176 n.291, on ch. 7 and the martyr stories as additions by the Epitomist.

[3]The identification of Jason of Cyrene with Jason, son of Eleazar, in II Mcc 8:17, by Tcherikover (1959) 385, is, however, pure guess-work. Cf. Hengel (1973) 176, 182.

[4]Surnames of the type Κυρηναιος usually indicate the place of birth or origin and are meaningful chiefly *outside* this place (in Cyrene Jason would hardly be called Jason of Cyrene!)—cf. e.g. Κυρηναιος and Κυπριος in Acts 4:36; 6:9; 11:20; 13:1; 21:16 and also e.g. Acts 2:11. Cf. Hengel (1973) 176.

[5]This is maintained by Tcherikover (1959) 383. Bunge (1971) 201 f., 328 f., 595-614.

[6]This is maintained by e.g. B. M. Metzger (1957) 140; Eissfeldt (1964) 719.

[7]E.g. Tcherikover (1959) 388; Eissfeldt (1964) 720; Bunge (1971) 201 f.

[8]Bunge (1971) 595-614.

[9]Cf. the treatment in Stemberger (1972) 13-23.

[10]About the text of the story, cf. e.g. P. Katz, Studia Patristica 4 (1961) 118-124.

[11]Gr. και το πνευμα και την ζωην υμιν παλιν αποδιδωσιν.

[12]For the interpretation and translation of the text here, see H. Bückers, Bibl 21 (1940) 406-412.

[13]Cf. Stemberger (1972) 17; Nickelsburg (1972) 94. Concerning Nickelsburg's treatment of II Mcc 7 *(ibid.* 93-109), I feel that the author forces some parallels too much in order to place the passage in his history of tradition.

[14]Cf. Stemberger (1972) 22.

[15]Alex. and a few other MSS read τα αυτα, which would even strengthen the literalism of the resurrection hope expressed here. There is no reason to believe that this was the original reading.

[16]Cf. n.13; Nickelsburg (1972) 94 f. n; Stemberger (1972) 23.

[17]So Stemberger (1972) 23. Wied (1965) 104 f., rightly suggests the possibility that ταυτα in 14:46 may refer to της ζωης και του πνευματος rather than to τα εντερα, and thinks that there may be an intentional ambiguity to cover both, but the parallel 7:10-11 decisively indicates τα εντερα. This is also the simplest way of understanding ταυτα in 14:46.

[18]This is also the original meaning of "spirit" in Ez 37. Cf also Rev. 11:11.

[19]Cf. *infra* 6.2, and for the relation between Sadducees and Maccabees, cf. e.g. Le Moyne (1972) 387-389, also 75, on the relation between I Mcc and the Sadducees.

[20]Some kind of intermediate state might seem to be required, if an atoning sacrifice would be of any value to the dead, but our text says nothing about it, and logical principles cannot be forced upon the text.

[21]In the second volume this parallel will be used to suggest a new interpretation of the baptism for the dead, mentioned in I Cor 15:29. According to my theory, partly based on this parallel, those νεκροι in Corinth were already baptized Christians, whose death in these early years was considered to be punishment for some serious sin, which excluded them from the communion of the Church. So their baptism was no longer functioning, they had lost "baptismal grace"; the idea of a vicarious repetition may have appeared in such a context.—Concerning the interpretation of Judas' action in the story, it is naturally possible to think that the resurrection equals salvation. The sacrifice is offered in order to give the sinners a share in the future resurrection with the whole of the people of Israel.

[22]Against Stemberger (1972) 11 f. n, concerning the interpretation of I Sm 28 and the corporeal *post-mortem* existence in OT, I agree with Stemberger's interpretation of the corporeal description of the vision. But his conclusion *Soll die Auferstehung leiblich sein, ist sie daher wohl auf Erden gedacht* is not supported by the texts of II Mcc.

[23]E.g. Beresford (1971) 41; Bunge (1971) 201 f.; Stemberger (1972) 6 f. But cf. for a balanced judgment e.g. Hoffmann (1966) 92; Hengel (1973) 182.

4.3 IV Maccabees

IV Mcc is a discourse[1] on the fate of Eleazar, the seven brothers and their mother, as an example of the superiority and sovereignty of religious reason over the passions and emotions (1:1)[2]. Its most important source is II Mcc 6-7[3], which is approximately a century older than IV Mcc[4]. The author is an orthodox Jew[5], perhaps from Alexandria[6], or Antioch[7] or even Asia Minor[8]. The comparison between II and IV Mcc must underline the difference that exists in their views on life after death[9]: Faith in the resurrection, conceived very literally, was the hope which the martyrs expressed before the king in II Mcc. All their statements on the resurrection have seemingly been carefully avoided by the author of IV Mcc. They have been replaced by expressions of belief in a spiritual type of immortality. We shall examine the more important passages in greater detail:

4.3.1
Concluding the description (ch. 5-6) and panegyric (ch. 7) of the old Eleazar's martyrdom, the preacher of IV Mcc states (*7:18-19*):

Those who take thought for religion (εὐσεβειας) with their whole heart (ἐξ ὁλης καρδιας), they alone are able to dominate the passions (παθων) of the flesh, believing that to God they die not, as neither did our patriarchs Abraham, Isaac, and Jacob, but live to God (ζωσιν τῳ θεῳ), ET: Hadas, 1953, is used unless otherwise stated).

This commentary is echoed in *16:25* by another comment. Following the mother's encouraging speech (16:16-23), the author emphasizes, concerning her seven sons:

They too knew well that those who die for the sake of God live to (Hadas: with) God (ζωσιν τῳ θεῳ)as do Abraham and Isaac and Jacob and all the patriarchs.

This is a striking parallel with the Lukan version of Jesus' reply on the question of the Sadducees concerning the resurrection (Lk 20:37 f.—cf. Mk 12:26 f. and Mt 22:32). It has been noted that TestXIIPatr gives special attention to the patriarchs' share in the resurrection (3.3.1). **(A)** These testimonies allow us to assert that Judaism around the beginning of CE gave special emphasis to the patriarchs' role in the resurrection and/or life to come. **(B)** Neither body nor soul are specifically mentioned. **(C)** The only qualification given to future life is "to God" $\vartheta\epsilon\tilde{\omega}$. This implies perhaps the antithesis "to men", i.e. "in the eyes of men" or "in the flesh" (cf. Wi 3:4). The present tense, "live" ($\zeta\tilde{\omega}\sigma\iota\nu$), is important, and it must mean that the patriarchs were already living the eternal life "to God" and that at least those who die the death of martyrs will attain that future life immediately after death. The same impression is given by the common reply of the seven brothers to the suggestions of the "tyrant" in *9:7-9:*

> If you take our lives and inflict upon us a death ($\tau\grave{\alpha}\varsigma$ $\grave{\eta}\mu\tilde{\omega}\nu$ $\psi\upsilon\chi\grave{\alpha}\varsigma$ $\epsilon\grave{\iota}$ $\vartheta\alpha\nu\alpha\tau\omega\sigma\epsilon\iota\varsigma$) for religion's sake, do not think that you are injuring us by your torments. We, by our suffering and endurance, shall obtain the prize of virtue; and we shall be with God ($\pi\alpha\rho\alpha$ $\vartheta\epsilon\tilde{\omega}$), on Whose account we suffer; but you, for our foul murder, will endure at the hand of divine justice the condign punishment of eternal torment ($\alpha\grave{\iota}\dot{\omega}\nu\iota\sigma\nu$ $\beta\alpha\sigma\alpha\nu\sigma\nu$) by fire.[10]

(A) Eternal life $\pi\alpha\rho\alpha$ $\vartheta\epsilon\tilde{\omega}$ is the promise in which those who suffer can trust. **(B)** The body is not mentioned. The term $\psi\upsilon\chi\eta$ is here more or less synonymous with $\zeta\omega\eta$ [11]. One might logically ask the question how eternal torment by fire could be effective without a body, but that question is probably most irrelevant to the mind of the author[12].

4.3.2

Several other passages contrast the eternal pains, which will be the fate of the wicked king in similar (10:11[13]; 12:12[13]; 13:15) or somewhat varying (10:15— $\grave{\sigma}\lambda\epsilon\vartheta\rho\sigma\varsigma$) terms, with the blessed life of the righteous after death. These expressions may indicate the idea that all men will have some kind of judgment after death, but there is no theoretical affirmation of such a statement in IV Mcc, where the tyrant king alone stands for the wicked ones. However, a general teaching about the blessed life of the pious comes from the mouth of the fourth brother in *10:15:*

> By the blessed death of my brothers, by the everlasting destruction of the tyrant, by the eternal[14] life of the pious, I will not deny our noble brotherhood.

In the same way *15:3* makes an affirmation about the mother:

> She loved religion better, which preserves to eternal life ($\sigma\omega\zeta\sigma\upsilon\sigma\alpha\nu$ $\epsilon\grave{\iota}\varsigma$ $\alpha\grave{\iota}\omega\nu\iota\alpha\nu$ $\zeta\omega\eta\nu$) according to God's promise ($\kappa\alpha\tau\alpha$ $\vartheta\epsilon\sigma\nu$).

This terminology ("eternal life"—"eternal destruction") reminds us of the "two-way theology", of which we found numerous examples in the Jewish writings already studied (3.3.4 and further references there; 4.1.3). The words of the fourth brother should be compared with what he is saying in II Mcc 7:14 (cf. 4.2.1.2 and Marchel, VD 34, 332). The negative statement in II Mcc 7:14 ("there will be no resurrection to life for you") has been changed to the positive affirmation of his eternal destruction, whereas the resurrection terminology has been replaced by the words about the eternal life. The tendency is clear, though we should not exaggerate the consciousness of the author of IV Mcc[15].

4.3.3

The Stoic ideal of the "mastery over suffering which comes from Divine reason" (13:16) is to be rewarded in a very Jewish fashion, according to *13:17:*

When we have died in such fashion, Abraham and Isaac and Jacob will receive us, and all the patriarchs will praise us.

We have already stated the important role of especially Abraham and all the patriarchs in after-life (4.3.1). This passage describes them functioning as hosts in the heavenly glory (cf. Mt 8:11; Lk 16:22 ff.). (A, B) The martyrs' life after death (C) is not portrayed by a concrete image; neither (D) is anything said about the "date" of the beginning of their life after death.

4.3.4

The term $\dot{\alpha}\vartheta\alpha\nu\alpha\tau\sigma\varsigma/\dot{\alpha}\vartheta\alpha\nu\alpha\sigma\iota\alpha$ is used on a number of occasions for the life after death[16] gained by martyrdom, e.g., in *14: 5-6:*

All as if running the course to immortality[17], sped onward to death by torture. Just as hands and feet move in harmony with the promptings of the soul, so did those holy youths, as if prompted by the immortal[17] soul[18] of religion, harmoniously accept death on its behalf.

(A) Immortality awaits the martyrs after their torture. (B) When the "soul" or the "immortal soul" is mentioned, it does not imply any doctrine of the immortality of the soul *per se.* The harmonious, completely solidaric willingness of the seven brothers to accept death is compared with the harmonious function of the limbs of the body under the guidance of the soul[19]. The religious inspiration is functioning as the soul of that body of the seven brothers. Thus, "immortal" is an attribute of religion, rather than a quality of the soul. In the actual context religion would be called "immortal" precisely because it grants immortality to those who adhere to it, especially if they have to sacrifice their lives in faithfulness to its commandments. (D) "Speeding onward to death" equals "running the course to immortality". Consequently, it is likely that death is considered the moment when immortality begins—as usual in IV Mcc.

The attitude of the sons has a perfect parallel in that of their mother, according to *16:13:*

As though her mind were of adamant, and as though she were again giving birth to her brood of seven sons unto immortality $(\dot{\alpha}\vartheta\alpha\nu\alpha\sigma\iota\alpha\nu)$ ... she encouraged them to death for religion's sake.

(A) Martyrdom is the way to immortality, which (D) seemingly is waiting immediately after death.

4.3.5

The last sentence of the book repeats this doctrine in *18:23:*

The children of Abraham (οἱ δε 'Αβραμιαιοι παιδες). with their mother, who bore off the prize, are ranged in the choir of their fathers; having received souls pure and immortal (ἀθανατους Hadas: "deathless") from God.

Townshend's commentary interprets these words as pointing "to an original difference between good and bad souls before their incorporation in the body", and compares them with Wi 8:19. We shall briefly return to the much disputed question whether this passage does at all imply a doctrine of the pre-existence of souls (4.4.9). There is no need, in any case, to find such Platonic doctrines in the text of IV Mcc. Ψυχας ἀγνας και ἀθανατους ἀπειληφοτες may just as well refer to **(A)** the reception of a new(form, and a)spiritual kind of existence after death, according to the interpretation of Hadas (1953) *ad loc.* This understanding which does not introduce a new idea in the last verses is preferable from a methodical point of view.[20] **(B)** Then our conclusion is that this passage does not teach the immortality of the soul as an inherent quality of the soul, as distinguished from the body. The consistent message of IV Mcc seems to be that immortality is given to the righteous after death, especially to those who died for the sake of righteousness.

(C) The martyrs are "ranged in the choir of their fathers" this phrase states their participation in the patriarchs' life "to God" (cf. 4.3.1 and 3). So the idea of future life found here has a strong Jewish characteristic: the righteous are not seen as isolated individuals of high moral qualities, but are seen as members of the chosen people, the descendants of Abraham. However, their relation to Abraham and the other patriarchs is, of course, no mere genealogical fact. The attribute 'Αβραμιαιος seems also to denote a similarity in the way of life. In order to attain the eternal glory, Abraham had to walk the way of faith and trust through all the sufferings and hardships by which God put him to the test. This is also the way in which the 'Αβραμιαιοι have to go, according to the description of the relation between the patriarch and both his genealogical and spiritual "children"[21]. Having suffered in the same manner as Abraham, they receive a share in his immortal life before God **(D)** immediately after death.

4.3.6
The description of the eldest brother's torture contains two verses, in which the teaching of the "Abrahamic" way is concentrated, *9:21 f.:*

Even when the frame of his body was already dissevered, that great-spirited youth, a true son of Abraham ('Αβραμιαιος νεανιας), uttered no groan. As though he were being transformed into incorruption by the fire (ἐν πυρι μετασχηματιζομενος εἰς ἀφθαρσιαν), he nobly endured the torments . . .

(D) The very act of martyrdom is described as **(C)** the transformation **(A)** into incorruption, very much like the story about the Martyrdom of Polycarp (MartPol 15):

The flames, bellying out like a ship's sail in the wind, formed into the shape of a vault, and thus surrounded the martyr's body as with a wall. And he was within it not as burning flesh but rather as bread being baked, or like gold and silver being purified in a smelting-furnace. And from it we perceived such a delightful fragrance as though it were smoking incense or some other costly perfume (ET: H. Musurillo, 1972, 15).

One source of inspiration behind the formulations of MartPol 15 is Wi 3:6 (cf. Musurillo, 1972, 15n). The sacrificial terminology of v.6b has a parallel in the last sentence of the quotation above. Also the context of IV Mcc 9:21 f. contains the idea of martyrdom as a sacrifice, 9:24 (cf. II Mcc 7:37). Although no direct literary dependance of IV Mcc upon Wi can be proven in this case, there is a certain similarity in the way of thinking and expressions. Both form the common background of Early Christian reflections on martyrdom[22]. Instead of ἀθανασια IV Mcc 9:22 employs ἀφθαρσια, another purely Greek term, which in LXX is used only by Wi and IV Mcc (Larcher, 1969, 280). Both are found in I Cor 15:50-54[23], where ἀφθαρσια/ἀφθαρτος describe the transcendental form of life (not "flesh and blood", v.50), which can only attained either by death and resurrection or by transformation (v.52). For the act of transformation IV Mcc 9:22 employs the verb μετασχηματιζω, [24]. The moment of transformation, which both in I Cor 15 and II Bar 51 (cf. *supra* 3.10.2 and 3.10.2.1.1) is the day of the resurrection, is the very act of dying according to IV Mcc 9:22.

'Aφθαρσια is used about the future life also in *17:12:*

> On that day virtue, proving them through endurance, set before them the prize of victory in incorruption (ἀφθαρσια) in a life of long duration ἐν ζωῃ πολυχρονιῳ. [25]

(A) 'Aφθαρσια must refer to life after death in spite of the strange qualification given by the last words, (ἐν ζωῃ πολυχρονιῳ) Some scholars have suggested that they represent a gloss,[26] but they may also be considered *lectio difficilior et probabilior,* since they look like an anti-climax to ἀφθαρσια, if they are interpreted literally, "a life of long duration". But the interpretation of Townshend ("everlasting life"—cf. n.25) is more likely to be correct. Ζωη πολυχρονιος is a synonym of ζωη αἰωνιος [27]. Unusual compounds are a characteristic feature of the Asianic style of IV Mcc[28]. 'Aιδιος in 10:15 is another example of a variant of αἰωνιος.

(B) Neither body nor soul is mentioned, but **(C)** ἀφθαρσια would qualify the future life as non-earthly, transcendent. **(D)** Probably the death of the martyrs is again regarded as the gateway to that life.

4.3.7
Pythagorean influence has been suspected in a description of the heavenly glory of the mother and her seven sons in *17:4-6:*[29]

> Be of good courage, then, mother of holy soul, who keep the hope of your endurance firm with God; not so majestic stands the moon in heaven with its stars, as you stand; lighting the way to piety for your seven star-like sons; honoured by God, and with them fixed in heaven. For your child-bearing was of our father Abraham.

(A) It is not absolutely clear that the expressions in these verses refer to the heavenly glory in a life after death. They might be interpreted as rhetorical phrases for the fame which the martyr family had won, but it is more probable that "with them fixed in heaven" also denotes **(B)** a real assumption after death, in the context of IV Mcc, bearing in mind the use of star-imagery in both Jewish and pagan Greek texts about the life of the righteous after death[30]. **(C)** The life to come for the righteous thus implies a transformation of mortal man to divine glory, without any precise information **(B)** about which part of man is to participate in the future life. **(D)** The text would seem to say that the glorification takes place immediately after death.

The last sentence about the child-bearing of Father Abraham is interpreted to be a statement on the mother as the mystical bride of Abraham by Dupont-Sommer (1939, *ad loc.*). This is an unnecessary theory. It is much more likely that Abraham is conceived as the model of the mother in his sacrifice of the only son (cf. 16:20; 18:11 and n.21). Of course, Abraham is also a partaker of that star-like life, receiving his sons in heaven (7:18 f.; 16:25; 13:17—*supra* 4.3.1; 4.3.3).

4.3.8

Another rather interesting expression of the same belief in the blessed after-life of the martyrs is found in *18:3:*

> Those men who yielded up their bodies to suffering for the sake of religion were in recompense not only admired by mankind, but were also deemed worthy of a divine portion ($\vartheta\epsilon\iota\alpha\ \mu\epsilon\rho\iota\varsigma$).

(A) $\Theta\epsilon\iota\alpha\ \mu\epsilon\rho\iota\varsigma$ must refer to that *post mortem* life and immortality which the martyrs received by their death, **(B)** without any statement about the future role of the body or of the soul. **(C)** $\Theta\epsilon\iota o\varsigma$ is used in that rather vague Greek way which implies immortality, glory, a blessed life (cf. H. Kleinknecht, TWNT III, 1938, 122 f.). Thus, the glorification of the martyrs in heaven is expressed,[31] and it is obvious that **(D)** it commences immediately after death.

4.3.9

A little more about the "divine portion" is said in *17:18 f.:*

> By (the constancy) they now have their stand before the throne of God, and live the life of eternal blessedness ($\tau o\nu\ \mu\alpha\kappa\alpha\rho\iota o\nu\ \beta\iota o\nu\sigma\iota\nu\ \alpha\iota\omega\nu\alpha$) · For Moses says, "All the holy ones are underneath Thy hands."

The last quotation (Dt 33:3b, LXX word for word) is of interest because it indicates that Biblical texts were used in the Greek speaking synagogue as a means of proving the doctrine of salvation after death for the righteous. The words $\upsilon\pi o\ \tau\alpha\varsigma\ \chi\epsilon\iota\rho\alpha\varsigma\ \sigma o\upsilon$ are given a literal interpretation, and they function as an argument for the statement that the saints stand before the throne of God. **(A, D)** The martyrs have reached the blessed age, eternity, the age to come, already at death. **(B)** The assertion that "they stand" would logically imply a body, but it does not, of course, prove anything about a resurrection of the body in such a vague context. Standing before the throne of God must rather imply a life very similar to divinity, the life of angels (cf. 7.2.1.4 ff.). This is a highly spiritualized and transcendent notion of the future life of the blessed, which neither includes nor excludes the body.

4.3.10

In the existing MSS and edd. of IV Mcc the final end of the book is preceded by some references to Scripture, which were obviously intended as a reinforcement of the teaching on the sufferings of the righteous and the salvation prepared for them even after death[32]: Abel killed by Cain, Isaac sacrificed as a holocaust, Joseph in prison, Ananias, Azarias and Misael, Daniel among the lions (cf. n.21 *supra*), further Is 43:2, Ps 33(34):20a, Prv 3:18 (adaptation to the present context, cf. Hadas, 1953, *ad loc.*), Ez 37:3 (with the addition of ξηρα from the preceding verse) and Dt 32:39b. Again, we find some examples of Bible texts being used to support the hope of immortality of the righteous, and especially the martyrs, after death. Some of the persons mentioned may be considered as types of martyrs, obviously sharing their sufferings. It is implicitly presupposed that they also share the blessed life after death, which is obtained by the patriarchs and the martyrs, according to IV Mcc. This may be especially true of Abel, who was actually killed, and of Isaac. It is interesting to find that the sacrifice of Isaac and his last minute salvation is regarded as a figure of the resurrection both by Rabbinic Jewish[33] and Early Christian[34] exegetes. The following Biblical persons (Joseph, etc.) are examples of the suffering righteous who are saved by the Lord in the end, but they cannot so naturally be seen as figures of the resurrection.[35]

4.3.10.1

The quotation from *Is 43:2* is very appropriate after the description of the torments and the use of the fire. The quotation would be meaningful here, however, only if the text is re-interpreted as a promise of future life for the righteous after death.

4.3.10.2

Ps 33:20a should be read in its original context (vv.20b-23) which contains promises about the future salvation of the righteous. V.21 asserts that the Lord preserves all the bones of the righteous, which might be interpreted as a statement on the resurrection of the body. V.23 states: "He will redeem the souls of his servants."

The adapted quotation from *Prv 3:18* tells us how sayings about "life" and "live" generally were very easily used and read with the meaning of "eternal life" after death.

4.3.10.3

Most interesting and surprising in the context of IV Mcc is the quotation from *Ez 37:3*, which also seems to presuppose that the readers are aware of its context. **(B, C)** One would not expect that the use of this very concrete and physical description of a resurrection would convey the hope of eternal life in the circles behind IV Mcc. A simple explanation may be that the immediate context and the quotation itself pertain to a later insertion (cf. n.32), where a more Biblical than philosophical outlook was brought into the text of IV Mcc. But it is also possible that those circles who produced IV Mcc were able to read Ez 37:1-14 in a very symbolic way. According to their interpretation, Ez 37 did not speak about resurrection, but spoke in general about life after death for the pious Israelites (cf. *supra* 4.1.6). If this later alternative is true, we are compelled to be even more cautious than ever about making definite conclusions about the ideas on resurrection/immortality among Jews of the Greek diaspora.

4.3.10.4

Finally, *Dt 32:39* has often been interpreted as an explicit reference to resurrection/future life (cf. 4.1.1 and further references there). It uses a language which would indicate resurrection rather than spiritual immortality.

4.3.11 *Summary*

(A) The doctrine of future life after death is very much in the centre of the interest of the author of IV Mcc. This life implies both the reward of the righteous who have suffered for their religion and the punishment of their oppressors.

(B) It seems that the resurrection terminology is consciously, but quietly avoided, but the resurrection of the body is never directly excluded. The immortality of the martyrs' souls is not considered as an inherent quality. It is instead a gift of God for their faithful endurance of the sufferings.

(C) The portion of the righteous after death is a divine existence in the presence of the Divine Majesty.

(D) The idea of an "end time", a "last day", is replaced by the death of the individual, as the moment of decisive change.

---

[1] E. Norden I (1898) 417; A. Deissmann, Kautzsch, AP II (1900) 151; M. Hadas (1953) 100-102; Nickelsburg (1972) 109 f., among others, use the term *diatribe*, thinking of the "strong philosophic coloring" (Hadas 102) of the book. A. Dupont-Sommer (1939) admits this designation only for the first part of the book (1:1-3:18). The writing should rather be described as a *panegyric*. He thinks that it was delivered as a real sermon at the Jewish shrine of the martyrs in Antioch (11-25).—This conjecture is interesting, indeed, but the case would be without clear parallels, therefore his theory has not yet been generally accepted. 1:1 defines the aim of the treatise in a way which is characteristic of the philosophical diatribe (Hadas *ad loc.*): φιλοσοφωτατον λογον ἐπιδεικνυσϑαι

[2] Cf. also Hoffmann (1966) 87. On the expression εὐσεβης λογισμος in 1:1 cf., S. Lauer, JJS 6 (1955) 170 f.

[3] Cf. Dupont-Sommer (1939) 26-32; Hadas (1953) 93; Tcherikover (1959) 390 f.; Hoffmann (1966 87, all of whom refuse to accept the suggestion of a direct relation between IV Mcc and the work of Jason from Cyrene: all differences between II Mcc and IV Mcc can be explained by the general tendencies of IV Mcc without the recourse to that theory.

[4]On II Mcc cf. 4, 2. There is no consensus as to the exact date of IV Mcc among the scholars. The suggestions vary between 63 BC—*terminus post quem* in Deissmann, Kautzsch, AP II, 150; R. B. Townshend, Charles AP II (1913) 654—and circa AD 120 (the suggested date in Dupont-Sommer, 1939, 75-85) and dates in between (before Vespasian, Deissmann 150; before AD 38, Townshend, 654; about AD 35, E. J. Bickermann, *In hon.* L. Ginzberg, 1945, 105-112, and Hadas, 1953, 95-98; before Hbr, which is literally dependent on IV Mcc, J. R. Harris, ExpT 32. 1920/1, 183-185; within the first century: Volz, 1934, 58; W. Marchel, VD 34, 1956, 328).

[5]Cf. Deissmann, Kautzsch, AP II,151; Townshend, Charles, AP II, 653; Dupont-Sommer (1939) 37 f.; Eissfeldt (1964) 832; Hoffmann (1966) 87.

[6]Deissmann, *ibid.* 151, suggesting Asia Minor as a plausible alternative; Townshend, *ibid.* 654.

[7]Dupont-Sommer (1939) 67-73; Hadas (1953) 108-113.

[8]Deissmann *ibid.* 150; Hadas (1953) 98.

[9]Cf. Marchel, VD 34, 332-334; Hoffmann (1966) 87.

[10] Διὰ πυρος, missing in one correction of Sin, is considered a gloss by Dupont-Sommer (1939) *ad loc.*

[11]Cf. LS s.v. and e.g. Mt 2:20; 6:25; 10:39; 16:25; 20:28; Mk 3:4 etc.

[12]Cf. Plato on the torments of the wicked in Hades, e.g. in Phaedo 113D-114B (explicitly called "myth" in 110B—cf. 114D: no sensible man would maintain that "this is just as I have described it").

[13]Though here only the punishment of the wicked is mentioned.

[14]I read ἀίδιος with Rahlfs (1962); Hadas (1953) *ad loc.* Townshend, Charles AP II; Dupont-Sommer (1939); Hadas (1953) translate "glorious", which would be more suitable to the variant reading ἀοίδιμος in Alex., followed by H. B. Swete III (1912) *ad loc.* The normal meaning of ἀίδιος is "eternal", "everlasting"—see LS s.v.

[15]Cf. Dupont-Sommer (1939) 48; Marchel, VD 34, 332-334; Hoffmann (1966) 87 f., and the summary *infra* 4.3.11.

[16]Cf. C. Larcher (1969) on the Greek character of this terminology, in LXX used only in Wi, IV Mcc and Sir 17:30.

[17] Ἀθανασια is rendered "deathlessness" ἀθανατος "deathless" by Hadas (1953) *ad loc.*, probably to emphasize the paradox of the statement, as in Gr.

[18] Ψυχη, rendered "spirit" by Hadas (1953) *ad loc.* This translation makes the similitude in the context less clear, so the usual way of translating ψυχη has been chosen.

[19]"Ordinary Stoic doctrine", Hadas comments *ad loc.* Although it may be disputed whether this is directly influenced by Stoicism, the general character of the book and its main idea about the dominion of τα παθη through λογισμος εὐσεβης has a strong Stoic flavour. Cf. also O. Perler, RivArchCrist 25 (1949) 63.

[20]Cf. Larcher (1969) 149.

[21]6:17: The sons of Abraham must show courage and cannot save themselves by hypocrisy; 6:22: The sons of Abraham must die nobly for the sake of religion; 7:19 as well as the preceding verse seems also to imply that the patriarchs could dominate their passions by their zeal for religion "of all their heart"; 9:21: In his terrible torture Ἀβραμιαιος νεανιας did not even sigh (cf. 4.3.6); 13:16-17: When we arm ourselves with the domination of passions from divine reason and die like that, Abraham, Isaac and Jacob shall receive us, and all the fathers praise us (4.3.3)—implying perhaps that the fathers lived and died with the same domination of passions; 15:28: the daughter (i.e. of Abraham) remembered the godfearing Abraham's endurance; 16:19-20: You ought to stand all sufferings for the sake of God—as Abraham, our father, for his sake hastened to sacrifice Isaac, the son who was to be the father of the people (the only time more concrete information is given about the sufferings of Abraham and his patience in trusting God); 16:25: Those who die for God, will live for him like Abraham, Isaac and Jacob; 17:6: The mother's child-bearing was of father Abraham—again

with a reference to patience and endurance in hope (v.4) in the context; 18:1: The Israelites as stemming from the seed of Abraham are encouraged to know religion (v.2)—that "the religious reason" is the master of the passions—both from within and from without; 18:20: with a new description of the sufferings of the seven brothers, the mother is called simply ἡ 'Αβρααμιτις • —Other Biblical heroes seem to be mentioned with similar intentions as maybe Aaron in the description of the sufferings of Eleazar in 7:11 f., and in the same context Isaac's reason; Daniel and his companions in 16:3, 21 and 18:12; Abel, killed by Cain, in 18:11 together with Isaac, "offered as a holocaust", and Joseph in prison; in 18:12 the "zealot" Phinees, and in v.13 again Daniel, among the lions.—The motif of *imitatio patrum* was also found in LAB 33:5. There, too, it is the way to heavenly glory (3.8.3). In IV Mcc this *imitatio patrum* is connected especially with suffering, since the theme of the *diatribe* is the domination of emotions through the religious reason (1:1). But it is hard to deny that the imitation of the fathers resembles the *imitatio Christi* as it is presented in e.g. Rm 8:17; Ph 3:10; II Tm 2:11 f.

²²Cf. e.g. Hadas (1953) 124-127; Musurillo (1972) xiv. On this subject H. v.Campenhausen (1936) 2-5, needs a complement. Cf. Perler, RivArchCrist 25 47-72; W. H. C. Frend (1965) 30-78.

²³ 'Αφθαρσια/αφθαρτος 4 times, ἀθανασια twice, is the "Greek" synonym of the "kingdom of God" in v.50.

²⁴Cf. Hadas (1953) *ad loc.* for some Philonic parallels and the relation to I Cor 15:51 ff.

²⁵I follow the translation of Townshend, Charles AP II, *ad loc.,* with the exception of his rendering of ἐν ζωῇ πολυχρονιῳ "in everlasting life", where Hadas is preferred, since the phrase has to be discussed a little, because of its literal meaning.

²⁶Thus Dupont-Sommer (1939) and Hadas (1953) *ad loc.*—with the suggestion that the expression may be a gloss by a reader who preferred a Biblical phrase (cf. 18:19) to the philosophic ἀφθαρσια • This is not a very natural explanation, since the later history of the tradition of IV Mcc did not usually mean a return to early Israelite expressions.

²⁷Only in the present context (but cf. the quotation of 18:19 and its meaning here—4.3.10.4). In LXX πολυχρονιος generally means long-lived, old, lasting for a long time—cf. Gn 26:8; Job 32:9; Wi 2:10; 4:8; Ep Jr 46—as in the Gr. literature in general—cf. LS s.v. A vaguely parallel use might be found in Phaedo 87D, where the soul is said to be πολυχρονιον in relation to the body. Cf. E. Jenni, IDB IV (1962) 644; J. Barr (1969) 73, 75; J. Guhrt, TBNT II/2 (1971) 1457—1458 for the denotation of the Hebrew עולם which often meant something similar to πολυχρονιος rather than "eternity" in a philosophically defined sense. The border between the two concepts may have been rather unclear to Jewish writers of the period of IV Mcc, who were used to LXX renderings of promises of long life to the righteous in the Bible, e.g. Ex 20:12; Dt 5:16; Ps 90(91):16; Prv 9:18d etc. and perhaps read them as statements on everlasting life—cf. 4.1 *supra.*

²⁸Cf. Norden I (1898) 416-420; Dupont-Sommer (1939) 57, 60-66.

²⁹E.g. by Dupont-Sommer (1939) 47. He refers also to 14:7-8.

³⁰Cf. *infra* 4.6.2.1 on BJ VI, 46-48 (Titus' speech) and further A. J. Festugiere (1932) 149-151; Hoffmann (1966) 44-47. A good example is quoted by Dupont-Sommer (1939) 47, from Inscr. Graec. XII, 7 n.123: ἀστηρ γαρ γενομην θειος ἀκρεσπεριος

³¹For the term μερις cf. 2.3 and Dn 12:13, where LXX translates δοξα, Theodotion κληρος for Hebr גרול For the use of this term in the Qumran documents cf. e.g. 3.5.1 (1QS XI, 7 f.); 3.5.4 (1QH XI, 11); 3.5.7 (4Q181 1 II, 3-6).

³²Some scholars think that this passage, as a whole, belongs to a later interpolation—because of the language and style, and above all because the passage 18:6-19 breaks the connection between the preceding and the following context. After a few verses which look like the beginning of the conclusion of the book, the present redaction suddenly returns to the teaching of the mother (and even the father of the sons). Cf. Dupont-Sommer (1939) 17, 153 f. n, referring to other authors as well. But even if this would be a later insertion by another hand than the original author, there are still good reasons to believe that these Biblical references point back to the teaching of the Greek-speaking

diaspora synagogues. Larcher (1969) 150, calls the passage a Jewish Alexandrian midrash before Philo.

[33]PRE 31 (Friedlander's ET p.228): When the sword touched the neck of Isaac, his soul did actually depart, but when the voice of God commanded Abraham to stop, it returned and then Isaac understood the resurrection of the dead and pronounced the second benediction of *Shemone esre, Mechayyeh hamethim.* See also Löwinger, Jahrb.f.jüd.Volkskunde 25, 117, for several other examples from later midrashim, preserving the same tradition (Shibbole ha-Leket, Buber 9b, 18a; Ozar Midr 584b; Menorath hamaor IV, 3-II, 80b, Vilna).

[34]Rm 4:17; Hbr 11:17-19—cf. e.g. J. F. Wood, NTS 14 (1957/8) 583-589—stressing the sacrificial motif more than the birth-resurrection side; E. Käsemann (1969) 159; O. Hofius, NTS 18 (1971) 93-94.

[35]Cf., however, 3.8.7 on Phinees (LAB 48:1).

4.4 The Wisdom of Solomon

The blessed immortality of the righteous after death has a central place in the theological conception of the Wisdom of Solomon, an Alexandrian Jewish tract of late second or early first century BC[1]. It supplies the answer to the burning question about the seeming temporal success of the wicked and the apparent defeat of the cause of justice. This is the theme of ch. 1-5. Since Wi is accepted as a canonical book by both the Roman Catholic and the Eastern Orthodox Churches, its views on afterlife have been more eagerly disputed than those of other Hellenistic Jewish writings of the same period. Wi speaks about the future life of the righteous without mentioning the resurrection. This is a problem for the theologians who try to harmonize the official doctrine of the Church with her canonical writings. Is the resurrection silently presupposed or silently denied? Are there other solutions to this problem? K. Romaniuk, BiLe 10, 1969, 200-204, gives a good summary of the discussion. By examining the important texts individually, I hope to establish an answer.

4.4.1

The introduction exhorts the rulers of the earth to love justice as the path to life, whereas wickedness leads to death. *1:15* states:

Justice ($\delta\iota\kappa\alpha\iota\sigma\sigma\upsilon\nu\eta$) is immortal ($\grave{\alpha}\vartheta\alpha\nu\alpha\tau\sigma\varsigma$, ET: NEB, throughout Wi).

(A) This statement, read in its context, implies that justice leads to eternal life[2]. Wi's teaching on immortality is well summarized in this statement, in spite of its brevity. This investigation shall prove that Wi regarded immortality as a reward of a righteous life rather than an inherent quality of the soul[3]. The hope of immortality is the righteous' consolation in a world which often seems to be completely dominated by the wicked.

4.4.2

The author returns to this theme after presenting the argument of the wicked in 2:1-20. In 2:21-22 the fault of the wicked way of thinking is summarized, and *v.22b* states:

They never expected that holiness of life would have its recompense; they thought that innocence had no reward.

126

4.4.3

The questions about the recompense of a righteous life are obviously very important for the development of the doctrine on life after death found in the following chapter. This doctrine is the anti-thesis to the faulty argument of the wicked. This will be expounded in 3:1-9. But first comes the presupposition: man was created for immortality but lost his eternal life by means of the devil's spite, which brought death into the world (2.23-24).

4.4.3.1

(A) The righteous, however, enjoy a blessed life after death (3:1-4):

> But the souls of the just are in God's hand, and torment shall not touch them. In the eyes of foolish men they seemed to be dead ... But they are at peace ... they have a sure hope of immortality ...

4.4.3.2

(B) Only the soul survives death. The body, in contrast to the glorified soul, is seen by foolish men as being chastened and dead. Efforts have been made to interpret *v.7f.* as a statement on a final resurrection, presupposing that the phrases about after-life in vv.1-3 refer to an intermediate state[4]:

> In the moment of their visitation ($\dot{\epsilon}\pi\iota\sigma\kappa\sigma\pi\hat{\eta}\varsigma$) [5] they will kindle into flame ($\dot{\alpha}\nu\alpha\lambda\alpha\mu\psi\sigma\nu\sigma\iota\nu$), like sparks that sweep through stubble; they will be judges and rulers over the nations of the world ...

It is true that there seems to be a distinction between the state of the souls immediately after death ("in God's hand", "at peace", "they have a sure hope of immortality[6]") and the future glorification "at the time of their visitation". But the silence of the resurrection remains a fact. Therefore, it is impossible to make any positive conclusions about the author's faith in the resurrection on the basis of this passage (cf. e.g. Romaniuk, BiLe 10, 201).

4.4.3.3

(C) The description in v.7 f. presents an image of the future glorification of the righteous, which, at least, resembles and may be inspired by Dn 12:3[7]. Here the shining splendour of the righteous is associated with a consuming fire, the fire of the judgment. Then they will function as judges and rulers under God, the eternal King (v.8b). The images and ideas are certainly more Jewish than Greek. Above all, Dn 7 (18, 27) may have been a source of inspiration or at least a parallel[8].

4.4.3.4

(D) As previously stated under **(B)**, there seems to be *two* distinct phases of after-life for the righteous: (1) the immediate *post mortem* state ("in God's hand", "at peace") and (2) the state following the $\dot{\epsilon}\pi\iota\sigma\kappa\sigma\pi\hat{\eta}$ in v.7—cf. also $\dot{\epsilon}\nu\ \epsilon\pi\iota\sigma\kappa\sigma\pi\hat{\eta}\ \psi\upsilon\chi\omega\nu$ in v.13. The corresponding verb $\dot{\epsilon}\pi\iota\sigma\kappa\epsilon\pi\tau\sigma\mu\alpha\iota$ in LXX normally renders פקד (Gehman, VT 22, 197 ff.). Here $\dot{\epsilon}\pi\iota\sigma\kappa\sigma\pi\hat{\eta}$ clearly refers to God's "coming", as expected in Jewish eschatological and apocalyptic traditions about the End (Mal 3:1; Zch 14:3 f., 9; Dn 7:9; I En 1:3b-4, 9). This $\dot{\epsilon}\pi\iota\sigma\kappa\sigma\pi\hat{\eta}$ will render judgment and punishment to the wicked, salvation and glory to the righteous. In 4:15 it is used as a synonym of χαρις and ἐλεος. This "date" represents the end of human history or the present age and the last judgment, and so it corresponds to a usual date of the resurrection of the dead[9]. When this eschatology is combined with the description of the souls "in God's hand" immediately after death, the logical conclusion would be a theory about an intermediate state. However, the two types of eschatology are apparently only juxtaposed without very much reflection on the tension between them (cf. Larcher, 1969, 316 ff.). Therefore, it would not be correct to postulate the idea of an intermediate state here. We have no indications that such an idea was at all in the mind of the author.

4.4.4

In 3:10 the reflections of Pseudo-Solomon reconsider the wicked. In 3:11-46 the wicked and the righteous are compared, especially as to their having a progeny, in the following manner:

The godless and their progeny	*The childless righteous*
3:10-12	3:13-15 (a eunuch)
3:16-19 (children of adultery)	4:1-2 (remembrance of virtue is a kind of immortality)
4:3-6 (the flourishing mass of the progeny of the wicked will soon disappear).	

This theme is not merely an occasional choice. The progeny is the immortality in the old religion of Israel. A man's name was preserved by his children (2.1.1). But here immortality is in the "remembrance of virtue" (4:1) which is acknowledged both by God in the eternal[10] triumph (4:2b) and by men who follow the good man's example (4:2a)[11].

4.4.5

A new section is begun in *4:7*. A righteous man, who dies an early death, is described in a way which alludes to the assumption of Enoch in Gn 5:24[12]:

> But the righteous[13] man, even if he dies an untimely death, will be at rest ... There was once such a man who pleased God, and God accepted him and took him while still living from among sinful men ... His soul was pleasing to the Lord, who removed him early from a wicked world ... Even after his death the just man will shame the godless who are still alive.

(A) Rest awaits the righteous man after death (a parallel to "peace" in 3:3). It seems likely that Wi interprets the assumption of Enoch as his death. Conversely, the death of a righteous man is interpreted as an assumption. **(B)** Then the assumption would probably no longer be interpreted as corporeal: death would mean that the soul is received by God, whereas the body is of no interest. **(C)** This passage does not say anything about a glorification of the righteous after death except the vague allusion to the shame which the righteous man will bring to the godless. **(D)** Perhaps this will be realized at the ἐπισκοπη of 3:7[14]. This passage does not, however, seem to be aware of any perfection of the righteous' salvation other than that which occurs at death.

4.4.6

The book continues in 4:17 ff. with the description of the dreadful fate of the ungodly. They will be both scorned (v.18) and "dried up", they will perish (v.19) and "they shall be in torment". It seems as if Wi speaks about a resurrection unto judgment and some sort of continued existence after death for righteous and wicked. *5:1 ff.* confirms our suspicion that the author thought of the day of judgment in v.16, κατακρινει for here this situation is described in more detail:

> Then the righteous man shall take his stand, full of assurance, to confront those who oppressed him ... at the sight of him there will be terror and confusion, and they will be beside themselves to see him so unexpectedly safe home (ἐκ στησονται ἐπι τῳ παραδοξῳ της σωτηριας)   ... they will say among themselves: This is he whom once we held as a laughingstock[14b] To think that he is now counted one of the sons of God and his portion is among the saints[15].

(A) So the premature death of the righteous is not the end, as the wicked believed in their temporal life. The wicked will once more be confronted with the righteous. **(D)** The description of that scene looks very much like a judgment, perhaps the last judgment. At least a final decision on the fate of the righteous and their persecutors is implied. This will be the great surprise for the wicked: those who were considered displeasing to God will be glorified by Him. This should remind us of Is 53, probably an important source of Wi 5:1 ff.[16]. **(B)** The description of the righteous man, "standing", would seem to require a body. The wicked "see" him! But, of course, this language could not be forced to prove that the author of Wi believed in the resurrection of the body. Although the sight of the righteous man is essential for his identification and recognition by the former persecutors, the important function of this motif is certainly his vindication rather than the restoration of his body (cf. Nickelsburg, 1972, 68). **(C)** His glorification is expressed in very lofty terms: "among the sons of God", "his saints"—i.e. (at least originally) the angels[17]. A simple identification is perhaps avoided   by   the   use   of   the   expressions   "counted   among"   and "portion" (κληρος, cf. 2.3). **(D)** As already remarked this is a scene of judgment, and it naturally causes us to think in terms of the last judgment. There is, however, no definite statement in the context on the "date" of the scene (cf. Nickelsburg, 1972, 88 f.). The confrontation of the righteous with his oppressors after his death must logically imply either a final judgment of both the living and the dead[18] or the death of the oppressors. The question of the "date" of the righteous man's eschatological vindication before his persecutors is obviously not important to the author. Only the fact that there will be such a vindication is of any importance. These texts serve to proclaim the final victory of justice and the reward of the righteous after death.

4.4.7

In 5:6 ff. the wicked return to the description of their own life (vv.6-7) and its vanity (vv.8-14). It seems rather difficult to imagine how the wicked could profess their own total annihilation which was already accomplished. Thus the strong words should probably be interpreted hyperbolically rather than literally, as an expression of the emptiness of the wicked's lives, which is in contrast with the blessed, immortal life of the righteous in *v.15 f.*:

> The righteous live for ever and their reward is in the Lord, and the care of them with the Most High. Therefore shall they receive royal splendour, and the diadem of beauty from the Lord's hand; for with his right hand shall he cover them, and with his arm shall he shield them[19].

V.16 introduces a detailed description (vv.17-23) of the Lord arming himself for a final eschatological battle, which has many analogies in the Jewish literature[20]. **(A)** In v.15 f. the immortal life of the righteous is once again described. Their death is really no death at all, as has been stated in Wi 3:4. Their immortal life is, in fact, already begun in their being righteous. Their righteousness, is their immortality (1:15) and so the present tense (ζωσιν) involves more than life after death[21], but in the actual context life after death is probably in the foreground of the mind of the author (Lindblom, 1914, 70). **(C)** The nature of the immortal life is described as a close communion with God in terms similar to those in certain Psalms (16:5 ff.; 73:23-26). Of course, the images of glorification and exaltation into royal dignity, το βασιλειον της εὐπρεπειας και το διαδημα του καλλους ἐκ χειρος κυριου, "the cover" of God's "right hand" and "the shield" of "his arm", should not be understood literally. They are instead images of the divine glory and communion with God. Perhaps their share in the divine rule is also stated in this manner, as in 3:7 f. (cf. Heinisch, 1912; Fichter, 1938, *ad loc.*). As has already been noted, the present tense of ζην denotes that the immortal life of the righteous is begun in the temporal life and is not broken by physical death. The reward of the righteous is the communion with the Lord, which is probably meant to be one aspect of their righteousness. It cannot be destroyed by death. But the use of the future tense in v.16 indicates further future glorification, like the "visitation" according to 3:7. This is also indicated by the description of the eschatological battle in vv.17-23. Thus, this passage again confirms our impression that Wi contains clear references to the basic ideas of the Jewish apocalyptic traditions, but there is a striking vagueness about the "time-table".

4.4.8

Ch. 6 begins a new section, resuming the exhortation to the kings in 1:1. They are encouraged to receive wisdom, above all (6:9 f.). That leads to a sort of aretalogy[22] of wisdom[23] (6:12-21), in which it is stated (*6:18b-19*).

> To keep her laws is a warrant of immortality (ἀφθαρσια) and immortality brings a man near to God.

'Αφθαρσια corresponds to חיים in the Hebrew Bible—as a consequence of obedience to God's law. Σοφια and δικαιοσυνη (Wi 1:15) are really identical according to the argument of the book against "the wicked". **(A)** We may presuppose that ἀφθαρσια implies life after death, since a blessed life after death, the final reward of righteousness, is precisely the basis of the argument for the identification of righteousness and wisdom in the former part of the book. (C) Ἀφθαρσια "brings a man near to God". This corresponds to the previous statements on communion with God and the divine glorification of the blessed righteous (4.3.1 and 4.4.7).

4.4.9
After an introduction (6:22-25) Pseudo-Solomon speaks about his own reception of wisdom (7:1-8:16). And in this context he repeats the teaching of the preceding quotation (*8:17c*):

In kinship with wisdom lies immortality (ἀθανασια) [24].

While describing his search for wisdom as a search for a bride, Pseudo-Solomon says about himself (*8:19-21a*):

> As a child I was born to excellence, and a noble soul fell to my lot (ψυχης δε έ-λαχον ἀγαθης); or rather, I myself was noble, and I entered into an unblemished body (ἀγαθος ὢν ἠλθον εἰς σωμα ἀμιαντον) but I saw that there was no way to gain possession of her except by gift of God ...

This passage has been regarded as an indication of Platonism, of belief in the pre-existence of the soul[25]. Since such a belief would contradict the previously stated opinion (4.4.1) that immortality is not an inherent quality of the soul but rather a gift of God on account of righteousness, the passage should be mentioned in this investigation of the views on after-life in Wi. Most of the modern scholars, who comment on this passage, seem, however, to doubt that it does say anything about an individual, personal pre-existence of the soul[26]. What is of most importance is again the stress on the gift of God, which excludes the view that wisdom is an inherent quality of the soul to be awakened by true *gnosis*. The passage remains rather obscure, but since there are no real parallels in Wi, we should not reconstruct a doctrine about pre-existence on the basis of this passage alone. (A) Wisdom as immortality is a gift of God to those who are prepared to receive it.

4.4.10
Another passage which seems to closely approach the Platonic ideas about the immortality of the soul is *9:15*:

> A perishable body weighs down the soul and the earthy tabernacle[27] (γεωδες σκηνος) burdens the mind so full of thoughts.

Indeed, the terminology of Plato is quite apparent[28], and it is hard to deny the influence of his anthropology, though it was perhaps mediated through later Greek philosophers (Reese, 1970, 86 f.). Yet, according to the following verses, the solution to this problem of man lies in the grace of God, the gift of his wisdom and his "holy spirit", rather than in man's own developing the slumbering qualities of his soul (cf. also Porter, *In hon.* Harper, 228 f.). The manner in which Platonic anthropology is thus combined with the theology of the main stream of

Jewish tradition is remarkable. Anthropology seems to be of secondary interest, and therefore the antropologies vary. But the message about the insufficiency and weakness of man without God's gifts returns again and again.

4.4.11

After the midrashic exposition of certain chapters of Israel's history (Wi 10-12), a lengthy polemic is developed against idolatry (Wi 13-15). Addressing the one true God (15:1-2) the Sage professes in *15:3:*

> To know thee is perfect[29] righteousness, and to acknowledge thy power is the root of immortality ($\dot{\rho}\iota\zeta\alpha$ $\dot{\alpha}\vartheta\alpha\nu\alpha\sigma\iota\alpha\varsigma$).

Again we find the equation righteousness = immortality, or, at least, that righteousness is the way to immortality. Both are founded on the knowledge of the true God, which is contrasted with idolatry. **(A)** Immortality probably means life after death, as in the rest of the book. **(C)** Its nature is defined as righteousness and as knowledge of God and communion with God[30], i.e., as being ethical and spiritual. **(D)** Thus, the eternal, immortal life is already begun in the temporal life by the very act of knowing God[31].

4.4.12

The midrashic interpretation of the history of Israel is continued in Wi 16. The idolaters and enemies of Israel and their punishment is set in opposition to the chosen people and their chastisements. The manner of the Lord's treatment is seen in the account of the biting of the snakes in the desert, when the Israelites were healed by (*16:12b-14*)

> thy all-healing word, O. Lord. Thou hast the power of life and death, thou bringest a man down to the gates of death and up again. Man in his wickedness may kill, but he cannot bring back the breath of life ($\pi\nu\epsilon\upsilon\mu\alpha$) that has gone forth nor release a soul ($\psi\upsilon\chi\eta\nu$) that death has arrested.

Here $\psi\upsilon\chi\eta$ and $\pi\nu\epsilon\upsilon\mu\alpha$ are seemingly identical and they are both used in the full meaning of the old Hebrew נפש and נשמה i.e. the breath of life. The passage does not actually express anything more than the conviction of the Lord's power over death and life which is found in quite early strata of the Hebrew Bible[32]. **(A, B)** Thus, these verses do not prove that the Sage believed in the future eschatological resurrection of the dead, only that he accepted the possibility of miraculous resurrections like those connected with Elijah and Elishah[33].

4.4.13 Conclusions

(A) There is no doubt that Wi distinctly advocates life after death. **(B)** But it neither teaches the resurrection of the body nor any other kind of resurrection. Neither does it directly exclude the idea. It is completely silent on that point. On the other hand, it states that immortality will be given to the souls of the righteous after death. We might even say that immortality is the immediate consequence of righteousness. Thus, the death of the righteous is no real death at all. Their *souls* are preserved "in God's hand", "in peace". (C) After death the righteous will be glorified and transformed into the glory of angels, enjoying a life in close fellowship with God and sharing his rule. (D) There will be a future eschatological confrontation of the righteous with their oppressors and persecutors. This will occur after the death of the righteous, but we are not told whether the persecutors are living or dead. In spite of the vagueness of these expressions they show us that the Greek diaspora writer of Wi is working with traditional Jewish apocalyptic ideas about a final universal judgment.

¹Cf. e.g. R. Schütz (1935) 7 f.; J. Fichtner (1938) 8; Pfeiffer (1949) 327 f.; L. H. Brockington (1961) 67-70; Eissfeldt (1964) 744; Russell (1967) 271; J. M. Reese (1970) 117-121. An exception is E. Zimmermann, JQR 57 (1966) 1-27, 101-138.

²Larcher (1969) 281, compares the statement of Wi 1:15 with Plato's fundamental idea about a relation between δικαιοσυνη and the true good of the soul—see e.g. Republic X, 608C-614A—but with a very important distinction: in Wi the immortality does not belong to the nature of the soul. It is instead a gift of God's grace.

³Cf. Larcher (1969) 241; Reese (1970) 62, 64 f.

⁴Cf. W. Weber, ZWissTh 53 (1911) 322-345; 54 (1912) 205-239, especially 211 (he presents the rather extreme interpretation that Wi was written in order to propagate the belief in the resurrection of the dead); Schütz (1935) 187-195; H. Bückers (1938) 26 f., 34-38; Schilling (1961) 98-101 (possibly); A. Hulsbosch, WKTN, Jb 1955, 145; R. J. Taylor, EThL 42 (1966) 124, 135, 137; Aalen, NTS 13, 12 f.

⁵For this term, see Larcher (1969) 316 ff.; H. S. Gehman, VT 22 (1972) 197-207—on Wi 206 f.; supra 3.4.1 (PsSol 3:11); 3.5.1 (1QS IV, 6b and 11b); 3.5.1.4, n.12.

⁶ Ελπις αθανασιας πληρης, indicating that this hope is not fulfilled immediately after death—or rather referring to the situation of the righteous, when they are being "punished in the sight of men", i.e. before death? The latter alternative may actually be more likely.

⁷Cf. e.g. Weber, ZWissTh 54, 211; J. Fichtner, ZNW 36 (1937) 125; Bückers (1938) 36 f.; A. Dupont-Sommer, REG 62 (1949) 80-86; Nickelsburg (1972) 60 n, and the following comm. ad loc.: J. A. F. Gregg (1909); P. Heinisch (1912); J. Reider (1957).

⁸Cf. also I En 1:4, 9 (the "saints" are probably angels rather than men, however); 24:29, and for OT statements about Israel's final exaltation above all the nations of the world e.g. Is 2:2-4; Mi 4:1-3; Is 54:3; 60. Cf. also the following NT passages: I Cor 6:2; Mt 19:28; Lk 22:30; Rev 20:4.

⁹See e.g. Dn 12:2; I En 51:1; 61:5; 92:2-4; TestSim 6:7; Jud 25:1; Zeb 10:2; Benj 10:6; PsSol 3:10-12; 15:12 f.; LAB 3:10; IV Ezr 7:16-28, 113 f.; II Bar 48-51.

¹⁰For the choice of this translation instead of NEB's "through all time" (which shows that "immortality" was interpreted by the NEB scholars rhetorically instead of referring to "eternal life"), see e.g. Heinisch (1912); A. T. S. Goodrick (1913); Fichtner (1938) ad loc.—4:2 tells us that God recognizes virtue by the reward of eternal life, given immediately after death, where a triumphant αιων awaits the righteous.

¹¹The structure of the transition from v.1 to v.2 is chiastic—cf. Schwyzer II, 702, for this rhetorical figure.

¹²Cf. e.g. Goodrick, Heinisch, Fichtner ad loc.; Nickelsburg (1972) 88 and n.

¹³This translation of δικαιος is preferred to the "good" of NEB.

¹⁴For the possible alternatives of interpretation, see e.g. Goodrick (1913) ad loc. He thinks of the Last Judgment, making references to Mt 12:41 and 19:28.

¹⁴ET of the New American Bible (1970) for the preceding sentence.

[15]"And his portion is among the saints", the rendering of Goodrick (1913) is more literal in relation to the Gr. καὶ ἐν ἁγίοις ὁ κλῆρος αὐτοῦ ἐστιν than the NEB: "and assigned a place of his own among God's own people". NEB's rendering of ἅγιοι seems very dubious to me, since they could be the angels in v.5a (cf. "sons of God", I En 1:4, 9 and O. Procksch, TWNT I, 111).

[16]Cf. Nickelsburg (1972) 58-66 and see also Heinisch (1912), Goodrick (1913) and Fichtner (1938) *ad loc.* Nickelsburg thinks that the form of Wi 2 + 4-5 can be defined as a "wisdom tale", which has been complemented by inspiration from Is 53. Wi 2 + 4-5 actually preserves a fuller form of this tradition, also found in Dn 12:3 (*ibid.* 68-70 and cf. also 71-92).

[17]See Gn 6:2; Ps 89:5-7; Job 1:6; 2:1; 38:7; Lk 20:36, and cf. Procksch, TWNT I, 111; G. Fohrer, TWNT VIII (1969) 348 f.; E. Schweizer, *ibid.* 356, further Fichtner (1938) *ad loc.* and *infra* 7.2.1.4-6, finally H. Riesenfeld, EuA 47 (1971) 508, for the relation between these expressions and Dn 7:27 as well as LXX Ps 88 (89):5-7.

[18]Cf. Heinisch (1912) and Goodrick (1913) *ad loc.*

[19]This translation is closer to Goodrick (1913) than to NEB, since a more literal translation is preferable for this analysis.

[20]Ez 38-39; Haggai 2:23 f.; Zch 12:2-9; Dn 11:40-12:1; I En 56:5-7; IV Ezr 13:27-35; OrSib III, 663 ff.; 101 ff. etc. Cf. Hartman (1966) 77-101.

[21]Cf. Nickelsburg (1972) 88 f., and also Heinisch (1912) *ad loc.,* (though he reads too much scholastic theology into the text); Lindblom (1914) 69-71; Bückers (1938) 18.

[22]Concerning this form, see, e.g. E. Norden (1913) 177 ff.; A. J. Festugiere, HTR 42 (1949) 209-234.

[23]For wisdom aretalogy in Wi, see e.g. W. L. Knox (1944) 38; Reese (1970) 43 f.

[24]8:13 is another example: ἔξω δι' αὐτὴν ἀθανασίαν
καὶ μνήμην αἰώνιον τοῖς μετ' ἐμέ ἀπολείψω.

The parallelism might suggest, however, that immortality is here synonymous with the good name, remembrance. Cf. Bückers (1938) 16, also for v.17.

[25]E.g. Lindblom (1914) 67 f.; Nikolainen I (1944) 154 (referring also to 7:3, which could hardly be relevant here—cf. Beresford, 1971, 53).

[26]E.g. F. C. Porter,, *In hon.* W. R. Harper (1908) 219-224, 249-269; (he refers to Rabbinic views that the souls of men are in the keeping of God before being allotted by him a body, as the background to the statement of Wi 8:19 f.); Heinisch (1912) and Fichtner (1938) *ad loc.*; Grelot, RQ 1, 120 (the expressions used about the soul are only intended to describe the preeminence of the soul); Taylor, EThL 42, 87; Beresford (1971) 50-53. Cf. also R. Meyer (1937) 56 f, further the interpretation of Reese (1970) 80-86, going back to E. Gärtner (1912): the situation described is happening in life, when wisdom first comes into the soul, "the perfect integration of human personality of the wise man, the fullest effective union of his body and soul" (85).

[27]The translation of Goodrick (1913) of this phrase, otherwise, NEB is followed. The paraphrase of NEB ("frame of clay") obscures the use of σκῆνος as a metaphor of the body, which is of interest in our context.

[28]Above all Phaedo 81C is quoted by e.g. Porter, *In hon.* Harper, 227; Heinisch (1912); Goodrick (1913); Fichtner (1938); Reider (1957) *ad loc.*

[29]Rendering ὁλόκληρος instead of NEB's "the whole of".

[30]For the relation and association between knowledge of God and communion with God in the general context of Biblical theology, cf. e.g. R. Bultmann, TWNT I, 701.

[31]Cf. on the interpretation of Wi 15:3 R. E. Murphy, CBQ 25 (1963) 88-93. Also e.g. Bückers (1938) 12 f.

[32]Cf. e.g. Bückers (1938) 37; Beresford (1971) 48 f., and *supra* 2.1.2.

[33]Cf. e.g. Heinisch (1912) *ad loc.* and *supra* 2.1.2.

4.5 Philo of Alexandria

The works of Philo, the Alexandrian Jewish philosopher and theologian[1], at least in volume by far excel the works by any other writer in the Hellenistic diaspora which are preserved to our days. So it is impossible to achieve an exhaustive analysis of his ideas about immortality within the framework of this investigation. We have to be content with a few typical passages.

4.5.1

Philo's thinking, above all his anthropology, is quite consistent in its basic structure[2]. One fundamental text is *Opif 135*, which describes the creation of man: Man is a composed being, consisting of earthly substance and of divine spirit. The body is made of dust ($\chi o \nu \varsigma$), whereas the soul is not made of anything created ($\dot{\alpha}\pi$' $o\dot{\nu}\delta\epsilon\nu o\varsigma$ $\gamma\epsilon\nu\eta\tau o\nu$ τo $\pi\alpha\rho\alpha\pi\alpha\nu$), but originates directly from the Father and Ruler of the Universe. He breathed into man.

Divine breath ($\pi\nu\epsilon\nu\mu\alpha$ $\vartheta\epsilon\iota o\nu$) that migrated hither from that blissful and happy existence for the benefit of our race, to the end that, even if it is mortal in respect of its visible part, it may in respect of the part that is invisible be rendered immortal. Hence it may with properiety be said that man is the borderland between mortal and immortal nature ($\vartheta\nu\eta\tau\eta\varsigma$ $\kappa\alpha\iota$ $\dot{\alpha}\vartheta\alpha\nu\alpha\tau o\nu$ $\varphi\nu\sigma\epsilon\omega\varsigma$ ... $\mu\epsilon\vartheta o\rho\iota o\nu$) partaking of each so far as is needful, and that he was created at once mortal and immortal, mortal in respect of the body, but in respect of the mind immortal (ET F. H. Colson—C.H. Whitaker, 1929).

(A, B) It is without a doubt that a doctrine on the immortality of the mind (here: $\delta\iota\alpha\nu o\iota\alpha$, otherwise: $\nu o\nu\varsigma$) is developed. The mind is "the soul of the soul" ($\psi\nu\chi\eta$ $\psi\nu\chi\eta\varsigma$)[3]. Sometimes he speaks only about "the soul" (Sacr 5; Gig 14, e.g.). The terms denote the centre of personality, the spiritual self. Now the important and striking difference between Philo and the other Jewish sources we studied, even the most Hellenized, as IV Mcc and Wi, is Philo's assertion that immortality is an inherent quality of the mind which is in the very nature of the human being as it was created.[4] Mortality is directly related to the body, immortality is related to the mind. **(C)** Immortality, infused by the Divinity, is an actual share of the Divinity[5]. **(D)** The consequence of such a way of thinking is that man is immortal in his temporal life, *before* physical death, in so far as his mind is dominating the mortal body. There are a number of examples of such a "realized eschatology" in Philo's writings, e.g., *SpecLeg I, 345:*

The knowledge ($\dot{\epsilon}\pi\iota\sigma\tau\eta\mu\eta$) of Him is true consummation of happiness. It is also agelong life. The law tells us that all who "cleave to God live", and herein it lays down a vital doctrine . . . For in very truth the godless are dead in soul, but those who have taken service in the ranks of the God who only I S are alive, and that life can never die ($o\dot{\iota}$ $\delta\epsilon$ $\tau\eta\nu$ $\pi\alpha\rho\alpha$ $\tau\omega$ $\dot{o}\nu\tau\iota$ $\vartheta\epsilon\omega$ $\tau\epsilon\tau\alpha\gamma\mu\epsilon\nu o\iota$ $\tau\alpha\xi\iota\nu$ $\dot{\alpha}\vartheta\alpha\nu\alpha\tau o\nu$ $\beta\iota o\nu$ $\zeta\omega\sigma\iota\nu$, ET Colson, 1937)[6]

Philo supports his equation of immortality and knowledge of God with a reference to Dt 4:4. The use of this passage also tells us what Philo means when he uses the terms "know", "knowledge", about the relation to God. They imply some kind of fellowship, some kind of communion on the personal level.[7] The Hebrew

Bible does supply us with a number of texts which represent similar ideas, or at least they can easily be interpreted in the same way as Philo and like-minded Jews of his time interpreted Dt 4:4[8].

Platonic influence may have contributed to the Philonic tendency of identifying righteousness with immortality[9]. Decisive in the thought of Philo, however, is the *personal* relation to God, whose essence is being and life. According to Philo, everyone who communicates with God shares His immortality, whereas, according to Plato, the more impersonal world of ideas is the source of endless life and happiness.[10]

4.5.2

In Philo's description the Therapeutae are those who already realize the immortal life of the soul, which comes to fulfilment after the death of the body (*Vita cont 13*):

> Then such is their longing for the immortal and blessed life that thinking their mortal life already ended (τετελευκεναι νομιζοντες ἠδη τον θνητον βιον) they abandon their property to their sons and daughters or to other kinsfolk . . .(ET Colson 1941).

The obvious implication of Philo's expression is that death is the gateway to the real immortal and blessed life, i.e., the death of the body. Yet death can be anticipated by man's freeing himself from earthly bonds. The more such a liberation is accomplished in the temporal life, the closer the temporal life comes to the ideal, bodyless immortal life[11].

On the other hand, death in its deep sense—its real darkness, Hades or Hell—is a present reality (before the death of the body) in the lives of those who are slaves of the evil desires and the passions of the flesh. We were told in the passage quoted from SpecLeg (I, 345) that "the godless are dead in soul". The interpretation of the Semitism θανατῳ ἀποθανειν found, e.g., in LA I, 107 f.,[12] conveys the same doctrine that the spiritual death already in the temporal life is the only real death of any importance. And according to *Congr 57,* the true Hades is

> not that mythical place of the impious in Hades. For the true Hades is the life of the bad, a life of damnation and blood-guiltiness, the victim of every curse (ET Colson—Whitaker, 1932).

4.5.2.1

(A) Actually, it is not so easy to decide if Philo is at all thinking of a continued existence of the wicked after the death of the body, or if he rather sees their death as a final annihilation. Some of his texts seem to speak about eternal torments and, consequently, a continued existence of the wicked after the death of the body, e.g., *Praem 60* as well as its context:

> Men think that death is the termination of punishment but in the divine court it is hardly the beginning[13].

On the other hand, he may speak about "the eternal death" (ὁ ἀιδιος θανατος), as in Posterit 39, and he expresses himself as if the death of the body denotes the total annihilation of the wicked.[14] Goodenough (HTR 39, 85 f.) tries to explain the surprising contradictory statements of Philo on this and other related questions from Philo's mystical experience. As a mystic, Philo is well aware of the fact that ordinary language cannot express the realities beyond the world of senses. The mystic, even consciously, employs paradoxical, contradictory assertions in order to communicate his transcendent experience to his hearers or readers. It is the "resultant" of the tensions that the mystic tries to convey. Without committing myself to defining Philo as a mystic (cf. e.g. the judgment of Feldman, 1963, 406), or to any far-reaching conclusions from such a definition, I think that this observation of Goodenough is quite important, as it regards statements on after-life in general in a culture which has reached some degree of philosophical or theological reflection. This includes both the Greek diaspora and the Palestinian Judaism of the period 200 BC-AD 100 (cf. *infra* 7.1.2-7.1.3).

4.5.3

Though Philo's anthropology leads to the conclusion that immortality is an inherent quality of the soul or mind as such (4.5.1), it is very clear—as stated in the preceding section—that immortality is a consequence of a virtuous life alone, in which the body is ruled by the soul or by reason. This is what Philo means when he refers to "philosophy", e.g., in *Opif 77:* By philosophy

> man, mortal though he be, is rendered immortal (καιτοι θνητος ὠν ἀνθρωπος ἀπαθανατιζεται), ET Colson—Whitaker, 1929).

A similar statement is found in *Gig. 14:*

> The souls of those who have given themselves to genuine philosophy . . . study to die to the life in the body, that a higher existence immortal and incorporeal in the presence of Him who is himself immortal and uncreated, may be their portion (μελετωσαι τον μετα σωματων ἀποθνῃσκειν βιον, ἱνα της ἀσωματου και ἀφθαρτου παρα τῳ ἀγενητῳ και ἀφθαρτῳ ζωης μεταλαχωσιν ET Colson—Whitaker, 1929).

4.5.4

There are several other passages which contain the same teaching[14]. It is clear that the body is identified with everything that is mortal and contrary to wisdom and virtue. **(B)** Within such a system of ideas, it is, therefore, obviously impossible to understand a resurrection of the body as anything other than a punishment. In spite of this, some authors have tried to defend the resurrection interpretation of one or two passages in Philo. One of them is *Exsecr 158*[15], in the context of the re-establishment of Israel after all the curses had been laid upon her:

> Then like a fond mother she will pity the sons and daughters whom she has lost, who in death and still more when in life were a grief to their parents. Young once more she will be fruitful and bear a blameless generation to redress the one that went before (ἐπ᾽ ἀνορθωμα της προτερας ET Colson, 1939; L. Cohn, 1906, reads ἐπανορθωμα τ.πρ.)

Then Is 54:1 is quoted, ὁπερ λογιον και ἐπι ψυχης ἀλληγορειται. It is remarkable to find this piece of genuine Jewish eschatology, describing the history of judgment and salvation of Israel, in Philo. It is possible that (ἐπ) ἀνορϑωμα did refer to the resurrection of the dead of Israel in the traditions which may have been used by Philo. But it is far more probable that he is only thinking of the fantastic fruitfulness of the Messianic days, which is described in some apocalyptic texts[16].

4.5.5

The patriarchs and heroes of faith in Israel are the great examples of immortalized wise men, above all Enoch[17], Abraham[18] and Moses[19]. It is obvious that the traditions about the assumptions of Enoch and Moses would easily lend themselves to such an interpretation. Their assumptions are described as the liberation of the soul from the fetters of the body and the transformation of the whole being of these men into immortal, spiritual nature[20].

4.5.6

(C) Though Philo does not conceive of any corporeal state after death, his idea that the soul is made out of the same matter as the stars and other heavenly bodies, i.e., ether[21], permits him to describe the wise and righteous men after death as being glorified and transformed into the likeness of stars and angels, which are more or less identical, e.g. in *Sacr 5:*

> When Abraham left this mortal life, "he is added to the people of God" (Gen. xxv. 8), in that he inherited incorruption and became equal to the angels, for angels—those unbodied and blessed souls—are the host and people of God (καρπουμενος ἀφϑαρσιαν, ισος ἀγγελοις γεγονως ἀγγελοι γαρ στρατος εἰσι ϑεου, ἀσωματοι και εὐδαιμονες ψυχαι, ET Colson and Whitaker, 1929).

This assimilation of the immortal or immortalized souls with the stars and the angels is found in several texts[22], and this recalls a Jewish apocalyptic tradition, of which we have seen several examples (cf. *infra* 7.2.1 ff. and further references there). A special Philonic version of this tradition is the re-interpretation of the stars/angels/souls as ideas or forms. This seems to have taken place, e.g., in *Gig. 61:*

> The men of God are priests and prophets who have refused to accept membership in the commonwealth of the world and to become citizens therein, but have risen (ὑπερκυψαντες) wholly above the sphere of sense-perception and have been translated (μετανεστησαν) into the world of the intelligible and dwell there registered as freemen of the commonwealth of Ideas, which are imperishable and incorporeal (ET Colson and Whitaker, 1929).

Such a re-interpretation of the immortality belief[23] really throws doubts on the personal character of *post-mortem* life in general in some strata of Philo's thinking; e.g. the analogy of music relates that music remains after the musician in its eternal patterns and structures (Det 75). However, the repeated exhortation to leave "oneself"[24], even for the mind to get out of "itself"[25], probably cannot be taken univocally and literally, but should rather be understood as metaphorical language of a mystic[26].

4.5.7

(D) In most passages touching the question of immortality, Philo regards death as the moment of change, the soul's liberation from the prison of the body[27]. On the other hand, the perspective of traditional Jewish eschatology, which includes an End time history and even the final glorification of Israel, is not completely abandoned (cf. 4.5.4 on Exsecr 158 in its context). But the hope of personal immortality is not connected with the expression of any national or universal collective eschatology[28].

4.5.8

In spite of these important and radical deviations from Jewish eschatology and anthropology, it is evident that Philo considers himself a faithful interpreter of the traditions of his people. As Legatio proves, he was accepted as such by, at least, the Alexandrian Jewish community. Nowhere do we find any polemics against the belief in the resurrection of the body. One does not even get the impression that Philo knew of such a belief[29]. It seems that his depreciation of the body is a matter of course. Yet it is rather impossible to imagine that he had not read II Mcc 7 or Dn 12:2 f. The relationship between the blessed souls and the stars in Philo's works indicates a possible acquaintance with Dn 12:3 or similar traditions[30]. Several statements of Legatio (117, 192 and 369) show the same spirituality of martyrdom as that shown in II Mcc (and IV Mcc). How conscious was Philo of his silently re-interpreting these traditions? Did he feel any opposition between the idea of the immortality of righteous souls and the belief in the resurrection of the body? Was a spiritualizing way of understanding the resurrection texts already so natural in Philo's environment that a clear distinction between resurrection and immortality was hardly possible to be established?

[1] He lived between circa 25 BC and AD 45-50—see e.g. E. R. Goodenough (1940) 2.

[2] For Philo's thought in general, cf. e.g. E. Bréhier (1907); H. Elmgren (1939); Goodenough (1940); H. A. Wolfson I-II (1962); L. Feldman (1963); Philon d'Alexandrie (1967); Früchtel (1968); S. Sandmel (1971).

[3] Opif 66; Heres 55. Cf. Hoffman (1966) 81; who quotes H. Schmidt (1933) 50 (and cf. 49-53).

[4] Though, according to Wi, too, man was created for immortality (2:23 f. and 4.4.3), but the original immortality is not especially related to the soul as it is in Philo.

[5] Det 90—cf. Hoffmann (1966) 82, who quotes Schmidt (1933) 52.

[6] Cf. also Gig 61; Mut 209, 213; and e.g., Elmgren, 1939, 150—however, Sacr 5 mentioned there does not seem clear to me: I think that it might refer to life after death as well, when it speaks about Abraham joining God's people, agreeing with Volz (1934) 268, against Hoffmann (1966) 83n, who also rightly states that Philo thinks of immortal life starting in the temporal life.

[7] Cf. Bultmann, TWNT I, 696 f., 700 f., 702 (but is the label "Gnostic" necessary?).

[8]Cf. Sanh 90b, R. Yochanan in the name of R. Shim'on b. Yehozadaq, and *infra* 5.4.1—and in general the Scripture quotations there, further 4.1 (LXX) and 5.8 (Tg). Cf. also Ps 63:4,9; 73:26; 91:14-16; Jr 22:16; 31:33-34; Ex 33:12-17.—For Philo's exegesis in general, cf. V. Nikiprowetzky, RHPR 53 (1973) 309-329.

[9]Cf. e.g. E. R. Goodenough, HTR 39 (1946) 107 f.

[10]Cf. e.g. Symposium 211D-212A; Phaedrus 247C-250C.

[11]Cf. Opif 77; 152; 165; La I, 105-108; II, 57; III, 41-44; Det 159; Gig 13-15;61; Heres 68-74; 85; 276; QGn I, 85; IV, 153.

[12]Cf. also Praem 70; Legatio 91; QGn I, 70, 75; IV, 46, 152 f.

[13]ET Colson 1939. Cf. also Exsecr 152; Cher 2; Somn I, 151 f.; II, 133—but the expressions are hardly clear and might be metaphorical. Cf. Elmgren (1939) 147-149.

[14]Det 141; Legatio 91.

[14bis] E.g. Opif 152; LA I, 108; II, 57; III, 44; Sacr 6 f.; 129; Det 75; 141; 159; Gig 61; Legatio 91; QGn I, 75; III, 11; IV, 46, 66, 152, 164; QEx I, 15. Cf. also J. G. Kahn, RHPR 53 (1973) 293-307.

[15]Quoted by Elmgren (1939) 173—though somewhat reservedly—as evidence for the statement that "Philo, among other eschatological future perspectives, reckoned upon the possibility that men would rise for new life" (ET from the Swedish text, by the present author). According to Elmgren, J. C. Schreiter, Philo's Ideen über Unsterblichkeit, Auferstehung und Vergeltung (1813) 132, also argues for Philo's belief in the resurrection, referring to Cher 114, rightly disapproved by Elmgren, 173 n.

[16]E.g. II Bar 29:5 (about the vine, not about women—cf. 3.10.2.2.4)—cf. also 73:7 (*supra ibid.*), also AbRN rec. B 43, 60B; CtR I, 14; Shab 30b; GnR 45:27—and here e.g. R. Mach (1957) 201-222.

[17]Posterit 43; Mut 38; QGn I, 86.

[18]Heres 276-282—cf. also Det 159, and QGn III, 11. For Isaac Sacr 6. For all the patriarchs, cf. Exsecr 166; QEx II, 114. See also Goodenough (1940) 186-193.

[19]Sacr 8; Virt 67 f.; 76; Mos II, 288; QGn I, 86. Cf. Goodenough (1940) 193-201.

[20]Posterit 43; Exsecr 166; Virt 67 f.; 76; Mos II, 288; QGn I, 86. Moses is deified—cf. Sacr 9—and addressed in prayer—Somn I, 164 f.

[21]Opif 146; LA III, 161; Det 90; Mut 223; Heres 240; 280-282. Cf. Goodenough, HTR 39, 89.

[22]Opif 139; 143 f.; Mos II, 108; Gig 6-11, 37; Cher 114; Somn I, 134 f.; QGn II, 8; QEx II, 114. Cf. Goodenough, HTR 39, 93 f.

[23]Cf. also Gig 31; Det 75-78; Mut 79 f.; QGn II, 8; QEx II, 114.

[24]LA III, 41-44; Heres 68 f.; 74; 85.

[25]LA III, 41, 43.

[26]Especially Heres 69; 74—and cf. e.g. Teresa of Jesus, Way of Perfection X (in Complete Works II, 1946, 43). For Philo as a mystic, cf. especially Goodenough (1940) 178-211.

[27]Cf. e.g. Migr 9: το παμμιαρον ... δεσμωτηριον, also Joseph 264; LA III, 42; Heres 68; 85.

[28]Cf. the following passages, which treat personal immortality: Opif 77; 113; LA II, 57; III, 42; Sacr 5; 8; 129; Det 45; Posterit 39; Gig 14; Plant 36-37; 44-45; Migr 37; Fuga 55; 58; 61; Joseph 264; SpecLeg I, 303; II, 262; Praem 110; AetMundi 46; Omnis probus 109; Vita cont 13; Legatio 91; 117-118; 192; 369; QGn I, 70, 75, 76, 85, 86; III, 27, 53-54; IV, 46, 66, 164, 169, 244; QEx I, 15; II, 38, 39, 114. And the following texts, where an eschatology of the nation or the world may be found: Praem 79-126; Exsecr 127-172 (and cf. Elmgren, 1939, 92-118); SpecLeg I, 208; Mos II, 263 (and cf. Elmgren, 1939, 164-175).

[29]Elmgren (1939) 172, says that "one may take it for granted" that Philo knew of the belief in the resurrection of the dead, though he concedes that we do not find any direct statement in Philo on the matter—cf. the following sentences in the text above.

[30]But cf. also the non-Jewish ideas of a similar kind, e.g. according to BJ VI, 46-48 (4.6.2.1). These may have influenced Philo's terminology and imagery as well.

4.6 Josephus

Though a Palestinian from the beginning[1], Josephus must be numbered among the representatives of the Greek-speaking diaspora. This is due not only to his geographical location in later years—in Rome[2], but above all to the fact that he is writing in Greek for a Hellenistic non-Jewish audience. So he is consciously expressing himself in a way that would be understood by his Gentile readers. This is very evident from references to Greek mythology[3] and comparisons with Hellenistic schools of philosophy[4]. When we consider his answers to our questions on a life after death, we have to presuppose that he inclines towards a Hellenizing interpretation of the Jewish beliefs about after-life which he may express[5].

4.6.1

In the discussions about the Qumran testimonies I quoted Josephus' descriptions of Essene eschatology (3.6.1). Although it is evident that Josephus greatly respects the members of this party, he declares himself to be a Pharisee (Vita 12). So one might expect to find his own beliefs expressed in the description of Pharisaic doctrine, as the short one of *BJ II, 163:*

> Every soul, they maintain, is imperishable ($\psi\upsilon\chi\eta\nu$ $\delta\epsilon$ $\pi\alpha\sigma\alpha\nu$ $\dot{\alpha}\varphi\vartheta\alpha\rho\tau\sigma\nu$), but the soul of the good alone passes into another body ($\mu\epsilon\tau\alpha\beta\alpha\iota\nu\epsilon\iota\nu$ $\delta\epsilon$ $\epsilon\dot{\iota}\varsigma$ $\dot{\epsilon}\tau\epsilon\rho\sigma\nu$ $\sigma\omega\mu\alpha$), while the souls of the wicked suffer eternal punishment (ET: Thackeray, 1926).

(A) Immortality, or rather the impossibility of non-existence, is described as an inherent quality of the human soul. **(B)** The decisive act of salvation for the righteous is the resurrection of the body, i.e., *another* body than the one that has died.[6] We are not told the manner in which the eternal punishments are administered to naked souls, though all the descriptions of the punishments *post mortem* are most concrete concerning the physical nature of such punishments. **(C)** Nothing is said about the nature of the new body. **(D)** Neither is anything said about the "date" of the resurrection.

4.6.2

The aspect of reward and punishment dominates the second text in the works of Josephus, which describes the Pharisaic eschatology, *Ant XVIII, 14:*

> They believe that souls have power to survive death ($\dot{\alpha}\vartheta\alpha\nu\alpha\tau\sigma\nu$ τ' $\dot{\iota}\sigma\chi\upsilon\nu$ $\tau\alpha\iota\varsigma$ $\psi\upsilon\chi\alpha\iota\varsigma$) and that there are rewards and punishments under the earth for those who have led lives of virtue or vice: eternal imprisonment is the lot of evil souls, while the good souls receive an easy passage to a new life ($\dot{\rho}\alpha\sigma\tau\omega\nu\eta\nu$ $\tau\sigma\upsilon$ $\dot{\alpha}\nu\alpha\beta\iota\sigma\upsilon\nu$), ET: L. H. Feldman, 1965).

(A) As in the former text, the Pharisees are said to believe that immortality (continued existence after death) is an inherent quality of the human soul. Thus, justice is finally distributed—"under the earth", a localization evidently inspired by the Greek tradition (cf. Feldman *ad loc.*). **(B)** Nothing is said about the fate of the body, but the term $\dot{\alpha}\nu\alpha\beta\iota\sigma\upsilon\nu$ alludes to the idea of a resurrection (II Mcc 7:9, Feldman *ad loc.*), as was clearly expressed in BJ II, 163. **(D)** The "date" of this resurrection is indefinite, but the word ῥαστώνη might intimate a certain distance in time between the moment of death and the entrance into new life. (C) Whereas the glorification of the righteous souls is not described, the punishment of the wicked is slightly suggested ("eternal imprisonment").

4.6.2.1

In the narrative about the death-bed of Herod the Great in BJ I, 647-664, Josephus tells the story about an attack against the golden eagle over the great gate of the temple. This is inspired by two Rabbis: Judas, son of Sepphoraeus, and Matthias, son of Margalus (648). These told their young students that,

> even if the action proved hazardous, it was a noble deed to die for the law of the fathers; for the souls of those who came to such an end attained immortality and an eternally abiding sense of felicity; it was only the ignoble, uninitiated in their philosophy, who clung in their ignorance to life and preferred death on a sick-bed to that of a hero (650; ET: Thackeray, 1926, for quotations from BJ).

When the students are arrested after the attack and brought before Herod, they are asked:

> And why so exultant, when you will shortly be put to death? They replied: Because after our death, we shall enjoy greater felicity (653).

We can rather safely presume that the Rabbis and their disciples were Pharisees. (A, B) They teach that the soul of a martyr "remains immortal" (τὴν ψυχὴν παραμενειν) (D) in the death of the body. (C) The *post mortem* state of the martyrs or heroes is described simply as ἀγαϑα. After-life distinctly means the reward of the heroes, who are prepared to sacrifice their lives for the laws or the nation. This is an especially important motif in BJ, and is also the general description of the Jewish attitudes in CApion 218 f. (4.6.5). In BJ it returns (with variations) both in Eleazar's speech on Masada (4.6.4) and, without relation to the Law of Moses, naturally, in Titus' exhortation to his soldiers before the decisive break-through into Jerusalem (VI, 46-58)[7]. Josephus' own effort to dissuade his followers at Jotapata from suicide (4.6.3) may be said to have presupposed the same basic conviction (cf. the protests of his comrades, III, 356-360), although it was modified by Josephus' speech (362-382). A common ideology of war, perhaps also expressed in a Hellenistic source to Titus' speech, forms the background of Josephus' thought[8] besides the Maccabaean martyr ideal.

4.6.3

The descriptions of Pharisaic doctrine may now be compared with those texts in which Josephus' own view on after-life is distinctly stated. His speech at Jotapata should be considered first of all (BJ III, 362-382).[9] Josephus' fundamental Pharisaic anthropology appears clearly in the introductory rhetorical question (362):

> Why set asunder such fond companions as soul and body?[10]

The difference between Josephus and Philo is obviously radical. But a little later Josephus approaches Philo and the Platonic tradition (372):

All of us, it is true, have mortal bodies, composed of perishable matter, but the soul lives for ever, immortal (ψυχη δ 'άθανατος άει): it is a portion of the Deity (θεου μοιρα) housed in our bodies.

(A) The "immortality" of the soul refers to good and evil alike. Those who commit suicide will not thereby escape the punishment, though their mortal bodies perish. Even the soul is in some way divine. This doctrine might be supported by Gn 2:7, which is about the spirit of God being breathed into Adam. But this divinity is morally neutral. **(B)** The body is simply said to die, whereas all souls live for ever. A little later this Platonic (cf. Michel-Bauernfeind, I, 1959, *ad loc.*) doctrine is further elaborated (374 f.):

> Know you not that they who depart this life in accordance with the law of nature and repay the loan which they received from God, when He who lent is pleased to reclaim it, win eternal renown (κλεος); that their houses and families are secure; that their souls, remaining spotless and obedient, are allotted the most holy place in heaven, whence in the revolution of the ages (έκ περιτροπης αίωνων), they return to find in chaste bodies a new habitation. But as for those who have laid mad hands upon themselves, the darker regions of the nether world receive their souls, and God, their father, visits upon their posterity the outrageous acts of the parents.

(A) After death the souls of both the righteous and the wicked are rewarded according to their deeds. (The only class of sinners mentioned are those who commit suicide—that is the crime against which the speech is directed.) The descendants, as well as they themselves, will be rewarded according to the Mosaic principle (Ex 20:5, e.g.). **(B)** It is only the soul which survives after death. Gn 2:7 (and Eccl 12:7?) may be one reason why the life or the soul is described as God's loan and death as his reclamation of the loan. In the end, however, the souls shall return to "chaste bodies". This is a resurrection, though no continuity between the earthly body and the new post-resurrection body is indicated. The "chaste bodies" given at the resurrection are "a new habitation" (corresponding to the Gr. verb άντενοικίζονται). Only the righteous participate in the resurrection or return to a body. **(C)** We are told that the souls of the righteous are glorified, being elevated to the highest possible position in heaven. But also their bodies are transformed (or exchanged), which could be vaguely indicated by the attribute "chaste" (άγνος). **(D)** The life of the soul continues after death. The resurrection will take place only at the "revolution of the ages".

4.6.4

Another speech in BJ, which treats both the immortality of the righteous and suicide, is quite contrary to Josephus' own speech at Jotapata. This speech, Eleazar's second speech at Masada, tries to *per*suade its hearers to commit suicide, or more precisely, to kill their own families and comrades (VII, 341 ff.)[11]. The title of Eleazar's speech, given by Josephus, is quite simply Περι ψυχης άθανασιας. [12] In the first part the thesis of the speech is "that life, not death, is man's misfortune" (343), the thesis is supported by the "Divine words of the fathers" and is confirmed by the examples of the ancestors. But it resembles Greek philosophy more than Hebrew traditions[13]. That is also true of the further argument for the thesis (*344*):

> For it is death which gives liberty to the soul and permits it to depart to its own pure abode, there to be free from all calamity; but so long as it is imprisoned in a mortal body and taunted with all its miseries, it is, in sober truth, dead, for association with what is mortal ill befits that which is divine.

At first, Eleazar's view of death and the relation between body and soul may seem similar to that of Philo (4.5.1), but there is this one important difference: The soul is divine and immortal, regardless of ethical qualifications. In any case, the statement on the immortality of the soul is formulated without any limitations and conditions. Death means immortality—without any respect to a moral judgment of the temporal life. Life in the body is death, without the further qualification given by Philo (4.5.2), i.e., life in vice, life dominated by the passions and desires of the body. Eleazar does concede, however, in the following sentences that "even while incarcerated in the body" the soul is a remarkable thing, which transcends "mortal nature", invisible, incorruptible, "of a nature one" (μιαν μεν αὐτη φυσιν ἐχουσα την ἀφθαρτον). It gives life to everything that it touches from its own abundant immortality (345, 347-348). "But", Eleazar asserts again (*346*),

> it is not until, freed from the weight that drags it down to earth and clings about it, the soul is restored to its proper sphere, that it enjoys a blessed energy and a power untramelled on every side, remaining, like God himself, invisible to human eyes.

Death is the return of the soul to its origin, a God-like existence, because death is liberation from the body. The final argument for preferring death to life is the comparison between death and sleep (349-350) in a way that resembles Socrates in the Apology[14]. The Jewish traditions, however, provide sufficient arguments for a readiness to die. Yet Eleazar also recalls the stories about "those Indians who profess the practice of philosophy" (*351-357*):[15]

> They . . . reluctantly endure the period of life, as some necessary service due to nature, but hasten to release their souls from their bodies; and though no calamity impels . . . from sheer longing for the immortal state . . . they commit their bodies to the fire, that so the soul may be parted from the body in the utmost purity . . .

If the Jews dare not choose death, they bring

> shameful reproach upon our country's laws, which are the envy of all mankind.

In the mouth of the zealous nationalist, Eleazar (if he ever said anything like this[16]), the last sentence would be a weighty argument. But Josephus himself, who formulates the speech[17], evidently shares the pride of his political enemy (BJ VII, 253-275), which is described as the heroic willingness of his people to choose death on account of her sacred laws[18]. Thus, he returns to this theme in CAp 218 f., again giving belief in life after death as a reason why Jews are so ready to die (*infra* 4.6.5).[19] But before this text is discussed, another passage, which in one way expresses the same basic attitude, may be cited:

4.6.4.1

Abraham's sacrifice of Isaac, his son, is described. This heroic act is somewhat comparable to those other deeds, referred to above, and especially the Masada Zealots' slaughter of their own families (BJ VII, 391-392). In Josephus' mind, of

144

course, Abraham's obedience to the divine will forms an absolute contrast with those wild rebels. In a total surrender to the hard command from heaven, Abraham, according to *Ant I, 231* (ET: Thackeray, 1930), asks that God

> amid prayers and sacrificial ceremonies would receive your soul and keep it near to Himself; and for me you shall be a protector and support of my old age—to which end above all I nurtured you—by giving me God instead of yourself.

(A) The hope expressed in these words is that the soul of Isaac will be received by God and brought into his presence after death. **(B)** Unlike Hbr 11:19 and Rm 4:17[20], no resurrection is mentioned in this description of the sacrifice of Isaac. Abraham's hope concerns only the soul of Isaac. **(C)** He asks that Isaac's soul be kept near to God. In some other Jewish texts concerning life after death this nearness to God is expressed in images as transformation into star-like glory, association with the angels, assumption, enthronement or exaltation (cf. 7.2.1-2 and 7.4.3). Abraham hopes and prays that Isaac, near to God, will protect him—but how? We might expect the answer: Through his intercession. But the answer given expresses a radical faith in God alone: "By giving me God instead of yourself." Such a radicalism must surprise the reader of Josephus, this man of world. He may, however, be drawing on an unknown source. **(D)** Obviously, Isaac is to protect Abraham in life, i.e., the soul will be received by God immediately after death.

4.6.5

In the apology for his people Josephus summarizes his narratives about deeds of heroism (*CAp 218 f.*):

> Each individual, relying on the witness of his own conscience and the lawgiver's prophecy, confirmed by the sure testimony of God, is firmly persuaded that to those who observe the laws and, if they must needs die for them, willingly meet death, God has granted a renewed existence and in the revolution of ages the gift of a better life (γενεσθαι τε παλιν και βιον ἀμεινω λαβειν ἐκ περιτροπης).

(A) All Jews believe in life after death, according to this description. No Sadducees are mentioned. Josephus may have thought that the nuances between the parties would not be of interest to his non-Jewish readers in this context. Above all, he is eager to present his people as being highly morally qualified. In this respect the motivation of future life after death is very important. **(B)** The expressions indicate a belief in a resurrection rather than a continued life after death. For παλιν γενεσθαι, we may refer to the eschatological term παλιγγενεσια, which is used for the resurrection and re-creation of the universe[21]. Josephus seems to have a certain preference for βιος in this context[22]. It has seldom been found in the texts of other authors about resurrected life. **(C)** This life will be "better" than the temporal one. **(D)** The "date" is denoted by περιτροπη, the revolution, namely of the ages (cf. BJ III, 374; *supra* 4.6.3). So Josephus gives a rather classical Jewish resurrection doctrine. The fact that he avoids the usual resurrection terminology may be due to his desire not to confront his readers with the most difficult parts of Jewish thinking, and, of course, also to his own assimilation of a popular Greek philosophy. Yet we cannot be sure that this was not the common way of expressing the belief in after-life in wider Jewish circles. We have found other examples of similar vague terminology for the resurrection or new life after death[23].

4.6.6 Summary

It is obvious that belief in a life after death is quite important for this Jewish historian. Its main importance is due to the desire for a final administration of justice, rewards and punishment. So it is characteristic of Josephus that he regards the soul as immortal by nature. This is true of both the righteous' and the wicked's soul. Eleazar's speech, which describes death as leading to a blessed immortality without exceptions, is probably not representative of Josephus' own thoughts, if we consider how contrary this would be to his own speech at Jotapata. Contrary to all the other texts, which might reflect Josephus' own ideas, Eleazar's speech does not contain any kind of reference to a resurrection, a *new* life after death, which is not a mere continued life of the soul, liberated from the bonds of the body. So Eleazar (who should be more Jewish than anyone else) is pictured as holding a very distinct dualistic view of man and a consistently "spiritual"—Platonic or "Greek"—belief in the immortality of the soul, whereas Josephus himself very cautiously but consistently alludes to some type of resurrection. The formulations are vague, but they indicate a new beginning of life after death which is combined with the change of the ages. Hardly anything is said, however, about the nature of resurrected life or the new life, which is given after death at the change of the ages.

---

[1]Cf. BJ I, 3; Vita 7-8, and e.g. H. St. J. Thackeray (1929) 6 f.; B. Schaller, DkP II (1967) 1440.

[2]Vita 422-423. Cf. Thackeray (1929) 15 f.; Schaller, DkP II, 1441.

[3]Cf. 3.6.1 for BJ II, 153-156, and Thackeray (1929) 124. Greek poetry is also well known to Josephus—cf. Thackeray (1929) 116-118.

[4]E.g. Ant XVIII, 11; Vita 12.

[5]See 3.6.1 about his image of the Essenes and, in general, e.g. W. Schmid (1920) II:1, 600, about Josephus' tendency to try to please Greek readers. Also v.d. Ploeg, BO 18, 121.

[6]This is the only text which contains the idea of "another body", although it is implied in the question of II Bar 49:3 (3.10.2)—but also explicitly denied by the answer in 50:2-3. Is the idea of a total discontinuity between the two bodies maybe a concession to the non-Jewish readers and their possibilities of understanding the concept of resurrection?—Cf., on the other hand, Bruce, ScJTh 24, 458 f., who observes the possibility that a non-Jewish reader might misunderstand this as a sentence on the re-incarnation.

[7]In Thackeray's translation (1926):

I refrain on this occasion from an encomium on the warrior's death and the immortality reserved for those who fall in the frenzy of battle, but for any who think otherwise the worst I could wish is that they may die in peace of disease, soul and body alike condemned to the tomb. For what brave man knows not that souls released from the flesh by the sword on the battlefield are hospitably welcomed by that purest of elements, the ether, and placed among the stars, and that as good genii ($\delta\alpha\mu\rho\nu\epsilon\varsigma$) and benignant heroes they manifest their presence to their posterity; while souls which pine away in bodies wasted by disease, however pure they may be from stain or pollution, are obliterated in subterranean night and pass into profound oblivion, their life, their bodies, aye and their memory, brought simultaneously to a close?

There is a certain similarity between this Roman soldier's spirituality (according to the Jewish historian) and old Nordic ideas about the reception of fallen warriors in Valhalla and the same of death in a disease (*sot*)—cf. e.g. H. Ringgren-Å. V. Ström (1967) 100; H. R. E. Davidson, HistRel I (1969) 624. The astral glorification is well known from Jewish eschatology, as we have seen (for references see *infra* 7.2.1-7.2.1.2). The deification in the ether reminds us of PsPhoc 104 and 108—cf. *infra* 4.8.1.

⁸Cf. O. Michel-O. Bauernfeind II:2 (1969) 162.

⁹Cf. H. Lindner (1972) 39 n.3, and for suicide as an act of heroism among Jewish nationalists and non-conformists, cf. e.g. Razis' case, *supra* 4.2.1.3, beside the Masada incident—*infra* 4.6.4, further Michel-Bauernfeind I (1959) *ad loc.*

¹⁰Gr: ἤ τι τα φίλτατα διαστασιάζομεν, σῶμα καὶ ψυχήν; A similar phrase is found in Plato, Leg IX, 873. Cf. Michel-Bauernfeind I (1959) *ad loc.*

¹¹Josephus' final suggestion in Jotapata, BJ III, 387-389.—Cf. Michel-Bauernfeind, II:2 (1969) 276-278; Lindner (1972) 39 n.3.

¹²Like a Hellenistic tractate—cf. Michel-Bauernfeind II:2 (1969) *ad* VII, 341. Lindner (1972) 35-40, thinks that a Hellenistic tractate on this theme may partly, at least, have been Josephus' source. Cf. also W. Morel, RheinMus 75 (1926) 106-114, with references to Plato and Poseidonius. See also V. Nikiprowetzky, In hon. A. Dupont-Sommer (1971) 469-473.

¹³Cf. Thackeray (1926) *ad loc.*, and n.12.

¹⁴40 DE, though Socrates refers to dreamless sleep, Eleazar to sweet dreams.

¹⁵Cf. Morel, RheinMus 75, 111, comparing with Poseidonius and Megasthenes' Ἰνδικα.

¹⁶Very unlikely, according to e.g. Morel, RheinMus 75, 107. Cf. also Lindner (1972) 38, 40.

¹⁷Cf. e.g. C. Thoma, Kairos 11 (1969) 43, 51 f.; Lindner (1972) 36-40. For the historic background of the episode, see e.g. O. Bauernfeind-O. Michel, ZNW 58 (1967) 274. For the *genre*, speeches by historic figures in the classical and Hellenistic history works, which characterize the speaker without being speeches which were ever actually made, see e.g. W. Schmid II (1948) 161-177, 212; OxfClassDict (1970) 1068. For Josephus and Thucydides, see Thackeray (1929) 110-114, with reservations about the theory which says that Thucydidean assistants were at work in Josephus' works.

¹⁸Cf. e.g. Thackeray (1929) 22, and BJ II, 174, 196-198. Another concrete example is found in Philo, Legatio 117, 192-198. IV Mcc and Hbr 11:35-37 also testify to the fact that the heritage of the Maccabaean martyrs was very much alive among Josephus' Jewish contemporaries. Cf. also Frend (1965) 50-55.

¹⁹Was this, perhaps, a weak point in Josephus' conscience after Jotapata? Cf. 4.6.2.1, further BJ III, 356-382, for the accusations of his fellow soldiers and his defence, and e.g. R. Laqueur (1920) 254-260, 266-274; Thackeray (1929) 19 f., for Josephus as a traitor of the Jews in his own time and in the judgment of later generations.

²⁰Cf. e.g. Wood, NTS 14, 588 f.; Käsemann (1969) 159-162, 172; Hofius, NTS 18, 93-94, for the sacrifice of Isaac and the resurrection of the dead.

²¹Cf. Mt 19:28; F. Büchsel, TWNT I, 687 f., on παλιγγενεσια, further Ant XI, 66. Also Philo, Cher 114; Mos II, 65; Posterit 124 ff.; Legatio 325, and Elmgren (1939) 167-170.

²²Cf. Ant XVIII, 14 (*supra* 4.6.2); BJ III, 374 (4.6.3), and K. H. Rengstorf I (1973) s.v.

²³Cf. e.g. *supra* 3.1.1; 3.2.3.4-6; 3.2.4.4; 3.2.5; 3.3.4; 3.5.1 (1QH IV, 6b-8); 4.3.1; 4.4.7; 4.5.1; 4.6.2.

4.7 The Sibylline Oracles

Using the Greek[1], Oriental[2] and Roman[3] pagan figure of the Sibylla for Jewish and Christian missionary purposes is a long and complicated story. The collections of oracles, preserved in MSS, are Christian. Yet it is possible, to some extent, to decide which of them are originally Jewish traditions. Most modern scholars agree that at least Books III, IV and V are Jewish[4], though this does not mean, of course, that they are free of Christian interpolations and other changes in the text[5]. These books are the only ones which are of any concern in this investigation.

Book III, in its original version[6], was written circa 150 BC[7] or 42 BC (Nikiprowetzky, 1970, 195-225, esp. 217). Book IV seems to describe both the destruction of Jerusalem (lines 115-118, 125-127) and the eruption of Vesuvius AD 79 (130-134). Therefore, it cannot be earlier than the end of the first century AD. Book V presupposes the beginning, at least, of the reign of Hadrian, and consequently cannot be written very much earlier than AD 150[8]. The place of origin of the collections is probably Egypt[9].

Using the form of oracles in the sense of sayings about the future (according to the presupposed fiction) agrees with an apocalyptic content. So we should expect sayings about the Last Events, the resurrection and the judgment. But comparatively, there is not very much said about these events. More is said about the works of God within a history, which has already partly transpired for the author[10]. So there are not many passages which mention the resurrection of the dead. The most explicit text is *IV, 171-190:*

4.7.1

(171) But if with evil mind you obey me not, but delighting in ungodliness (172) you receive all these words with ill-affected ears, (173) then fire shall come upon the whole world, and a mighty sign (174) with sword and trumpet at the rising of the sun. (175) The whole world shall hear a rumbling and a mighty roar. (176) And he shall burn the whole earth, and consume the whole race of men, (177) and all the cities and rivers and the sea. (178) He shall burn everything out, and there shall be sooty dust. (179) But when at least everything shall have been reduced to dust and ashes (180) and God shall quench the giant fire, even as he kindled it, (181) then God himself shall fashion again the bones and ashes of men, (182) and shall raise up mortals once more as they were before   (ὀστέα δε και σποδιην αὐτος ϑεος ἐμπαλιν ἀνδρων μορφωσει, στησει δε βροτους παλιν ὡς παρος ἠσαν).   (183) And then the judgment shall come wherein God himself shall give sentence, (184) judging the world again. And all who have sinned with deeds of impiety (185) a heap of earth shall cover again   (τους δ᾽ αὐτε χυτη κατα γαια καλυψει),   (186) and murky Tartarus and the black recesses of hell   (γεεννης)·   (187) But all who are godly shall live again on earth[11] when God gives breath and life and grace to them, (188) the godly. And then all shall behold themselves[12] (189) beholding the lovely and pleasant sunlight, (190) Thrice blest the man who lives until that time.

This comparably full description of the Last Events is introduced with a threat against the wicked, but there does not seem to be any chance for the non-fulfilment of that threat, for the earth and all of mankind are destroyed by fire, **(A)** being followed by the resurrection. IV Ezr has a similar view (*v. supra* 3.9;

3.9.4.2; 3.9.4.2.1): everybody has to die and nobody reaches the eternal life without dying. **(B)** Faith in the resurrection is expressed very concretely, in terms which slightly resemble Ez 37:1-14 (4.1.6). **(C)** It is true that the Age to Come is an age of light and glory, but the light is that of the sun. The good men who are saved will live their blessed life "on earth" (187). Those who are raised will be "as they were before". Nothing is mentioned about a glorification into a heavenly state. **(D)** The resurrection takes place in the immediate context of judgment, which brings breath, life and grace to the righteous but condemns the wicked to Tartarus and Genenna. These terms are obviously synonymous here[13] and show that the ways of thinking within the two cultures are inter-assimilated.—Nothing is said about the soul or about any intermediate state.

So the image given by this document from the Greek diaspora, using a pagan "prophetess" as mouth-piece, is very typical of the Jewish apocalyptic. It also employs such details of the apocalyptic scenery as the eschatological trumpet, known from several other apocalyptic text (cf. *infra* 5.8.3 and further references there, in the treatment of Is 27:12 f.). The passage is quoted in the Apostolic Constitutions, however, and this is a rather important source in establishing the original text[14]. This reminds us that we cannot be absolutely certain that the quoted passage does not stem from a Christian pen or is not heavily overworked by Christian tradition.

4.7.2

In III, 705 ff. a description of the future glorification of Israel is given: the temple is in the centre and the "sons of God" shall live around it in peace, being protected with a wall of fire by the Lord himself (cf. V, 247-252 and n.11). A parallel is found somewhat further on in *III, 767-784*, which mentions the immortality of the righteous in the Holy Land:

(767 And then indeed he will raise up his kingdom for all ages (768), he who once gave a holy law (769) to godly men, to all of whom he promised to open out the land[15] (770) and the world, and the portals of the blessed, and all joys, (771) and everlasting sense ($\nu o \upsilon \nu$) and eternal gladness.

(A) Nikiprowetzky in his recent work on OrSib III (1970, 167-176) finds an expressed belief in immortality, but since the context describes a very earthly messianic or divine kingdom and only $\nu o \upsilon \varsigma$ is mentioned as living for ever, it is expressed somewhat ambiguously. He mentions the possibility that the one (or the circle) who formulated these verses thought of both an immortality of the righteous souls and a final resurrection. He also considers the alternative that the Kingdom itself would be eternal, whereas the righteous, living in the Kingdom, would live very long, but not for ever (*ibid.* 175 f.). **(D)** Here as elsewhere in OrSib the perspective is world history, not any eschatology of the individual. Immortality and/or the glorification of the Chosen People belong to the Age to Come after the destruction of the old world and the divine judgment (663-697, 741-743).

4.7.3 Summary

We may say that the eschatology of the collective, i.e. the universe or the people, totally dominated the message of OrSib concerning the last things, and we learn hardly anything about the ideas about personal life after death for the individual in the circles which produced OrSib. So we might say that this Alexandrian Jewish work (cf. n.9) is the extreme opposite of Philo. In the perspectives of future salvation history, the life of the individual seems to lose some of its importance, and thus faith in the resurrection is clearly expressed in only one passage. But then it is stated in a very literal form, further in the context of the Last Judgment. This passage is comparatively late (cf. *supra* 4.7 and n.8), more or less contemporary with LAB, IV Ezr and II Bar, where a similar development in eschatology is represented[16]. The vague allusions in OrSib to a more spiritual type of immortality do not tell us very much, and, furthermore, they belong to the context of a national eschatology[17]. That may be considered to be rather remarkable in a work, which in its form and style is so thoroughly Hellenized.

[1] Cf. e.g. J. Geffcken (1902) 1-30; A. Kurfess (1951) 5-14; Denis (1970) 111 f.; V. Nikiprowetzky (1970) 2-7.

[2] Cf. e.g. Denis (1970) 113 f.; Nikiprowetzky (1970) 8-36.

[3] Cf. e.g. Kurfess (1951) 14 f.; Denis (1970) 112; Nikiprowetzky (1970) 7 f.

[4] See Kurfess (1951) 307; B. Noack (1963) 445; Russell (1964) 54 f.; Denis (1970) 111, 118-120.

[5] Cf. e.g. Russell (1964) 55; Denis (1970) 118 f.

[6] Cf. e.g. Geffcken (1902) 4-16; Russell (1964) 55; Denis (1970) 120; Nikiprowetzky (1970) 60-70, 206, 217-225.

[7] Cf. Geffcken (1902) 4-16; Russell (1964) 55; Denis (1970) 120; J. J. Collins, diss. Harvard, according to HTR 65 (1972) 593 f.

[8] Cf. e.g. Russell (1964) 55; Denis (1970) 120 f., for these dates.

[9] Cf. e.g. Kurfess (1951) 307; B. Noack, SEÅ 31 (1966) 73 f.; Nikiprowetzky (1970) X; Denis (1970) 122, considering Asia Minor as an alternative for book IV.

[10] Cf. e.g. Kurfess (1951) 80; Noack, SEÅ 31, 67 f.; Denis (1970) 114 f.; Nikiprowetzky (1970) 86-88, 105-109.

[11] Gr. γαιαν, translated *Erde* by Kurfess (1951) and *jorden* by Noack (1963) *ad loc.* "Land", i.e. the land of Israel, might be an alternative worth consideration. Cf. the descriptions of the final salvation given to the Jews who live around Jerusalem, in III, 705 ff., 767-784; (*infra* 4.7.2), and V, 247-252. The latter passage does not belong to the period which is investigated here. Its eschatology is very national and earthly, although the Jews are described as a "godlike ϑειος and heavenly race". In V, 269-270 there may be a vague allusion to eternal life after death for the righteous, but the text is very uncertain and its meaning is quite unclear. CF. H. C. O. Lanchester, Charles AP II (1913) *ad loc.* (whose conjecture καλων instead of καλον is unconvincing; perhaps the phrase refers only in general terms to the new turn in the fate of the righteous in the Age to Come.) See also Kurfess (1951) who reads καταλλαξουσι and Noack (1963) *ad loc.* instead of καλον αρξουσι.

[12] Gr. τοτ᾽ εισοψονται εαυτους, Thus Lanchester (whose ET is followed) with the text of the Apostolic Constitutions V, 7:13—see e.g. Kurfess (1951); Noack (1963) *ad loc.* for the different readings.

[13] Does Tartarus/Gehenna denote some kind of miserable continued existence, or, rather, merely eternal death? There was probably no clear alternative for those who formulated this oracle. They may not have been able at all to conceive an absolutely extinguished existence.

[14]Cf. lines 179-190 with Apost.Const. V, 7:13, and Geffcken (1902); Kurfess (1951) and Noack (1963) *ad loc.*

[15]Lanchester renders γαια "earth", Kurfess *Erde* and Nikiprowetzky *terre*, but it would also be possible to think of the γαια as the land of Israel. Cf. n.11.

[16]Cf. 3.8-10 and Nickelsburg (1972) 140-141. I EnSim show a similar resurrection doctrine and may belong to the same period (3.2 and 3.2.4). Cf. the survey of Stemberger (1972) 119 f.

[17]Cf. III, 767 ff., *supra* 4.7.2.—As an Anti-Messiah Beliar is to raise the dead according to III, 66. This is merely a sign of his power.—Rome is condemned to "the nether region of Hades", according to V, 178, which seems to refer to the idea of the wicked being punished in a future existence after death—cf. however, also Is 14, about Babylon, a passage which does not tell us anything about life after death or even about individual punishment after death.—Cf. also P. Dalbert (1954) 118-123 on the eschatology of OrSib, emphasizing that future life will be lived on earth, according to OrSib.

4.8 Pseudo-Phocylides

This hexametric collection of "the counsels of God" (line 1), which are largely ethical maxims, belongs to a *genre* of Hellenistic Jewish pseudepigraphy similar to that of OrSib. As in OrSib the chosen pseudonym is not a name from the traditions of Israel. It is instead the name of an ancient Greek sage, which is used to propagate Jewish ethics[1]. The original Phocylides was a poet and author of proverbs from Miletus in the sixth century BC[2]. Our document skilfully mixes Jewish and Greek concepts in such a way that it is difficult to determine even whether he was himself a Jew, influenced by Greek philosophy or rather a Greek imbued with Jewish ideas[2]. According to modern scholars, however, he was more likely a Jew[4], who may have lived in the first or second century AD[5], perhaps in Egypt[6]. Christian interpolations, or even Christian authorship, have also been discussed as a possibility[7]. But there is no evident sign of Christian influence in these maxims[8].

4.8.1

In the context of an exhortation to fulfil the duties towards the dead in the right manner, we find an interesting eschatological and anthropological section in *99-115:*

> Cover the unburied dead with earth.
>
> (100) Do not dig up a tomb of the dead and what may not be seen (ἀθεατα cf. LS s.v.;
> do not show it to the sun, thus inciting the wrath of a demon.
> It is not a good thing to dissolve the human frame (ἁρμονιην cf. LS s.v.)
> The remains of the departed will soon (ταχα) [9], we hope, come from the earth to the light.
> Afterwards they become gods (θεοι τελεθονται) [10].
>
> (105) For souls remain unharmed in the dead.
> The spirit is namely God's loan (χρησις) [11] to mortals and his image.
> For we have a body of earth and afterwards we are dissolved into earth,
> and so we are dust. But the air above has received the spirit.
> Be not chary of[12] riches. Remember that you are mortal.
>
> (110) It is impossible to bring wealth and fortune to Hades.
> All who die are equal in death[13], but God rules the souls.
> The eternal dwelling-places are common and the father land of Hades,
> a place common to all, both poor people and kings.
> Not a long time do we men live, but a limited period (ἐπικαιρον) [14].
>
> (115) However, the soul is immortal and lives on unaging[15] for ever.

4.8.1.1

The paraenetic context determines the function of these eschatological and anthropological statements. This may be the explanation why this section seems to express at least *three* different views on life after death: **(A)** The old Hades-Sheol notion of totally dark equality between all dead (2.1.2) is found in 111-114; **(B)** A very literalistic doctrine of the resurrection is taught in 102-103, where the precept not to remove any part of the body is based on the future resurrection of the departed's remains. But, on the other hand, belief in the immortality of the soul as an inherent quality, distinguishing it from the body that will be dissolved without any resurrection seems to be maintained in 105-108 and 115. Finally, a simple ghost-notion, invoked to guarantee the peace of the tomb with the warning not to incite the wrath of a demon, is found in 101. These widely divergent views are merely juxtaposed without any efforts to harmonize them[16]. **(C)** Thus the literalistic doctrine of the resurrection in 102-103 is combined with the idea of a deifying transformation in 104.

4.8.1.2

The anthropology in PsPhoc 106-108 is clearly based on the teaching of Gn 1-3. Gn 2:7 relates that the *spirit* gives life from God to the body, which is earth itself[17]. The spirit is also the image (εἰκών) of God in man, as required by Gn 1:26[18]. Finally, the dissolution of the body into dust echoes Gn 3:19[19]. The contrast between the return of the body to the dust of the earth and the return of the spirit to "the air", as well as the term "loan" (χρῆσις), reminds us of the description of death in Eccl 12:7[20]. The prayer אלהי in Ber 60b (5.3.2) shows us another example of an anthropology dependent upon Gn 2:7. The literalistic resurrection doctrine, with the special reluctance against taking any limb from the body, also indicates that the author was Jewish[21].

4.8.1.3

The last remark brings us back into the paraenetic context of these sayings on death and life after death. Actually only one type of eschatology seems to have an independent function in the context, namely the immortality of the soul, for the ghost-notion is used as an argument for fulfilling the duty of burying the dead (99-102), the literalistic resurrection concept is invoked as the reason why corpses should be left as they are, and the old Hades idea functions in the warning against avarice. That leads me to the conclusion that immortality as an inherent quality of the soul is probably the view on after-life which dominates the mind of the author. We found the same phenomenon in Philo, who also based himself upon Gn 2:7, although Philo emphasizes the ethical conditions for immortality, which are not mentioned in this section of PsPhoc. Another difference between Philo and PsPhoc is that in PsPhoc the different after-life notions are combined without any effort to harmonize them.

4.8.1.4

(D) The resurrection of the body, according to 103-104, occurs in an eschatological future—"soon" (cf. n.9), and "afterwards" (ὀπίσω) followed by

152

the deifying transformation. Since the immortality of the soul is regarded as an inherent quality, she is not touched by death, but immediately upon death she returns to her rightful element, the air. No distinction is made between the righteous and the wicked. The idea of any kind of judgment or retribution after death is completely absent in this passage. Thus it forms a rare exception among Jewish texts (cf. 7.1.11 and the tabular survey of 7).

4.8.2 *Summary*

PsPhoc, an example of a thoroughly hellenized Judaism (or of Judaized Hellenism), manages to combine a literalistic resurrection language with a clear dichotomic anthropology, based upon Gn 1-3, which he interprets in a Hellenizing or, perhaps, a Stoicizing way, with the reference to the spirit's or soul's reception by the air[22]. In any case, the unharmonized juxtaposition of contradictory ideas about after-life obliges us to examine the context of each saying and its function in this context. I presume that the author emphasizes the type which is not functionalized by the paraenesis. On the other hand, in the author's mind, the paraenesis, which is able to use so many different and partially contradictory ideas about after-life, is likely to be more important than those ideas themselves[23].

[1]Other examples of the same *genre:* Pseudo-Heraclitus (cf. Denis, 1970, 220-222); Pseudo-Hecataeus (*ibid.* 263 n). For the *Sitz im Leben* of this type of literature cf. e.g. J. Bernays (1885) 250; P. Dalbert (1954) 9 ff.; K. Lincke (1903) 47-61; F. Dornseiff (1939) 37-51, tried to defend the authenticity. A. Dieterich (1913) 180 f., suggests a nucleus of authentic sayings of Phocylides, which was revised and developed in the course of tradition.

[2]Cf. e.g. K. Lincke, Philologus 70 (1911) 438; B. S. Easton, AnglThR 14 (1932) 222; E. Lohse, RGG V (1961) 362; M. S. Hurwitz, EncJud XIII (1971) 1335.

[3]Easton, AnglThR 14, 222. Dalbert (1954) 9-11, refrains from using PsPhoc, since the uncertainty about its authorship is so great. Cf. also Dieterich (1913) 180 f.; A. Farina (1962) 8-15. The latter alternative was preferred by M. Rossbroich (1910) 23, 102. (Denis, 1970, 218, does not give correct information on Rossbroick, whom he has not read—217 n.7.) Lincke (1903) 47-61, believes that the work represents the influence of Parsism in Asia Minor during the 6th century BC.

[4]In 1856 Bernays published a work, which contained this conclusion, cf. *id.* (1885) 192-254. A. Beltrami, RFIC 41 (1913) 513-548, after preparatory work, RFIC 36 (1908) 411-423, suggested an Essene author. (I have not been able to consult his *Studi pseudofocilidei,* Firenze 1913.) Cf. further A. Kurfess, ZNW 38 (1939) 171; Lohse, RGG V, 362; Denis (1970) 219; Hurwitz, EncJud XIII, 1335. Farina (1962) 8-15, however, believes that new sentences have been added by different authors through the centuries and so it is hardly possible to speak of one "author".

[5]Cf. Rossbroich (1910) 23-25, 103; Denis (1970) 219, with further references. Bernays (1885) 249-251, suggests a date between 150 BC and AD 70.

[6]Cf. e.g. Bernays (1885) 251 (Alexandria); Dieterich (1913) 181 f.; Denis (1970) 219.

[7]Cf. e.g. Lohse, RGG V, 362; Denis (1970) 218.

[8]Cf. Rossbroich (1910) 102; Easton, AnglThR 14, 222.

[9]Cf. LS s.v.: There are two possible meanings of $\tau\alpha\chi\alpha$ registered here. The first, used in our translation, is found in Homer, in the Attic prose, in papyri, and also in the Tragedies, but not in LXX. The second meaning is "perhaps, probably", including everything from probability to possibility, used with the optative. The first meaning is more sensible with $\dot{\epsilon}\lambda\pi\dot{\iota}\zeta o\mu\epsilon\nu$.

[10]Cf. LS s.v. $\tau\epsilon\lambda\epsilon\vartheta\omega$. $\Theta\epsilon o\iota$ is an obvious difficulty for those who believe that the author was a Jew. So Bernays (1885) 205, emendates $\vartheta\epsilon o\iota$ to $\nu\epsilon o\iota$. But the change is hardly necessary—cf. e.g. IV Mcc 18:3 (4.3.8). See also Lincke (1903) 53; Rossbroich (1910) 68 f.; Farina (1962) ad loc. Probably, $\vartheta\epsilon o\varsigma$ has more the meaning of "divine", than of "god" in the polytheistic sense. Cf. 7.2.1.4-6.—Kurfess, ZNW 38, 171n, suggests a deletion of the line 104, which is missing in certain MSS and which disturbs the connection between 103 and 105.

[11]For this meaning of $\chi\rho\eta\sigma\iota\varsigma$, cf. LS s.v. Cf. $\chi\rho\epsilon o\varsigma$ in Wi 15:8 and Josephus BJ III, 374 (4.6.3 supra). Cf. also Bernays, 1885, 203 f.; Rossbroich (1910) 70.

[12] $\Phi\epsilon\iota\delta o\mu\alpha\iota$ with gen.—cf. LS s.v. and Rossbroich (1910) 71; Easton, AnglThR 14, 225 ad loc.

[13]Gr. $\pi\alpha\nu\tau\epsilon\varsigma$ $\iota\sigma o\nu$ $\nu\epsilon\kappa\upsilon\epsilon\varsigma$. With my paraphrase I try to render the adverbial $\iota\sigma o\nu$, as defining $\nu\epsilon\kappa\upsilon\epsilon\varsigma$ —cf. Easton's version, AnglThR 14, 225, ad loc. For a Cynical background of the sentence see Rossbroich (1910) 72.

[14] $'E\pi\iota\kappa\alpha\iota\rho o\nu$ means "in due time", but here the meaning is defined by the contrast of $\pi o\lambda\upsilon\varsigma$ $\chi\rho o\nu o\varsigma$ —cf. Easton, AnglThR 14, 225, ad loc. Also Rossbroich (1910) 73, with parallels.

[15]This translation of $\dot{\alpha}\gamma\eta\rho\omega\varsigma$ $\zeta\eta$ $\delta\iota\alpha$ $\pi\alpha\nu\tau o\varsigma$ is inspired by the one of Easton, ibid. ad loc.

[16]Cf. Rossbroich (1910) 72: Stupidus diversas opiniones permiscuit neque animadvertit se paucis versibus antea contrarium dixisse—One solution, suggested by Dieterich (1913) 180-182, and Farina (1962) 13, is the hypothesis of a long development, during which many different elements were added to the core of the text.

[17]LXX uses $\pi\nu o\eta$ instead of $\pi\nu\epsilon\upsilon\mu\alpha$ as here and also in Philo, Opif 135—cf. 4.5.1. But $\pi\nu\epsilon\upsilon\mu\alpha$ is the only possible expression in the hexameter here, so this is not an argument against the connection with Gn 2:7.

[18]For the $\pi\nu\epsilon\upsilon\mu\alpha$ or $\nu o\upsilon\varsigma$ as the Divine $\epsilon\dot{\iota}\kappa\omega\nu$ in man cf. e.g. Philo, Heres 57; 231, and J. Jervell (1960) 28 f. (concerning PsPhoc) and 58-60 (concerning Philo). The reference to Gn 1:26 also conceded by Rossbroich (1910) 70, in spite of Gentile parallells.

[19]Rather than 3:20, to which Rossbroich (1970) 71, refers.

[20]On the relation between Eccl 12:7 and Gn 2:7, cf. e.g. R. E. Murphy, JeBiCo (1968) 540. God has "given" the spirit, who returns to him. Bernays (1885) 204 n.; Rossbroich (1910) 71, also give Eccl 12:7 as a parallel. Cf. also BJ III, 374—supra 4.6.3. None of these passages is listed in Beltrami, RFIC 36, 411-423, esp. 417 f., where a number of references and allusions to both O and NT are enumerated.

²¹Cf. Bernays (1885) 203: The reluctance in itself is not particularly Jewish, but the reason for the reluctance according to 103, the hope of the resurrection of the body, could not have been formulated by a Gentile.

²²Is ἀηρ ἀνα a synonym of αἰϑηρ, the matter of the soul according to Stoic doctrine (cf. e.g. M. P. Nilsson II, 1961, 263 ff.; S. Sambursky, 1965, 343-345), and is its reception by ἀηρ ἀνα an allusion to a kinship in nature between the soul and the ἀηρ ἀνα?

²³An alternative explanation of the juxtaposition of contradictory ideas in PsPhoc's eschatological section is, of course, the possibility that the work from a purely Greek (even Phocylidean?) core grew unto the present collection of γνωμαι by the addition of both Jewish and, later, Christian interpolations through the centuries. Cf. supra n.1 for Dieterich's position and n.4 for Farina's. It is obvious that in such a case PsPhoc would be much less interesting in our investigation. The position taken here, that PsPhoc is the work of a Jew, may be regarded as a working hypothesis.

4.9 Joseph and Asenath

This novel[1] about the marriage between Joseph, the son of Jacob, and Asenath, the daughter of Pentephres, a priest of Heliopolis-On, is now more generally regarded as a basically Jewish work[2], though, perhaps with Christian interpolations[3]. M. Philonenko believes that he can describe the author more closely: He is an Egyptian Jew, belonging to a group rather similar to, but not identical with the types of Essenes or Therapeutae, which Philo relates (cf. n.1 to 3.6), and he worked with an already existing Hebrew legend (1968, 102-109). According to Philonenko, the references to a sacred meal (8:5, 11; 15:4, 14-17:6) concern an initiation communion, which is strongly influenced by Hellenistic mystery rites, in that particular community which forms the *Sitz im Leben* of JA (1968, 93-98). C. Burchard (1965, 125-133) even finds Rabbinic parallels to the terminology in JA. Thus he believes that JA 8:5 and 15:4 do not refer to any other meal than the daily meal of a Jew, which is always blessed by the recitation of the *berakah*. So the allusions to "the bread of life and the cup of immortality" do not concern the Christian Eucharist, as the older authors thought[4]. Burchard (1965, 142 f.) and Philonenko (1968, 35-37, 55) both agree that Asenath is described as the ideal proselyte. Philonenko compares the role of Asenath with the Rabbinic Jewish traditions, in which she is Jewish: a descendant of Dinah, the daughter of Jacob. This is not at all mentioned in JA, where, on the contrary, her purely Gentile origin is stressed. So JA seems to be one example of the literary propaganda of Hellenistic Judaism[5]. Certainly JA was originally written in Greek[6], though, perhaps, the Greek novel was based on a Hebrew legend[7].

4.9.1
The following is a quotation of one of the passages which describe the above-mentioned meal, *15:3-4:*

Your name has been written in the book of life and shall not be blotted out for ever. But from this day you will be renewed (ἀνακαινισϑησῃ) and refashioned (ἀναπλασϑησῃ) and requickened (ἀναζωοποιηϑησῃ), and you will eat the bread of life (ἀρτον ζωης) and drink the cup of immortality (ποτηριον ἀϑανασιας) and be anointed with the unction of incorruption (χρισματι της ἀφϑαρσιας) [8].

The interpretation of this text is, of course, very much dependent on the question whether it contains a Christian interpolation, and if so, how far it can be extended[9] But when Asenath is promised that her name shall not be blotted out from the "book of life", this refers to an ancient Jewish and Israelite concept, which originally regarded the temporal life (Ex 32:32; Ps 69:29; 139:16), and was later used in connection with the resurrection (Dn 12:1 f.—see 2.2). **(A)** In the present context "the book of life" seems to be related to an eternal life that conquers death[10]. This eternal life is the gift given to the proselyte, according to the promise of the angel mystagogue (cf. n.8), which is emphasized and explicated by the following affirmation on a recreation of new life.

(B) The terminology used in the three verb forms implies a threefold repetition of the prefix ἀνα, again, which indicates the idea of a *re*surrection rather than a continued spiritual life after death. The last expression (ἀναζωοποιειν) uses ἀνα with a common term for the resurrection, corresponding to Hebrew pi'el of היה [11]. The two first compounds with are more unusual. Baptismal language in the Early Christian literature shows examples of the use of ἀνακαινιζειν, or related terms, which may have to do with the idea of baptism as an anticipation of the final resurrection and new creation[12]. The word "refashion" (ἀναπλασσειν) suggests a body, but the term was used in mystery cults for initiation, among other things (Philonenko, 1968, 94-98, 182 f. n.), so we must be aware of its possible metaphorical meaning.

(D) The angel tells Asenath that the new life is to start "from this day". Thus, resurrection is already realized by the entrance into the Jewish community, or, rather, "resurrection" and "new creation" are used as metaphors of the new life after the conversion. If this passage is not a Christian interpolation (cf. n.9), then it is an interesting example of a Hellenistic Jewish way of thinking, represented at least in the Greek-speaking diaspora perhaps before it was connected with the Christian sacraments[13]. In such a case it would be an important part of the background of early baptismal theology in the Greek-speaking Christian communities.

4.9.2

In the same context as 15:3-4, we find in *16:16 f.*[14] a strange description of the death and resurrection of a swarm of bees which has appeared in the honeycomb. This is actually the meal of initiation, which is prepared for Asenath by the angel in a miraculous way (16:1 ff.). The bees cover Asenath, but at the command of the angel they fall dead to the ground, leaving Asenath. Then, in v.17, a second command is given:

156

And the man said: Rise (ἀναστητε) and depart to your place. And they all rose (ἀνεστησαν) and departed to the court that adjoined the one belonging to Asenath.

(A, B) A resurrection from the dead is described as being followed, perhaps, by the gathering into Paradise. The term "place", which is singular, and is based on Hebrew מקום makes this allusion, according to a suggestion of Philonenko (1968, *ad loc.*). But whom do the bees symbolize? Philonenko refers to some parallels in his comm. *ad loc.*, but he does not answer this question. He thinks (187 n.) that the comparison between the manna and honey (Ex 16:31) was one gateway for the introduction of the bees. He suggests also that the bee-goddess Neith plays a certain role in the background of JA (cf. Philonenko, 1968, 66-79). A reasonable guess would be that the bees represent the people of God to whom Asenath had come.[15] The fate of the bees is, perhaps, one way of symbolizing the truth in the statement made by the angel about the communion with the honeycomb[16] in *16:8:*

> For this honey the bees of the paradise of delight have made, and the angels of God eat of it, and whosoever shall eat of it, shall not die for ever[17].

(D) Again, the eternal life is given to the communicant immediately at the communion. **(C)** As a result, a visible transformation takes place in the face of Asenath, the penitent and convert who is now received and initiated into the people of God, according to *18:7:*

> Her face was like the sun, and her eyes as the morningstar, when it rises (cf. *infra* 7.2.1.3).

4.9.3

When Dan and Gad, conspiring against Joseph and Asenath with the son of Pharaoh, attack the chariot of Asenath and Benjamin, Asenath prays, according to at least one part of the textual tradition of *27:8*[18]:

> Lord, my God, who quickened me (and delivered me) from death (ὁ ζωοποιησας με ἐκ του θανατου), you who said to me: Your soul shall live for ever, save me from these men.

(A) Philonenko (*ad loc.*) finds this to be a particularly clear reference to and affirmation of the doctrine of the immortality of the soul. But, of course, nothing is said about life *after* death. Rather it is the life given at the conversion which is promised not to be extinguished, apparently not even physically. It seems that, at least in this case, the promise is fulfilled literally, since the swords of the adversaries fall from their hands and are turned into ashes.

4.9.4

In her prayer of 27:8 Asenath appears to refer back to Joseph's prayer in *8:10 f.*:

> Lord, God of my father Israel, the Most High and the Mighty, who quickened (ζωοποιησας) all things and called them from the darkness to the light and from error to truth[19] and from death to life, may you yourself, O Lord, quicken (ζωοποιησον) and bless this virgin. And renew (ἀνακαινισον) with your holy spirit, and reform (ἀναπλασον) her with your hidden[20] arm, and quicken (ἀναζωοποιησον) her with your life that she may eat the bread of your life[21] and drink the cup of your blessing (ποτηριον εὐλογιας σου). Let her whom you chose[22] enter the rest[23] which you have prepared for your elect[24].

157

Philonenko (1968, 55, 158 n.) recognizes traces of a liturgy for the admission of proselytes, which, again, is very interesting as a possible background of Early Christian baptismal theology[25].

In the same way the parents of Asenath, on seeing her clad for the marriage feast with Joseph, praise God "who quickens the dead", according to the longer recension of 20:5. **(D)** In both cases we have examples of a resurrection which is realized by the initiation of the proselyte.

4.9.5 Summary

JA appears to represent a rather remarkable use of resurrection terminology as compared to the other documents of the Hellenistic-Jewish diaspora. The reception of a proselyte signifies her resurrection to new life, including a transformation and glorification which resembles the one expected for the righteous in the new world in more futuristic eschatological texts. Nothing is actually said about death, and so this resurrection is not a resurrection of the dead in the literal sense. The eternal life of the soul is mentioned once, in connection with the initiation into the chosen community, but the statement seems to imply a general promise of salvation *from* death, not *after* death. A special quickening and immortalizing function is attributed to some kind of communion (with a bread, a cup or a honey-comb) or unction in several passages. These might be, at least partially, Christian interpolations, but it is just as likely that they are originally Jewish. The comparison of this "realized eschatology" with that in the Qumran community (*supra* 3.5.4) is especially interesting in the context of a study of the background of Early Christian thinking about the sacraments.

[1]For this designation cf. e.g. M. Philonenko (1968) 1, 27, 43-48; Denis (1970) 40.

[2]Cf. e.g. C. Burchard (1965) 99-107, who goes as far as declaring (99): "Es gibt . . . in ihr keinen Satz, der nicht jüdisch sein könnte." Further also, basically, T. Holtz, NTS 14 (1967/8) 482-497, though with reservations against the position of Burchard and suggestions of Christian interpolations, and Philonenko (1968) 99-109, finally Denis (1970) 45 f.

[3]Cf. Holtz, NTS 14, 482-497, against Burchard (1965), who is joined by Philonenko (1968) 91.

[4]As e.g. E. W. Brooks (1918) xi, who thinks that JA in its present shape is the result of a Christian revision of an earlier Jewish production (xi-xv). P. Batiffol (1889-1890) 18-29, had a similar view. Holtz, NTS 14, 486-493, believes that the Jewish source before the Christian revision had some reference to a communal meal, which was then developed by the Christian reviser.

[5]Burchard (1965) 143-151; Philonenko (1968) 53-61; Denis (1970) 45.

[6]Burchard (1965) 91-99; Philonenko (1968) 27-32, 53-61; Denis (1970) 45.

[7]Philonenko (1968) 32; Denis (1970) 45.

[8]ET here and in general for quotations from JA: Brooks (1918), somewhat modernized in its English, compared with the Gr. texts of Burchard (1965) 122 (for the passages which mention the sacred meal) and Philonenko (1968). Cf. also *8:5:*

> . . . eats the blessed bread of life and drinks the blessed cup of immortality and is anointed with the blessed unction of incorruption . . .

This is said about Joseph, the pious Jew. Cf. also 8:11, quoted *infra* 4.9.4. The text of Batiffol (1889-90), followed by the translations of Brooks (1918) and Riessler (1928) gives a parallel formulation in a longer recension of *16:9 ff.* (according to the verse numbers used by Philonenko), which is also found in Burchard (1965) 122, as *64:14 f.:*

> Lo! you have eaten the bread of life, and you have drunk the cup of immortality, and you have been anointed with the unction of incorruption; lo! now to-day your flesh produces flowers of life from the fountain of the Most High, and your bones shall be made fat like the cedars of the paradise of delight of God and unwearying powers shall maintain you; accordingly your youth shall not see old age, nor shall your beauty fail for ever, but you will be as a walled mother-city of all.

The formulation that ends this quotation seems to be connected with a tendency in JA to make Asenath an image of Zion (cf. Burchard, 1965, 118 f.; Philonenko, 1968, *ad* 15:6, where Asenath receives the new name "City of Refuge"). And so it is quite difficult to decide, how far the statements above are directed to an individual type proselyte or concern Jerusalem. **(A, B)** As a saying about an individual it might be interpreted as stating the resurrection of the body **(C)** in a very physical way, **(D)** even without death intervening, but undoubtedly a more symbolical understanding should be applied here. The formulations might allude to Ps 92:13 ff. (for the unction cf. also v.11, and for the tree metaphor, see also Ps 1:3 etc.). As 15:4, this passage stresses the already realized immortality of the proselyte. The statements on the bread, the cup and the unction are identical with those in the two other passages. It is obvious that the textual uncertainty does not allow one to make far-reaching conclusions at all, based on this quotation.

[9]Cf. n.4, and, concerning this passage, e.g. Holtz, NTS 14, 486 n.1, for the interpolation theory, but also the opposite view represented by Burchard and Philonenko, described *supra* 4.9.

[10]Cf. Philonenko (1968) *ad loc.* with several references to texts using the term and concept of "the book of life": Is 4:3; I En 47:3; 104:1; 108:3; Job 30:22; 36:10; ApcSoph 4; Rev 3:5; 13:8; 17:8; 20:12, 15; 21:27, and cf. Bousset-Gressmann (1926) 258; H. Odeberg (1928) 63 n.; L. Koep (1952) 31-39.

[11]For the use of this verb, cf. the references in the note of Philonenko (1968) *ad loc.*: TestAbr A 18; OdSol 11:12. For ζωοποιειν / החיה pi'el), cf. Shemone esre II (5.3), further I Cor 15:22; Rm 8:11, and e.g. Kegel (1970) 18.

[12]Cf. Philonenko (1968) *ad loc.* for the use of the term in LXX. Another example is 1QH XI, 13 f. (3.5.4 *supra*). Cf. also A. v.Harnack, TU 42 (1918) 101-103.

[13]For the date of JA, cf. Burchard (1965) 1511 (before the end of the first century BC); Philonenko (1968) 108 f. (in the beginning of the second century AD); Denis (1970) 47 (contemporary with the NT writings, after 100 BC, before AD 100).

[14]In the ed. of Philonenko—cf. n.8 *supra*.

[15]Cf. n.8 for the identification between the people of God—or Zion—and Asenath.

[16]Cf. the Byz. longer reading in Lk 24:42.

[17]This agrees with the text of Philonenko. Batiffol's is much longer and seems full with secondary additions.

[18]Her prayer is omitted by the MSS B and D, cf. Philonenko (1968) *ad loc.*

[19] Και απο της πλανης εις την αληθειαν is omitted by BD, cf. Philonenko *ad loc.*—who has placed it within parenthesis.

[20] Τῃ κρυφαιᾳ with Philonenko's cj.

[21]From "and reform ... to ... your life" is omitted by BD. Cf. Philonenko (1968) *ad loc.*

[22] 'Εξελεξω must be the second person singular of aorist middle indicative, and not the first person, as the translation of Philonenko (1968) presupposes. Cf. also Brooks (1918) *ad loc.*

[23] Καταπαυσις, "rest", is connected with Ps 94(95):11 by Philonenko (1968) *ad loc.*, but it is also an important Gnostic term. Cf. e.g. EvTh 51; 60; Exc. ex Theod. 65:2, and B. Gärtner (1961) 265-267. On JA and Gnosis, cf. Philonenko (1968) 85-89.

[24]This is the text of Philonenko (1968). Batiffol's has a number of secondary additions.

[25]Cf. *supra* 4.9.1. The possibility of a Christian interpolation is also a factor to include—cf. Holtz, NTS 14.

4.10   The Testament of Job

D. Rahnenführer[1], M. Philonenko[2] and M. Delcor (Bibel und Qumran, 1968, 57 f.) have reached the consensus that this midrash on the book of Job[3] is of pre-Christian origin and that it was written in the Hellenistic Jewish diaspora. It is closely related to JA (Rahnenführer, ZNW 62, 92 f.) in that it has a similar background and approximately the same date, i.e. 40 BC (Delcor, Bibel und Qumran, 1968, 72 ff.), or some decades later[4]. Just as Asenath is presented as the ideal proselyte (4.9—cf. also 3.11.5 on Abraham), so might the same thing be said about Job in TestJob (Rahnenführer, ZNW 62, 88). Thus the book may have been employed for missionary purposes[5] like JA (4.9) and OrSib (4.7). References to the resurrection and heavenly exaltation of this ideal proselyte, Job, are well suited to such a *Sitz im Leben*, such as *4:9:*

4.10.1

You shall be raised ($\dot{\epsilon}\gamma\epsilon\rho\vartheta\eta\sigma\eta$) at the resurrection ($\dot{\alpha}\nu\alpha\sigma\tau\alpha\sigma\epsilon\iota$) [6].

This verse is placed in the context of Job's conversion from idolatry to faith in the one true God. An archangel gives the promise about his resurrection as a response to his decision to destroy the idol he had worshipped. Thus, the hope of future life outweighs the terrible trials that Job/Jobab[7] shall have to undergo and which are also predicted by "the archangel of God" in the preceding verses. **(A)** In 3:5 Job recognizes that the words of the voice, informing him about the true nature of the idol, "are for the salvation of my soul". Job may already refer to a *post-mortem* life of the soul, but this is not a necessary interpretation of his words. 4:9 is evidently a promise about resurrection after death. Perhaps these words of the archangel reveal something of the interepretation of Job 19:25-27, which was current in the milieu that produced TestJob[8]. **(B)** Resurrection terminology is used, **(C)** but the mode of resurrection is not developed. **(D)** The term $\dot{\alpha}\nu\alpha\sigma\tau\alpha\sigma\iota\varsigma$ obviously refers to a general, final resurrection in the future, since we find it in the definite form.

Another resurrection statement may be found in the words of Job's wife, who, when she sees the heavenly glory of her children, exclaims before her death (*40:4*).

Now I know that my memory remains with the Lord[9]. I shall then rise ($\dot{\alpha}\nu\alpha\sigma\tau\eta\sigma\sigma\mu\alpha\iota$) and I shall enter the city, and I will slumber a little. Then I shall receive the reward for my slavery.

Provided that this longer text is correct[10], the hope of **(A, B, D)** a future resurrection, following an intermediate state of unconsciousness, "slumber", would be expressed (cf. e.g. Philonenko, Sem 18, 19 f.). **(C)** We may guess that the city, which Job's wife will enter after her resurrection, is then the (either heavenly or earthly) eschatological Jerusalem. But the statement is quite isolated in the context, and so its precise meaning and consequences for the way in which resurrection is conceived cannot be defined.

4.10.2

(A) Another group of statements about after-life, Job's own and that of his children, **(B)** uses *assumption* terminology rather than resurrection language. One example is *39:12 f.,* where Job answers his friends, the kings, who want to find the bones of his children for him: His children will not be found

since they have been taken up $(\grave{\alpha}\nu\epsilon\lambda\eta\varphi\vartheta\eta\sigma\alpha\nu)$ into the heavens by the King, their Maker[11] . . . My children have been taken up $(\grave{\alpha}\nu\epsilon\lambda\eta\varphi\vartheta\eta)$ into heaven[12].

An assumption of their bodies is implied in that the statement is given as an explanation to the fact that the bones of Job's children have disappeared. **(C)** Their bodies have been taken up into "heaven"—an assumption into a transcendent state. **(D)** This followed immediately upon death.

(C) This assumption is, of course, accompanied by a divine glorification. Job's children are *(40:3)*:

crowned near $(\pi\alpha\rho\alpha)$ the glory of Him who is in heaven $(\grave{\epsilon}\pi o\upsilon\rho\alpha\nu\iota o\upsilon)$ [13].

(D) Since this is stated immediately before the above (4.10.1) quoted words of Job's wife, the assumption of Job's children is obviously realized directly at death. She will slumber and rise again—they are already crowned in heaven.

Job's own assumption **(D)** at the moment of death is described in *52:2 ff.*: The angels come to fetch his soul (v.2) and finally God himself arrives ("He who sits on the great chariot"—v.9) and kisses Job (*v.9*). Then,

he took the soul of Job and He soared upward $(\grave{\alpha}\nu\epsilon\pi\epsilon\tau\alpha\sigma\vartheta\eta)$ taking her by the arm and carrying her upon the chariot, and He went towards the East. His body, however, was brought to the grave . . .

(A) Job is brought to a new life at the moment of death in a way which reminds us of the assumption of Elijah in II Ki 2:11[14]. **(B)** But in the case of Job it is quite clear that the *body* is *not* taken up into heaven. The burial of the body is contrasted with the assumption of the soul. One reason for this might be that Job's resurrection had already been affirmed. Further the Biblical book of Job speaks explicitly about his death (42:17). **(C)** God's kiss intimates the close relation between Job and his Maker. According to 33:2-9 this will be perfected in the life to come, where Job is enthroned on the right hand of the Father in heaven.

4.10.2.1

(C) In *33:2-9,* i.e. in Job's first reply to the kings, his friends who visit him in his affliction, he makes a contrast between his own divine glory, which will be close to the Father in heaven, and the whole of the temporal order. **(B)** We are not told whether it is Job's body that is to share in this glorification or if it is only the soul.

Obviously, a "throne", in the normal sense of the word, requires a body, but to what extent is the terminology to be taken literally? In TestJob 52 the *soul* is carried upon a chariot, so an enthroned soul would be possible, too! But this kind of mixed language probably indicates a symbolical understanding of both "throne" and "chariot". The same would be true about the "strings" given to the daughters of Job, which, according to 47:3, are to bring them into a better world, the heavens[15].

4.10. *Summary*

We should especially notice the juxtaposition of different descriptions of death with what comes after death: resurrection in the eschatological future, assumption of the whole man (body and soul) at the moment of death, assumption of the soul, while the body is left in the grave[16]. No efforts to harmonize these notions have been made; the problem of their inter-relations does not seem to have been observed. Yet via the idea of an intermediate state, resurrection may be reconciled with an assumption of the soul without the body. But this could hardly apply to a corporeal assumption, if the resurrection is to occur in the eschatological future.

[1]Diss. Halle-Wittenberg, 1967, a typewritten manuscript, not available to the present author, but a summary by the author is found in ZNW 62 (1971) 68-93, where a possible publication in the series *Corpus Hellenisticum Novi Testamenti* is announced.

[2]Sem 18 (1968) 12 f., 21-23. He defends Gr. as the original language, basing himself upon the use of LXX in TestJob, but he concedes one exception, ch. 43, which appears to be a translation from Hebrew. The same argument for an original Gr. text is used by Rahnenführer, ZNW 62, 77. Gerleman I (1946) 62, describes TestJob as a paraphrase of a Hebrew original. Also Riessler (1928) 1333, speaks of a Hebrew original, whereas C. C. Torrey (1945) 142 f., and Pfeiffer (1949) 70, suggest Aramaic.

[3]For this designation cf. Philonenko, Sem 18, 13; Denis (1970) 100.

[4]Philonenko, Sem 18, 24: During the first century BC; Delcor, Bibel und Qumran 72: possibly later within the first century BC. Cf. Denis (1970) 103, for references to older works, which date TestJob at later dates, until AD 200.

[5]Rahnenführer, ZNW 62, 88. Cf. e. g. Dalbert (1954) 21-26, on the missionary spirit of Hellenistic Judaism in the diaspora. However, he does not include TestJob (*ibid.* 7) in his list of Jewish missionary literature, cf., however, also M. Hengel, Pseudepigrapha I (1972) 307, for a sceptical view of the concept "missionary literature".

[6]S. P. Brock's text (1967) is used. The MS V (13th century Gr. MS, preserved in the Vatican Library—see Brock, *ibid.* 3) here adds εἰς ζωὴν αἰώνιον, which might allude to Dn 12:2. This MS' is followed by A. Mai (1833), reproduced in the ed. and ET of K. Kohler, *In mem.* A. Kohut (1897) 264-338. But the longer reading is certainly due to a later gloss of a scribe, who probably did not understand the promise of resurrection as a promise of salvation in itself, since he apparently thought of resurrection both for salvation and for eternal damnation.

[7]TestJob identifies Job with an Edomite king, mentioned in Gn 36:33 f. and I Chr 1:44 f.

[8]Cf. Philonenko, Sem 18, 19-21, and *supra* 4.1.4.

[9]So far Kohler's ET, It follows *in mem.* Kohut 295) Cardinal Mai's text (and cod. V), which does not contain any allusion to the resurrection. In Kohler's ET it continues:

And after she had spoken this, and the evening came, she went to the city, back to the master whom she served as a slave, and lay herself down at the manger of the cattle and died there from exhaustion.

This text is really more clear than that of Brock, which I translate in the rest of 40:4. Especially the reference to the city is more easily understood, since the idea of the heavenly Jerusalem is not otherwise represented here.

[10]With the ed. of Brock (1967), supported by P, the oldest MS, 11th century, Paris; I am not very sure of this—cf. n.9—though one might argue that Brock's and P's text represents the *lectio difficilior*.

[11]This is my ET, based upon Brock's text. Mai's ed. says, in Kohler's ET:
They are in the keeping of $(\pi\epsilon\varphi\nu\lambda\alpha\gamma\mu\epsilon\nu\alpha\ \epsilon\dot{\iota}\sigma\iota\ \pi\alpha\rho\alpha)$ their Maker and King.
Did the scribe(s) behind this tradition want to avoid the bodily assumption of the children of Job, which is found in the tradition represented by P? Cf., however, the following note.

[12]Cod. V, followed by Mai, says: $\dot{\alpha}\nu\epsilon\lambda\eta\varphi\vartheta\eta\sigma\alpha\nu\ \kappa\alpha\iota\ \dot{\epsilon}\varphi\nu\lambda\alpha\chi\vartheta\eta\sigma\alpha\nu$ a combination of the two verbs used in v.12, one by P and the other by V. Thus, it is probably a secondary conflation.

[13]Mai's ed. with MSS SV employs the genitive of $\delta o\xi\alpha$ and adds with V $\beta\alpha\sigma\iota\lambda\epsilon\omega\varsigma$ after $\dot{\epsilon}\pi o\nu\rho\alpha\nu\iota o\nu$..

[14]For "chariot" LXX uses $\dot{\alpha}\rho\mu\alpha$ in IV (II) Ki 2:11 as TestJob 52:9.

[15]Cf. Philonenko, Sem 18, *ad loc.*, referring to the Iranian *kusti,* and G. Widengren (1965) 351-353.

[16]Volz (1934) 269, has not seen the difference between the two modes of assumption.

4.11 II Enoch

The Book of the Secrets of Enoch is commonly called II En or the Slavonic Book of Enoch, since it is preserved only in the Slavonic versions[1] which can be traced to an old Slavonic translation of Greek text from the tenth century.[2] It might be a Jewish Christian work of the early second century[3]. But the arguments employed for the Christian origin of the document[4] are not altogether convincing[5]. So it is very possible that the author was a non-Christian Jew, probably from Alexandria or some other place in the Greek-speaking diaspora. The date would then be circa AD 70[6]. Accepting this latter theory, I have had some doubts in my mind as to whether I should include II En among the works of the Greek-speaking diaspora, in light of its origin, or among the apocalyptic texts in ch. 3 (with e.g. Russell, 1964, 38, 61 f.), in regard to its contents. I give priority to the language criterium (cf. 3.0.4). Thus the fact that Jewish apocalyptic may be found in the Greek-speaking diaspora, as well as in Palestine, is emphasized. Even if the author was a Jewish Christian, his eschatological ideas and symbols would probably be so close to general Jewish apocalyptic thinking that they may be regarded as testimonies of Jewish beliefs in certain circles in or before the first century AD.

4.11.1

In ch. 8-10 the paradise of the righteous and the hell of the wicked are described. Paradise is a wonderful garden prepared for the righteous, who suffer offence in their lives and spite in their souls, and avert their eyes from injustice and make righteous judgment, to give bread to the hungering, to clothe the naked and cover them with a garment, to raise the fallen, and help the wronged, who walk before God's face and serve him alone; now for these is this place prepared for an eternal inheritance (Vaillant, 1952, 9 f. ET: N. Forbes—R. H. Charles, AP II, 1913, *B 9:1*).

The striking similarity between this passage and Mt 25:34 ff. does not necessarily lead to the conclusion that they are directly influenced upon each other (*vs.* Vaillant, 1952, 9, n.15). The inspiration of Is 58:6-14 is probably common to the two texts and gives sufficient explanation for the similarities[7].

(A) It is obvious that the distribution of rewards pertains to a *post mortem* situation (9:1; 10:4). (B) The nature of the joys of Paradise and the torments of Hell would seem to require bodies, but nothing is explicitly stated about that. (D) Both places are shown to Enoch, at his ascension, in the third heaven (including Hell—cf. also *supra* 3.2). Afterwards he reports to his sons what he has seen (1:10). Consequently, Paradise and Hell existed already in the days of Enoch, according to the fiction in the book. Probably this description implies that Paradise and Hell function immediately after death.

Again, in the context of Enoch's speech to his children, "the place of judgment", with the terrible guardians of Hell, and the Paradise of the righteous (apparently considered as pre-existent, cf. 49:2 and Mt 25:34) are described:

And I saw there a blessed place, and all blessed creatures, and all were living in joy and infinite happiness in eternal life (*42:13* B, ET in Charles AP II, 1913; cf. Vaillant, 1952, 44-45).

The macarisms which follow this description again seem to allude to Is 58:6 ff. (A) In Vaillant's translation though not in Forbes-Charles', one of them explicitly states the death of those blessed righteous (52:11) (D) They are promised eternal life after death (B) without any references to body or soul, neither to a day of judgment.

4.11.2
A rather unique idea is found in *II En 58:4-6:* Even the souls of the animals will be alive on the day of judgment and they will then accuse men, whose souls alone are to be judged. (D) The motif of the "great judgment" is found here, too. (B) Only the souls are vaguely mentioned.

4.11.3
II En 61:2-3 speaks of the many mansions prepared for men (cf. Jn 14:2)

in the great time . . . good for the good, and bad for the bad (Forbes-Charles, rec. A), and concludes: Blessed is he who departs into the sweet houses (Forbes-Charles, rec. B).

(D) The "great time" seems to be combined with the idea that the pious enter the "mansions" of the "great time" immediately after death. The "great time" is obviously the eschatological future. How can the mansions of this great time then be entered immediately after death, before the appearance of the "great time"? This question does not appear to be relevant at all to the author or redactor. It is the idea of a definite separation between the wicked and the righteous after death which seems to be his concern. The expressions and images of this idea may vary, as well as the "date" of realizing the separation, immediately after death or future day of judgment.

4.11.4

II En 65:8 (rec. B) has a more univocal end time perspective:

> And all the righteous shall be collected together in the great age . . . and they shall be eternal and incorruptible. And thenceforward there shall be no labour amongst them, nor sickness, nor humiliation, nor anxiety, nor need, nor night, nor darkness, but great, endless and indestructible light. And the great paradise will be their shelter and eternal dwelling-place . . .[8]

(B) The resurrection is not directly mentioned, but in view of the fact that the ingathering of the elect is so often combined with the resurrection (cf. *supra* 3.2. 1; 4.1.6 n.32; *infra* 5.8.3) and the clear statements on after-life in the rest of II En, we may rather safely assume that the author has some sort of revivification in his mind. **(C)** The "great age" denotes a radical transformation of this life, for the new, transformed mode of existence, "endless and indestructible light", is an important traditional symbol[9].

(C) The traditional imagery of transformation is again found in *66:7:*

> Blessed are the righteous who will escape the great judgment of the Lord, because their faces will shine like the sun[10].

4.11.5 *Summary*

II En expects a future life of the individual after death. This life is transformed to joy and supernatural light for the righteous, whereas the wicked are to suffer everlasting pain. There are neither any explicit statements on the resurrection of the body, nor on the survival of the soul after the death of the body.

---

[1]Cf. e.g. the ed. of A. Vaillant (1952) pp. III-VIII, XIII-XXVI; Denis (1970) 28 f.: the two versions are the shorter and the older Bulgarian, and the longer and the younger Russian.

[2]It may be even later. Cf. Vaillant (1952) VIII, XIII-XV; Denis (1970) 28.

[3]E. Schürer I (1901) 292; Vaillant (1952) VIII-XIII; J. Daniélou (1958) 25-27. N. Forbes-R. H. Charles, AP II (1913), 429; C. Bonwetsch (1922) 7; Eissfeldt (1964) 843-844, think of an Alexandrian Jew of the first century AD. Cf. Denis (1970) 28 f.

[4]E.g. by Vaillant (1952) X-XI: II En knows of forgiveness even for the Watchers (rec. A 18); benedictions precede the maledictions borrowed from I En (II En 52:1-14); in 42:6-16 rec. B there is a list of eight beatitudes like those of Mt 5:3-10; there are several allusions to NT passages in the style of II En (B 9:1—Mt 25:34; 61:2—Jn 14:9; 21:3—Mt 14:27); Melchizedek replaces Noah in the end of the book, not found in Charles, AP II, but ch. 23 in Vaillant's ed.

[5]The argument of forgiveness is wholly irrelevant, the rest of the allusions could be explained differently—cf. the works of Bonwetsch etc., quoted in n.3.

[6]Cf. Denis (1970) 28 f.; the works of Bonwetsch and others, cited in n.3.

Cf. the following synopsis:

II En	Is 58:6b-14
Prepared for the righteous,	
who suffer offence in their lives	those who have been crushed
and spite in their souls,	
and avert their eyes from injustice	to loose the fetters of injustice
and make righteous judgment	
to give bread to the hungering,	sharing your food with the hungry ...
to clothe the naked	clothing the naked ...
and cover them with a garment,	
to raise the fallen and help	and satisfy the needs of the wretched
the wronged,	the Lord will be your guide
who walk before God's face	continually ... you shall
and serve him alone;	find your joy in the Lord.
. . . . .	your father Jacob's patri-
this place prepared for an eternal inheritance.	mony shall be yours ... (ET NEB)

[8]The shorter version in ET of Forbes-Charles, AP II (1913)—cf. Vaillant (1952) 63.

[9]Cf. *supra* 2.2.3 (Dn 12:3); 3.2.3 (I En 92:4 and 104:2); 3.2.4 (I En 39:7; 51:4 and 58:3); 3.2.5 (I En 108:11-15); 3.4.1 (PsSol 3:12); 3.5.1 (1QS IV, 8); 3.5.5 (4Q Amram); 3.8.8 (LAB 19:4); 3.10.2 (II Bar 51:3, 10), and also *infra* 7.2.1.

[10]An allusion to Jg 5:31—cf. *infra* 7.2.1.3, with further references. Vaillant's translation is followed—p. 63. The passage is not found in Forbes-Charles' rec. B. Rec. A says:

> Blessed are the just who shall escape the great judgment, for they shall shine forth more than the sun sevenfold.

4.12 Jewish tombs—inscriptions and symbols

It has been asserted that "the hopes of beyond are to be read on almost all Jewish funerary inscriptions" (J. B. Frey, CIJ I, 1936, p. CXXXII). A closer look at the tombs of the Roman Jews, however, leads the same author to state in another context (Bibl 13, 153 f.) that the resurrection of the dead is not mentioned very often. He believes, however, that the very refusal to cremate the bodies of the Jews is evidence in itself (*ibid.*). Actually, it seems to me that the Jewish tombs do not say very much about after-life at all. Theories about burial customs and the use of certain symbols may be interesting, but without the support of literary sources they often appear to be mere speculations and loose combinations[1]. In this context I will concentrate on those tombs which may be dated before AD 100. Hebrew inscriptions in the diaspora, as well as Latin, will also be used here (cf. 3.0.9).

4.12.1

(A) A very large number of inscriptions use the phrase ἐν εἰρήνῃ ἡ κοίμησις αὐτοῦ (-ης, -ων) [2]. It may just as well refer to the undisturbed rest of the body in the tomb, which is stressed by some sharp formulations on a number of sepulchres[3].

It is also possible that any interpretation is an over-interpretation of this vague phrase, which may have been used very differently among various groups of Jews, both by such as believed in a life after death and by the sceptics (cf. the modern secularized use of similar phrases in a funeral context). The same is, of course, true of inscriptions where the phrase is reduced to ἐν εἰρήνῃ, [4], other formulations with εἰρήνη [5], or םולש [6]. We might suspect that the wish or prayer to "sleep with the righteous"[7] (or parallel designations, perhaps indicating above all the patriarchs—cf. *supra* 3.3.1 and 4.3.1, *infra* 7.2.3.1-4—and other OT figures) would express a little more of a hope of life after death. But we cannot be sure that such a phrase does say something more than OT formulations such as "sleep with the fathers" (I Ki 2:10; 11:21, 43; 14:31 etc.). If it would express some belief in life after death, unlike the OT phrase, **(B)** it would, of course, be impossible to tell whether a resurrection hope or ideas about a spiritualized immortality lie behind the formulation. This is also true of the exhortation to *pray* for the repose in peace (CIJ 126, 132, with the comm. of Frey *ad loc.*) or of the direct, but similarly vague, formulations of prayer for those placed in the tomb[8].

4.12.2

On the other hand, we cannot presuppose that the common phrase in sepulchral inscriptions θαρσει, οὐδεις ἀθανατος [9] tells us that the Jew buried there would have been a Sadducee or that he would have shared the hopelessness in front of death of those pagans from whom the expression was borrowed[10]. This inscription, found in Beth Shearim, close to the eastern entrance of the necropolis[11], is immediately combined with a clear expression of resurrection belief[12] of the kind we may expect to find at a burial place of the patriarchs of Jewish orthodoxy[13]. This combination disproves any suggestion that θαρσει, οὐδεις ἀθανατος tells us anything about a denial of after-life. It is also combined with the common phrase ἐν εἰρήνῃ ἡ κοιμησις (CIJ 401—cf. also 527).

4.12.3

Thus, a very narrow selection of inscriptions of this relevant period remain for a closer examination. One, a Greek text, can be dated on the very day of January 28, 5 BC, found in Leontopolis, Egypt (*CIJ 1510*). It concerns a young wife, Arsinoe, who died giving birth to a child. It is a long text, and I am content to quote the following sentence:

> This tomb conceals in its bosom my body, which was raised in purity (ἀγνοτραφες) but the soul went (ἐπετε = ἐπεται) to the saints (ὁσιους).

(A) It seems clear that a belief in after-life is expressed, **(B)** which presupposes the dichotomy between the body and the soul. The soul (of excelling beauty, according to the preceding lines) of the virtuous Arsinoe has been taken up to be among "the saints"—which might refer to the patriarchs (cf. 4.12.1 and n.7)—**(D)** at death.

Another Leontopolis inscription (*CIJ 1513*), on the tomb of a certain Rachelis, tells us that she was short-lived, but, as she says in the text:

I expect a good hope of mercy (ἐλεους ἐλπιδα ἀγαϑην).

(A) The one who wrote this line must have been mindful of some kind of after-life **(D)** which was to be realized some time after death. It was the future hope of Rachelis at her death. That might be an allusion to a resurrection to come (cf. also 3.14.2 and n.9).

4.12.4

The wooden "identity disk" of the Jewish mummy Sitorah, found in Middle Egypt[14], says in Hebrew:

Peace be on her place of rest (משכבה) her soul to life eternal (נשמתה לחיי עולם *CIJ* 1536).

4.12.5

A unique exception is the long Latin inscription on the tomb of *Regina* in Rome (the Monteverde catacomb) from the early second century AD. In spite of its late date we may quote it (Müller-Bees, 1919, 134; *CIJ 476*) as a contrast of the other quotations above:

Hic Regina sita est . . . rursum victura, reditura ad lumina rursum. Nam sperare potest ideo quod surgat in aevum promissum, quae, vera fides, dignisque piisque, quae meruit sedem venerandi ruris habere. Hoc tibi praestiterit pietas, hoc vita pudica, hoc et amor generis, hoc observantia legis, coniugii meritum, cujus tibi gloria curae. Horum factorum tibi sunt speranda futura, de quibus et coniunx maestus solacia quaerit.

(A, B) The belief in the resurrection is clearly expressed. **(C)** By her resurrection Regina will have a place in the holy land (*sedem venerandi ruris*)[16]. **(D)** It will take place in the age to come. Thus, this inscription states what might be called a classical later Jewish resurrection faith. The ground of hope is the observance of the Law and the good deeds, which were performed by this wife of a faithful Roman Jew. But this only example of a clear confession of the resurrection found on a Jewish tomb does not belong to the period which is covered by this investigation.

4.12.6 *Summary*

These archaeological finds do not contribute very much to the knowledge of Jewish beliefs about after-life, which can be reconstructed from the written sources. The border-line to general Hellenistic formulas and expressions is not very clear. If there is any indication of a conviction about life after death, it looks more like an immortality of the soul than a resurrection in most cases[17].

---

[1]Here some examples of such theories: Frey, Bibl 13, 153 f.: The refusal to burn the dead must indicate belief in resurrection among the Jews; A. Marmorstein, ZNW 32 (1933) 32-41: The ark with open doors, two arks, *torah*-scrolls, the *menorah,* stars (with ref. to SDt § 10; Dn 12:3), the turnip

(which dies again and again and returns to life); E. R. Goodenough IV (1954), 71-98; the *menorah* stands for light and life, also immortality; B. Lifshitz, RB 68 (1961) 402 f., supporting Goodenough; W. Wirgin, IEJ 14 (1964) 102-104: bare tombstones or graves mean belief in the resurrection of the body, the use of the *menorah* signifies belief in the resurrection of the soul (cf. the criticism of E. M. Meyers, 1971, 87 f.); Meyers (1971) 72-95: the custom of reburying the dry bones after the first burial, and to send ossuaries from the diaspora to the Holy Land would express a (not too literal) belief in the resurrection and the Holy Land as the Land of the living, the land of resurrection, as in Rabbinic sayings; an ossuary on the Mount of Olives in the Dura Europos fresco (cf. *supra* 4.1.6) would be another expression of the belief in the Mount of Olives as the place of the resurrection. But we must underline above all the statement of Meyers (1971) 87: without direct "inscriptional aids, it seems methodologically hopeless to identify a specific custom with a particular view of afterlife". E.g. the sending of bones to the Holy Land does not necessarily tell us very much about the faith in the resurrection there, when we remember the orders of Jacob (Gn 49:19) and especially of Joseph (Gn 50:25) to bury them (the bones) in the tomb of the fathers or at least in the Promised Land (Joseph is not explicit, but that must be the intention)—and Gn does not contain any faith in the resurrection of the dead. Cf. here the rev. of F. Christ, RB 80 (1973) 140-142: The ossuaries do not tell us anything about resurrection faith that we do not know already from contemporary documents.

²N. Müller—N. A. Bees (1919) 21, 23, 27, 34, 37 (27 and 28), 41, 43, 49, 59, 66, 67, 68, 69, 82, 97, 100, 106, 107, 109, 118, 121, 126, (127), 145, 154, 155, 160. 161 (nr. 117), 164, 167, 169, 170—in the Monteverde catacombs in Rome; CIJ 3, 7, 13, 16, 18, 24, (31?), 32, 35, 41, 44, 50, 62, 63, 69, 76, 81, 84, 85, 86, 88, 89 (?), 90, 92, 93, 95, 99, 100, 101, 102, 103, 104, 105, 106, 109, 111, 117, 121, 124 ($\kappa o \iota \tau \eta$ instead of $\kappa o \iota \mu \eta \sigma \iota \varsigma$). 126, 131, (132), 135, 136 (*menorah*), 137, 138, 140, 144, 145, 146, 147, 148, 149, 151, 152, 154, 156, 157, 158, 159, 167, 168, 171, 172, 178, 180, 184, 185, 192, 195, 198, 201, 203, 206, 212, (Latin), 224, 228 (=212), 212), 229, 232, 248, 250 (=212), 262, 264, 265, 277 ($\kappa o \iota \mu \eta \sigma \iota \nu$), 286, 301, 304, 307, 314 (with $\vartheta a \rho \sigma \varepsilon \iota, o \dot{v} \delta \varepsilon \iota \varsigma \, \dot{a} \vartheta a \nu a \tau o \varsigma$) 315, 317, 321, 322, 323, 325, 328, 337, 338, 343, 349, 351, 355, (358), 359, 361, 363, 364, 365, 370, 372, 373, 374, 381, 383, 384, 385, 390 ($\dot{\varepsilon} \nu \, \varepsilon \dot{\iota} \rho . \kappa o \iota \mu a \sigma \vartheta \omega$) 392, 396, 397 (+ שלום על י שראל), 401, 403, 405, 407 (?), 408, 413, 415, 417, 418, 430, 432, 433, 454, (Latin except the phrase), 458 (Latin: QUIECET IN PACE with *menorah*), 464 (as 454), 498, 501, 503, 506, 507, 509, 511, 512, 523, 536, 542, 547, 551 b, 577, 582, 587, 588, 594, 627, 629 a, (Latin), 732, 869 (Hebrew), 900 (Hebrew), 903, 1405, 1535 (the last from 869 Palestinian).

³E.g. CIJ 650. Cf. n. 11 to 3.14 *supra*, and J. and L. Robert, REG 69 (1956) 181 f.

⁴CIJ 20, 89, 133, 255, 316, 391, 394, 459, 477 (*in pace*), 485, 494, 495, 496, 535, 543, 558 (*Hic requiescit in pace* . . .), 559 and 568 (as 558), 568 also with a Latin transcription of $\,$ שלום $\big)$ 644 with 645 and 646 as 558, 644 also with a $\,$ שלו $\big($ רד $\,$ 660 (*in pace*).

⁵CIJ 800, 804, 867 (for a synagogue); 630 (Latin); 526 (cf. also n. 7—Latin).

⁶CIJ 283 (with *shofar*, *menorah* and palm-branch), 293 $\big($ על $\big($ י $\big)$ שו $\big($ ר $\big)$ אל $\big)$ 296, 319, 397 $\big($ על י שראל $\big)$ 497 (4 times, Greek and Latin inscription, two *menoroth*), 499, 552, 558 $\big($ שלום למנורחת $\big)$ 570 (Latin and Hebrew), 572 (*menorah*), 573, 574, 575 (Greek transcr.), 578, 579, 584 $\big($ על משכבב $\big)$ 586, 595, 596, 597, 599 $\big($ על ישראל אמי ן $\big)$ 600 (twice with *menorah*, palmbranch and shofar), 606, 607, 609, 611 (Latin inscription + *menorah* + נבורח נבפש 613, 622 $\big($ יהי שלום על 626, 630 (a) b $\big($ מנורחת $\big($ אמי ן $\big($ שלום על מנורחתם אמי ן $\big)$ 632, 644 (with Latin inscription), 650 (Catania, שלום על ישראל 659 (with Latin), (668. 670 with later blessings), 671, 732, 739, 857, 858, 859, 866 $\big($ שלום על כל ישראל $\big)$, 874, 887 $\big($ על י שראל $\big)$, 892, 893, 895, 897, 908, 914, 920, 922, 933, 934, 937 943, 948. 951, 956, 959, 961, 970, 994 1028, 1034, ($\Sigma \Lambda \Lambda O M$) as 1036, 1037, 1038, 1039 $\big($ שלו רד ם $\big)$, 1071 ? (ΣA ... E) 1076, 1078, 1079, 1080, 1086, 1087, 1090, 1113 ($\Sigma A \Lambda \Lambda O M$), 1175 $\big($ לעולם $\big)$ על ישראל לעולם $\big)$, 1195, 1200, 1208, 1226, 1391 $\big($ על ישראל $\big)$, 1414 $\big($ על משכבב $\big)$, 1421, 1437, 1438 ($\dot{v} \pi \varepsilon \rho \, \sigma \omega \tau \eta \rho \iota a \varsigma$). Cf. 3.14!

[7]CIJ 78, 110 $(εὐψυχει\cdot)$, 118, 210 (Latin, *menorah*), 281, 526 (Latin) 632 (Hebrew, in Calabria). Cf. also 340 with $μετα των ὁσιων$ instead of $μετα των δικαιων$, and G. Delling, ThLZ 76 (1951) 523 and n. See also 3.14.3.

[8]CIJ 358, a prayer of a father for his four-year-old son: $νυν, δεσποτα, ἐν ειρηνῃ κο[ι]-μησιν αὐτου Ἰουστον, ιηπιον ἀσυ[γ]κριτον, ἐν δικαιωματι σου.$ Cf. Delling, ThLZ 76, 522.

[9]Müller-Bees (1919) 56, 114, 164; CIJ 314, 335, 380, 401, 450, 539, 544, 551 c, 782, 788, 1005, 1209. Cf. Delling ThLZ 76, 522 with n.

[10]Thus Delling, ThLZ 76, 521 f. But cf. Frey in CIJ on 1005.

[11]Cf. N. Avigad, IEJ 7 (1957) 246; *supra* 3.14.3.

[12] $εὐτυχως τῃ ὑμων ἀναστασ[ε]ι$ see Avigad, IEJ 7, 247. Cf. n. 11 to 3.14.

[13]Cf. e.g. Enc.Jud. (1971) IV, 766, 771—referring to e.g. the fact that R. Simeon, the son and successor of Jehudah ha-Nasi, is probably buried there.

[14]Cf. Frey in CIJ *ad loc.* for these "identity disks", and the date: First or second century AD.

[15]Another somewhat later Egyptian inscription in Hebrew (Antinoopolis, early second century AD, CIJ 1534) reads: "His soul in the bundle of life $\left(\text{נ פ ש ו ב צ ר ו ר ה ח י י ם}\right)$ and a probably sixth century Spanish tomb (CIJ 661) with the *magen Dawid* and the *menorah*, includes a combination of these two wishes:

נשמתה לחיי עולם הבא נפשה בצרור החיים אמן שלום

Similar expressions are found in Venosa inscriptions (CIJ 569 and 571—third to sixth century AD). Cf. *infra* 5.6.

[16]Frey, CIJ *ad loc.*, interprets this land as the Paradise. But cf. Delling, ThLZ 76, 523 f., with his reference to Bill III, 828; IV, 1198.

[17]Cf. *supra* 3.14.3 on Milik's suggestion about *Athanasii* etc.;— further Delling, ThLZ 76, 523; CIJ 298, 364, 398?, 516, 576, 675.—It is astonishing to find the pagan Roman inscription *Dis Manibus*, sometimes shortened D.M., on a number of Jewish graves in Rome (CIJ 524; 578; Müller-Bees, 1919, 52, 90, 91—DIS alone—93, 94, 95, 150). Other expressions of a pagan kind of disillusion (as one might think) are: CIJ 761 $(ὁ βιος ταυτα)$ and, even in Beth-Shearim חבל (CIJ 1148, 1151, 1156). Cf. also CIJ 1511, 1530, 527.

5 Early Rabbinic Traditions

In NT exegetical work Rabbinic texts are often quoted without any deliberations about the age of the quotations or their possible relation to ideas and phenomena in the Jewish environment of the Primitive Christian Church. This may be one of the dangers in the indiscriminate use of the material gathered in the commentary of P. Billerbeck[1]. A full description of the Rabbinic Jewish views on after-life would also require, of course, a monograph of its own. I am quite content to refer to those which are already existing[2]. Instead, I shall try to select the material that rather safely or at least possibly may be derived from teachers that flourished before or just around 100 CE, i.e. in the period preceding the destruction of the Temple and the age of the reconstruction and consolidation of Judaism after the national and religious catastrophe. This later period is marked by the work of the academy at Jabneh, which, among other things, meant the drawing of a clear-cut line of demarcation between Judaism and Jewish Christianity[3]. My selection of the material involves many source-critical and traditio-historical problems. In the treatment of these I shall start from the critical analyses of J. Neusner[4]. His judgments on the age of the different pericopes are normally accepted as working hypotheses. On this basis I will try to apply my own four questions to those pericopes that may be accepted as plausibly older than 100 CE. Considering Paul's Rabbinic training[5], the examination of this particular section of the Jewish background is obviously rather important in the general context of my work.

5.1 The Houses

Among the earliest relevant texts for our study are some of the traditions that treat the discussions between the Schools of Shammai and of Hillel. One is very revealing for question **(B)** and also **(C)** , and is preserved in two passages of the Midrash Rabba, *GnR 14:5* and *LvR 14:9*.[6] A synoptic comparison will help us to discuss the pericope:

GnR 14:5	LvR 14:9
‏וייצר‎ :two formations, one in this world and one in the future world.	
The School of Shammai and the School of Hillel disagree.	The School of Shammai and the School of Hillel held differing views.
The School of Shammai maintain: His formation in the next world will not be like that of this world.	The School of Shammai said: Unlike the formation of the embryo in this world is to be the formation thereof in the Time to Come.
In this world skin and flesh are formed first, the sinews and bones last; but in the future he will commence with sinews and bones and finish with the skin and flesh, for thus it says in connection with the dead of Ezekiel:	In this world it begins with flesh and skin, and ends with sinews and bones, but in the Time to Come, it is to begin with sinews and bones and end with skin; for thus it is written of the dead of (the vision of) Ezekiel, as it is said:

171

And I beheld, and, lo, there were
sinews upon them, and flesh came up,
and skin covered them above (Ez 37:8)
Said R. Jonathan ...

(Ez 37:8, as in the left column,
is quoted.)

R. Chiyya b.Abba said ...

(The same objection of a later Rabbi, though different names are given.)

The School of Hillel said:
Just as he is formed in this world,
so will he be formed in the next world.
In this world the skin and flesh
come first,
the sinews and bones last;
so in the future will he begin with
the skin and flesh and end with the
sinews and bones.
For thus says Job:
Wilt thou not pour me out as milk
and curdle me like cheese?
Thou wilt clothe me with skin and flesh,
and knit me together with bones and sinews
(Job 10:10 f.).
He does not say,
"Thou didst pour me out ... and
didst curdle me," but
Thou wilt pour me out ...
and wilt curdle me."
It is not written here,
"Thou hast clothed me with skin
and flesh,"
but *Thou wilt clothe me,* etc.;
it is not written,
"And with bones and
sinews Thou *hast* knit me together",
but *Thou wilt knit me together.*

The School of Hillel said:
Like the formation of the embryo in
this world,
will be the formation thereof in the
Time to Come:
In this world it begins with skin and flesh
and ends with sinews and bones;
in the Time to Come it will be
likewise.
for thus said Job ...
surely Thou wilt pour me out as
milk (Job 10:9 f.).

It does not say,
"Thou hast poured me out", but

Thou wilt pour me out
And thou wilt curdle me like cheese
It does not say,
"Thou hast curdled me", but
Thou wilt curdle me. Thou wilt
clothe me with skin and flesh (v.11).
It says not, "Thou *hast* clothed me",
but "*Thou wilt clothe me. And*
thou wilt cover me with bones and
sinews (ibid.).
It says not "Thou *didst* cover me",
This then was (the speaker's meaning
when he said:)

Imagine a bowl full of milk:
before rennet is put into it
the milk is loose (liquid)
but when rennet is put into it,
the milk curdles and sets.
Thus Job said:
Wilt thou not pour me out as milk ...
skin and flesh ...
Thou hast granted me life and favour

Thou hast granted me life and
favour

(ET H. Freedman, 1939).

(v. 12, ET J. Israelstam, 1939).

172

5.1.1

(A, B) The resurrection of the body seems to be conceived of in a very literal way by both schools. But perhaps one might say that the Shammaites are the more extreme literalists, in light of their interpretation of Ez 37:1-14 as a description of the future general resurrection. We have been able to state that some parts of the diaspora, at least, interpreted Ez 37:1-14 to deal with the eschatological resurrection (4.1.6). The present example of the same interpretation in Palestinian Judaism is not unique[7]. But there are also a number of texts which show us that EZ 37:1-14 was understood as a historical narrative, and in this case the Rabbis try to identify the people who were raised to life by Ezekiel[8], or they refer to the text as an example of a resurrection which had already taken place in history, proving the future resurrection at the end of time[9].

On the other hand, the Hillelites, who refer to Job 10:10-12, might also be interpreted as extreme literalists. But do they think of the resurrection as a new conception? The version of LvR 14:9 could convey such an understanding, but there the formation of the embryo is especially mentioned and emphasized, because the context (14:9) treats this subject. GnR 14:5, which departs from the interpretation of וייצר in Gn 2:7, avoids, perhaps, the idea of the resurrection as a new conception by combining the "pouring out" and the "curdling", in the quotation from Job and the argument, with the formation of man in its two stages, from that which is soft and loose to that which is fixed, skin-flesh to sinews-bones. This image function of the comparison with the milk-cheese procedure is strenghtened in GnR 14:5 by the additional summons to imagine the procedure of curdling. Thus, it seems to me that the Hillelite point of view may be interpreted to be less literalistic and more "spiritual" than the Shammaite position.

5.1.2

Likewise, according to Beth-Hillel's opinion, there is no relation between the material remains of the dead and their resurrected bodies, as there is in the view of the School of Shammai. It seems that the Hillelites consider the resurrection to be a new creation of the body, *ex nihilo*. I am aware of the danger of over-interpretation here, but in this way the difference between the two schools is given some meaning.

(C) In this tradition none of the schools mention or even consider a transformation of the body for the future age. Resurrected life is a life in an earthly body, which is either identical with the old one (Ez 37:1-14 in the interpretation of Beth-Shammai: the bones represent the identity and continuity)[10], or an entirely new body (Beth-Hillel, interpreting Job 10:10-12[11]).

(D) The resurrection will take place at some indefinite point "in the future" or "in the Time to Come".

5.1.2

Another controversy between the two schools concerning eschatology is reported in *RH 16b-17a* and in *TSanh 13:3-5*. The question is the fate of the intermediate, those neither righteous nor wicked. The following synopsis gives us the basis for our discussion:

TSanh 13:3

The House of Shammai say,
"There are three groups.

One
(. . . one . . .)

is for eternal life (עולם   לחיי)
(These are the completely evil
people—see below!)

One is

for reproach, for everlasting
abhorrence.[13] These are the completely evil
people. That (ש) the last of them
(קרליהו) descend to Gehenna and
squeal and rise again and are healed.
As it is said, *And I will bring
the third part through fire
and will refine them as silver
is refined and will try them
as gold is tried.
And they shall call on my name
and I will answer them* (Zch 13:9). Concerning
them Hanna said, *The Lord kills and resurrects,*

*brings down to Sheol
and raises up* (I Sm 2:6).
The House of Hillel say, "He that
abounds in grace inclines (the
scales) towards grace."
And concerning them, David said,
*I love that the Lord should hear
my voice and my supplication.*
And concerning them

the entire passage (of David)
was said.

RH 16b-17a

It has been taught:
The House of Shammai say,
"There will be three groups
at the Day of Judgment
—one of thoroughly righteous,
one of thoroughly wicked,
and one of intermediate.
The thoroughly righteous will forthwith
be enscribed[12] definitively as entitled
to everlasting life (עולם   לחיי)
the thoroughly wicked will forth with
be inscribed definitively as doomed to
Gehinnom, as it says,
*And many of them that sleep in the dust
of the earth shall awake, some to everlasting life
and some
to reproach and everlasting abhorrence*[13]
(Dn 12:2).
The intermediate will go down
to Gehinnom and squeal and rise again
as it says, *And I will bring
the third part through the fire,
and will refine them as silver
is refined, and will try them
as gold is tried.
They shall call on my name
and I will answer them* (Zch 13:9).
Of them, too, Hanna said,
*The Lord kills and resurrects,
brings down to Sheol
and raises up* (I Sm 2:6).
The House of Hillel say, "He that
abounds in grace inclines (the scales)
towards grace,"
and of them David said,"
*I love that the Lord should hear
my voice and my supplication* (Ps 116:1).
And on their behalf
David composed
the whole of the passage,
I was brought low and he saved me
(Ps 116:6; ET Neusner, 1971, 238 f.).

5.1.2.1

In his commentary Neusner (*ibid.*) emphasizes that this pericope is highly developed and complex as compared to the basic structure of the "Houses-form". He does not at all comment upon the relation between the above quoted pericope and that which follows in the parallel traditions. I shall return to it in the treatment of the exclusion statements, where it really belongs (5.2.2).

The point of the dispute is the existence of a purgatory for the intermediate, which is affirmed by the Shammaites and denied by the Hillelites. If there is a balance between good deeds and sins, then grace will outweigh the sins, according to Hillelite teaching. Perhaps the redactor of RH 16b-17a missed that point, however. The statement of the House of Hillel seems to be understood as a mere comment on the belief in purgatory in RH 16b-17a. The quotation of Ps 116:6, which is added by RH, functions as a scriptural argument *for* the belief in purgatory, or may easily be so understood.

5.1.2.2

(A) The introduction of a purgatorial state by the Shammaites may reveal that the condemnation of the wicked according to the words of Dn 12:2 is regarded not as annihilation but as ever-lasting torments. **(B)** The thoroughly wicked rise from the dead to be punished and, finally, according to the Shammaites, the intermediate will rise after their period in Gehinnom. Thus, a universal resurrection is probably taught here, (though the limited meaning of "many of . . ." in Dn 12:2 is used to introduce the intermediate group, cf. *supra* 2.2 n. 10). **(C)** The emphasis is not at all, however, placed on the manner in which this resurrection or life after death appears. **(D)** Only the version of Babli mentions the "date" of the Day of Judgment, which is probably secondary, since it is required by contrast to the context in RH, where the New Year's *Day* is the theme. So without the reference to Dn 12:2, the statements might just as well be related to a judgment immediately after death (cf. Wahle, Kairos 14, 300). The Rabbinic interest actually concerns only the problem of retribution.

5.2   Dogma and Anathema

One of the classical formulations of Rabbinic orthodoxy—one of the few[14]—is the anonymous statement found in MSanh 10:1a:

> All Israelites have a share in the world to come, for it is written: *And thy people also shall be all righteous; they shall inherit the earth for ever* (Is 60:21). And these are they that have no share in the world to come: he that says that there is no resurrection of the dead (prescribed in the Law) and that the Law is not from Heaven, and an Epicurean . . . (ET H. Danby, 1933).

The context that immediately follows this statement enumerates some other exceptions from the share in the world to come, which are generally maintained or asserted by individual Rabbis. We shall return to some of those formulations, but first some considerations about the formulation of the dogma itself shall be given:

The positive statement concerns Israel and the whole of Israel, i.e., it includes all of the generations of Israel. It even concerns the criminals sentenced to death, according to the paragraphs that precede this statement in its present context[16]. The formulations of the dogma is not the theme of this part of MSanh. 10:4 b returns to the original subject, which is capital punishment (cf. e.g. Blackman, 1965, *ad loc.*). **(A)** It is clear, then, that the sentence quoted on a "share in the world to come" concerns, at least partly, life after death in its present context.

5.2.1

(B) Those who deny the resurrection of the dead are the first exception from the general rule about the salvation of all Israelites, or, rather, according to the present editions, those who deny that the resurrection of the dead is התורה מן , may be derived from the Law. But the text is uncertain. Some MSS and e.g. Maimonides did not read the addition מן התורה [17]. It is neither known to the Tosefta-parallel (TSanh 13:4—cf. RH 17a and *infra* 5.2.2). The first explanation of the Gemara (Sanh 90b), "he denies the resurrection of the dead, therefore he shall have no share in the resurrection of the dead", seems to presuppose the shorter reading. A little later, in sayings by R. Yochanan and R. Simay, the question is asked: Where in the Torah do you find the resurrection of the dead? Towards the end of the treatment of the resurrection (91b) the same question is asked and answered by R. Meir and others. But the main part of this section discusses the more general question about the proofs for the resurrection of the dead from Scripture in general or from nature. The most natural explanation is the theory that מן התורה is a secondary addition which strengthens the anathema against those who deny the resurrection[18]. It may have crept into the Mishnah from discussions of the early Tannaitic period, like the one between Rabban Gamaliel and the Sadducees (see 5.4.1 *infra*). The Synoptic tradition about the confrontation between Jesus and the Sadducees (Mk 12:18-27 parr) silently seems to presuppose that a proof-text has to be found in the Pentateuch. Thus the question of the resurrection of the dead is connected with the possibility of proving it from the Torah at a very early stage. The anathema also combines those who deny the resurrection of the dead with those who deny the Law and its heavenly origin in both the Mishnah and the Tosefta/RH-Gemara-traditions.

5.2.2

A list of individuals or groups excluded from the life of the world to come (MSanh 10:1-3) is introduced by the anathema on those who deny the resurrection of the dead (or its derivation from the Torah). This list has a parallel (lacking the introducing statement of MSanh on those who deny the resurrection) in TSanh 12:9-13:12. The pericope quoted in 5.1.2 is inserted in this context of TSanh (13:3) as well as its extension in both TSanh and RH on the punishment of the transgressors and the heretics in Gehenna (TSanh 13:4-5 // RH 17a). The point of this pericope is the same as the point of the whole list of exclusions from future life, at least in its present context: sins on a "religious" level, i.e. heresy, idolatry, etc. are much more serious than criminal or ethical transgressions in general. Even the executed criminals are admitted to the life to come. The transgressors of Israel and the nations (TSanh 13:4-5//RH 17a), those who sin "with their bodies" (בגופן) are punished only twelve months in Gehenna and then they are annihilated. But the heretics, etc. suffer eternal torments (TSanh 13:5//RH 17a); they are excluded from the Age to Come (MSanh 10:1-3//TSanh 12:9;[19] 13:6-12). Different traditions are obviously combined here and quite different statements on punishment after death are juxtaposed. This did not seem to be a problem to the redactors and the transmitting community before them. Was the reason for this unharmonized juxtaposition a consciousness of the mere symbolic value of the details of the descriptions of the future judgment? However, the essential meaning and message of these descriptions appear to be constant in the variety of symbols.

5.2.3

(C) The positive terms used to express resurrection and the new life after death do not relate very much about the nature of the eternal life הבא עולם denotes the radically changed conditions of life (D) in an eschatological future (cf. 2.2.4 n. 23 *supra*). (B) המתים תחיית refers to *renewed* rather than continued life (D) at some point after death. The noun תחיה is derived from the pi'el of חיה which is found in the main liturgical formulation of the resurrection dogma in Shemone esre II (*infra* 5.3.1).

5.2.4

This Mishnah quotation is transmitted anonymously. The traditional Rabbinic rule says that anonymous statements in Mishnah should be attributed to R. Meir[20]. This assertion is of little value in a critical historical context. The conviction of the universal salvation of Israel, which is expressed by the introductory statement of MSanh 10:1, seems to be presupposed by John the Baptist in his preaching of repentance according to the Q-tradition of the Synoptic Gospels (Mt 3:9//Lk 3:8): "We have Abraham for our father". And is not this tradition one explanation of Paul's hope, as expressed in Rm 11:26[21]? The anathema-formulations may plausibly be dated from the period of the Academy at Jabneh (i.e. the last decades of the first century CE), when Judaism was reconstructed on a Pharisaic foundation and the Pharisaic dogma was identified with Jewish orthodoxy[22].

5.3 Liturgy

Among the various expressions of belief in new life after death in the prayers of the synagogue I have selected two examples[23] In both cases the date cannot be determined with any certainty. However the final redaction of the *Tefillah (Amidah, Shemone esre)* seems to have taken place during the patriarchate of Gamaliel II[24]. Still, this gave the individual worshipper or reader a certain freedom to formulate the contents that were fixed in his own words (cf. e.g. Heinemann, EncJud II, 839). The second benediction has a polemical tone which was probably directed against the Sadducees (cf. e.g. Elbogen, 1913, 29 f.; D. Hedegård, 1951, 85 n), when it proclaimed the dogma of the revivification:

Thou art mighty for ever, JHWH, thou quickenest the dead (מתים מחיה מחיה) thou art mighty to save ... and keepest faith to that sleep in the dust(עפר ישני cf. Dn 12:2) ... who killest and quickenest (רמחיה ממית cf. Dt 32:39: I Sm 2:6) and causest salvation to spring forth. And faithful art thou to quicken the dead (המתים להחיות נאמן) Blessed be thou, JHWH, who quickenest the dead (המתים מחיה) [24bis] .

(A, B) A resurrection after death is stated, **(C)** without providing any answers as to *how* the resurrection life would present itself, **(D)** or *when* the dead would rise. By reciting this benediction (with the rest of the *Amidah*—cf. EncJud II, 839 f.) three times a day the dogma of the resurrection was engraved in the Jewish mind, at least from the period of the reconstruction after 70 CE.[25] God's sovereign power as the Lord of life and death in the early traditions of Israel (cf. 2.1.2) is the basis of the hope of resurrection (cf. the formulations of the prayer in JA 20:5 *supra* 4.9.4).

5.3.2
Another central prayer which expresses the faith in the resurrection is the morning benediction אלהי (*Ber 60b*), whose date, however, is uncertain[26]:

My God, the soul נשמה which thou hast placed in me is pure. Thou hast fashioned it in me, thou breathed it into me, and thou preservest it within me, and thou wilt one day take it from me and restore it to me in the time to come. So long as the soul is within me, I thank thee, O Lord, my God, and the God of my fathers, Sovereign of all worlds.
Blessed art thou, O Lord, who restorest souls to dead corpses. (ET M. Simon, 1948).

(A, B) The doctrine of the resurrection of the dead is clearly maintained **(C)** in quite a literal form: the dead corpses are to be revived by the restoration of the נשמת . The נשמה is a rather impersonal part of man, more or less equivalent to "life" itself, breath and life, as expressed in OT by the terms נשמה, נפש and רוח (e.g. Eccl 12:7). This is the basic anthropology found in Gn 2:7 (cf. also *supra* 4.8.1.2). **(D)** The soul is thus not a part of man which survives death, but is instead the life-giving principle which is taken from man in death by God, to whom it really belongs, and given back to man in the future resurrection. Thus, regardless of the actual date of the formulation of this prayer, its anthropology has an archaic ring[27].

5.4 **Apology**

Of special interest in this investigation are naturally the early pericopes and traditions about the debates between the Sadducees (and others who deny the resurrection) and the early Rabbis on the question of the resurrection. This special interest is the reason why some pericopes which are connected with names later than our "dead-line" (AD 100) are cited here. The following questions can be asked in order to distinguish three classes of discussions:

I.   Where is the resurrection found in the Torah (cf. *supra* 5.2.1)?

II. In what manner will the dead rise?

III. How can it be reasonable to believe in the resurrection?

5.4.1

I. A number of later traditions in Sanh 90b-92b belong to the first category in its pure form[28]. Though the question concerns the Torah itself, the answer in at least half of the cases is taken from other parts of the Scriptures. Another form of these statements offers the positive conclusion that the resurrection can be derived from the Torah at the end of the argument, which starts with the Bible quotation and its interpretation[29]. Yet another form contrasts two quotations with each other[30]. It is obvious that the formulated question: Where is the resurrection found *in the Torah*? belongs to a somewhat later stage of the discussions. Even then, however, the answers presuppose a wider definition of the concept Torah, extending it to all the Scriptures in many cases.

The impression that the formulated precise question about the *Torah* belongs to a somewhat later stage of the development is confirmed by one of the controversies, reported in Sanh 90b-91a, R. Eliezer b. R. Jose's report on his refutal of the Samaritans and their assertion that the resurrection of the dead is not found in the Torah: He is a *tanna* of the *third* generation[31]. The two remaining controversies on this theme do not directly formulate the question about the Torah, though the decisive answer is found in the Pentateuch. The Rabbies quoted in these controversies both belong to the first century CE. The story about R. Gamaliel's[32] discussion with the Sadducees is the most important example of this *genre*. Therefore, I give the following summary of the story (*Sanh 90b*):

> The Sadducees asked R. Gamaliel: Whence can it be derived that the Holy One, blessed be He, shall revive the dead? He answered: From the Law, the Prophets and the Hagiographa. From the Law he quoted Dt 31:16:   הנך שכב עם אבותיך וקם   The Sadducees replied that וקם more naturally belongs with   העם הזה   (they are, of course, right from a philological point of view).
>
> From the Prophets Gamaliel quoted Is 26:19, which the Sadducees related to the resurrection of the Durah valley (Ez 37:1-14), regarded, then, as a historic event (cf. 5.1.1 and n. 8 *supra*).
>
> From the Hagiographa Gamaliel cited Ct 7:10, which the Sadducees interpret literally, whereas Gamaliel seems to think of the "sleep" of death, where the dead still live in some sense.[33] Finally Gamaliel quoted Dt 11:9, stressing the fact that the promise of the Land is given to "the fathers" (להם) not to "you" (לכם) : the fathers had to go through the resurrection in order to have a fulfilment of this promise. Then the conclusion is drawn: מיכן לתחיית המתים   מן התורה .   An addition to the tradition says that he quoted Dt 4:4 with the interpretation that those who were alive then, would be alive in the world to come.

The reference to the "fathers" appears to be decisive (cf. *infra* 7.2.3.1-7.2.3.6). Immediately following the Gamaliel pericope, R. Joshua b. Chananiah (a contemporary of Gamaliel II and Eliezer b. Hyrkanus—cf. e.g. Strack, 1920, 123) is asked by "the Romans"[34]:

> Whence that the Holy One, blessed be He, shall revive the dead and that He knows what is to be?

Like Gamaliel, Joshua refers to Dt 31:16. Like the Sadducees the Romans object with the more natural interpretation of the verse. Then Joshua is content to state that at least half of his thesis is proven true, namely that God knows what will happen. God's power is the important issue, obviously.

5.4.2

II. In the second class I would include some pericopes of varying content, which contain answers to questions regarding the details of the manner of resurrection. An example is the dialogue between R. Meir and Queen Cleopatra on the question: "Will the dead rise naked or with clothes?" R. Meir replies with a conclusion ר חומר קל from the seed of wheat, which is buried naked but appears in manifold clothing. So much more will the righteous be clothed at the resurrection, since they are buried in their clothes. The story is later than our deadline, since Meir was the disciple of Akiba (cf. e.g. Strack, 1920, 128 f.). Cleopatra cannot be the correct name of the dialogue partner. She seems to be pictured as a believing Jew, who quotes Ps 72:16, as she expresses her faith in the resurrection and only asks the complementary question of how the resurrection would take place. Bacher (II, 1890, 68) believes that the question is ironical, but this is not indicated by the context. In any case, the last Queen Cleopatra died almost two centuries before Meir. Bacher (*ibid.* n.), followed by Stemberger (Kairos 15, 239 f.), suggests the reading "patriarch of the Samaritans" instead of Cleopatra. Parallel variants of the story mention other names than Meir (Keth 111 b: Chiyya b. Joseph; PRE 33, Friedlander p. 245: Eliezer), who appears in similar discussions with Samaritans, however (EcclR 5:12 to Eccl 5:10; Jalq II, 140—cf. Stemberger, Kairos 15, 239-242, 260-263). All this indicates a rather late origin of the story. But it comes so close to I Cor 15:36 that I cannot refrain from quoting it here. However, the use of the same image is strikingly different in the two traditions. The Rabbinic variant employs it to prove an extremely concrete interpretation of the resurrection, Paul to demonstrate the possibility of a spiritual body.

The dialogue between Antoninus and Rabbi in Sanh 91b pertains to the same *genre,* dialogues between Jewish Sages and Roman dignitaries (cf. n.34), and more or less to the present category of discussions about the resurrection. Although the connection with the name of Rabbi indicates a late second century date, the fact that the same story is found in ApEz probably proves an earlier origin of the parable about the blind man and the lame man and their joint action in the king's garden.[35]

5.4.3

III. This class of dialogues on the resurrection of the dead, where the question "how?" is really an objection against the possibility of this faith, is represented first by a discussion in 90b-91a between Rabban Gamaliel (II, cf. Bacher, 1903, 82, suggesting Rome as the place of the discussion, n. 5), or rather his daughter, and the emperor:

The emperor said to R. Gamaliel: You say that the dead will come alive—but they will be changed into dust, and how could dust come alive?! Then his daughter said to him . . . I want to reply . . . We have two pot-makers in our town. One makes them from water, the other from clay. Who deserves more praise? The emperor replied: The one who makes them out of water. She replied: When he creates (men) out of water, so much the more from clay[36].

The parable is taken from nature like R. Meir's in the discussion with Cleopatra (5.4.2). We recognize the comparison between the conception and the resurrection (*supra* 5.1.2 and 3.9.4.1.5): resurrection is a new creation. Determining the historicity of the pericope or the true age of its origin is naturally difficult. A similar parable is used by R. Ammi, Palestinian Amoraean of the third generation (Strack, 1920, 140), in a discussion with a heretic[37]. That does not indicate an early date of the story about Gamaliel's daughter and the emperor (cf. also Herr's work, cited in n.34, on the historicity of stories of this *genre* in general).

The next pericope also applies the argument קל וחומר (Sanh 91a):

Once a מין said to Gebina b. Pesisa[38]:
"Woe to you, ye wicked, who maintain that the dead will revive;
if even the living die, shall the dead live!"
He replied:
"Woe to you, ye wicked, who maintain that the dead will not revive: if what was not, (now) lives, surely what has lived, will live again."
"You have called me wicked," said he, "If I stood up I could kick you and strip you of your hump!"
"If you could do that," he retorted, "you would be called a great doctor, and command large fees."
(ET Freedman 1935).

The implied argument, God's power to create new life, is the same here as in the preceding pericope about Gamaliel's daughter, though God is not mentioned. Therefore, the demonstration looks purely rationalistic. Maybe מין signifies "Sadducee" (cf. *infra* 6.2.1).

5.4.4

There are striking similarities and dissimilarities between these three classes of arguments concerning the resurrection of the dead in Sanh 90b-92b and the two most important NT pericopes which argue for this belief, Mk 12:18-27 parr and I Cor 15. I intend to publish my observations about this relationship in the context of my treatment of these texts in the second volume of this work.

5.5 A death-bed

The scene of the death-bed of Yochanan ben Zakkai (Ber 28b; AbRN 25) has often been quoted as a rather early example of Rabbinical belief in judgment, Paradise and Hell immediately after death (Bill IV, 1138; Hoffmann, 1966, 162). Yochanan weeps when his disciples come to see him in his illness. They ask him why he is weeping. He answers with a parable. He would weep even though he would only be taken to a mortal, human king.

Now that I am being taken before the supreme King of Kings . . . who lives and endures for ever and ever, whose anger, if He is angry with me, is an ever-lasting anger, who if he imprisons me imprisons me for ever, and whom I cannot persuade with words or bribe with money—nay, more, when there are two ways before me, one leading to Paradise and the other to Gehinnom, and I do not know by which I shall be taken, shall I not weep? They said to him: Master, bless us. He said to them: May it be (God's) will that the fear of heaven shall be upon you like the fear of flesh and blood . . .[39]

(A, D) Judgment seems to await man immediately after death with two possible sentences, Paradise or Hell. **(B)** No reference is made to a future resurrection or a future judgment. So this scene is an example of an eschatology which involves a decision for the individual person immediately after death without describing a general resurrection and judgment. However, Neusner, in his investigation of the Yochanan b.Zakkai legend (1970, 224), comes to the conclusion that this part of the story about Yochanan's death represents a late addition to a much shorter narrative, whose author is Joshua b.Levi according to jAZ 3:1 (with a parallel in jSota 9:16). So the value of the pericope is very limited in this context.

5.6   The bundle of life

A *baraitha* in *Shab 152b,* attributed to R. Eliezer, quotes a passage in Scripture which seems to have been quite important as a support for belief in life after death for the righteous, I Sm 25:29[40]:

> It was taught, R. Eliezer said: The souls of the righteous are hidden under the Throne of Glory, as it is said, *yet the soul of my lord shall be bound up in the bundle of life* (I Sm 25:29a). But those of the wicked continue to be imprisoned, while one angel stands at one end of the world and a second stands at the other end and they sling their souls to each other, for it is said, *and the soul of your enemies, them shall he sling out as from the hollow of a sling* (I Sm 25:29b).

(A, B, D) After-life is considered only in the respect of a continued existence of the souls, whether righteous or wicked. The wicked are punished in a way that would seem to presuppose some corporality. The distinctions are not very clear, of course. The souls of the righteous, however, enjoy an existence in close fellowship with the Divine Majesty, which seems to be indicated by the statement on their being hidden under the Throne of Glory. Whether the R. Eliezer quoted here is really the Eliezer b.Hyrkanus or not, and whether the quotation is authentic or a later interpretation in his name, the widespread use of I Sm 25:29 speaks for the assumption that the application of this text to the fate of the souls after death is likely to be quite early.

5.7   Varia and summary

There are, of course, other passages in the Rabbinic literature that may or may not belong to the period under consideration, which would give us some answers to our questions. They may be anonymous or they may be preserved under the heading "our Rabbis taught" and similar expressions[41]. There is the *haggada* in LamR I, 16 § 45 about the profession of faith by Vespasian's captives, who understand that even those who drown themselves (to avoid the condemnation to the brothels) or those who are devoured by lions are brought back to God.[42] With references to Ps 44:21-23 and 68:23 this answers some difficult questions for those who believe in the resurrection. The whole of PRE 34 treats the resurrection and, according to the names listed there, delivers a number of early Tannaitic traditions. But the redaction of PRE (early eighth century, cf. e.g. M. D. Herr, EncJud XIII, 1971, 559) is too late. It cannot be considered to be a source for the present investigation. There is a saying attributed to Hillel in MAb 2:7 about gaining life in the world to come through the words of Torah, but its authenticity is very dubious[43]. Since the uncertainty of the date and origin is so great in many cases, I am content to present this little collection of examined passages, which clearly demonstrates the variety in such a narrow circle and also the dominating tendency: belief in a resurrection (or new life after death) without being more precise about the body, though it is usually included. (Cf. index III for a survey.) The materialistic ideas of the future world often attributed to the Rabbis are hardly found in the period under consideration. With some, but with no overwhelming consistency, we find references to the eschatological future and the judgment in general terms.

[1]Cf. e.g. the section on Rabbinic texts in Hoffmann (1966) 156-174, Hoffmann's declaration in the foot-note p. 156 and the severe judgment of NT scholars in general in J. Neusner (1971) 1 f.

[2]Cf. the works referred to in 1.1.4 and the foot-notes there, further e.g. A. Marmorstein, AmJTh 19 (1915) 577-591; H. Wahle, Kairos 14 (1972) 291-309; G. Stemberger, Kairos 15 (1973) 238-266. S. Liebermann, In hon. H. A. Wolfson II (1966) has unfortunately not been available to me.

[3]Cf. e.g. Schürer I (1901) 656-659; II (1970) 383; EncJud IX (1971) 1176 f.; Kirche und Synagoge I (1968) 35-37; K. Hruby (1971) 21-24.—Of course, one might object against my limiting the material to the period prior to 100 CE, since one might maintain that many of those sayings or Scripture interpretations attributed to teachers later than 100 CE can reflect earlier traditions and ways of thought. This possibility is naturally admitted—cf. supra 1.3.3. But without any "dead-line", how can we distinguish between later developments, perhaps even partly the result of the debate between Christian and Jewish teachers—such as Justin and Trypho, and that which has really helped to shape the background of Paul's thinking? Analogical limitations of the period under consideration are found in e.g. Schubert, WZKM 56 (1960) 154-167, and Neusner (1971)—cf. id. Kairos 14 (1972) 57-70.

[4]See his works on Yochanan ben Zakkai (1970) and the Pharisees before AD 70 (1971).

[5]Gal 1:14; Ph 3:6; Acts 22:3, and cf. e.g. M. Dibelius—W.G. Kümmel (1951) 30 f.; G. Bornkamm (1969) 34 f.

[6]For these disputes and their form in general, see Neusner II (1971) 1-4. Cf. also I. Konovitz (1965), an apparently complete collection of the pericopes, according to Neusner's judgment. Neusner does not treat the following pericope, which is summarized in modern Hebrew in Konovitz, 30.

[7]SDt § 306; jShab 1:3; jKil 9:6; Shab 152b; GnR 13:11; 14:8; 96:5. TgEz 37 does not show any clear traces of this interpretation.

[8]Sanh 92b (where R. Judah b.Bathyra even expresses his conviction of having an ancestor among those raised by Ezekiel; PRE 33, Friedlander pp. 248-251); TanchNoah 10; EcclR III, 15 § 1; CtR 7:9; midrPs 78:5.

[9]There is some similarity between this argument (referring also to Elijah's and Elisha's miracles) and the idea of Christ as the "first fruits of those who have fallen asleep" in I Cor 15:20 ff.—see e.g. GnR 73:4; ExR 48:4; LvR 27:4; EcclR III, 2 § 1; III, 15 15 § 1; IV, 3; V, 10 § 1; VIII, 10 § 1; JalqEz 375 f.; NischmChaim 7 (39b) according to Löwinger, Jahrb.f jüd.Volkskunde 25, 42n. Cf. here Molin, Jud 9, 238.

[10]It might be possible that they also think of a new creation, starting with *new* bones, but the image of Ez 37, with the dry bones, suggests rather a continuity between the remains of the earthly body and the resurrected body.

[11]I do not exclude the possibility that some continuity between the earthly body and the body of the resurrection was accepted by Beth-Hillel, but the imagery that is used suggests a new creation.

[12]This formulation as also "the day of judgment" in the text of RH is dependent on the preceding context, a saying about three books opened on New Year's Day, one for the righteous, another for the wicked, and another for those in between. The following context in RH 17a develops the theme of the Lord's mercy and judgment. In TSanh 13 our pericope belongs in the enumeration of those who have no share in the Age to Come, parallel to MSanh 10:1-4 (cf. *infra* 5.2).

[13]Here I deviate from the ET of Neusner to follow the one used above 2.2.

[14]Cf. e.g. Moore II (1950) 323; D. Boyarin and S. Siegel, EncJud XIV (1971) 96, 98 f.

[15]This part of the quotation, the positive statement of the dogma, is not found in the Cambridge MS, which forms the basis of W. H. Lowe's edition of 1883, and in Kauffmann's MS of the Budapest Academy—cf. H. Danby (1919) xvif and 120 n.2. See also S. Krauss (1933) 397 f. Krauss accepts the longer text, as also P. Blackman (1965), whereas Danby (1919) 120, only quotes it in a foot-note. In the Mishnah-edition (ET) of 1933 Danby accepts the longer text, however.—These words are recited in the reading of Pirqe Aboth in the beginning of each chapter.

[16]Cf. Krauss (1933) *ad loc.*; Blackman (1965) *ad loc.*—Cf. also *infra* 7.2.3.6 on the salvation of the patriarchs and the people.

[17]Danby (1919) drops the clause without any comments. See Löwinger, Jahrb.f.jüd.Volkskunde 25, 28; Krauss (1933) *ad loc.*; H. Loewe (1937) 25 f.; J. Le Moyne (1972) 171-173.

[18]Thus Loewe and Le Moyne *ibid.*

[19]TSanh 13:1-2 does not suit this pattern quite well. I shall return to the discussion of these verses in the context of a special examination of the whole list of exclusions from the Age to Come.

[20]According to R. Yochanan (Sanh 86a) and R. Simeon b.Laqish (jYeb 4:10/11). The majority of the Sages, according to R. Yochanan in jYeb 4:10 (11). Cf. C. Albeck (1971) 145.

[21]Cf. *supra* n. 16 and *infra* 7.2.3.6

[22]I argue for this date on the basis of an attempt at a form critical analysis of the list of exclusions from the Age to Come in the paper mentioned in n. 19.

[23]More references are found in the articles of EncJud XIV (1971) 99, and of Stemberger, Kairos 15, 249.

[24]jBer 4:6 (7); Ber 28b-29a; Meg 17b, and here I. Elbogen (1913) 28-30; J. Heinemann, EncJud II (1971) 839 f.; Maier (1972) 139.

[24bis]ET Hedegård, 1951, 85 f.—for the Hebrew text (identical with that used in the Synagogue to day) cf. *ibid.* See also Stemberger, Kairos 15, 243-244, where a good discussion of the interpretation is found.

[25]Cf. *infra* 6.2.1 for another example of a liturgical and polemical way of expressing the dogma of resurrection or, at least, the fact of an Age to Come, MBer 9:5c.

[26]It is transmitted with the introduction: "Our Rabbis taught . . ." Elbogen (1913) 89, speaks of its rather late introduction into the liturgy of the synagogue, but does not speak of its actual origin, Cf. also Stemberger, Kairos 15, 247 f.

[27]Cf. Wahle, Kairos 14, 292-294, with ref. to MChul 2:6; Shab 23:5 (2); 151b; Yeb 16:3-4; 120b; Nid 31a; EcclR 5:12 to 5:10, 121c. See further Porter, *In hon.* W. R. Harper (1908) 251 f.; Stemberger, Kairos 15, 248.

[28]Here is a list of the Sanh-passages, the Rabbis cited and the passages of the "Torah" quoted:

Sanh	90b	Yochanan	Nm 18:28
	91b	Meir	Ex 15:1; Jos 8:30
	91b	Joshua b.Levi	Ps 84:5
	91b	Chiyya b.Abba	Is 52:8
	92a	Raba	Dt 33:6
	92a	Rabina	Dn 12:2
	92a	Ashi	Dn 12:13.

[29]Sanh 91b	Rabbanan	Dt 32:39
Sanh 92a	Tabi in the name of Joshiah	Prv 30:16.

[30]Sanh 91b	Resh Laqish	Jr 31:17 - Is 35:6
	Ula	Is 25:8 - Is 65:20
	Raba	Dt 32:39c - Dt 32:39d.

[31]Cf. H. Strack (1920) 130.—He quotes Nm 15:31.

[32]This Rabban Gamaliel ought to be the teacher of Paul, if there would be serious possibilities for a discussion with Sadducees, but Neusner I (1971) 341 f., emphasizing the difficulty of distinguishing between the sayings of Gamaliel I and II, does not count this tradition among those which he attributes to Gamaliel I (treated pp. 341-376). For the attribution of this tradition to Gamaliel II, see W. Bacher (1903) 82.

[33]Here follows an inserted commentary by R. Yochanan in the name of R. Simeon b.Yehozadaq on Ct 7:10: when a *halakah* is pronounced in the name of a dead Rabbi, his lips murmur in the tomb!

[34]Cf. M. D. Herr, Scripta Hierosolymitana 22 (1971) 140; for the whole of this *genre,* dialogues between Jewish Sages and Roman Dignitaries, *ibid.* 123-150.

Cf. *supra* 3.13 and Stemberger, Kairos 15, 250-254.

[35]A third example of "class II" in Sanh 90b-92b is quoted as טנא דבי אליהו in Sanh 92a-b. On the writing called sometimes טנא דבי אליהו cf. e.g. Strack (1920) 220; J. Bowker (1969) 90: "Some of its midrashic material is at least as early as the third century". Whether this also concerns the tradition cited in Sanh 92a-b, I am not able to discuss here. The טנא quotes Is 4:3 to prove **(B)** that the righteous who are raised **(C)** will not return to the dust any more but shall live for ever in a renewed world (Is 2:11 is quoted here), where they will have wings like the eagles and fly above the waters (quotation of Ps 46:3 and Is 40:31). This is then followed by a discussion between some second and third generation Tannaites whether the story of Ez 37:1-14 is "truth" (אמת) or "parable" (משל). A decisive argument is the assertion of R. Judah b.Bathyra that his grandfather was among those raised by Ezekiel.

[36]The school of R. Ishmael adds a second parable:

> If a glass piece may be broken and repaired again, though it is made by flesh and blood—how much the more flesh and blood that was created by the spirit of the Holy One, blessed be He.

(B, C) This is a clear example of the doctrine of the resurrection of the body—almost directly contrary to Paul's teaching in I Cor 15:50.

[37]A king commands his servants to build palaces for him in a place where there is neither earth, nor water. They do so but their buildings fall down after a while. Then the king commands them to build in a place with earth and water. But this time they say: We are not able to do so. Actually, they ought to be able so much the more!—Further proofs of the possibility of resurrection are taken from the mysterious formation of mice (moles) out of earth and flesh and snails (immediately after rain they suddenly appear) (Sanh 91a).

[38]Who lived before the destruction of the temple, according to Marmorstein, AmJTh 19, 584, though hardly at the time of Alexander the Great as the following context asserts. On the form of a dialogue between a Jewish leader and Alexander, see Neusner I (1971) 34.

[39]ET Simon, 1948. Cf. also J. Neusner (1970) 221-223, for an English synopsis, containing Ber 28b, AbRN 25, jAZ 3:1 and jSota 9:16.

[40]Cf. 4.12 n.15, for quotations of the same phrase in sepulchral inscriptions, further, in the Rabbinic literature e.g. SNm § 139, a parallel tradition, here attributed to R. Eliezer b.R. Jose Hagelili, (cf. 5.4.1 *supra*). Perhaps the R. Eliezer cited in Shab 152b is this later *tanna* rather than Eliezer b. Hyrkanus (which is the usual identity of Eliezer without a surname—cf. Strack, 1920, 123). Further the phrase is cited in the Rabbinic literature in Pes.r. 2:3; LvR 18:1—and, anonymously, "our Rabbis taught", in Shab 152b, just before the present pericope for the state of the souls after death, contrasted with that of the bodies (for the bodies of the righteous Is 57:2 is quoted); and "it has been taught" in EcclR III, 21 § 1. Cf. Wahle, Kairos 14, 297.

[41]E.g. Ber 28b: A *berakah* to be said on departure from the Beth ha-Midrash (cf. Lk 18:11 f.):

> I give thanks to Thee O Lord my God, that thou hast set my portion with those who sit in the Beth ha-Midrash and Thou hast not set my portion with those who sit in (street) corners, for I rise early and they rise early, but I rise early for words of Torah and they rise early for frivolous talk; I labour and they labour, but I labour and receive a reward and they labour and do not receive a reward; I run and they run, but I run to the life of the future world and they run to the pit of destruction (ET Simon, 1948).

Cf. also the following story about Eliezer's death-bed and spiritual testament about winning the future life, leading into the narrative about Yochanan b.Zakkai's death, quoted *supra* 5.5. Cf. also Pes 68a, quoting DT 32:39. Further, "it has been taught", EcclR III, 21 § 1.

[42]This reminds us of the Maccabaean martyrs' attitude, especially Razis' (*supra* 4.2.1.3), and of Eleazar and his people at Masada (*supra* 4.6.4). Whether the *haggada* has anything to do with history or not, it reflects an attitude which was found among Jews in that period. Cf. W. R. Farmer (1956) 65-70.

[43]Neusner I (1971) 225 f., concludes that the saying originated in Amoraic times.

5.8 Targum

Unfortunately, it is very difficult to determine the origin of the targumic traditions in each case (cf. e.g. Bowker, 1969, 14-16). Therefore, here the examination of Tg is only given a confirming (or non-confirming) function in relation to that which is found in other sources concerning a "relecture" of certain OT texts (cf. *supra* n.4 to 4.1), interpreting them as statements of eternal life and/or resurrection after death.

5.8.1

Dt 32:39, apparently interpreted as a resurrection statement by LXX (4.1.1), is rendered by TgJ II (ET Etheridge):

> I kill the living in this world, and make alive the dead in the world that comes.

By this interpreting translation this phrase **(A)** the resurrection of the dead **(D)** in the eschatological future, at the change of the ages. The same interpretation is represented by TgJ I (ET Etheridge):

When the Word of the Lord shall reveal himself to redeem his people, He will say to all the nations: ... I, in my Word, kill and make alive; I smite the people of the Beth Israel, and I will heal them at the end of the days.

For similar Rabbinic interpretations see n.3 to 4.1.

5.8.2

1 Sm 2:6, quoted by Beth Shammai in TSanh 13:3/RH 17a (cf. *supra* 5.1), for teaching the purgatory of the intermediate[1] is thus rendered in TgJon:

All these are the mighty deeds of the Lord, who Himself lives forever: He kills and by His word revives (עלמא חיי). He brings down to Sheol, and He shall also bring out in eternal life

(A, B) The resurrection of the dead by the Word of the Lord is clearly taught by the additions to and changes of the original Hebrew text. **(D)** A future resurrection after an intermediate state in Sheol seems to be implied by these formulations which are, of course, both bound to the original Hebrew text and the expressions of the ideas of the *meturgeman* himself.

1 Sm 25:29, often quoted for the salvation of the righteous and the punishment of the wicked after death, has the following counterpart in TgJon:

And may my lord's soul be deposited (גניז) in the treasury (גנז) of eternal life חיי עלמא before the LORD, your God, but the soul of your enemies may He let it fly as people do with stones of a sling.

The Hebrew bundle (צרור) is here the treasury[2] of eternal life. This seems to allude to an idea of an intermediate state or immediate salvation of the righteous souls into a deeper fellowship with the Lord after death **(A, B, D)**, as the quotation is otherwise used in the Rabbinic traditions.

5.8.3

Is 25:8a: בלע המות לנצח.

These words in the Hebrew text are widely held to be a secondary addition[3]. But they do belong to the Bible of Paul and his Jewish and early Christian environment (cf. I Cor 15:54b; Rev 21:4[4]). The Masoretes read בלע as pi'el, by which (in the context) this translation is rendered: He swallowed up death for ever. If before בלע is understood as conjunctive, it signifies a futuristic meaning, which is natural in the context (cf. most translations, ancient and modern, with the exception of Theodotion, syro-hexapla, Paul). An early alternative way of reading בלע denotes pu'al, and this is read by Paul and Theodotion (κατεπόθη ὁ θάνατος εἰς νικος) and also Peshitta(ואתבלע מרתא לנכר לעלמין). Then המות is the subject, whereas the pi'el interpretation rather unnaturally understands המות as the object of the action of בלע [5], with the exception of LXX κατεπιεν ὁ θανατος ἰσχυσας [6]. This interpretation of LXX seems to announce the terrible power of death rather than its annihilation, and may suit the preceding context in LXX, where the judgment of the nations is a more dominating theme than in the Hebrew text. Whatever the original meaning of the words may have been[7], the tradition of understanding the words as a proclamation of death's destruction and annihilation is otherwise fairly unanimous, both in the other ancient versions, as we have seen above, in the Rabbinic exegesis[8], and finally in TgJon:

יתנשון מרתא לעלמין (they shall forget death for ever).

This is an eschatological interpretation which proclaims the end of death after the resurrection or, more generally, in the world to come, as is clearly seen in the context[9]. TgJon well expresses the general understanding of this saying in the Jewish exegetical tradition of the period under investigation.

Is 26:19 is possibly a resurrection statement in the original Hebrew text and certainly asserts the resurrection in LXX (cf. 4.1.5). (A) It is even more explicit in TgJon:

> It is thou that bringest the dead to life, thou raisest up the bones of their dead bodies; all that were cast to the dust shall live and sing praises before thee; for thy dew is a dew of light unto them that observe thy law, but the wicked to whom thou gavest might, but who have transgressed thy Memra shalt thou deliver unto Gehinnom. (ET J. F. Stenning, 1949).

(B) The physical character of the resurrection has received a stronger expression, (D) likewise the aspect of judgment, which is administered at the revelation of the Lord "from the house of his Shekinah" (Is 19:21 TgJon). In the mind of the מתורגמן the resurrection and the judgment at the *parousia* of the Lord God must have been closely related to each other, though the exact relationship is not defined.

The Tg understanding of "the dew of light" is hardly clearer than the Hebrew text.

It is no surprise to find Is 26:19 as *the* quotation from the Prophets used by R. Gamaliel in support of the belief in the resurrection of the dead (Sanh 90b—*supra* 5.4.1).

Is 27:12-13 is likely to lie behind the idea of the eschatological trumpet which gathers the people of God in the dispersion[10]:

> On that day the LORD will beat out the grain, from the streams of Euphrates to the Torrent of Egypt; but you Israelites will be gleaned one by one. On that day a blast shall be blown on a great trumpet (שו פר) and those who are lost (ע ו ב ד י ם, who are getting lost, strictly) in the land of Assyria and those dispersed in the land of Egypt will come in and worship the LORD on the holy mountain, in Jerusalem (ET NEB).

TgJon gives the following interpretation (ET Stenning):

> And it shall come to pass at that time (ב ע ד נ א ה ה ו א) that the slain (ק ט ל י ן)shall be cast before the Lord from the rock of the river Euphrates unto the brook of Egypt, but ye shall be brought near, one by one (lit. to the side of the other), O house of Israel. And it shall come to pass at that time that a great trumpet shall be blown; and they that were exiled (ד ג ל ו) to the land of Assyria, and they that were cast forth into the land of Egypt, shall come and worship before the Lord in the holy mountain, in Jerusalem.

The Aramaic version may express the idea of the eschatological ingathering of the people of Israel by using the verb ג ל א for the Hebrew ע ב ד —ג ל ו ת א//ה ג ל ו ת/ה ל ה is the technical term for the exile, see e.g. Shemone esre and cf. e.g. Bill II (1924) 490; K. L. Schmidt, TWNT II (1953) 99; EncJud VI (1971). I suggest that the "slain" who are "cast before the Lord" in v.12 are the dead of the people of Israel, especially those who died in the exile, who are to share in the resurrection in the land of Israel. However, I admit the possibility that the slain could be the enemies of Israel, who are killed on the day of triumph for God's people. In later traditions the trumpet remains associated with both the gathering of God's dispersed Israel[11] and the end time resurrection of the dead[12]. Originally, the trumpet sound belongs to the scene of a theophany[13]. So it is not difficult to understand why it appears in descriptions of the final theophany (cf. also TgJ I to Ex 20:18). The fact that Is 26:19 is situated in the greater context of Is 27:12-13 may have led the interpreter to combine the end time resurrection with the eschatological trumpet[14]. The combination of the gathering of the diaspora with the resurrection may also be inspired by an eschatological interpretation of the scene described in Ez 37:1-14 (cf. *supra* 4.1.6). It is a common feature of the Jewish expectation of the resurrection[15].

5.8.4

Hos 6:2 is probably in the mind of Paul, and even the tradition before him, when he states (I Cor 1 5:4) ὅτι ἐγήγερται τῇ ἡμέρᾳ τῇ τρίτῃ κατα τας γραφας [16] The Synoptic sayings about "on the third day, after three days" probably also refer to Hos 6:2:[17]

He will revive us after two days, on the third day he will raise us and we shall live in his presence.

Even in its original context, being, perhaps, a quotation from a penitential liturgy[18], the resurrection may be more than a casual metaphor for the restoration of the people. Perhaps the formulations of Hos 6:2 presupposed a consciousness of some idea of resurrection not unknown in Canaanite and general West Semitic vegetation cults[19]. TgJon definitely interprets it as a prophecy **(A, B)** about the end time resurrection of the dead:

He will revive us for the days of consolation which are to come; on the day of the resurrection of the dead he will raise us and we shall live in his presence.

(D) The third day has become "the day of the resurrection of the dead" **(C)** After the resurrection life "in his presence" may imply fellowship with God in a heavenly world[20]. The Targumic interpretation is echoed by the Rabbinic use of Hos 6:2. This passage as well as several other texts in the Bible[21] is used as a proof-text for the assertion that God's salvation occurs on "the third day"[22]. It is also used more precisely for identifying "the third day" with "the day of the resurrection"[23] The Rabbinic combination of the power of the Creator both to send the rain and to revive the dead[24] may also be inspired by Hos 6:2, together with the following verse[25].

5.8.5 *Ps. 1:5,*[26] Tg:

Therefore the wicked shall not be declared righteous on the great day (אבר אמוי בר) nor the sinners in the company of the righteous.

(A) The reference to the resurrection is not so clear as it is in LXX (4.1.2), but the Hebrew original text has been eschatologized: **(D)** "The judgment" has been interpreted as "the day of judgment". The comparison with LXX shows that Tg represents an independent tradition of interpretation. In LXX the "judgment" is retained, whereas the verb ἀναστησονται expresses the eschatologization of the Hebrew original. Such a process was probably rather spontaneous in the minds of Jewish readers in a later period.

Ps 22:30 (cf. 4.1.2) is rendered in a way which implicitly shows a later belief in the resurrection:

"he will not give life to the soul of the wicked".

Ps 49:16 is paraphrazed rather freely:

David said in a prophetic spirit: O that God would redeem my soul from the judgment of Gehenna, for He shall teach me his law for ever.

(D) Gehenna replaces Sheol and an act of judgment is introduced here, which is found neither in the Hebrew nor in the Greek version although both may already be a prayer for a salvation from death (cf. *supra* 4.1.2).

Ps 65:9, which was slightly developed in LXX (4.1.2) towards the concept of personal immortality, explicitly affirms the hope of future life in Tg:

He counted our soul to the life of the age to come (בחיי דעלמא דאתי)

(B) נפשא can be understood in the old Hebrew sense as "the whole man" or, rather, in the framework of a basic dichotomy of man as the surviving part of man at death.

5.8.6
The resurrection denial of the Hebrew text of *Job 14:12-14* has been deleted in Tg:

(12) A son of man sleeps and he shall not rise, *until there are no heavens* the wicked shall not be roused
(14) ... If a *wicked* man dies, can he live again?

(A) The resurrection of the *wicked* is denied in the Aramaic interpretation by the additions which are italicized. Thus, the text remains open for the resurrection of the righteous.

Tg*Job 19:25-26* may express some sort of belief in life after death, or a resurrection:

And I know that my redeemer lives, and after this his redemption shall rise above the dust. And when my skin is inflated(אתפח) **,** this will be so. And from my flesh I shall see God again.

The passage is extremely obscure like the Hebrew original (cf. 4.1.4), and no sure interpretation can be given.

5.8.7 Summary

It would be interesting to go through all of the targumic material with the aim of studying the re-interpretation that may have taken place in relation to the Hebrew Bible regarding life after death. That is obviously not possible within the framework of this investigation. Moreover, since the date of the origin of the preserved targumic material is so uncertain, the fruitfulness of such a work for the study of the background of NT could be questioned.

[1]I Sm 2:6 is also quoted by R. Joshua (b. Chananiah, the contemporary and frequent opponent of Eliezer b.Hyrkanus, who is quoted in the preceding context) in Sanh 92b: this is the song sung by those revived through Ezekiel. Cf. *supra* 5.1.1 and n.8.

[2]Cf. SNm § 139, the tradition attributed to R. Eliezer b.R. Jose Hagelili
   If he has died, she (the soul) is given to the treasury (אוֹ צָר) . For it is said (I Sm 25:29b is quoted)—and I hear: The righteous as well as the wicked. Then it is further taught (I Sm 25:29c is quoted, concerning the wicked)

[3]First of all, a general suspicion towards any far-reaching statements on the victory over death in the period of the history of Israelite-Jewish religious thought which is covered by the books of the Hebrew Bible is an argument against the "authenticity" (within the framework of the Israiah apocalypse); further, the fact that the saying stands somewhat isolated in the context is another argument. Above all, it breaks the parallelism of the rest of the verse—and neither suits the preceding saying. The introductory verb בָלֵע is also found in the opening of v.7—the point of departure for making a gloss? On the other hand, one might well argue that 1QIsa, LXX and I Cor 15:54b presuppose that the sentence existed at least one century BC. For the negative judgment on the "authenticity", see e.g. Martin-Achard (1956) 102; Wied (1965) 36; M. L. Henry (1957) 176; Fohrer, KuD 14, 258, for a positive judgment see e.g. Sutcliffe (1946) 125-128, and, denying the necessity of a negative judgment, G. W. Anderson, SupplVT 9 (1963) 126.

[4]The first words of Rev 21:4 και ἐξαλειψει παν δακρυον are unmistakably an allusion to Is, 25:8. So it seems clear to me that the words ὁ θανατος οὐκ ἐσται ἐτι (cf. *infra* for the understanding of this phrase). Cf. G. E. Gray—A. S. Peake (1912) *ad* Rev 21:4; O. Procksch (1930) and E. J. Young (1969) *ad* Is 25:8.

[5]Thus Aquila: καταποντισει τον θανατον εἰς νικος Symmachus: καταποθηναι ποιησει τον θανατον εἰς τελος Vulgate: *praecipitabit mortem in sempiternum.* And also TgJon—cf. *infra*—it would seem.

[6]And Theodotion, according to syro-hexapla: κατεπιεν ὁ θανατος εἰς νικος, מן תה ל נ ב ן וכ בל ע.

[7]H. Ringgren in an oral communication: This may simply have been something similar to "What is death?", not at all any proclamation of everlasting victory over death.

[8]Sanh 91b = Pes 68a (cf. 5.4.2 and n.30); GnR 26:2; ExR 15:21; LamR 1:13. Cf. Bill III, 481 f., and jMQ 3:9; MekEx 12:28-30; PRK Achereth (p. 458, 20 f.); ExR 30:3; DtR 2:30; EcclR 1:4:3.

[9]E.g. v.7, a destruction of an Anti-Christ figure.

[10]Cf. Hartman (1966) 135, 166, especially on Mt 24:31.

[11]PsSol 11:1 f.; ApcAbr 31:1; Shemone esreX; jSanh 10:5. IV Ezr 6:23 and OrSib IV, 174 (cf. *supra* 4.7.1) mention the eschatological trumpet, too, but more in general as a signal of the last time. Cf. Friedrich, TWNT VII (1964) 71-88; Hartman (1966) 135, 166.

[12]Above all in Christian texts: I Th 4:16; I Cor 15:52; Did 16:6; DescMariae 3 (2.2 n.26 *supra*); Thomas of Celano's hymn Dies irae v.3 (probably dependent on OrSib IV, 174) etc.—later hymns with this motif are numerous. In OrSib IV, 174, the sound of the trumpet is rather closely though not immediately followed by the resurrection. Cf. also; Sanh 10:5; TgJ I to Ex 20:18; Akiba according to Jellinek, Beth-ha-Midr III, 31:28 ff.: God himself sounds the trumpet and revives the dead successively with seven blasts of the trumpet.

[13]Ex 19:13, 16, 19; 20:18 and cf. Friedrich, TWNT VII, 71-88.

[14]Cf. here Leqach tob to Nm 24:17: There a tenth apocalyptic voice from heaven proclaims (in the words of Ps 24:17): "Lift up your heads, O gates!" Then the dead rise, and in this connection Is 26:19 is quoted. After that the exiles are gathered, and here the midrash refers to Is 27:13. The midrash Leqach tob is very late, of course, about 1100 (cf. Strack, 1920, 224) but may reveal the possibility that the two passages were combined at an earlier stage.

[15]Cf. *supra* 4.1.6 and n.32 with the idea of the ג ל ג ל   the return of the righteous to the Holy Land in subterranean tunnels—see jKil 9:6; Keth 111a-b. For the special relation between the resurrection and the land of Israel, see further Pes.r.1:4-6; Tanch Wayasa' 23 B; JalqShimBeresh 131:42-43: The land of Israel is אר ץ הח י ים   Cf. Bonsirven (1934) 480 f.—TgEz 37:1-14 does not tell us whether the passage was interpreted as a prophecy of the final resurrection, but e.g. Neofiti Gn 30:22 gives us an example of such an understanding of Ez 37:12—cf. also Stemberger, Kairos 14, 282.

[16]Cf. e.g. F. C. Burkitt, JThS 2 (1901) 113; H. E. Tödt (1959) 171; B. Lindars (1961) 61-66; Wood, NTS 14, 588 f.; G. Strecker, Interpr 22 (1968) 429n; Wendland (1968) *ad loc.*; H. Conzelmann (1969) *ad loc.*; M. Black, ZNW 60 (1969) 4; *id.* NTS 18 (1971) 5 f.; H. K. McArthur, NTS 18 (1971/2) 81-86.

[17]Mk 8:31 parr   δει   ; Lk 18:31-33; 24-46, and cf. Lindars (1961) 61-66; C. F. Evans (1970) 48-50; Black, *loc.cit.*

[18]See e.g. E. Sellin (1929)V; H. W. Wolff (1961); J. M. Ward (1966); J. L. Mays (1969) *ad loc.* W. Rudolph (1966) *ad loc.,* is somewhat reluctant, and stresses the existing relations between these verses and their context.

[19]The resurrection terminology is used here with reference to a national restoration, according to comm. by Sellin, Wolff, Ward, Mays and further Charles (1899) 129; Nötscher (1926) 138-146; Sellin, NKZ 30, 241-246; Birkeland, StTh 3, 74; Schilling (1951) 45 f.; Martin-Achard (1956) 64-73; König (1964) 220-227; Wied (1965) 16; J. Wijngaards, VT 17 (1967) 227 ff.; Fohrer, KuD 14, 158 f.; Beresford (1971) 8-19. T. H. Robinson (1954) *ad loc.*, thinks that the prophet or the author of the penitential liturgy thought of a real resurrection, based on Canaanite cultic ideas. On the presupposed consciousness of Canaanite resurrection ideas, see W. Baudissin (1911) 403-406; Riesenfeld (1948) 4-7; Martin-Achard 64-73, esp. 70-73; Sellin, *loc.cit.*; Eichrodt II (1961) 352 f.; Schilling, 46; Mays (1969) *ad loc.*; W. Zimmerli (1971) 91; Stemberger, Kairos 14, 284 f.

[20]Cf. IV Ezr 7:97 f.; Ber 17a; Men 43b; Sota 42a; Shab 152b; I Cor 13:12; II Cor 3:7-18; I Jn 3:2 and e.g. E. Lohse, TWNT VI (1959) 769-779, esp. 775 f., for the meaning of "before God's face".

[21]Gn 22:4; 42:18; Ex 15:22; 19:16; Jos 2:16; II Ki 20:5; Jonah 2:1, 11; Est 4:16; 5:1. Cf. also C. Barth, EvTh 28 (1968) 521-533, for the pattern of a "new beginning on the third day" in OT.

[22]GnR 56:1; 91:7; EstR 9:2; midrPs 22:5.

[23]jSanh 11:6; Sanh 97a; RH 31a; PRE 51 (Friedlander p. 411).

[24]MBer 5:2; DtR 7:6 jBer 5:2; Chag 12b; Shemone esre II with additions on certain days. Cf. Stemberger, Kairos 15, 239-247.

[25]Cf. jBer 5:2 with an explicit reference to Hos 6:2-3 for this combination, and R. Mach (1957) 197 f.

[26]With the obvious exception of 11 QTgJob, which, however, does not contain the crucial passages of Job, the Tgs preserved for the Hagiographa are generally later than any other (cf. e.g. R. Le Déaut, EthL 44, 1968, 20 f.; A. Sperber, IV A, 1968, VIII; B. Grossfeld, EncJud IV, 1971, 848). But older material may be retained in the later editions, with great uncertainty about the real age.

6 Silence—or denial of life after death

When we have gone through all of these texts with varying formulations and assertions about life after death, the impression might remain that these beliefs were generally accepted, and that they even dominated Jewish thinking both in the Greek-speaking diaspora and in the homeland of the centuries around the emergence of Christianity. This is, of course, not the case, though it would be possible to trace a development from the documents of the second century BC to the sources dating from around AD 100, when the expectation of life after death was accepted as Jewish dogma (5.2-3). In an unpublished dissertation of 1971 A. J. Beresford has examined most of the Jewish documents of the period under consideration with the question whether they speak about life after death. In many cases the answer was negative. It is not necessary to repeat this work. I will just enumerate the following Jewish writings from the period under consideration which are silent on after-life: Sir[1], Judith[2], Tob[3], Aristeas[4], I Bar[5], I Mcc[6], III Mcc[7], III Ezr[8], ParJr[9], AssMos[10] and MartIs[11].

6.1
Some of them may presuppose a belief in life after death, and in others the silence may be significant, since the general contents of the book would give occasion for statements on after-life, e.g. Sir, Tob or I Mcc. We cannot discuss each single case here. It is enough to state the fact that a fairly large number of sources from our period are silent on the question of life after death. The problem of the Qumran scrolls has been discussed above (3.5), but it may be mentioned to underline one result of this investigation, which is only negative: Life after death is by no means a central theme in all of the Jewish thinking in the time of Paul[12].

6.2
A special case is represented by the conscious denial of the resurrection of the dead and immortality after death by the *Sadducees*. Now our sources for the knowledge about this Jewish group which once was the leading party in the nation, are with a few possible exceptions, only found in the descriptions of their sharpest opponents among the Pharisees or Christians. Josephus' testimony is probably the least biased one of those which are preserved[13]. It is found twice, with the description of the other Jewish parties, in BJ II, 165, and in a shortened form in Ant XVIII, 16.

6.2.1
The first passage states that the Sadducees deny both the survival $\delta\iota\alpha\mu\omega\nu\eta$ of the soul and the retribution $\tau\iota\mu\omega\rho\iota\alpha\iota\ \kappa\alpha\iota\ \tau\iota\mu\alpha\iota$ in Hades; the second says that their doctrine $\lambda\omega\gamma\omega\varsigma$ makes the soul disappear $\sigma\upsilon\nu\alpha\varphi\alpha\nu\iota\zeta\epsilon\iota$ with the body. They denied any form of after-life, but apparently Josephus described their attitude as, above all, a denial of the immortality of the soul.

193

6.2.2

In NT (Mk 12:18 parr; Acts 4:2; 23:8) and in the Rabbinic sources (Sanh 90b—cf. 5.4.1; TanchBeresh 5[14]) the Sadducaean attitude is described as, above all, a negation of the resurrection of the dead (implicitly in Acts 4:2 and Sanh 90b). Acts 23:8 also describes the Sadducees as being critical of any belief in angels and spirits (which is probably more or less synonymous here—cf. Le Moyne, 1972, 135). According to AbRN, rec. A, 5 (also rec. B), their denial concerned retribution after death[15].

6.2.3

This unanimity of the different sources speaks for the assumption that the Sadducees did actually refuse to think of any form of after-life. Then we find a number of texts where the same scepticism about life after death is attributed to (5.4.3). In one case the MSS vary between מיניך and צדוקיך[16] (MBer 9:5c): The מיניך or צדוקיך) denied the existence of another world during the period of the Second Temple, and that is why it was ordained that the benedictions should end with העורלם ועד העורלם–מןrather than לעלם alone. The Sadducees may be indicated by the designation מיניך in all these cases. The tendency in Tg and midr to picture deniers of the resurrection may also belong to anti-Sadducee polemic (Le Moyne, 1972, 174), and, thus, indirectly testifies to the fact that the Sadducees did deny after-life.

6.2.4

The attitude of the Sadducees as regards life after death should probably be connected to their general conservatism (cf. Le Moyne, 1972, 41, 363 f.) and to their reluctance to the introduction of any ideas that could not be proven from the Pentateuch[20] in its literal sense[21]. Further, the fact that they represented, above all, the aristocracy and were well adapted to the requirements of this world[22] may also have been an explanation of their lack of interest in the question of life after death[23].

6.3

How wide-spread was the Sadducaean way of looking at life after death in relation to the beliefs of the Pharisees on the other hand? In light of the revision of earlier descriptions of the Pharisees and their importance before the destruction of the Second Temple by e.g. J. Neusner[24], one might guess that their belief in the resurrection was restricted to relatively small sections of the people in the pre-70 period. Josephus, however, asserts that belief in the resurrection of the dead was the firm persuasion of "each individual" of the Jewish people (CAp 218 f., *supra* 4.6.5). Admittedly this is very panegyrical and is found in a definitely apologetic context[25]. Further, it was written by somebody who considered himself a Pharisee (4.6.1) and it is quite late (in the nineties CE[26]). But in spite of the hyperbolic language there should be some truth in the statement. It seems likely that a belief in life after death was shared by rather wide circles among Jews both in Palestine and the diaspora (Josephus, at this point a diaspora Jew, makes no distinction) in the latter half of the first century AD. But the discussion on the acceptance of the resurrection dogma was not yet finished in the last decades of the first century of CE. The disputes on the subject which are preserved in Sanh 90b-92b (cf. 5.4) testify to this fact and the fact that *the* Jewish belief in the resurrection of the dead was not established until some decades after Paul.

[1]This is true for the Hebrew original-cf. Wied (1965) 137-141, and Beresford (1971) 58-62. The Greek version may contain some vague references to reward and punishment in the beyond—cf. e.g. Bückers (1938) 64 f.; König (1964) 210 f., 252; Aalen, NTS 13, 10 f.; Beresford, 59, on 7:17, and 61, on 48:11. The work of C. Kearns (1951) has not been available to me. Cf. n.13 for the relation between Sir and the Sadducees.

[2]With Beresford (1971) 36, against König (1964) 211, who wuld find an allusion to punishment beyond death in 16:17. For the date cf. Eissfeldt (1964) 796 (250-200 BC).

[3]Cf. Beresford (1971) 42 f. Eissfeldt (1964) 793: Probably pre-Maccabaean, at least before 20 BC. Originally Aramaic.

[4]For a discussion on the date, cf. Denis (1970) 109 f. Eissfeldt (1964) 818, suggests around 130 BC.

[5]Cf. Eissfeldt (1964) 804, referring to 2:17. The date of I Bar given here: First half of the first century BC.

[6]Cf. Beresford (1971) 36: "Nowhere . . . the slightest trace of a belief in any sort of after-life."—On the relation between I Mcc and the Sadducees, cf. n.13.

[7]Cf. Beresford (1971) 43; Nickelsburg (1972) 90-92. According to Eissfeldt (1964) 788 f., it should be dated in the end of the first century BC, at least before AD 70.

[8]Eissfeldt (1964) 777-781. Date between 165 BC and AD 90.

[9]I presume that ch. 9 is a Christian addition. There Jeremiah proclaims his own assumption, but the death and resurrection of the prophet after three days is also described. Cf. Denis (1970) 74. Date: between AD 70 and 132/5.

[10]The common opinion about the date of AssMos depends on references to Herod the Great and his three heirs and sons in ch.6, and then determines the date as somewhere between AD 7 and AD 30 see e.g. R. H. Charles (1897) lv-lviii; AP II (1913) 4ll; Volz (1934) 33; Eissfeldt (1964) 846; Russell (1964) 58 f.; E. M. Laperoussaz, Sem 19 (1970) 96-99. Following a suggestion by J. Licht, JJS 12 (1961) 103, Nickelsburg (1972) 43-45, argues for the view that ch.6 is a later Essene interpolation, and then concludes that the date of the original document is about the same as Dn, earlier than the Maccabaean revolt. For our conclusion about the silence on after-life in AssMos, cf. also Volz (1934) 33 f.; Laperoussaz, Sem 19, 85 f. Beresford (1971) 36 f., thinks that the author of AssMos "held to a purely spiritual view of the after-life", whereas Nickelsburg (1972) 29-31 and 38, believes that a resurrection or exaltation of the righteous after death may be presumed by the formulation in 10:9 about the exaltation of Israel to the stars, and in v.10, its viewing of the enemies in Gehenna behind. That is, of course, possible, but since it makes no direct references to life after death, it is included in this list.

[11]Cf. the ed. of R. H. Charles (1900) xliii-vi; id. (1918) xiiif on the Jewish character of MartIs within the otherwise Christian AscIs, and *ad* 2:9 (also *id.* AP II, 1913, 160) on the editorial addition which suggests belief in the ascension. On the Jewish origin of AscIs, cf. also Denis (1970) 175.

[12]Cf., however, Le Moyne (1972) 67-73 on Sir as pre-Sadducaean, and *ibid.* 73-75, on I Mcc as being close to the Sadducees. See, on the other hand, Schubert (1970) 48.—On Josephus as a Pharisee, at least at the end of his life, cf. e.g. Vita 12 and *supra* 4.6.1. For a possible earlier adherence to the Sadducees see e.g. Le Moyne (1972) 27-31. On the source problems in general, *ibid.* 27-153. Concerning grounds for scepticism regarding Josephus' value as a source in this matter, see Le Moyne, 59.

[14]The Sadducees deny [the resurrection] and say: *As the cloud breaks up and disperses, so he that goes down to Sheol never comes back* (Job 7:9). Cf. Raba's assertion (BB 16a) that Job denied the resurrection. See Le Moyne (1972) 173n, as to the possible מ י נ י ך instead of צ ד ו ק י ך in the original text; also *ibid.* 359n.

[15]On the two recensions, cf. e.g. the ET of J. Goldin (1955). AbRN 5, commenting on the description of Antigonus of Soko, given in MAb :3, says that this sage had two disciples, who studied his words about serving the Divine Master as slaves without expecting any reward and started asking (ET Goldin):

> Why did our ancestors see fit to say this thing? Is it possible that a laborer should do his work all day and not take his reward in the evening? If our ancestors, forsooth, had known that there is another world and that there will be a resurrection of the dead, they would not have spoken in this manner. So they arose and withdrew (from the Torah, excluded by B) and split into two sects, the Sadducees and the Boethusians: Sadducees hamed after Zadok, Boethusians after Boethus.

The members of these groups often used vessels of gold and silver in their lives, and the reason seems to be, according to the Sadducees, at least, that

> it is a tradition amongst the Pharisees to afflict themselves in this world; yet in the world to come they will have nothing.

So the social status of the Sadducees is linked to their denial of after-life. They had received their good in this life—as the rich man of the Gospel parable (Lk 16:25). It is hard to distinguish the Boethusians, as a group, from the Sadducees. The distinction may be of a political character: the Boethusians, named after the high priest Simon b. Boethus, appointed by Herod in 24 BC, supported Herod and his dynasty, whereas the Sadducees were pro-Hasmonaean. Thus the Boethusians would be identical with the group called "Herodians" in the Gospel tradition (Mk 3:16; 12:13; Mt 22:16)—thus EncJud IV (1971) 1169; Le Moyne (1972) 340-343.

[16]Cf. e.g. Le Moyne (1972) 170 f.: the change from מ י נ י ך to צ ד ו ק י ך was due to Christian censorship.

[17]TgJ I and II; Neofiti to Gn 4:8. Cf. Le Moyne (1972) 174.

[18]TgJ I and II; Neofiti to Gn 25:29, 34; GnR 63:14 to Gn 25:34. Le Moyne *ibid.*

[19]The servant of Elisha (cf. II Ki 6:20-27 in jSanh 10:2; Le Moyne *ibid*)Some of the righteous ancestors, who have sinned in some way according to the Hebrew Bible, are also pictured as denying the resurrection, as Moses in ExR 44:6 to Ex 32:13 (R. Levi) and Job in GnR 65:11; BB 16a. Cf. Le Moyne *ibid.*

[20]Ant XIII, 297. See e.g. K. Budde (1900) 42-43; Moore I (1927) 68; J. Z. Lauterbach (1951) 120 f. n; Le Moyne (1972) 41, 357-360, on the canon of the Sadducees and the probably lower authority of the Prophets and the Hagiographa in Saducaean circles.

[21]Cf. e.g. Lauterbach (1951) 31 f.; M. Mansoor, EncJud XIV (1971) 621.

[22]Cf. e.g. Ant XVIII, 298, and Le Moyne (1972) 41.

[23]Cf. *supra* n.15 for the description of AbRN 5 and Le Moyne (1972) 41.

[24]Especially III (1971) 304-306, 318 f., and also *id.* Kairos 14 (1972) 57-70: After the massacre of the Pharisees by Alexander Jannaeus they were only a sect, a group, that practiced ritual table fellowship and debated certain rules for eating. Cf. also Le Moyne (1972), 357-363 esp. 361-363.

[25]Cf. e.g. Thackeray I (1926) xiii, xvi.

[26]Cf. e.g. Thackeray I (1926) xiif.

7   A survey and a tentative synthesis

It will be useful to summarize the results with all their possible vagueness and their variations and to concentrate them in a form which is easily available to the reader. For this reason, a statistical table is presented and some conclusions are drawn that are not based upon the table itself but upon the results which are summarized there (cf. 1.3.2). The danger of using statistics is greater than ever in a context like this. A reliable statistic work would in any case require that every single eschatological text of the period had been analyzed with this questionnaire. Now this has not been done, though the selection is rather wide. Many of the numbers given in the columns on the table will be questionable. This is emphasized in certain cases by the question-marks and parentheses. But only if the table as a whole is read *cum grano salis* can it serve its purpose of summarizing and visualizing the results of the analysis of each single text in order to prepare some conclusions and a tentative synthesis of the investigation.

	(A)		(B)							(C)										(D)		
	Real[1]		R	RB	IS	Int	Co	Wic	InQ	Ri	E	TE	T	TH	H	Ass	Ex	Enth	LD	ADe	J
Dn	2[2]		1	1										1+1?					2		1
Jub	1				1			1			(1)								1		1
I En 83-90	1		1																1		
I En 1-36	4		2		3	1	2												1	3	3
I En 91-104	4+1		2+1?		2			1				2	1						3	1	3
I En 37-71	3		1	2	1?	1?				1	4	1				1			3	1?	2
I En 108	1		1		1			1						1					1	1	1
TestXIIPatr	7		4		1			1				1	1					1	5	1	3
PsSol	1		1											1					3		4
Qumran	1+2?	3	1+2?								2			5		1			1+1?		4
Essenes	2		1		2			1	2										1	1	
VAE+ApcMos	8		5	1	3?	3?				1		1	1				1		4	3?	
LAB	8	(1)	2	1?	3+2?	1				2			2		1	1+1?	1		2	2+1?	1
IV Ezr	3		2	1	2	2	2	1		1			2						2	2	2
II Bar	4		2	2	2	2					(2)		1				1		5	2	3
ApcAbr	1+1?			1?							1		1						1		2
TestAbr	4				4											1				4	1
ApEz	1		1																		1
InscrPalest	24?? +(3)		(3)																		
LXX	5+6?		2+2?	3	1+1?					1				1					3+1?	1+1?	6
II Mcc	5		1	2	1?	1													1		1+1?
IV Mcc	11				1						1			3	2	1				7	4
Wi	3		2						6		2			1					2+1?	3	4
Philo	18	9			*17*		5	2			4			3	1				1	20	5
Josephus	6+(2)		2	2	5+(2) 3		1? 3	3		2	(2)	2							2	6+	3
							(1)		(1)											(2)	
OrSib	2			*1*	1						2								2		1
PsPhoc	2			*1*	2			1			2								1	2	
JA		5	4	1	1					1			1								
TestJob	4+2?		1+1?		1+1?		1?				1	2					2		1	2	
II En	4+(1)		1?		(1)								2						3	1	3
InscrDiaspora	2+2 etc? (1)		(1)+ 1?		*1+1*						(1)								1?+ (1)	2	(1?)
Rabbinica	10+ (1)		6	3	1+ (1)			1+ (1)			(1)					1+ (1)			3+ (1)	1+ (1)	3+ (1)
Tg	9		5	1	3	1?								1					7	1?	4
SUMMARY	137	17	46	21	40	8	4	16	8	20	6	2	2	35	7	10	4 3		60	63	67
	37?	(1)	(4)	2?	9?	5?		1? 1?	(1)		(1) (4)			(2)	(1) 1?				(2)	7?	(1)
	(8)		8?	*2*	(4)			(1)						1?					4?	(3)	(1?)
					18																1?

¹The **(A)**, **(B)**, **(C)** and **(D)** above are the usual four questions (1.3.4.1-4, as rubrics for the various answers on this line, where the abbreviations stand for the following contents:

Real = "Realized eschatology", i.e. eternal life starting already within the precincts of the temporal life. Resurrection (assumption or exaltation) terminology is used about initiation into Judaism, the community of the righteous, an ethical and "philosophical" life.

R = "Resurrection" without any precise statements about the fate of the body.

RB = Clear statements about the resurrection of the body.

IS = "Immortality of the soul", i.e. denoting different forms of non-corporeal after-life, starting immediately after death in most cases or, at least, with no mention of a *revivification*. It also serves different kinds of ideas on an intermediate state. The italicized numbers stand for the texts where the salvation of the soul is stressed and contrasted with the destruction of the body at death.

Int = "Intermediate state", texts where both the continued life of the soul after death and the resurrection in the eschatological future are expressed in such a way that a harmonization between the two ideas seems to have taken place. The cases below represent the "store-house" type of intermediate state, i.e., the souls are either explicitly said to dwell in special "store-houses", preserved there until the resurrection, or nothing is said about any consciousness of the souls in this state.

Co = "Consciousness of the soul in the intermediate state", the souls are considered as living a real personal life between death and resurrection, already enjoying heaven or hell in some measure.

Wic = "Wicked", the souls of the wicked are also considered as "surviving" death. Usually their punishment in after-life is described or asserted.

InQ = "Inherent quality", i.e., regarding immortality as a quality which naturally and necessarily belongs to the soul, irrespective of its moral standard. Death is considered as an automatic liberation of the soul to a blessed state (though the idea of punishment of base souls may be juxtaposed with InQ—e.g. BJ II, 154-157—just as in Plato, cf. e.g. Phaedo 105B—106E and 111E-114B).

Ri = "Righteousness" leads to immortality, contrasted with the preceding type of belief in immortality of the soul. Such a way of thinking would logically require the annihilation of the wicked at death, but it is sometimes juxtaposed with the idea of punishments for the wicked in Hades or Gehenna.

E = Resurrection is described as a return to "earthly life", or the immortal life (without any mention of the resurrection) is pictured as merely very good earthly life.

TE = "Transformed earthly"; though life after the resurrection or eternal life generally is seen as new earthly life, it is also transformed into supranatural dimensions of light, glory, the presence of God in the Holy Land, etc.

T = "Transformed" life after the resurrection or after death, of the body or of the soul, without any answer to the question: On earth or in heaven?

TH = "Transformed heavenly", life in a transcendent glory, Divine or angelic, with the imagery of stars and heavenly light.

Ass = The beginning of new life is described as an "assumption" of body and/or soul into heaven before death, at death or on the last day.

Ex = "Exaltation", though not explicitly an assumption as the reward of the righteous after death.

Enth = Enthronement and/or coronation on God's right hand.

LD = A "last day", a day of resurrection, salvation and/or judgment is mentioned, or an eschatological future at the end of history, when the change of the ages is realized.

ADe = Life after death, immortality or punishment, begins immediately "after death".

J = A final "judgment" is directly mentioned or presupposed by the description of the retribution of righteous or wicked respectively.

²The numbers given in this table refer to the number of pericopes or textual units of some kind (often chapters) where any belief in life after death (the first column) or related ideas may be mentioned. The numbers correspond to the list in the third index *infra* ("answers to questions"),

where references to chapters (and corresponding subdivisions, usually not verses) of the passages under consideration are given. These references can be explained by the discussion in the contents concerning each text *supra* (or in the foot-notes). I want to emphasize the fact that these numbers are recognized by the author as being quite debatable and questionable in many cases. Nevertheless, they give some idea about the importance given to thoughts about after-life in the various texts. A question-mark after the number indicates doubts about the interpretation given in the table. A parenthesis means that the reference within the parenthesis does not belong to the period under consideration in this work.

7.1 Some theses

The conclusions drawn from the analyses of each single text, summarized and visualized in the preceding table, are presented in the form of theses for the discussion.

7.1.1
There is obviously no single Jewish doctrine about life after death in the period under consideration; there is rather a great variety and pluralism of ideas both about the end of world history and about death and about that which follows the death of the individual person.

7.1.2
These ideas, partly contrary, partly possible to harmonize, but seldom actually harmonized, do not only change from one stream of tradition to another, but appear simply juxtaposed in the same writings and even in passages very close to each other. Thus, resurrection (of the body) and immortality (of the soul) are combined, perhaps only by juxtaposition[1]. They may also be harmonized or systematized into an intermediate state of the dead souls between death and the final resurrection of the body[2]. Different images express the newness of the life beyond death[3]. Sometimes this new life of the righteous (and the punishment of the sinners) is considered to commence immediately after death,[4] sometimes on the Last Day[5] or in an eschatological future which is not precisely defined[6].

7.1.3
This leads me to the conclusion that the single ideas, images, visions, symbols, teachings and intimations about after-life in Early Judaism were not of great importance to the authors themselves, nor, probably, to their first readers. The texts themselves[7] require a sort of "demythologizing", if we wish to apprehend their *message,* the common underlying motifs and the intentions expressed in all the variations of symbols and concepts about life after death. It is the task of the interpreter to try to transpose or translate the various symbols into a language of

abstraction and theory concerning the human person and his relation to God, the meaning of human existence and death. This is what I mean, when I use the term "demythologizing".

7.1.4

"The Jewish doctrine of the resurrection of the dead"—more particularly "of the body"—is indeed a "myth". The idea that the Jews in general shared a common doctrine of this kind, as opposed to "the Greek doctrine about the immortality of the soul", may be quite useful for pedagogic simplification or for the construction of hermeneutic models (1.1-1.1.1 *supra*). It is true that such a doctrine seems to be well established both in Palestinian and Greek-speaking diaspora Judaism towards the end of the first century CE, and was definitely canonized by the Rabbis of Jabneh. But it does not dominate our sources from Judaism of the period as a whole—and the role of the body is hardly particularly stressed even by the canonical formulas (MSanh 10:1a; Shemone esre II). Statements on an immortality of the soul which excludes the resurrection of the body are almost as common as those which explicitly state the resurrection of the body, and the same proportions can be asserted for statements on the soul's life after death without exclusion of the body and texts which state the resurrection without explicit reference to the body. The two main types of beliefs about after-life are easily combined, with or (more often!) without the harmonizing concept of the intermediate state.

7.1.5

The popular idea about the grossly materialistic and naive thoughts concerning the resurrection and *post-mortem* life in Early Judaism has very little foundation. Throughout the sources we find suggestions about the heavenly, transcendent, glorified and spiritual state of the righteous in the new life after death.

7.1.6

What we have previously said applies to both Palestinian and Greek diaspora texts. But there is an undeniable difference: the emphasis on the immortality of the soul, *excluding* the body, is not found in the Palestinian sources; it is only found in some of the texts from the diaspora (including then Josephus, who quotes Eleazar of Masada, the Jewish nationalist, for such an extremely "Greek" view on after-life, cf. 4.6.4). However some of the clearest expressions of the belief in the resurrection of the body are also found in the texts from the Greek-speaking diaspora[8].

7.1.7

A special group of texts presents the idea of a resurrection already realized or an immortality achieved by initiation into the chosen people or the elect community or by the exercise of true philosophy and righteousness. These are the Dead Sea texts[9] and some of the most Hellenized documents[10].

7.1.8
The motif of a coming end of history, a Last Day, or a similar point of eschatological future, when God's righteousness will be vindicated, in the salvation of those who trust in him and the punishment of the sinners, is very consistent. Even Philo preserves this idea (cf. 4.5.4 and 7). IV Mcc, however, has replaced it by the death of the individual (4.3.11). This is also the dominating trend in Philo, of course. Also, TestAbr is silent concerning the eschatological future of the people or the world and concentrates wholly on the fate of the individual. But these exceptions rather confirm the rule and the consistent trend in our sources.

7.1.9
The motif of a common end of history does not at all exclude, but may very well include the hope of immediate salvation for the righteous after death. In most cases this does not imply a doctrine on the intermediate state between the two "dates" of final salvation and judgment.[11] Both aspects seem to be accepted side by side without any need of harmonization.

7.1.10
Even when the idea of the intermediate state is introduced, it functions very much as a secondary harmonization between two perspectives. This is proven by the fact that its position is hardly ever well balanced: either the intermediate state tends to become the definite, final blessed or damned state[12], or it is pictured as a treasury or treasuries where the souls are preserved until the resurrection, i.e., practically without importance: this state is comparable to the "sleep" of the bodies in the earth[13], although the souls in the treasuries may be said to invoke God for the establishment of Divine justice.[14]

7.1.11
Finally, the most consistent theme in all of the types of texts is obviously the one of judgment and final retribution. That must be a very important motif in the varying forms of expressing life beyond the limits of this life in Early Judaism. Judgment may function as the final act of decisions which determine the fate of the righteous and wicked people[15], or as a decision for the individual immediately upon death[16], or as the fact of punishment of the wicked in Sheol/Gehenna and a blessed life in heaven for the righteous[17], or merely as salvation of the righteous from the destruction of the mass of perdition[18]. There are also mixed forms of these ideas[19]. This does not seem so important in comparison to the basic motif of final justice and reward for righteousness/punishment for wickedness.

7.1.12
The establishment of the belief in the resurrection of the dead as a dogma in Rabbinic Judaism represents the final result of a development, which started with unclear and tentative formulations in the early inter-testamental literature.[20] The systematized version of the concept of an intermediate state also belongs to a later part of the period under consideration[21]. Otherwise, the age of the texts does

in no way coincide with a certain type of belief in after-life: testimonies to both the resurrection of the body and a spiritual immortality appear from at least 100 BC[22] until AD 100[23].

[1]Cf. the table for texts, where the columns R and IS are both marked without any marking in the column Int, I En 91-104; 108; LAB; II Mcc and PsPhoc 99-115.

[2]E.g. I En 22; IV Ezr 7:28-114; II Bar 21:23; 30; Josephus, BJ II, 163; III, 374 f.

[3]Cf. 7.2.1 for the astral imagery, but see also the texts which describe a transformation of the earth into overwhelming fruitfulness and a kingdom of peace and joy, e.g. I En 51:4-5; TestDan 5:11 ff.; II Bar 29 and 73-74; 1QS IV:6 ff; 4QPsDn; ApcAbr 21; OrSib III, 767 ff.; IV, 171-190.

[4]See the column ADe in the table—the numbers may be checked in index III and the contents of my text in each case.

[5]Cf. e.g. I En 51; PsSol 15:12; ApcMos 10:2; 13:3b; 43:2; IV Ezr 7:26-28; II Bar 49:2; 51:1; OrSib IV, 171-190.

[6]E.g. Jub 23:30 f.; I En 108; TestJud 24-25; TestBenj 10:5-10; LAB 3:10; Philo, Exsecr 158; TestJob 4:9.

[7]Cf. 1.1.1 supra, concerning NT, and 7.4 infra. This task of "demythologizing" is not given by the need of "preaching" the message of these texts today, but by the very task of interpreting, i.e., understanding the texts and the intentions of their authors.

[8]LXX: Job 19:25 f.; Is 26:19; Ez 37:1-14; II Mcc 7; 14:46; OrSib IV, 181 f.; PsPhoc 103.

[9]See 1QS XI, 7b-9a; 1QH III, 19-23; XI, 10-14.

[10]Philo, Congr 57; SpecLeg I, 345; Vita cont 13; LA I, 107 f.; Praem 70; Legatio 91; QGn I, 70, 75; IV, 46, 152 f.; JA 8:10 f.; 15:3-4; 16:9 ff.; 18:7; 27:8.

[11]I En 91-104; LAB 3:10; 19:12 vs. 32:9; Wi 3:1-8; PsPhoc 103-108, 115; TestJob 4:9, vs. 52:9; II En 8-10 vs. 61:2-3; 65:8; 66:7; GnR 14:5//LvR 14:9; Shemone esre II; Ber 60b vs. Shab 152b; Ber 28b.

[12]I En 22; IV Ezr 7:78 ff.; Josephus, BJ II, 163; III, 374 f.; Ant XVIII, 14.

[13]II Bar 21:23; 30:2.

[14]IV Ezr 4:35 ff. Cf. also I En 9:10.

[15]I En 22:13b; 91:7-11; 63:10; TestBenj 10:8; PsSol 15:12; LAB 3:10; IV Ezr 7:33 ff.; LXX Ps 1:5; Wi 3:7 f.; OrSib IV, 183 f.; RH 16b.

[16]I En 103:3-7; TestAsher 6:5-6; Josephus' Essenes, BJ II, 154 ff.; IV Ezr 7:78 ff.; TestAbr A 11-13// B 8-11; Philo, Praem 60, Cher 2; Shab 152b; Ber 28b.

[17]I En 22; IV Mcc 13:14-17; Somn I, 151 f.; II En 8-10.

[18]Dn 12:1 f.; II En 66:7.

[19]I En 22; II En 8-10; 61:2-3; 65:8; 66:7; II Bar 29-30; Wi 3:1-8.

[20]Dn 12:2; Jub 23:30 f.

[21]IV Ezr; II Bar; Josephus, BJ II, 163; III, 374 f.—but see also I En 22.

[22]Dn 12:2 and Jub 23:30 f.; I En 102:4 f.; 103:3-7.

[23]ApEz; II Bar 49-51 and IV Mcc.

7.2 Three recurrent motifs

Some themes or motifs have recurred again and again in the different texts. I have selected three of them for a special survey and a few comments, since they are only partly covered by the table (7).

7.2.1 I. *The association between the immortal blessed and stars, angels, and other heavenly bodies or beings.*

Even as early as Dn 12:3 the righteous teachers are promised a future glory "like the stars". The statement of Dn 12:3 appears to apply the suffering Servant's exaltation and glorification (Is 52:13 and 53:11) to the somewhat larger group of "the wise leaders" (cf. 2.2.3). In I En 104:2 (3.2.3.6) and IV Ezr 7:97, 125a (3.9.3) *all* the righteous who have suffered in this life receive a similar consolation: they will shine like the stars or even brighter than the stars. The statement of Wi 3:7a that the righteous will "shine" at "the time of their visitation" (4.4.3.2-3) and other similar promises concerning the future glory of the righteous also represent a process of "democratization" (cf. n.22 to 2.2.3) of the motif of glorification (probably *post mortem*) by heavenly light.[1]

7.2.1.1

In LAB 33:5 the "fathers" are implicitly said to be like the stars in their glory (3.8.3), for Deborah tells the people to imitate these fathers and thus become like the stars. These stars fought on the side of Israel cf. Jg 5:20), i.e., they are personalized beings, who are associated with the angels. This association, approaching identification, between stars and angels is also seen in LAB 10:5, further in EthEn 104:2 (3.2.3.6)[2] and in II Bar 51:10: By the transformation after the resurrection the righteous will be "like unto the angels" and "equal to the stars" (3.10.2—cf. 3.10.2.2.2 and 3, on v.12).

The association between stars and angels has old roots. *Job 38:7* describes how

the morning stars sang together and all the sons of God shouted aloud (NEB),

at the creation of the world. This is probably a trace of "fragment of myth" (cf. e.g. G. A. Smith, 1927, 432, for this term) from wide-spread astral religion in the ancient Near East[3]: the stars (as well as the sun and the moon) are divinities which are reduced to "sons of God" or "angels" in one stream of Israelite tradition[4]. That the "son of God" on the throne of Jerusalem (Ps 2:7; 110:3[5]) is also described as a star (cf. Nm 24:17[6]), as well as the Divine king of Babylon (Is 14:12-14[7]), is no surprise in light of this general background. The same imagery is applied to the Messianic priest (TestLevi 18:3, cf. Hultgård, 1971, 125-135) and king (TestJudah 24:1, cf. Hultgård, 1971, 155, 159) in Jewish apocalyptic traditions, and to Jesus in NT (Rev 1:16; 22:16; cf. Mt 2:2, 9 f.; 17:2). Thus, the wider application of the image of the star may also be regarded as a sort of "democratization": from a royal attribute to a promise for all the righteous.

7.2.1.2

In IV Mcc 17:5 the martyred mother and her sons are likened to the moon and the stars in their *post-mortem* glorification (4.3.7); perhaps it is Pythagorean influence (cf. Dupont-Sommer, 1939, 47), though it is also within the tradition from Dn 12:3. The introduction of the *moon* here depends upon the concrete situation, of course, the *mother* with her sons.

7.2.1.3

IV Ezr 7:97 compares the future glory of the righteous both with the stars[8] and with the *sun* (3.9.3), as JA 18:7 does (4.9.2) in the case of the already risen and transformed new convert. In II En 66:7 (4.11.4) the faces of the righteous who are saved "will shine like the sun". This comparison may also be inspired by *Jg 5:31:*

All who love you, shall be like the sun rising in strength (cf. NEB).

In Rabbinic traditions the same image is used about the future glory of the righteous with reference to this text[9].

7.2.1.4

The fact that these images are used to symbolize the angelic or Divine glory as well as the glory of the risen righteous reveals that these are considered to share a status similar to that of the angels, close to God himself (cf. *infra* 7.4.3). However, the angels also appear alone in connection with the risen righteous. The Qumran texts emphasize the unity of the congregation of the righteous with that of "holy angels" (lQSb III, 6—cf. lQH XI, 11 f.; 4Q181 1 II, 3-4—*supra* 3.5.3, 3.5.4 and 3.5.7), a glorification which is already realized in the community. Philo says that Abraham, having left this mortal life, became equal to the angels, unbodied souls, (Sacr 5, 4.5.6), who are more or less identified with the Ideas (Gig 61, 4.5.6). According to II Bar 51:5 (3.10.2 and 3.10.2.2.2) the risen righteous will be transformed into the splendour of angels (cf. 7.2.1.1 on vv.10 and 12[10]). According to one possible translation, the final step is taken by I En 51:4: the risen righteous will become angels, but we cannot be sure of this translation (3.2.4.1)[11]. Anyhow, we may assert that our texts contain a definite trend towards a blurring of the border between men who share in the resurrection of the righteous, and the angels,

7.2.1.5

In Job 38:7 (7.2.1.1) the angelic beings were called "sons of God", as often in OT (Gn 6:2; Ps 89:5-7; Job 1:6; 2:1-cf. 4.4.6 n.17). A similar designation is found in the Dead Sea Scrolls: "the sons of heaven" (1QS XI, 8—3.5.1.6—1QH III, 22) with which the members of the community are associated[12]. Once they are even called "gods" (אלים) 4Q181 1 II, 3 f.). The wicked exclaim at the sight of the exalted righteous in *Wi 5:5:*

He is now counted one of the sons of God (4.4.6).

This is a vindication of a truth, which is asserted by the just already in his life on earth (2:16-18—cf. also v.13 παις κυριου) · This means that the righteous is not only similar to the angels, but that he is one of them, or, at least, rightly can be called "son of God. So the meaning of "sons of God" is applied from angelic beings to the faithful of the Lord. This may be observed in LXX Ps 88(89):6-8 (cf. Riesenfeld, EuA 47, 508). The same reinterpretation of "sons of God" may be the basis for the designation of the Qumran Community as בני אור (1QM *passim;* 4QAmram—*supra* 3.5.5) or the righteous of I En 108:11 as "spirits of the good of the race of light" (3.2.5)[13]. Above all, this concerns the term "holy ones" (ἅγιοι קדושים) used as a synonym of "sons of God" in Ps 89(88):6, 8.

7.2.1.6

"The *saints* of the Most High"(קדישי עליונין)appear in the interpretation of the vision of the Son of Man in Dn 7:22, 25, 27. The Son of Man figure seems to symbolize "the people of the saints of the Most High", at least in the present redaction of the vision narrative.[14] The "holy ones", originally heavenly beings, who were more or less identical with the angels[15], were thus in the redaction of Dn 7 identified with the faithful Jews. The ambiguity of the term is still clearly visible in Wi 5:5 and (7.2.1.5 and 4.4.6), where ἅγιοι is used as a synonym of υἱοι θεου, likewise in Ps 89 (88):6, 8 (*supra* 7.2.1.5). The same phenomenon reappears in 1QS XI, 8, though "sons of heaven" has replaced "sons of God" (3.5.6; 7.2.1.5). This passage combines the term with "lot"(גורל)just like Wi 5:5 (κλῆρος) 1QH XI, 11 f. and some NT passages[16]. The new meaning of "holy ones" is univocally represented by TestDan 5:11 f., where it is the synonym of "righteous" and by TestLevi 18:11, 14, where it denotes all those who are saved with the patriarchs, or, perhaps, "the saints" in the later Christian Church's understanding.

7.2.2   II. *Assumption or exaltation*

The transcendent glorification of the righteous may also be expressed in terms of assumption or exaltation before or after death. The stories of Enoch's and Elijah's assumptions (2.1.2) are early examples, which inspired Jewish meditation (cf. *infra* 7.3.2). The Servant of Yahweh is "highly exalted" (Is 52:13). Expressions of assumption or exaltation may be combined with resurrection statements, as in II Bar 51 (3.10.2). Or they may function as alternatives of resurrection, when the beginning of the new life at death or after death is to be described (e.g. TestAbr, 3.12).

7.2.2.1

Some Psalms (cf. 2.1.3 with further references) may already apply the assumption idea to the individual believer or they may have been used with this understanding by Jews who hoped for a life after death. Enoch is the type of the righteous in *Wi 4:10 f.* (4.4.5).

ζων μεταξυ ἀμαρτωλων μετετεθη, ἡρπαγη μη κακια ἀλλαξῃ την συνεσιν αὐτου.

The death of a young righteous man (cf. 4:17) is presented as the assumption of his soul (4:14). I En 71 describes the assumption of Enoch, elaborating the short allusion to this extraordinary action in Gn 5:24b (3.2.4.7). This is probably also

205

the foundation of Philo's statement in Gig 61 on the translation of the men of God from this world to the world of Ideas, though Abraham is the example given in the following context (4.5.6). Also according to LAB 4:11, Abraham is exalted *super excelsa* (3.8.2). Another assumption story is told about Phinees. He is identified with Elijah in 48:1, as in PRE 29 and 47: At his death he is transferred to a mountain, where God's eagle feeds him, until he is revealed again as Elijah. Then he is exalted to heaven, to those who are there before him (the patriarchs and other "fathers"?), in order to return at the end of time (3.8.7—cf. James, 1917, *ad loc.*). Moses entered heaven at his death according to LAB 32:9 (3.8.7). Israel's glory is described as a sort of realized assumption in LAB 30:5 (3.8.4).

7.2.2.2
Even the bodies of Job's children are taken up into heaven, according to TestJob 39:12 f. (4.10.2), whereas Job's soul alone is brought to heaven (52:2 ff.—*ibid.*). He is also enthroned in heaven (33:2-9) as his children are crowned near the Divine glory (40:3—4.10.2)[17].

7.2.2.3
The point of these statements on the assumption or exaltation of the righteous is above all the conviction that those who trust in God will finally be preserved in the communion with him which they enjoyed in this life and, beyond death, be brought into an even closer relation, a more immediate experience of his presence (cf. Wi 3:1, 9; 5:15; TestJob 40:3; 52:9; TestAbr A20//B14 and *infra* 7.4.3).[18]

7.2.3   III. *The saints of Israel*

The conviction of a new life of the righteous after death is usually not based on a rational argument for the immortality of the soul (as in Plato's Phaedo) or the resurrection of the body (though there are some analogies in Sanh 90b-91a—cf. 5.4.3). Rather it is deeply related to the sacred traditions of Israel and its religious leaders through the centuries (more or less historical). Philo, too, refers to Abraham as a prototype of immortalized men of God (Sacr 5, 4.5.6). Even in pre-exilic traditions some vague notions about personal life after death are related to a prophet and holy man of God (I Sm 28:11 ff.), who somehow continues his work for the people even after death (cf. I Sm 9:6 ff.; 15:10-16:13). The traditions about the assumptions of Enoch and Elijah[19] or the *post mortem* exaltation of the Suffering Servant of Is 53[20] show us how Israelite reflection, in spite of its dark view of death and Sheol (2.1) could not accept that an outstanding man of God, who in the temporal life lived in unbroken communion with God (cf. Gn 5:22a, 24a) disappeared in a state of anonymous eternal darkness and separation from God. This emphasis on the resurrection or immortality of the holy men is another recurrent motif in the Jewish texts studied. Thus, in Dn 12:3, the statement about the future glory of the מַשְׂכִּלִים does not concern the people in general, only their wise leaders[21]. In Dn 12:13 Daniel himself receives the promise about his future resurrection (2.3).

7.2.3.1
The Gn statement on Enoch's assumption is the basis of the description of his assumption and transformation in I En 70-71 (3.2.4). He is naturally the first of the holy fathers mentioned among those who are to be seen as risen on the day of final salvation according to Test Benj 10:6 (3.3.1).

7.2.3.2
Other Biblical figures, whose life after death and final exaltation are directly stated in the passages we have examined, include Adam (3.7.1-2), Moses (3.8.7-LAB 19:16[22]), Phinees (3.8.7), Job (4.10.1-2), some of the twelve sons of Jacob, at least (3.3.1), and, above all, the triad of Abraham, Isaac and Jacob (3.3.1; 4.3.1; 4.3.3)[23].

7.2.3.3
Among the three patriarchs, *Abraham* is more important than the others and sometimes stands alone in a similar context (3.8.2; 3.11; 3.12; 4.5.6). In IV Mcc Abraham is the type of the Maccabaean martyrs, who suffer and are glorified after death (4.3.5-4.3.7, n.21).

7.2.3.4
When "the *fathers*" or "the ancestors" are mentioned in the same way, the term may include the rest of the "saints" of Israel, as, probably, in IV Mcc 13:17, where it is used together with Abraham, Isaac and Jacob, or in 18:23. LAB 33:5 (3.8.3; 7.2.1.1) implicitly seems to state the glorification of the fathers as "stars".

This idea of the immortal and glorified "fathers" and holy men of God may be briefly alluded to in the inscription on Arsinoe's tomb in Leontopolis (CIJ 1510-4.12.3): "The soul went to the saints" (ὁσίους cf. also 4.12 n.7).

7.2.3.5
We noticed the element of *suffering* in the image of Abraham in IV Mcc. The saints who receive the promise of resurrection and eternal life are, above all, those who have suffered, as already the Servant of Is 53, the archetype of the מַשְׂכִּלִים of Dn 12:3 (cf. 11:33, 35 and *supra* 2.2.3), of the righteous man in Wi 2-5, of the persecuted and oppressed people in I En and II Bar (cf. Nickelsburg, 1972, 62-129) and, perhaps, also the martyrs of II Mcc 7 (Nickelsburg, 103-106). The martyr stories in II Mcc, and also their use for homiletical purpose in IV Mcc, link suffering and resurrection/immortality even more closely to each other[24]. The eschatology of II Bar and IV Ezr is, of course, strongly marked by the national suffering after the fall of Jerusalem (3.9; 3.10).

7.2.3.6
It is no mere coincidence that the "fathers", above all the patriarchs, whose lives and death had been elaborated in midrashic legend, play a special role for the hope of life after death. The fathers stand for the whole of the people[25]. John the Baptist's attacks on trusting in the status as a "child of Abraham" (Mt 3:9/Lk 3:8) may reveal popular notions about sharing the merits of the patriarchs[26] As

the resurrection is linked with the fate of the whole of the people, it is also closely related to the re-gathering of the diaspora[27]. So the importance of these individuals lies precisely in the fact that they represent the community, the people, its hopes for all the members of the people. They function, indeed, as the first-fruits of the resurrection[28]. But such a doctrine, similar to Paul's, is never explicitly stated in the written traditions which are preserved to-day. There is obviously no single individual person in Early Judaism who plays the role attributed to Jesus by Paul. One reason is, of course, that the resurrection of the fathers is still expected for the *future* or their eternal life, which they already experience[29], is realized only in "heaven", beyond history and the temporal world, whereas the *kerygma* about the resurrection of Jesus "on the third day", i.e. already realized and experienced within history, forms the foundation of Pauline thinking (I Cor 15:1-11).

[1]Cf. also for the symbolism of I En 92:4 (3.2.3.2); 39:7 (3.2.4.4); 50:1 (3.2.4.1); 58:3 (3.2.4.4); 108:12-14 (3.2.5); PsSol 3:12 (3.4.2); 1QS IV, 8 (3.5.1 and 3.5.1.3); 4Q Amram (3.5.5); LAB 19:4 (3.8.9); 51:5 (3.8 n.26); IV Mcc 9:22 (4.3.6); OrSib IV, 189 (4.7.1); II En 65:8 (4.11.4); TgIs 26:19 (5.8.3). More or less explicitly the "light" denotes the glory of the post-resurrection state and/or of future life.

[2]Cf. also I En 72-75; 80:1-6; 82. Cf. also Dn 8:10 for the identification of stars and angels, and J. J. Collins, CBQ 36 (1974) 33 f.

[3]Cf. besides comm. *ad loc.*, e.g. Sellin, NKZ 30, 261 f.; H. S. Nyberg (1938) 59 f.; F. Cumont (1949) 142-145; O. Rühle-C. M. Edsman, RGG I, 662 f.; F. M. T. de Liagre Böhl, RGG II, 815 f.

[4]Another effort of more radical "demythologization" of astral myth is the subtle polemic of the "priestly" Creation narrative in Gn 1:15-19—cf. here e.g. the comm. by G. v.Rad (1949) *ad loc.*

[5]Cf. e.g. G. Widengren (1941) 9, 17 f.; Coppens, EThL 32, 9-15; S. Mowinckel I (ET 1963) 53 ff., 62 ff.; Dahood I (1966) 11 f.; R. E. Murphy (1968) 596.

[6]Cf. N. H. Snaith (1967); M. Noth (1966) *ad loc.* TgOnk has מלכבא, TgJ I has תקיף מליך TgJ II מלכן for כורכב.

[7]See e.g. Smith I (1927) 428-432; S. Erlandsson (1970) 123.

[8]Cf. IV Ezr 7:125a: those who have practiced self-discipline are promised faces brighter than the stars—3.9.3.

[9]See e.g. SDt § 47 to Dt 11:21; § 10 to Dt 1:10; BB 8b; GnR 12:6; LvR 28:1; LamR 23; EcclR I, 7 § 9. Cf. Bacher. II (1890) 146; Bill IV, 940 f. See also TgJon which has a clear eschatological interpretation (ורחמוהי יהון עתידין לאזהרא). Cf. also the conclusion of the Matthaean interpretation (J. Jeremias, 1965, 79-84; J. Schniewind, 1950, and J. Schmid, 1956, *ad loc.*) of the parable of the wheat and the tares, about the future glory of the righteous, Mt 13:32. This logion seems to be dependent on Jg 5:31 + Dn 12:3—cf. e.g. A. Jones (1966) *ad loc.* Cf. also Mt 17:2.—In light of this background it seems probable that Paul, in his argument for the resurrection body in I Cor 15:40 f., does not create his analogy merely *ad hoc.* but rather employs traditional metaphors for the glory of the blessed immortal righteous.

[10]Cf. also LAB 30:5 for the motif of exaltation above the angels.

[11]The saying attributed to Jesus in the Synoptic tradition (Mk 12:25 parr) that the risen righteous will be "like the angels" obviously belongs to the same tradition.—A looser association with death and immortality has the angel-psychopomp of TestAsher 6:6 (3.3.4) and TestAbr (3.12.1, Michael). Cf. also the punishing angels of 1QS IV, 12 (3.5.1).

[12]Cf. also 1QH XI, 11—3.5.4—and the designation "the sons of your truth".

208

[13]The remarkable formulation of Lk 20:36, deviating from the parallels of Mk and Mt, should be seen in light of this background (cf. E. Klostermann, 1929; J. M. Creed, 1930; W. Grundmann, 1961, *ad loc.*). The phrase is obviously purely Jewish in its formulation, though the explicit identification of those who share in the resurrection for eternal life and the "sons of God" is not made anywhere in the Jewish material, as far as I have seen.

[14]Cf. e.g. Schmid, Jud 27, 192-220, on the possibility of several redactions and a change of the meaning of the Son of Man figure between the redactions.

[15]Cf. supra 7.2.3 and e.g. P. Vielhauer, *In hon.* G. Dehn (1957) 73.

[16]Col 1:12; Acts 26:18 ($\dot{\eta}\gamma\iota\alpha\sigma\mu\dot{\epsilon}\nu\omega\iota$ instead of $\dot{\alpha}\gamma\iota\omega\iota$) For $\kappa\lambda\tilde{\eta}\rho\omicron\varsigma$ as a designation of the congregation, cf. I Pt 5:3 and also Acts 8:21. For $\dot{\alpha}\gamma\iota\omega\iota$ as a designation for the members of the Church cf. the Pauline letter addresses and I Cor 6:2, e.g. Concerning the term "lot": Does Dn 12:13 already presuppose its eschatological connotation of a blessed state in heaven—or did it contribute to the development of this connotation? Cf. W. Foerster, TWNT III (1938) 761.

[17]I refer to the table in the beginning of ch. 7 for further references to the theme assumption/exaltation and to the corresponding passages in the index III. Besides, it may be mentioned here that ApcMos 32:4 and PsPhoc 108 describe the ascension of the spirit in a way which vaguely reminds us of Eccl 12:7 (3.7.1 and 4.8.1.2). But the anthropology is different: In ApcMos 32:4 the soul represents the person itself, and in PsPhoc 108 the soul is at least more personal than the (divine) breath of life, the principle of life, in Eccl 12:7—and Gn 2:7. Cf. also 5.3.2.

[18]Cf. also ITh 4:17: $\dot{\alpha}\rho\pi\alpha\gamma\eta\sigma\dot{\omega}\mu\epsilon\vartheta\alpha$ (cf. Wi 4:10), denotes the assumption of all the faithful, both living and the dead who have risen, $\dot{\epsilon}\nu$ $\nu\epsilon\varphi\dot{\epsilon}\lambda\alpha\iota\varsigma$ (cf. LAB 30:5) $\epsilon\dot{\iota}\varsigma$ $\dot{\alpha}\pi\alpha\nu\tau\eta\sigma\iota\nu$ $\tauο\tilde{\upsilon}$ $\kappa\upsilon\rho\dot{\iota}\omicron\upsilon$ $\epsilon\dot{\iota}\varsigma$ $\dot{\alpha}\dot{\epsilon}\rho\alpha$ (cf. PsPhoc 108), and the assumption brings them into a deeper fellowship $\sigma\dot{\upsilon}\nu$ $\kappa\upsilon\rho\dot{\iota}\omega$. Cf. further Ph 2:9; Jn 3:14; 8:28; 12:32, 34; Acts 2:33; 5:31, passages where the terminology of exaltation has replaced that of resurrection from the dead in the case of Jesus.

[19]The story about the resurrection of the man who touched the relics, the bones of Elisha (II Ki 13:21), may be another example of a belief in a victory over death, connected with a holy man of God, even though he had himself died in this case . . .

[20]For the view that the Suffering Servant is exalted *after* his death, by a resurrection of some kind, cf. e.g. Volz (1934) 230; Schilling (1951) 60 f.; H. W. Robinson (1955) 97; Cazelles, SoOr 4, 115 f.; further, referring to ancient Canaanite ritual as a background of Is 53, F. M. Th. Böhl (1923) 20-53; Engnell, BJRL 31, 77, 87, 89; Riesenfeld (1948) 9; H. J. Kraus, RGG I, 693; G. R. Driver, *In mem.* P. Kahle (1968) 90-105. Cf. also more cautious suggestions in the same direction, by Nötscher (1926) 154; H. Gressmann (1929) 331; Nyberg, SEÅ 7, 20, 64-68; Molin, Jud 9, 230; Martin-Achard (1956) 100 f.; S. Mowinckel (1956) 234 f.; W. Zimmerli-J. Jeremias (1965) 35; C. Westermann (1966) *ad loc.*; Frost, Interpr 26, 441. Cf. also C. North (1956) 147-149; *id.* (1964) *ad loc.* This is denied by e.g. J. Lindblom (1951) 45; Kaiser (1959) 119-123; König (1964) 223 f.; Wächter (1964) 194n; Fohrer, KuD 14, 360.

[21]Cf. 2.2.3 *supra* and n. 19, further Cavallin, SEÅ 37-38, 54 and nn. 54-54, on the change of meaning in LXX, compared to the Hebrew original.

[22]For the possibility that AssMos told the story about Moses' assumption after 12:36, see Schreiner (1969) 47 f. In this context we may also mention Asenath (4.9), related to Joseph.

[23]Cf. 4.3.1 on the relation between the formulation of IV Mcc and Jesus' reply to the Sadducees according to Mk 12:26 parr, above all the Lukan version. The triad is also pictured as participating in the life to come and the eschatological feast in the Q-logion, Lk 13:28/Mt 8:11.

[24]Concerning the role of "the saints", cf. also II Mcc 15:12-16 and 4.2.3.

[25]An appeal to the notion of "corporate personality"—cf. e.g. H. W. Robinson, Beihefte ZAW 66 (1936) 49-62—may not be unjustified here.

[26]Cf. 5.2.4 *supra*, Bill 1 and Schmid (1956) *ad* Mt 3:10.

[27]Cf. 5.8.3 on Is 27:12-13, 4.1.6 and n.32 on Ez 37:1-14.—In Rm 11:14 Paul, linking the resurrection to the reunion of Israel according to the flesh with the spiritual people of God (a re-interpretation of the gathering of the diaspora?), seems to work with these Jewish traditions.

[28]Cf. 1 Cor 15:20, 23 about Christ as the ἀπαρχη —but of greater importance here cf. Rm 11:16 where the term ἀπαρχη is employed to signify the patriarchs (cf. O. Michel, 1963, *ad loc.*): their holiness sanctifies all of the people, the φυραμα.

[29]Cf. e.g. TestAbr (3.12.3); ApcAbr (3.11); LAB (3.8.2 and 7); Lk 16:22 ff.; Mk 12:26 f.

7.3 The central texts

The different passages, which have been discussed above, have been selected and arranged only after their contents (that they contain some assertion about life after death), their supposed original language and their date of origin. No evaluation of their importance has been made.So it will be necessary to ask, in the end: Are any of the texts more important for the future development than others? Have they been read more often, quoted and reworked in new combinations and contexts? Can we follow a main road through the mass of material?

7.3.1

It is obvious from all of our remarks on the allusions to Dn 12[1] that the question can be answered in the affirmative. These verses work with Isaianic material, above all with Is 53, but also with Is 26:19 and 66:24 (2.2.2-3, with further references). The allusions to Is 53 emphasize the fact that the wise leaders and the righteous who are to be glorified have suffered as martyrs. Suffering and martyrdom also prepares the way to the glory of the resurrection according to II Mcc 7, which also may be working with Is 53 (cf. Nickelsburg, 1972, 102-104). IV Mcc develops the meditation on the fate of the seven brothers and their mother with new anthropological presuppositions. Wi 2-5 also seems to employ Deutero-Isaianic material, especially Is 53 (4.4.6; 4.4 n.16), and appears to presuppose Dn 12[2]. In the description of the rule of the nations given to the righteous at the day of the "visitation" Dn 7 (vv.14, 18, 27) may be recognized[3]. Wi 5:5 describes the "lot" of the righteous "among the saints", which is again Danielic terminology[4]. In Dn 7:13 f. the Son of Man is the symbol of these "saints" (cf. *supra* 7.2.6).

7.3.2

The reference to Enoch's assumption in Gn 5:24b (2.1.2) is another Biblical text which seems to have been important for the early Jewish meditation on resurrection and life after death. We have already been able to follow the use of the motif of his assumption in different texts (7.2.2.1). It is obviously the foundation of all the traditions about Enoch's visions (I En, with its various sources—cf. 3.2, II and III En). He is among those saints of Israel who will appear in glory on the day of the resurrection, according to TestBenj 10:8 (cf. 7.2.3.1 and 3.3.1). We might expect to find Elijah in a similar role. But in the texts which have been examined here Elijah only appeared twice, in LAB 48:1, where Phinees is apparently identified with Elijah (3.8.7) and in the description of Job's assumption in a chariot. Enoch, however, seems to be identified with the Son of Man in I En 70-71 (cf. 3.2.4.7 *supra*). In the last instance the Enoch literature seems to be inspired by Dn, more or less directly,[5] and by Is 53[6], but quotations from I En are found in possibly several writings which can be dated a little later within the same period[7].

7.3.3

I conclude that it is possible to say that there is a centre in the variety of testimonies concerning immortality and resurrection in the Jewish literature between circa 200 BC and AD 100. In this centre we find Dn 12, re-interpreting Is 52:13-53:12, with Wi 2-5 and II Mcc (inspiring the willingness to accept the death of the martyr as related by Josephus, 4.6.2.1; 4.6.5, as well as by IV Mcc), and the Enoch traditions, developed from the brief notice of Gn 5:24b. It is, of course, characteristic for all of the apocalyptic and pseudepigraphic literature that its heroes and fictitious authors are chosen among "the saints of Israel" in ancient times (Abraham, Isaac, Jacob, his twelve sons, Moses etc.—cf. 7.2.3). Thus, the developing faith in a life after death is linked with the central sacred traditions of the Hebrew Scriptures.

[1]3.2.3 (I En 91:10; 92:3-4); 3.2.3.6 (I En 104:2); 3.3.1 (TestJud 25:1); 3.3.2 (TestJud 25:4; Benj 10:8); 3.3.4 (TestAsher 6:6); 3.3 n.14 (TestJud 25:4), n.18 (TestBenj 10:8); 3.4.1 (PsSol 3:12); 3.5.4 (1QH VI, 34—cf. 3.5 n.28); 3.5.6 (4QPsDn 38-40—cf. 3.5 n.42); 3.5.7 (4Q181 1 II, 4-6); 3.9.2 (IV Ezr 7:32); 3.9.3 (IV Ezr 7:97); 3.10.3 (II Bar 42:7); 4.4.3.3 (Wi 3:7); 4.10 n.6 (TestJob 4:9 v.l.); 5.1.2 (TSanh 13:3/RH 16b); 5 n.28 (Sanh 92a).

[2]See 4.4.3.3 on Wi 3:7 and Dn 12:3. Cf. further Nickelsburg (1972) 68-70 on Wi 5 and Dn 12.

[3]See 4.4.3.3 and also P. Grelot (1961, 1971) 192 f.

[4]Dn 12:13 and 7:18, 22, 25, 27—cf. Riesenfeld, EuA 47 508.

[5]Cf. e.g. Nickelsburg (1972) 120-122, on I En 102-104 and Dn: he thinks above all of a possible earlier tradition behind Dn 12:1-3, which might have been known by the author of I En 102-104. Concerning EnSim and the Son of Man cf. e.g. Sjöberg (1946); T. W. Manson, BJRL 32 (1950) 171-93; J. Muilenburg, JBL 79 (1960) 197-209; Borsch (1967) 145-56; R. Leivestad, NTS 18 (1971/2) 246.

[6]Cf. recently, Nickelsburg (1972) 70-78, who refers briefly to the earlier discussion between Sjöberg (1946) 116-32; and J. Jeremias, TWNT V (1954) 686 f. Cf. also M. Rese, ZThK 60 (1963) 21-41; I. Engnell, BJRL 31 (1948) 54-93; *id.* (1970) 240.

[7]Explicitly I En 1:9 in Jud 14b-15—cf. further Denis (1970) 20-24 for a survey of the possible quotations from I En in TestXIIPatr, Jub, etc.

7.4   A tentative synthesis

If there is a sort of centre or focus among all the different texts and traditions which we have tried to examine (7.3), the final question of this investigation of the Jewish background of Paul's argument for the resurrection of the dead will be: Is it possible to distil, at least in "the central texts", a common message of any kind by "demythologizing" (7.1.3) the varying images for the hope of individual life beyond death which we have found in those texts which do express such an expectation?¹ A tentative and briefly summarizing answer may follow the four questions which have been used as instruments of analysis in the examination of the different texts:

7.4.1

(A) The old Israelite appeared to be able to accept death as meaning the practical extinction of his individual conscious personality in the conviction that his "name"—i.e. his personality in some way²—was preserved for future generations through the "seed" (2.1.1). The emergence of belief in an individual life after death implies a new responsibility and a new importance of both the *individual* person and of the *individual* life before death. This may be expressed symbolically by the idea that the names of the righteous are written in a heavenly book (Dn 12:1; JA 15:3). The offspring on earth is no longer so important as compared to the conviction that the individual personality is preserved for ever in God's care (Wi 3:1 ff.).

7.4.2

(B) No common anthropology, at least no common view on the relationship between the body and the soul, has been found in these texts. Rather, the different texts have different anthropological presuppositions and often no anthropological consciousness at all (cf. 7.1.6). In the same writings, and even the same passages, concepts and symbols from widely differing anthropologies are used in order to express the hope of personal survival of death: immortality of the soul or resurrection of the body. The writers intend to state that the *personality* survives. If the concept of a human person implies a body, it is necessary to state the resurrection of the body, in order to ensure the preservation of the person beyond death. But if the substance of the personality is defined as "the soul", "the spirit" or "the mind", then it is this substance alone which will live after death. When the dichotomy in the human existence—the tensions between the promptings of the body and the innermost craving of the centre of will and reflection of man—is emphasized, maybe under the influence of the Greek philosophical tradition (above all in the case of Philo), then salvation must consist of a liberation from this struggle. Since the body is seen as that which distracts man from his true destination, which is the search for spiritual truth, the destruction of the body at death is salvation, at least for those who have freed their spirits from the slavery of the passions of the body. But there is a unity in the expressions of varying anthropologies: the conviction that the personality survives death in that which constitutes the personal identity³. This is expressed by II Bar 51:2-3 (3.10.2 *supra*) by the idea that those who rise first have to recognize each other, and therefore they have to rise with their old bodies before the transformation for the final future state. The inscription of the names of the righteous in a heavenly book states their personal identity across the experience of death. This personal identity may both guarantee the final righteous judgment and the indestructibility of the believer's communion with God, being the source of life.

212

7.4.3

(C) This essential identity of the human personality before and after death is, however, radically modified by the radical discontinuity or difference between the old life before death and the new life after death. This discontinuity and the newness of *post-mortem* life for the righteous is expressed by various images, some of which recur fairly often, particularly those which are connected with the righteous' exaltation or assumption (7.2.2) to an existence of Divine light and glory similar to that of stars or angels (7.2.1), so that the immortal righteous are identified with "the sons of God". They stand before the throne of God (IV Mcc 17:18) or are enthroned with God (LAB 33:2-9; 40:3). The elect are under the wings of the Lord and shine before him (I En 39:7). In all the variety of images there is a common theme which may be described as nearness to God or even "a divine lot" (IV Mcc 18:3, *supra* 4.3.8) or as "becoming gods" (PsPhoc 104, *supra* 4.8.1.1; 4.8.1.4) or "be counted one of the sons of God" (Wi 5:5, *supra* 4.4.6). This means that the radical difference between "flesh" and "spirit", mortal man and the living God, which marks early Israelite religion[4], is in one way overcome. The expression of II Pt 1:4 about sharing in "the divine nature" is not far from the ideas which are expressed in the symbolism of the stars and the mythical language about the sons of God. The author of one of the Qumran hymns expresses his amazement at this change of conditions for a human being who has been "purified . . . that he may be united with the sons of your truth and in a lot with your holy ones, to raise the worm of the dead from the dust to eternal council" (1QH XI, 11 f.). The Qumran writer emphasizes that this elevation of a human being is sheer grace. Others (Philo, Wi) consider the glorification to be the consequence of a righteous life. Above all, the exaltation is given to the righteous who suffer. God's action implies a revolution of human conditions and the vindication of the demands of righteousness. Through the hope for final glorification, the *skandalon* of the seeming power of the godless tyrants, and the suffering and death of the righteous are overcome (Dn 12:2 f.; Wi 2-5; II Mcc and IV Mcc *passim*). The Suffering Servant who is highly exalted becomes the model for the fate of all the servants of God. Thus suffering and death may be conceived as victory instead of final defeat. Death becomes the gateway to transcendent glorification.

7.4.4

(D) Righteousness is finally vindicated, a just balance of the order of the world is restored and God is proven to be just. This theme is one of the most essential motifs of the Early Jewish descriptions of life after death, as we have seen (cf. the table of 7 and 7.11). It may be expressed in various ways regarding the fate of the wicked: annihilation,[5] eternal torments,[6] continued shadowy existence in dark Sheol,[7] resurrection for judgment.[8] The varying and often rather vague expressions again show us that the essential message of the texts is not these descriptions of future punishment of the wicked but the common motif of future retribution and final justice.

The ideas about the "date" of this final vindication of Divine justice vary. Sometimes it is placed immediately after the death of the individual. Even when this is the case, the expectation of a day of judgment, an end of history, "a last day" of some kind, normally is preserved (7.1.8). In both of these alternative perspectives the common motif is that of radical discontinuity, a necessary break between the present life in the old order of the world on one hand, and the blessed life in glory for the righteous in a transformed world on the other hand. This break may be represented only by the death of the individual and the new life of the soul after death in the presence of God[9]. It may be expressed by the hope that the exiles of Israel are finally gathered to the land of Israel, where also former generations will rise[10]. Essentially the same hope is proclaimed in the fantastic descriptions of the overwhelming fruitfulness of the Messianic age[11] and in statements about a completely new creation and/or concerning a resurrection of all men[12] with a subsequent transformation of their bodies as well as all of their existence[13]. Life after death is in any case never merely a return to the life lived before death. The point of the hope of life after death in Early Judaism is this transformation of the weak, imperfect, unjust, and often miserable existence of the righteous in the present world to the glory and joy in God's presence, in a situation of justice and undisturbed peace.

7.4.5

The hope of a radically transformed life after death was born or at least planted in Israel in a period of suffering for those who trusted in God's promise and tried to keep his laws. By this hope, at least in the case of the martyr, death itself can be identified with the very act of transformation (IV Mcc 9:21 f., *supra* 4.3.6).

7.4.6

This great variety of expressions of the hope of the suffering righteous for a transformed existence after death, which in Paul's time was developing to become the canonized dogma of Judaism, but was far from being so, offers a background of the study of primitive Christian reflection on the death and resurrection of Jesus and Paul's formulation of a Christian view concerning life after death.

---

[1] J. J. Collins, CBQ 36 (1974) 21-43, works with a similar approach.

[2] Cf. e.g. H. Bietenhard, TWNT V (1954) 242 f., 253, 265; R. Abba, IDB III (1962) 501, 505 f.

[3] Cf., on the other hand, 4.5.6 and Gig 61 with several other passages in Philo (n.23), where the purest souls seem to become almost identified with the Ideas. Thus, the personal character of life after death is pushed aside or disappears. However, Jewish eschatology in general would tend to emphasize the salvation of the people (MSanh 10:1-5.2), rather than individual, personal life after death. Or rather, the salvation of the individual person is guaranteed by his (faithful) membership in the elect people.

[4] With exceptions among the holy men, as Enoch, Abraham and Moses—cf. e.g. Ex 34:29-35.

[5] E.g. PsSol 3:10-12a; II Bar 30:4; 51:5b (in IQS IV, 14; these three cases in immediate combination with statements about future torments); II Mcc 7:14; IV Mcc 10:15; Ps 1:5 LXX; MSanh 10:3.

214

⁶E.g. I En 103:7-8; TestAsher 6:5; 1QS IV, 11b-13: BJ II, 155; II Bar 30:5; 51:2, 6; IV Mcc 9:9; TSanh 13:5 / RH 17a.

⁷E.g. OrSib IV, 184-186; I En 108:11-15; PsSol 14:9.

⁸E.g. ApEz; TestBenj 10:8; LAB 3:10; IV Ezr 7:32-38; II Bar 50; OrSib IV, 181-184; MSanh 10:3.

⁹As in Wi, Philo, IV Mcc and TestAbr.

¹⁰As in the "re-read" versions of Ez 37:1-14 or Is 26:19, in OrSib III, 757 ff. or in the inscription CIJ 476 (cf. 4.12.5).

¹¹E.g. Jub 23:26 ff.; II Bar 29:4-8 (cf. 3.9 n.26); 73 (3.9 n.27).

¹²E.g. I En 51 (3.2.4); LAB 3:10 (3.8.1); IV Ezr 7:26-32 (3.9); OrSib IV, 171-90 (4.7.1).

¹³Above all II Bar 49-52 (3.10.2)—but cf. also the columns TH, T and TE in the table, 7.

Bibliography

This bibliography has been arranged following the manner of text and literature citation in this book. Only references which are found in this book are included in this bibliography. In Part I, "Texts", I have only included: (a) *editions* of the original text (or ancient versions), (b) *collections* of ancient texts in modern translations. Modern translations of *individual* ancient writings are found in Part II, since they are quoted in the name of the translator. Part II, "Literature", contains the names of all modern authors and editors quoted in this book, with the titles of those of their works which have been used here, or with a reference to Part I, in the case of editors.

I. *Texts*

Biblia hebraica . . . ed. *R. Kittel.* 16th ed. by P. Kahle, A. Alt, O. Eissfeldt. Stuttgart 1971.

Biblia Hebraica Stuttgartensia . . . ed. *K. Elliger,* W. Rudolph. Stuttgart 1968-

    I. Genesis, ed. *O Eissfeldt* (1969).

    II. Exodus, Leviticus, ed. *G. Quell* (1973).

    III. Numeri, ed. *W. Rudolph,* Deuteronomium, ed. *J. Hempel* (1972).

    IV. Josua et Judices, ed. *R. Meyer* (1972).

    VII. Liber Jesaiae, ed. *D. Winton Thomas* (1968).

    VIII. Liber Jeremiae, ed. *W. Rudolph* (1970).

    IX. Liber Ezechiel, ed. *K. Elliger* (1971).

    X. Liber XII Prophetarum, ed. *K. Elliger* (1970).

    XI. Liber Psalmorum, ed. *H. Bardtke* (1969).

Die Weisheit des Jesus Sirach, hebräisch und deutsch, ed. *R. Smend.* Berlin 1906.

SS. Biblia polyglotta I-IV, ed. *B. Walton.* London 1657.

Targum

The Bible in Aramaic I-IV B, ed. *A. Sperber.* Leiden 1959-1973.

Thargum Jonathan ben Usiel zum Pentateuch, ed. *M. Ginsburger.* Berlin 1903.

Das Fragmententhargum, ed. *M. Ginsburger.* Berlin 1899.

Targum Onkelos I-II, ed. *A. Berliner.* Berlin, Frankfurt, London 1884.

Neophyti I. Targum Palestinense Ms de la Biblioteca Vaticana I-III, Génesis, Exodo, Levitico . . . ed. *A. Diez Macho.* (Textos y Estudios 7.) Madrid-Barcelona 1968-1971.

[The Targums of Onkelos and Jonathan ben Uzziel on the Pentateuch; with the Fragments of the Jerusalem Targum from the Chaldee . . . by *J. W. Etheridge I-II. London 1862-1865.*]

The Targum of Isaiah, ed. *J. F. Stenning.* Oxford 1949.

Le Targum de Job de la grotte XI de Qumran . . ., ed. *J. P. M. van der Ploeg,* A. S. v.d. Woude, B. Jongeling. Leiden 1971.

LXX

The OT in Greek . . . I-III, ed. *H. B. Swete.* 2nd ed. Cambridge 1895-99.

Septuaginta . . .I-II, ed. *A. Rahlfs.* 7th ed. Stuttgart 1962,

Origenis Hexaplorum quae supersunt . . . I-II, ed. *F. Field.* Oxford 1875.

Septuaginta. Vetus Testamentum Graecum auctoritate Societatis Litterarum Gottingensis editum. Göttingen 1931-

    IX,1.   Maccabaeorum liber 1, ed. *W. Kappler* (1936).

    X.   Psalmi cum Odis, ed. *A. Rahlfs* (1931).

    XII,2.   Sapientia Iesu Filii Sirach, ed. *J. Ziegler* (1965).

    XIII.   Duodecim prophetae, ed. *J. Ziegler* (1943).

XIV.	Isaias, ed. *J. Ziegler* (1939).
XV.	Ieremias, Baruch, Threni, Epistula Ieremiae, ed. *J. Ziegler* (1954).
XVI,1.	Ezechiel, ed. *J. Ziegler* (1954).
XVI,2.	Susanna, Daniel, Bel et Draco, ed. *J. Ziegler* (1954).

The Third and Fourth Book of Maccabees, ed . . . *M. Hadas*. (Jewish Apocryphal Literature.) New York 1953.

Les psaumes de Salomon . . . ed. *J. Viteau*. (Documents pour l'étude de la Bible.) Paris 1911.

The Odes and Psalms of Solomon I-II, ed. *R. Harris*, A. Mingana. Manchester, London, New York 1916-20.

Other versions

Biblia Sacra iuxta *Vulgatam* Versionem I-II, adiuvantibus B. Fischer, J. Gribomont, H. F. D. Sparks, W. Thiele . . . ed. *R. Weber*. Stuttgart 1969.

The OT in Syriac according to the *Peshitta* Version, ed . . . Peshitta Institute, Leiden 1972-

IV,3 Apocalypse of Baruch, ed. *S. Dedering*; 4 Esdras, ed. *R. J. Bidawid* (1973).

IV,6 Canticles or Odes, ed. *H. Schneider*; Prayer of Manasseh, ed. *W. Baars* and *H. Schneider*; Apocryphal Psalms, ed. *W. Baars*; Psalms of Solomon, ed. *W. Baars*; Tobit, ed. *J. C. H. Lebram*; 1 (3) Esdras, ed. *W. Baars* and *J. C. H. Lebram* (1972).

The New American Bible, Cleveland, New York 1970.

The New English Bible. Oxford, Cambridge 1970.

Collections of pseudepigrapha etc.

Apocalypses apocryphae Mosis, Esdrae, Pauli, Iohannis . . . ed. *C. v. Tischendorf*. Leipzig 1866.

Monumenta sacra et profana V. . . . ed. *A. M. Ceriani*. Milano 1868-71.

Anecdota graeco-byzantina I, ed. *A. Vassiliev*. Moscow 1893.

Fragmenta pseudepigraphorum graeca, Collegit *A. M. Denis*. (Pseudepigrapha Veteris Testamenti Graece III, pp. 46-246.) Leiden 1970.

[Die Apokryphen und Pseudepigraphen des ATs . . . I-II, ed. *E. Kautzsch*. Tübingen 1900.]

[The Apocrypha and Pseudepigrapha of the OT in English I-II, ed. *R. H. Charles*. Oxford 1913.]

[Altjüdisches Schrifttum ausserhalb der Bibel . . . ed. *P. Riessler*. Augsburg 1928.]

[De Gammeltestamentlige Pseudepigrafer (trans. into Danish) . . . I-IV, ed. *E. Hammershaimb*, J. Munck, B. Noack, P. Seidelin. Copenhagen, Oslo, Lund 1953-63.]

[Jüdische Schriften aus hellenistisch-römischer Zeit I, 1; II, 1, ed. *W. G. Kümmel*, C. Habicht, O. Kaiser, O. Plöger, J. Schreiner. Gütersloh 1973-   ]

Individual writings

The Homily on the Passion by Melito Bishop of Sardis with some fragments of the *A*pocryphal *E*zekiel, ed. *C. Bonner*. (Studies and Documents 12.) London, Philadelphia 1940.

The *As*cension of *I*saiah' . . ., ed. *R. H. Charles*. London 1900.

The *As*sumption of *Mo*ses . . ., ed. *R. H. Charles*. London 1897.

Die Himmelfahrt des Mose, ed. *C. Clemen*. (Kleine Texte . . ., ed. H. Lietzmann 10.) Bonn 1964.

Liber apocalypseos *Ba*ruch filii Neriae . . . ed. *M. Kmosko*. (Patrol.syriaca I, 2, pp. 1055-1206). Paris 1907.

Liber Henoch, aethiopice . . . ed. *A. Dillmann*. Leipzig 1851.

Das Buch Henoch . . . ed. *J. Flemming*, L. Rademacher (GCS). Leipzig 1901.

The Ethiopic Version of the Book of *En*och . . . with the fragmentary Greek and Latin Versions, ed. *R. H. Charles*. (Analecta Oxon. Sem. Ser. 11.) Oxford 1906.

The Book of Enoch or 1 Enoch, translated . . . with a Reprint from the Editor's text of the Greek fragments, ed. *R. H. Charles*. Rev.ed. Oxford 1912. 1st ed. 1893.

218

The Last Chapters of Enoch in Greek, ed. *C. Bonner*, H. C. Youtie. (Studies and Documents 8.) London 1937.

Apocalypsis Henochi Graece, ed. *M. Black*. (Pseudepigrapha Veteris Testamenti Graece III, pp. 1-44.) Leiden 1970.

Le livre des secrets d'Hénoch, texte slave . . . ed. *A. Vaillant*. (Textes publiés par l'Institut d'Etudes slaves 4.) Paris 1952.

3 Enoch or The Hebrew Book of Enoch ed . . . *H. Odeberg*, Cambridge 1928.

Die *Esra*-Apokalypse I-II, ed. *B. Violet*. (GCS.) Leipzig 1910-24.

Le livre de la priére d'Aséneth, ed. *P. Batiffol*. (Studia Patristica I-II, 39-115.) Paris 1889-90.

Joseph et *Aséneth* . . . ed. *M. Philonenko*. (Studia Post-Biblica 13.) Leiden 1968.

Pseudo-Philo's *Liber Antiquitatum Biblicarum*, ed. *G. Kisch*. (Publications in Mediaeval Studies of the University of Notre Dame 10.) Notre Dame, Indiana 1949.

Die *Oracula Sibyllina* . . ., ed. *J. Geffcken*. (GCS.) Leipzig 1902.

Sibyllinische Weissagungen, ed. *A. Kurfess*, München 1951.

Die Weisheitslehre des Phokylides . . . see *Lincke*, K. F. A (1903).

Pseudo-Phocylides, Anthologia lyrica Graeca II, ed. *E. Diehl*, R. Beutler (Bibliotheca . . . Teubneriana). Lipsiae 1936, 3rd ed. 1950, V-VI, 91-108.

Theognis Megarensis, Ps.-Pythagoras, *Ps.-Phocylides* . . ., ed. *D. Young*. (Bibliotheca . . . Teubneriana). Lipsiae 1961.

Silloge Pseudofocilidea . . ., ed. *A. Farina*. (Collana di studi greci 37.) Napoli 1962.

The *Testament of Abraham* . . . ed. *M. R. James*. (Texts and Studies 2:2.) Cambridge 1892.

The *Testament of Job*. An Essene Midrash on the Book of Job reedited and translated . . . *K. Kohler*. Semitic studies in Memory of A. Kohut, ed. G. A. Kohut. Berlin 1897, pp. 264-338.

Testamentum Iobi, ed. *S. P. Brock*. Pseudepigrapha Veteris Testamenti II, Leiden 1967, pp. 1-59.

The Greek Versions of the *Testaments* of the *Twelve Patriarchs* . . ed. *R. H. Charles*. Oxford 1908.

Testamenta XII Patriarcharum, ed . . ., *M. DeJonge*. (Pseudepigrapha Veteris Testamenti Graece I.) Leiden 2nd ed. 1970.

See also James, M. R., JThS 28.

Vitae Adae et Evae, ed. *W. Mayer*. Abhandlungen der philosophisch-philologischen Classe der königlichen bayerischen Akademie der Wissenschaften 14:3, München 1878, pp. 185-250.

VAE ed. *Mozley*—cf. Mozley, J. H.

Essenica

Antike Berichte über die Essener, Ausgewählt von *A. Adam*, (Kleine Texte für Vorlesungen und Ubungen 182.) Berlin 1961. (2nd rev.ed. by C. Burchard, Berlin, New York 1972.)

The Zadokite Documents . . ., ed . . . *C. Rabin*. Oxford 1954. (2nd ed. 1958.)

The Dead Sea Scrolls of St. Mark's Monastery. I: The Isaiah Manuscript and the Habakkuk Commentary; II:2: Plates and Transcription of the Manual of Discipline, ed. *M. Burrows*, J. C. Trever, W. H. Brownlee. New Haven 1950-51.

Discoveries in the Judaean Desert I, ed. *D. Barthélemy, J. T. Milik* . . . Oxford 1955.

-V, Qumran Cave 4, I, ed. *J. M. Allegro*, A. A. Anderson. Oxford 1968.

Die Texte vom Toten Meer I-II, ed. *J. Maier*. München, Basel 1960.

Die Texte aus Qumran, hebräisch und deutsch . . ., ed. *E. Lohse*, München 1964.

J. Licht, *The Thanksgiving Scroll*. A. Scroll from the Wilderness of Judaea (Hebrew). Jerusalem 1957.

The Thanksgiving Hymns . . ., ed. *M. Mansoor*. (Studies in the Texts of the Desert of Judah 3.) Leiden 1961.

Philo

Philonis Alexandrini opera quae supersunt I-VII, ed. *L. Cohn*, P. Wendland. Berlin 1896-1930.

Philo In Ten Volumes (and Two Supplementary Volumes) With an ET by *F. H. Colson* (alone VI-X), G. H. Whitaker. Supplement I-II Questions and answers on Genesis and Exodus, ed. R. Marcus. (The Loeb Classical Library.) London, Cambridge; Mass. 1929-1962.

L'ancienne version latine des questions sur la Genése de Philon d'Alexandrie I-II, ed. *F. Petit*. Berlin 1973.

Josephus

Flavii Josephi opera omnia I-IV, ed. *S. A. Naber*. Leipzig 1888-96.

Josephus with an ET by *H. St. J. Thackeray* in Nine Volumes (I-V, ed. Thackeray . . . IX, ed. *L. H. Feldman*. (The Loeb Classical Library.) London, Cambridge, Mass. 1926-65.

Flavius Josephus, De Bello Judaico, I-II, 2, ed. *O. Michel, O. Bauernfeind*. Darmstadt 1959-69.

Rabbinica

Die Mischna. Text, Ubersetzung und ausführliche Erklärung . . . *G. Beer*, D. Holtzmann, S. Krauss . . . Giessen, Berlin 1912-

Mishnayoth, ed. *P. Blackman*. 2nd ed. New York 1964.

[The Mishnah ET, see also *Danby, H.* (1933).]

תוספתא על פי כתבי יד ערפורט רוריען ... משה שמואל

צוקרמאנדל. פאזעוראלק 1879-82

Der babylonische Talmud mit Einschluss der vollständigen Misnah I-IX, ed. *L. Goldschmidt*. Berlin, Leipzig, Haag 1897-1934.

[The Babylonian Talmud translated into English I-XXXV, ed. *I. Epstein*. London 1935-48.]

Der Jerusalemische Talmud . . . (Hebrew), Krotoschin 1886.

תלמוד ירושלמי 1-2. ברלין 1928.

[Le Talmud de Jérusalem traduit . . . par *M. Schwab*, I-XI. Paris 187-89.]

Aboth de Rabbi Nathan, ed. *S. Schechter*. Wien 1887.

[ET AbRN, see Goldin, J. (1955).]

[Bibliotheca Rabbinica. Eine Sammlung alter Midraschim . . ., ed. *A. Wünsche*. Leipzig 1880-85.]

(*JalqShim*). 1876

קרט שמעוני מדרש על תורה נביים וכתובים ... ווארשא 1876.

Beth ha-Midrasch. Sammlung kleiner Midraschim und vermischter Abhandlungen aus der älteren jüdischen Literatur, I-VI, ed. *A. Jellinek*. Wien 1853-82.

Mechilta, der älteste halachische und haggadische Commentar zum zweiten Buche Moses . . ., ed. *I. H. Weiss*, Wien 1865.

*Mek*ilta—de rabbi Ishmael . . ., ed. *J. Z. Lauterbach*. Philadelphia 1933.

[Midrash Rabba translated into English I-IX . . ., *ed. H. Freedman*, M. Simon. London 1939.]

(*midrPs*). 1875   1875   מדרש שוחק טוב על תהלים ... ווארשא 1875.

[The *Midr*ash on *Ps*alms I-II, translated by *W. G. Braude*. (Yale Judaica Series 13.) New Haven 1959.]

*Pes*ikta *R*abbati. Midrasch für den Fest-Cyclus . . ., ed. *M. Friedmann*. Wien 1880.

[*Pesikta Rabbati*. Discourses for Feasts, Fasts and Special Sabbaths, I-II, translated from the Hebrew by *W. G. Braude*. (Yale Judaica Series 18.) New Haven, London 1968.]

(*PRE*) ווארשא ד.לוריא. ... ספר פרקי רבי אליעזר

[ET see *Friedlander, G.*]

Pesikta, die älteste Haggada, redigiert in Palästina von *Rab Kahana*, ed. *S. Buber*, Lyck 1868.

Pesikta de *Rav Kahana* . . . I-II, ed. *B. Mandelbaum*. New York 1962.

220

Seder R. Amram Ga'on, I . . ., ed. *D. Hedegård.* Lund 1951.

*S*ifre debe Rab, der älteste halachische und haggadische Midrasch zu *N*umeri und *Deut*eronomium, I . . ., ed. *M. Friedmann.* Wien 1864.

*S*iphre ad *N*umeros . . . adjecto Siphre Zutta, ed. *H. S. Horowitz.*(Schriften hrsg.v.d.Gesellschaft zur Förderung der Wissenschaft des Judentums.) Frankfurt a.M. 1916.

[*S*ifre zu *N*umeri. Unter Verwendung einer Ubersetzung von . . . J. Winter und mit Beiträgen von . . . H. Windisch . . ., ed. *K. G. Kuhn,* I-X. (Rabbinische Texte. Zweite Reihe. Tannaitische Midraschim. Ubersetzung und Erklärung, 2-3.) Stuttgart 1933-59.]

*S*ifre on *Deut*eronomy, Published originally by the Gesellschaft zur Förderung der Wissenschaft des Judentums [1939] and now republished by the Jewish Theological Seminary of America . . ., ed. *L.* Finkelstein. New York 1969.

(*Tanch*). 1879 ‏ר ו א ר ש א‏   1.‏ • • • • ‏ ‏ת ו ר ה‏ ‏ח ו מ ש י‏ ‏ח מ מ ש ה‏ ‏ע ל‏ ‏מ ד ר ש ת נ ח ו מ א‏

Midrasch *Tanch*uma I-III, ed. S. *B*uber, Wilna 1885.

Jewish Inscriptions

*C*orpus *I*nscriptionum *J*udaicarum. I-II., ed. *J. B. Frey.* Roma 1936-52.

Die Inschriften der jüdischen Katakomben am Monteverde zu Rom . . ., ed. *N. Müller, N. A. Bees.* (Schriften herausgegeben von der Gesellschaft für die Wissenschaft des Judentums.) Leipzig 1919.

Early Christian texts

Novum Testamentum Graece, ed. *E. Nestle,* K. Aland. 25th ed. Stuttgart 1963.

The Greek New Testament, *K. Aland,* M. Black, C. M. Martini, B. M. Metzger, A. Wikgren . . . 2nd ed. Stuttgart 1968.

[Neutestamentliche Apokryphen in deutscher Ubersetzung I-II, ed. *E. Hennecke,* 3rd ed. *W.* Schneemelcher, Tübingen 1959-64.]

Desc Mariae, ed. *H. Pernot,* REG 13 (1900). See also Pernot.

The Gospel according to *Thom*as. Coptic Text established and translated by *A. Guillaumont,* H. C. Puech, G. Quispel, W. Till, Y.'Abd Almasih. Leiden 1959.

Didascalia et *Const*itutiones *Apost*olorum, I-II, ed. *F. X. Funk.* Paderbornae 1906.

Die apostolischen Väter. Neubearbeitung der *Funk*schen Ausgabe, I, ed. *K. Bihlmeyer,* W. Schneemelcher. (Sammlung ausgewählter kirchen- und dogmengeschichtliche Quellenschriften II:1:1.) 2nd ed. Tübingen 1956.

Hermas, Le Pasteur, ed. *R. Joly.* (Sources chrétiennes 53.) Paris 1958.

The Acts of the Christian Martyrs, ed. *H. Musurillo.* (Oxford Early Christian Texts.) Oxford 1972.

Clemens Alexandrinus, Werke II-III, 3rd ed. *L. Früchtel,* Berlin 1960-70.

The *Exc*erpta *ex Theod*oto of Clement of Alexandria (Studies and Documents 1), ed. *R. P. Casey.* London 1934.

Hippolytus, Refutatio omnium haeresium, ed. *P. Wendland.* (GCS 26.) Leipzig 1916.

Origenes, Werke IX. Die Homilien zu Lukas in der Ubersetzung des Hieronymus und die griechischen Reste der Homilien und des Lukaskommentars, ed. *M. Rauer.* (GCS 49.) Berlin 2nd ed. 1959.

Synesius, Dio, PG 66. Paris 1859.

Thomas of Celano, The Hymn *Dies irae,* Nr 609 in "Den svenska psalmboken" (1937).

Other ancient authors

Hesiodi Theogonia, Opera et Dies, Scutum, ed. F. Solmsen. Fragmenta selecta ed. *R. Merkelbach,* M. L. West. (Scriptorum Classicorum Bibliotheca Oxoniensis.) Oxonii 1970.

*I*nscr*i*ptiones *G*raecae XII:7. Inscriptiones insularum maris Aegaei praeter Delum, ed. *I. Delamarre.* Berolini 1908.

*Plato*nis Opera, I-V, ed. *I. Burnet.* Oxonii 1900-07.

Platon, Oeuvres complétes IV:1, Phédon, ed. *L. Robin.* (Collection des universités de France . . . Budé.) Paris 1965.

C *Plin*ii Secvndi *Nat*uralis *Hist*oriae Libri XXXVII, vol. I, Libri I-VI, ed. C. *Mayhof.* (Bibliotheca . . . Teubneriana.) Lipsiae 1906.

*Xenophon, Mem*orabilia and Oeconomicus with an ET, by *R. C. Marchant.* (The Loeb Classical Library.) London, Cambridge, Mass. 1923.

II. Literature

Aalen, S., St. Luke's Gospel and the Last Chapters of Enoch, *NTS* 13 (1966-67), 1-13.

Abba, R., Name, *IDB* III (1962) 500-508.

Adam, A., see Essenica, Antike Berichte, under *Texts*.

Ahlbrecht, A., *Tod und Unsterblichkeit in der evangelischen Theologie der Gegenwart*. (Konfessionskundliche und kontroverstheologische Studien 10.) Paderborn 1964.

Albeck, C., *Einführung in die Mischna* (German translation of Hebrew original מבוא למשנה Tel Aviv and Jerusalem 1960). (Studia Judaica—Forschungen zur Wissenschaft des Judentums 6.) Berlin, New York 1971.

Alfrink, B., L'idée de Résurrection d'aprés Dan XII, 1, 2, *Bibl* 40 (1959) 355-371.

Allegro, J. M., Further Light on the History of the Qumran Sect, *JBL* 75 (1956) 89-95.

Anderson, G. W., Isaiah XXIV-XXVII reconsidered, *SupplVT* 9 (1963) 118-126.

Avigad, N., Excavations at Beth Shearim, 1955. Preliminary report, *IEJ* 7 (1957) 73-92, 239-55.

Bacher, W., *Die Agada der Tannaiten* I-II. Strassburg 1884-1890. (I, 2nd ed. 1903.)

Balz, H. R., *Methodische Probleme der neutestamentlichen Christologie*. (Wissenschaftliche Monographien z.AuNT 25.) Neukirchen 1967.

Bardtke, H., *Die Handschriftenfunde am Toten Meer*, I (2nd ed.)-II. Berlin 1958.

Barr, J., *Biblical Words for Time*. (Studies in Biblical Theology, First Series.) 2nd (rev.) ed. London 1969.

-, *Old and New in Interpretation*. A Study of the Two Testaments. (The Currie Lecture . . . 1964). London 1966.

Barrett, C. K., Immortality and Resurrection, *LondQuart* (vol. 190, ser.6) 34 (1965) 91-102.

Barth, C., *Die Errettung vom Tode* in den individuellen Klage-und Dankliedern des ATs. Zollikon 1947.

- Bundschliessung und neuer Anfang am dritten Tage, *EvTh* 28 (1968) 521-533.

Barthélemy, D., *Les devanciers d'Aquila*. Premiere publication intégrale du texte des fragments du Dodécaprophéton trouvés dans le désert de Juda . . . (SupplVT 10.) Leiden 1963.

[Batiffol, P., see JA, under Texts.]

Baudissin, W. v., *Adonis und Esmun*. Eine Untersuchung zur Geschichte des Glaubens an Auferstehungsgötter und an Heilgötter. Leipzig 1911.

Bauernfeind, O., see Michel, O.

Becker, J., *Untersuchungen zur Entstehungsgeschichte der Testamente der zwölf Patriarchen*. (Arbeiten zur Geschichte des antiken Judentums und des Urchristentums 8. Inst. Jud. Tübingen.) Leiden 1970.

Beek, M. A., Ein Erdbeben wird zum prophetischen Erleben (Jesaja 24-27), *Archiv Orientàlni* 17 (1949) 31-40.

- De opstanding in de apokalyptische Literatuur. *Geref TT* 68 (1968) 15-26.

Beltrami, A., Ea quae apud Pseudo-Phocylidem *Veteris et Novi Testamenti* vestigia deprehenduntur, *RFIC* 36 (1908) 411-423.

- Spirito Giudaico especialmente essenico della silloge pseudofocilidea, *RFIC* 41 (1913) 513-548.

Bentzen, A., *Daniel*. (HAT 19.) 2nd ed. Tübingen 1952.

Beresford, A. J., *The NT Concept of Resurrection Against Its Background*. Unpublished diss. Oxford 1971.

Berger, K., Der Streit des guten und des bösen Engels um die Seele. Beobachtungen zu 4Q Amrb und Judas 9, *JSJud* 4 (1973) 1-18.

223

Bernays, J., Ueber das phokylideische Gedicht. Ein Beitrag zur hellenistischen Litteratur, id. *Gesammelte Abhandlungen I:*19- Berlin 1885,192-261. (First published as *Jahresbericht* des jüdisch-theologischen Seminars „Fraenkelscher Stiftung". Breslau, am Gedächtnistage des Stifters, dem 27. Januar 1856.)

Bertholet, A., Zur Frage des Verhältnisses von persischem und jüdischem Auferstehungsgaluben, *Festschrift Friedrich Carl Andreas* .... Leipzig 1916, 51-62.

Bertram, G., ζαω κτλ. ζωη und βιος in der Septuaginta, *TWNT* II (1935) 853-856.

Bianchi, U., Le probleme des origines du gnosticisme, *StHRel* XII (1967) 1-27.

E. J. Bickerman, The Date of Fourth Maccabees, *Louis Ginzberg Jubilee Volume* ... New York 1945, 105-112.

Bietenhard, H., ὀνομα *TWNT* V (1954) 243-281.

Billerbeck, P., see Strack, H. L.

Birkeland, H., The Belief in the Resurrection of the Dead in the OT, *StTh* 3 (1949) 60-78.

Black, M., The Account of the Essenes in Hippolytus and Josephus, *Studies in Honour of C. H. Dodd*, ed. W. D. Davies and D. Daube. Cambridge 1956, 172-175.

- *The Scrolls and Christian Origins.* Studies in the Jewish Background of the NT. London, Edinburgh ... 1961.

- The Son of Man Passion Sayings in the Gospel Tradition, *ZNW* 60 (1969) 1-8.

- (1970), see *I En*, under *Texts*.

Blackman, P. (1965), see *Mishnah*, under *Texts*.

Böhl, F. M. T., *De "Knecht Des Heeren" in Jezaja 53.* Haarlem 1923.

Böklen, E., *Die Verwandtschaft der jüdisch-christlichen mit der Parsischen Eschatologie.* Göttingen 1902.

Bogaert, P., *Apocalypse* (syriaque) *de Baruch.* Introduction, traduction du syriaque et commentaire, I-II (Sources chrétiennes 144.) Paris 1969.

Bonner, C., (1937), see *I En*, under *Texts*.

- (1940), see *ApEz*, under *Texts*.

Bonnet, H., *Reallexikon der ägyptischen Religionsgeschichte.* Berlin 1952.

Bonsirven, J., *Le judaisme palestinien. Sa théologie. I. La théologie dogmatique.* Paris 1934.

Bonwetsch, G. N., Die Apokalypse Abrahams, *Studien zur Geschichte der Theologie und der Kirche* I, 1. Leipzig 1897, 1-90.

- Die Bücher der Geheimnisse Henochs, Das sogenannte slavische Henochbuch. (TU 44,2.) Leipzig 1922.

Bornkamm, G., *Paulus*, (Urban Bücher. Die Wissenschaftliche Taschenbuchreihe 119 D.) Stuttgart 1969.

Borsch, F. H., *The Son of Man in Myth and History.* (The NT Library.) London 1967.

Bousset, W., *Die Religion des Judentums im neutestamentlichen Zeitalter.* 2nd ed. Berlin 1906. 3rd ed. by H. Gressmann, entitled *Die Religion des Judentums im späthellenistischen Zeitalter.* (Handbuch z.NT 21.) Tübingen 1926.

Bowker, J., *The Targums and Rabbinic Literature.* An Introduction to Jewish Interpretations of Scripture. London, New York 1969.

Box, G. H., 4 Ezra, *Charles AP II* (1913) 542-624.

- *The Apocalypse of Abraham* ... with the assistance of J. I. Landsman, (Translations of Early Documents, Series I, Palestinian Jewish Texts, Pre-Rabbinic.) London 1918.

Boyarin, D., Siegel, S., *Resurrection, Rabbinic Period,* EncJud XIV (1971) 98-101.

Bréhier, E., *Les idées philosophiques et religieuses de Philon d'Alexandrie.* (Etudes de philosophie médiévale 8.) Paris 1908, 2nd ed. 1925.

224

Brock, S. P. (1967), see *TestJob*, under *Texts*.

Brockington, L. H., *A Critical Introduction to the Apocrypha*. (Studies in Theology.) London 1961.

Brooks, E. W., *Joseph and Asenath*. The Confession and Prayer of Asenath Daughter of Pentephres the Priest. (Translations of Early Documents, Series II, Hellenistic-Jewish texts.) London 1918.

Brownlee, W. H., The Servant of the Lord in the Qumran Scrolls I, *BASOR* 132 (1953) 8-15.

Bruce, F. F.,The Book of Daniel and the Qumran Community, *Neotestamentica et Semitica*, Studies in honour of *Matthew Black,* ed. E. E. Ellis, M. Wilcox. Edinburgh 1969, 221-35.

- Paul on Immortality, *ScJTh* 24 (1971) 457-72.

Brueggemann, W., From Dust to Kingship, *ZAW* 84 (1972) 1-18.

Budde, K., *Der Kanon des ATs*. Giessen 1900.

Büchsel, F., παλιγγενεσια , *TWNT* I (1933) 685-88.

Bückers, H., *Die Unsterblichkeitslehre des Weisheitsbuches*. Ihr Ursprung und ihre Bedeutung. (Alttestamentliche Abhandlungen XIII, 4. Diss. Pont.Inst.Bibl.Roma.) Münster 1938.

- Das "ewige Leben" in 2 Makk 7:36, *Bibl* 21 (1940) 406-12.

Buitkamp, J., *Die Auferstehungsvorstellungen in den Qumrantexten* und ihr alttestamentlicher, apokryphischer, pseudepigraphischer und rabbinischer Hintergrund. Unpublished diss. Groningen 1965.

Bultmann, R., γινωσκω κτλ. *TWNT* I (1933) 688-715.

- NT und Mythologie. Das Problem der Entmythologisierung der neutestamentlichen Verkündigung (1941), *KuM* I (1960) 15-48.

- *Theologie des NTs*. (Theologische Grundrisse.) 5th ed. Tübingen 1965. ET:*Theology of the NT,* New York 1951-55.

Burchard, C., *Untersuchungen zu Joseph und Aseneth*. Uberlieferung-Ortsbestimmung. (Wissenschaftliche Untersuchungen zum NT 8.) Tübingen 1965.

- Neues zur Uberlieferung der Testamente der zwölf Patriarchen, *NTS* 12 (1965/6) 245-58.

- Zur armenischen Uberlieferung der Testamente der zwölf Patriarchen, *Studien zu den Testamenten der zwölf Patriarchen,* ed. W. Eltester. (Beih.z.ZNW 36.) Berlin 1969, 1-29.

Burkitt, F. C., St. Mark viii 32: A neglected various reading, *JThS* 2 (1900/1) 111-13.

Burns, J. B., The Mythology of Death in the OT, *ScJTh* 26 (1973) 327-340.

Burrows, M., *The Dead Sea Scrolls* With Translations, New York 1955.

- *More Light on the Dead Sea Scrolls*. New Scrolls and New Interpretations With Translations of important recent discoveries, New York 1958.

Campenhausen, H.Frh.v., *Die Idee des Martyriums* in der alten Kirche. Göttingen 1936.

Carmignac, J., Retour du docteur de Justice à la fin des jours, *RQ* 1 (1958) 235-248.

Causse, A., *Der Ursprung der jüdischen Lehre von der Auferstehung*. Eine religionsgeschichtliche Untersuchung. Cahors 1908.

Cavallin, H. C. C., De visa lärarnas död och uppståndelse. Ett bidrag till teckningen av Jesu referensramar, *SEÅ* 37-38 (1972/3) 47-61.

Cazelles, H., Le jugement des morts en Israel, *SoOr* 4 (Le jugement des morts), Paris 1961, 103-142.

Ceriani, A. M., see Monumenta . . . under *Texts, Collections* . . .

Charles, R. H. (1897), see *AssMos* under *Texts*.

- A Critical History of the Doctrine of a Future Life In Israel, In Judaism and in Christianity, or Hebrew, Jewish and Christian *Eschatology*. (Jowett Lectures 1898-99.) London 1899, 2nd ed. 1913.

- (1908), see *TestXIIPatr* under *Texts*.

- (1912), see *I En* under *Texts*.

- (1913), see under *Texts, Collections*. ET of Jub (1-82), MartIs (155-62), I En (163-281), TestXIIPatr (282-367), AssMos (407-424), II Bar (470-526); with N. Forbes, II En (425-469).

- *The Ascension of Isaiah*. (Translations of Early Documents, Series I—cf. Box, ApcAbr *supra*.) London, New York 1918.
- A critical and exegetical commentary on the book of *Daniel* . . . Oxford 1929.

Christ, F., rev. of E. M. Meyers, Jewish Ossuaries . . . *RB* 80 (1973) 140-142.

Cohn, L., An Apocryphal Work ascribed to Philo of Alexandria, *JQR* 10 (1898) 277-332.

- *Die Werke Philos von Alexandria* in deutscher Ubersetzung, I-V. (Schriften der jüdischhellenistischen Literatur in deutscher Ubersetzung.) Breslau 1909-29.

Cohon, S. S., *Jewish Theology*. A historical and systematic interpretation of Judaism and its Foundations. (Collected Writings of Samuel Cohon.) Assen 1971.

[Collins, J. J., *Studies in the Sibylline Oracles*. Unpublished diss. Harvard.] Summary *HTR* 65 (1972) 593 f.

- Apocalyptic Eschatology as the Transcendence of Death, *CBQ* 36 (1974) 21-43.

Colson, F. H., see *Philo, Texts*.

Conzelmann, H., *Der erste Brief an die Korinther* übersetzt und erklärt. (Kritisch-exegetischer Kommentar über das NT . . . V, 11th ed.) Göttingen 1969.

Coppens, J., La portée messianique du Ps. 110, *EThL* 32 (1956) 9-15.

- Het onsterfelijkheidsgeloof in het Psalmboek, *Mededelingen van de Koninkl. Vl. Academie voor Wetenschappen* . . . Klasse de Letteren . . . 19 (1957) nr 3. *Brussel*.

Creed, J. M., *The Gospel according to St. Luke*. London 1930.

Cullmann, O., La foi à la résurrection et l'espérance de la résurrection dans le NT, *EThRel* 18 (1943) 3-8.

- *Immortality of the Soul or Resurrection of the Dead*. (The Ingersoll Lecture for 1955.) Published London 1958 and in *Immortality and Resurrection*. Four Essays . . ., ed. K. Stendahl, New York 1965. 9-53.

- Unsterblichkeit der Seele und Auferstehung der Toten. Das Zeugnis des NTs, *ThZ* 12 (1956) 126-156 (German edition of the preceding lecture with minor changes).

Cumont, F., *Lvx perpetva*. Paris 1949.

Dahood, M., *Psalms*, I. (The Anchor Bible.) New York 1966.

Dalbert, P., *Die Theologie der hellenistisch-jüdischen Missionslitteratur* unter Ausschluss von Philo und Josephus, (Theologische Forschung 4. Wissenschaftliche Beiträge z. kirchlich-evangelischen Lehre.) Hamburg 1954.

Dalman, G., *Der leidende Messias* nach der Lehre der Synagoge im ersten nachchristlichen Jahrtausend. Diss. Leipzig 1887.

- *Aramäisch-neuhebräisches Handwörterbuch* zu Targum, Talmud und Midrasch. 2nd ed. Frankfurt a.M. 1922.

Danby, H., *Tractate Sanhedrin Mishnah and Tosefta*. The Judicial Procedure of the Jews as codified Towards the End of the Second Century A. D. Translated . . . (Translations of Early Documents, Series III, Rabbinic Texts.) London, New York 1919.

- *The Mishnah*. Translated . . ., Oxford 1933.

Daniel, C., Esséniens et eunuques (Matthieu 19, 10-12), *RQ* 6 (1963) 353-90.

Daniélou, J., *Théologie du judéo-christianisme*. (Bibliotheque de théologie. Histoire des doctrines chrétiennes avant Nicée 1.) Tournai 1958.

Davenport, G. L., *The Eschatology of the Book of Jubilees*. (Studia Post-Biblica 20.) Leiden 1971.

Davidson, H. R. E., Germanic Religion, *Historia Religionum*, ed. C. J. Bleeker, G. Widengren, I. . . ., Leiden 1969, 611-28.

Deissmann, A., Das vierte Makkabäerbuch, *Kautzsch, AP* II (1913) 149-77.

Delcor, M., L'eschatologie des documents de Khirbet Qumran, *RSR* 44 (1952) 363-86.

Philon (Pseudo-), *SDB* VII (1966) 1354-75.

-, Le Testament de Job, la priére de Nabonide et les traditions targoumiques, *Bibel und Qumran*, ed. S. Wagner. Berlin-Ost 1968, 57-74.

-, Le livre de *Daniel* (Sources bibliques.) Paris 1971.

Delling, G., Speranda futura. Jüdische Grabinschriften Italiens über das Geschick nach dem Tode, *ThLZ* 76 (1951) 521-526. Also in *id.* Studien zum NT und zum hellenistischen Judentum. Göttingen 1970.

Denis, A. M., *Introduction aux pseudépigraphes grecs d'AT.* (Studia in Veteris Testamenti Pseudepigrapha.) Leiden 1970.

Dhorme, E., A Commentary on the Book of *Job.* ET . . . London . . . 1967.

Dibelius, M., Kümmel, W. G., *Paulus,* (Sammlung Göschen 1160.) Berlin 1951.

Dieterich, A., *Nekyia.* Beiträge zur Erklärung der neuentdeckten Petrusapokalypse. 2nd ed. Leipzig-Berlin 1913.

Doeve, J. W., Oscar Cullmann. Immortalité de l'ame ou résurrection des morts? *NovTest* 2 (1958) 157-61.

Dornseiff, F., *Echtheitsfragen Antik-griechischer Literatur.* Rettungen des Theognis, Phokylides, Hekataios, Choirilos. Berlin 1939.

Driver, G. R., *The Judaean Scrolls.* The Problem and a Solution. Oxford 1965.

- Isaiah lii, 13-liii, 12: The Servant of the Lord, *In memoriam P. Kahle,* ed. M. Black, G. Fohrer. (Beih. z.ZAW 103.) Berlin 1968, 90-105.

Driver, S. R., Gray, G. B., A Critical and Exegetical Commentary on the Book of *Job* together with a new translation. Edinburgh 1921.

Dubarle, A.-M., Une source du livre de la Sagesse, *RSPT* 37 (1953) 425-43.

Du Mesnil du Buisson, R., *Les peintures de la synagogue de Doura-Europos* 254-256 aprés J.-C. (Scripta Pontificii Instituti Biblici 86.) Roma 1939.

Dupont-Sommer, A., *Le Quatriéme Livre des Machabées* . . . . (Bibliotheque de l'Ecole des Hautes Etudes . . . Sciences historiques et philologiques 274.) Paris 1939.

- De l'immortalité astrale dans la "Sagesse de Salomon", *REG* 62 (1949) 80-86.

- Apercus préliminaires sur *les Manuscrits de la Mer Morte.* (L'Orient ancien illustré.) Paris 1950.

Easton, B. S., Pseudo-Phocylides, *AnglThR* 14 (1932) 222-28.

Edelmann, R., *Zur Frühgeschichte des Mahzor.* Genizafragmente mit Palästinischer Punktation. (Bonner Orientalistische Studien 6.) Stuttgart 1934.

Edsman, C. M., Eschatologie, *RGG* II (3rd ed. 1958) 650-55.

Eichrodt, W., *Theologie des ATs* II-III 4th ed. Stuttgart, Göttingen 1961.

- *Der Prophet Hesekiel* I-II. (Das AT Deutsch 22) Göttingen 1959-66.

Eissfeldt, O., *Einleitung in das AT* unter Einschluss der Apokryphen und Pseudepigraphen sowie der apokryphen- und pseudepigraphenartigen Qumranschriften. Entstehungsgeschichte des ATs. (Neue theologische Grundrisse.) 3rd ed. Tübingen 1964.

- Zur Kompositionstechnik des pseudo-philonischen Liber Antiquitatum Biblicarum, *NTT* 56 (1953) 53-71.

Elbogen, I., *Der jüdische Gottesdienst in seiner geschichtlichen Entwicklung.* Leipzig 1913. (New impression: Hildesheim 1962.)

Elmgren, H., *Philon av Alexandria* med särskild hänsyn till hans eskatologiska föreställningar. Diss. Lund 1939.

Engnell, I., The Ebed Yahweh Songs and the Suffering Messiah in "Deutero-Isaiah", *BJRL* 31 (1948) 54-93.

-, The Son of Man, *Critical Essays on the OT.* London 1970.

227

Erlandsson, S., *The Burden of Babylon.* A Study of Isaiah 14:2-14:23. (CB. OT Series 4.) Diss. Uppsala. Lund 1970.

Etheridge, J. W., see *Targum*, under *Texts*.

Evans, C. F., *Resurrection and the NT.* (Studies in Biblical Theology Series II, 12.) London 1970.

Farina, A., see *PsPhoc*, under *Texts*.

Farmer, W. R., *Maccabees, Zealots, and Josephus.* An Inquiry into Jewish Nationalism in the Greco-Roman Period. New York 1956.

Feldman, L., *Scholarship on Philo and Josephus* (1937-62.) (Studies in Judaica 1.) New York without date—probably 1963.

Feldman, L. H., see *Josephus*, under *Texts*.

Festugiére, A. J., *L'idéal religieux des Grecs et l'Evangile.* (Etudes Bibliques.) Paris 1932.

- A propos des arétalogies d'Isis, *HTR* 42 (1949) 209-34.

Feuillet, A., Le Fils d l'Homme de Daniel et la tradition biblique, *RB* 60 (1953) 170-202, 321-346.

- Le "ravissement" final des justes et la double perspective eschatologique (résurrection glorieuse et vie avec le Christ aprés la mort) dans la Premiere Epitre aux Thessaloniciens, *Rev Thom* 72 (1972) 533-59.

Fichtner, J., Die Stellung der Sapientia Salomos in der Literatur- und Geistesgeschichte ihrer Zeit, *ZNW* 36 (1937) 113-32.

- *Weisheit Salomos.* (HAT II, 6.) Tübingen 1938.

Finkelstein, L., *The Pharisees.* The Sociological Background of Their Faith. (The Morris Loeb Series 2.) 3rd ed. Philadelphia 1962.

Fisch, S., *Ezekiel.* Hebrew Text and ET with an Introduction and Commentary. (Soncino Books of the Bible.) London 1950.

Flemming, J., Rademacher, L., See *I En, Texts*.

Flusser, D., Apocalypse, *EncJud* III (1971) 179-181.

Foerster,W., κλῆρος *TWNT* III (1938) 757-63.

Fohrer, G.—Galling, K., *Ezechiel.* (HAT I, 13.) Tübingen 1955.

Fohrer, G., Das Buch *Jesaja* II, Kapitel 24-39.)Zürcher Bibelkommentare.) Zürich, Stuttgart 1962.

- Der Aufbau der Apokalypse des Jesajabuches, *CBQ* 25 (1963) 34-45.

- Das Buch *Hiob.* (Kommentar z.AT.) Gütersloh 1963.

- Das Geschick des Menschen nach dem Tode im AT, *KuD* 14 (1968) 249-62.

- υἱός B. AT; C. Judentum, I. Hell. Judentum, *TWNT* VIII (1969) 340-357.

Forbes, N., Charles, R. H., The Book of the Secrets of Enoch, *Charles* AP II (1913) 425-69.

Freedman, H., Genesis I-II, *Midrash Rabba* (1939)—see *Texts*.

Frend, W. H. C., *Martyrdom and Persecution in the Early Church.* A Study of a Conflict from the Maccabees to Donatus. Oxford 1965.

Frey, J.-B., La vie de l'au-delà dans les conceptions juives du temps de Jésus-Christ, *Bibl* 13 (1932) 129-68.

- (1936) CIJ, see *Texts, Jewish Inscriptions*.

Friedlander, G., *Pirke de Rabbi Eliezer.* (The Chapters of Rabbi Eliezer the Great.) According to the Text of the Manuscript Belonging to A. Epstein . . . translated and annotated . . . London. , New York, 1916.

Friedmann, M., see *Sifré*, under *Texts*.

Friedrich, G., σαλπιγξ κτλ. *TWNT* VII (1964) 71-88.

Frost, S. B., The Memorial of the Childless Man. A Study in Hebrew Thought on Immortality, *Interpr* 26 (1972) 437-50.

Früchtel, U., *Die kosmologischen Vorstellungen bei Philo von Alexandrien*. Ein Beitrag zur Geschichte der Genesisexegese. (Arbeiten zur Literatur und Geschichte des hellenistischen Judentums 2.) Leiden 1968.

Fuchs, H., Abrahams Testament, *JüdLex* I (1927) 48.

Gärtner, B., *The Theology of the Gospel of Thomas*. London 1961.

Gärtner, E., *Komposition und Wortwahl des Buches der Weisheit*. (Schriften der Lehranstalt für die Wissenschaft des Judentums II, 2-4.) Berlin 1912.

Galling, K., see Fohrer, G. (1955).

Geffcken, J., see *OrSib*, under *Texts*.

Gehman, H. S., Ἐπισκεπτομαι, ἐπισκεψις, ἐπισκοπος and ἐπισκοπη in the LXX in Relation to פקד and other Hebrew Roots. A Case of Semantic Development Similar to that of Hebrew, *VT* 22 (1972) 197-207.

Gerleman, G., Studies in the LXX, I-III. (Lunds Universitets Årsskrift N.F. I: 43:2-3; 52:3.) Lund 1946-56.

Ginsberg, H. L., The Oldest Interpretation of the Suffering Servant, *VT* 3 (1953) 401-04.

Ginzberg, L., *The Legends of the Jews* I-VII . . . Philadelphia 1910-28.

Glasson, T. F., *Greek Influence in Jewish Eschatology* With Special Reference to the Apocalypses and Pseuepigrapha. London 1961.

Gnilka, J., Die Auferstehung des Leibes in der modernen exegetischen Diskussion, *Conc* 6 (1970) 732-38.

Goldin, J., *The Fathers According to Rabbi Nathan*, translated from the Hebrew. (Yale Judaica Series 10.) New Haven, London 1955.

Goodenough, E. R., *An Introduction to Philo Judaeus*. Oxford 1940.

- Philo on Immortality, *HTR* 39 (1946) 85-108.

- *Jewish Symbols* in the Greco-Roman Period, IV. (Bollingen Series 37.) New York 1954.

Goodrick, A. T. S., *The Book of Wisdom* with Introduction and Notes. (The Oxford Church Bible Commentary.) London 1913.

Grassi, J., Ezekiel xxxvii. 1-14 and the NT, *NTS* 11 (1964/5) 162-64.

Gray, G. B., The Psalms of Solomon, *Charles, AP* II (1913) 625-52.

Gray, G. B., Peake, A. S., A Critical and Exegetical Commentary on the Book of *Isaiah* . . . (The International Critical Commentary.) Edinburgh 1912.

Gregg, J. A. F., *The Wisdom of Solomon* In the Revised Version with Introduction and Notes. (The Cambridge Bible to Schools and Colleges.) Cambridge 1909.

Grelot, P., L'eschatologie des Esséniens et le livre d'Hénoch, *RQ* 1 (1958) 113-31.

- *De la mort à la vie éternelle*. Etudes de théologie biblique. (Lectio Divina 67.) Paris 1971.

Greshake, G., *Auferstehung der Toten*. Ein Beitrag zur gegenwärtigen theologischen Diskussion über die Zukunft der Geschichte. (Koinonia 10.) Diss. Münster. Essen 1969.

Gressmann, H., see Bousset, W.

- *Der Messias*. (FRLANT 43, NF 26.) Göttingen 1929.

Grossfeld, B., Bible, Translations, Aramaic, the Targumim, *EncJud* IV (1971) 841-51.

Grundmann, W., *Das Evangelium nach Lukas*. (Theol.Handkommentar z.NT 3.) 2nd ed. Berlin 1961.

Grunwald, M., *Abraham* als jüdischer Proselytenname, *JüdLex* I (1927) 38.

Guhrt, J., αἰων , *TBNT* II, 2 (1971) 1457-62.

Guillaumont, A., A propos du célibat des Esséniens, *Hommages à A. Dupont-Sommer*. Paris 1971, 395-419.

Gunkel, H., Das vierte Buch Esra, *Kautzsch, AP* II (1900) 331-401.

Haag, E., Ez 37 und der Glaube an die Auferstehung der Toten, *Trierer ThZ* 82 (1973) 78-92.

Hadas, M., see *III* and *IV Mcc, Texts.*

Haller, W., Die Lehre von der Auferstehung des Fleisches bis auf Tertullian, *ZThK* 2 (1892) 274-342.

Hammershaimb, E., *Første Enoksbog, De Gammeltestamentlige Pseudepigrafer* (II). København, Oslo, Lund 1956 (69-174).

- Das Martyrium Jesajas, *Jüdische Schriften* . . . II, 1 (1973) 1-34.

Hanhart, K. *The Intermediate State in the NT.* Diss. Amsterdam 1966.

Harnack, A. v., Die Terminologie der Wiedergeburt und verwandter Erlebnisse in der ältesten Kirche. *TU* 42:3, Leipzig 1918, 97-103.

Harnisch, W., *Verhängnis und Verheissung der Geschichte.* Untersuchungen zum Zeit- und Geschichtsverständnis im 4. Buch Esra und in der syrischen Baruchapokalypse. (Diss. Marburg 1967. FRLANT 97.) Göttingen 1969.

Harrington, D. J., The Original Language of Pseudo-Philo's *Liber Antiquitatum Biblicarum*, HTR 63 (1970) 503-14.

- The Biblical Text of Pseudo-Philo's *Liber Antiquitatum Biblicarum*, *CBQ* 33 (1971) 1-17.

Harris, J. R., Some Notes on 4 Maccabees, *ExpT* 32 (1920/1) 183-85.

Hartman, L., *Prophecy Interpreted.* The Formation of Some Jewish Apocalyptic Texts and of the Eschatological Discourse Mark 13 par. (CB. NT Series 1.) Diss. Uppsala. Lund 1966.

Hartman, L. F., Daniel, *JeBiCo* (1968) 446-60. (= 26).

Hedegård, D., see *Seder,* under *Texts.*

Heinemann, J., Amidah, *EncJud* II (1971) 838-45.

Heinisch, P., Das Buch der *Weisheit* übersetzt und erklärt. (Exeget. Handbuch z.AT 24.) Münster 1912.

Hengel, M., *Judentum und Hellenismus.* Studien zu ihrer Begegnung unter besonderer Berücksichtigung Palästinas bis zur Mitte des 2 Jh.v.Chr. (Wissenschaftliche Untersuchungen zum NT 10.) 2nd ed. Tübingen 1973 (1st ed. 1969).

- Anonymität, Pseudepigraphie und "Literarische Fälschung" in der jüdisch-hellenistischen Literatur, *Pseudepigrapha I,* Fondation Hardt, Entretiens 18. Genève 1972, 291-308.

- Ist der Osterglaube noch zu retten? Friedrich Lang zum 60.Geburtstag gewidmet, ThQ 153 (1973) 252-69.

Henry, M.-L., *Glaubenskrise und Glaubensbewährung* in den Dichtungen der Jesajaapokalypse. Versuch einer Deutung der literarischen Komposition von Jes, 24-27 aus dem Zusammenhang ihrer religiösen Motivbildungen. (Beiträge zur Wissenschaft vom AuNT. Folge 5:6. Habil. Rostock 1952.) Stuttgart 1967.

Herr, M. D., Pirkei de-Rabbi Eliezer, *EncJud* XIII (1971) 558-60.

- The Historical Significance of the Dialogues between Jewish Sages and Roman dignitaries, *Scripta Hierosolymitana* 22 (1971) 123-50.

Hindley, J. C., Towards a Date for the Similitudes of Enoch, *NTS* 14 (1967/8) 551-65.

Hölscher, G., Das Buch *Hiob.* (HAT I, 17.) 2nd ed. Tübingen 1952.

Hoffmann, P., *Die Toten in Christus.* Eine religionsgeschichtliche und exegetische Untersuchung zur paulinischen Eschatologie. (Neutestamentliche Abhandlungen N.F.2. Diss. München 1959.) Münster 1966.

Hofius, O., Eine altjüdische Parallele zu Röm. IV.17b, *NTS* 18 (1971) 93-94.

Holl, K., Das Apokryphon Ezechiel, *Gesammelte Aufsätze zur Kirchen-geschichte* II. Tübingen 1928 (first published in Festschrift A. Schlatter 1922, new impression Darmstadt 1964), 33-43.

Holm-Nielsen, S., *Hodayot.* Psalms from Qumran. (Acta Theologica Danica 2.) Aarhus 1960.

Holtz, T., Christliche Interpolationen in "Joseph und Aseneth", *NTS* 14 (1967/8) 482-97.

Hruby, K., *Die Stellung der jüdischen Gesetzeslehrer zur werdenden Kirche.* (Schriften zur Judentumskunde 4.) Zürich 1971.

Hulsbosch, A., De eschatologie van het Boek der Wijsheid, *Studia Catholica* 1952, 113-123.

- Onsterfelijkheid en opstanding, *WKTN Jb* 1955, 129-44.

Hultgård, A., *Croyances messianiques des Test. XII Patr.* Critique textuelle et commentaire des passages messianiques. Unpublished diss. Uppsala 1971.

Humbert, P., La rosée tombe en Israel. A propos d'Esaie 26, 19, *ThZ* 13 (1957) 487-93.

Hurwitz, M. S., Pseudo-Phocylides, *EncJud* XIII (1971) 1335 f.

[Hutton, D. D., The Resurrection of the Holy Ones (Mt 27:51b-53): A Study of the Theology of the Matthaean Passion Narrative. Unpublished diss. Harvard 1969.] Summary HTR 63 (1970) 518 f.

Iersel, B.v., Auferstehung Jesu Information oder Interpretation? *Conc* 6 (1970) 696-702.

Immortality and Resurrection. four Essays by O. Cullmann, H. A. Wolfson, W. Jaeger, H. J. Cadbury, ed. *K. Stendahl*, New York 1965.

Israelstam, J., Leviticus, *Midrash Rabba* (1939)—see *Texts*.

James, M. R. (1892)—see *TestAbr*, under Texts.

- The Apocryphal Ezekiel, *JThS* 15 (1913/4) 236-43.

- Notes on Apocrypha. i. *Pseudo-Philo* and *Baruch, JThS* 16 (1914/5) 403-05.

- *The Biblical Antiquities of Philo,* now first translated from the Old Latin Version. London 1917. (New impression, prolegomena by L. H. Feldman, H. M. Orlinsky, The Library of Biblical Studies. New York 1971.)

- The Venice extracts from the Testaments of the Twelve Patriarchs, *JThS* 28 (1927) 337-48.

Jaubert, A., Le calendrier des Jubilés et de la secte de Qumran. Ses origines bibliques, *VT* 3 (1953) 250-64.

Jenni, E., Das wort 'olam im AT, III, Hauptteil, *ZAW* 65 (1953) 1-35.

- Eschatology of the OT, *IDB* II (1962) 126-33.

- Time, *IDB* IV (1962) 643-49.

Jeremias, G., *Der Lehrer der Gerechtigkeit.* (Studien z.Umwelt des NTs 2.) Göttingen 1963.

Jeremias, J., παις δεου C. Im Spätjudentum ... D. Im NT, *TWNT* V (1954) 676-713. See also W. Zimmerli.

- πολλοι *TWNT* VI 1959) 536-45.

- *Die Gleichnisse Jesu.* 7th ed. Göttingen 1965.

Jervell, J., *Imago Dei.* Gen. 1, 26 f. im Spätjudentum, in der Gnosis und in den paulinischen Briefen. (FRLANT, N.F. 58.) Diss. Oslo. Göttingen 1960.

Jones, A., *The Gospel According to St Matthew.* A Text and Commentary for Students. London, Dublin 1965.

Jonge, M. de, *The Testaments of the Twelve Patriarchs.* A Study of their Text, Composition and Origin. Diss. Leiden. Assen 1953.

- The Testaments of the Twelve Patriarchs and the NT, *StEv* 1 (TU 73) 1959, 546-56.

- Christian Influence in the Testaments of the Twelve Patriarchs, *NovTest* 4 (1960) 182-235.

- Once more: Christian Influence in the Testaments of the Twelve Patriarchs, *NovTest* 5 (1962) 311-19.

- (1970)—see *TestXIIPatr,* under *Texts*.

Käsemann, E., Der Glaube Abrahams in Röm 4, *Paulinische Perspektiven.* Tübingen 1969, 140-77.

Kahn, J. G., "Connais toi toi-meme" à la maniere de Philon, *RHPR* 53 (1973) 293-307.

Kaiser, O., *Der königliche Knecht.* Eine traditionsgeschichtlich-exegetische Studie über die Ebed-Jahwe-Lieder bei Deuterojesaja. (FRLANT 70.) Göttingen 1959.

Kaminka, A., LXX und Tg zu Proverbia, *HUCA* 8-9 (1931/2) 169-91.

Katz, P., Eleazar's Martyrdom in 2 Maccabees: The Latin Evidence for a Point of the Story, *Studia Patristica 4* (TU 79, 1961) 118-24.

Kearns, C., *The Expanded Text of Ecclesiasticus:* its teaching on the after-life as a clue to its origin. Unpubl. diss. Roma 1951. (This was not available to me.)

Kees, H., *Totenglauben und Jenseitsvorstellungen der alten Ägypter.* Grundlagen und Entwicklung bis zum Ende des mittleren Reiches. Leipzig 1926. (2nd ed. 1956.)

Kegel, G., *Auferstehung Jesu—Auferstehung der Toten.* Eine traditionsgeschichtliche Untersuchung zum NT. Gütersloh 1970.

Keulers, J., *Die eschatologische Lehre des vierten Esrabuches.* (Biblische Studien 20:2-3.) Freiburg i.Br. 1922.

Kirche und Synagoge. Handbuch zur Geschichte von Christen und Juden. Darstellung mit Quellen, I. Ed. *K. H. Rengstorf,* S.v. Kortzfleisch, Stuttgart 1968.

Kisch, G.—see *LAB,* under *Texts.*

Kittel, R.—*see Biblia Hebraica,* under *Texts.*

- Die Psalmen Salomos, *Kautzsch AP* II (1900) 127-148.

Kleinknecht, H., ϑειος *TWNT* III (1938) 122-23.

Klijn, A. F. J., The Sources and the Redaction of the Syriac "Apocalypse of Baruch", *JSJud* 1 (1970) 65-76.

Klostermann, E., *Das Matthäusevangelium.* (Handb.z.NT 4.) 2nd ed. Tübingen 1927.

- Das Lukas-evangelium. (Handbuch z.NT 5.) 2nd ed. Tübingen 1929.

Knox, W. L., *Some Hellenistic Elements in Primitive Christianity.* The Schweich Lectures of the British Academy 1942 (35). London 1944.

Koch, K., *The Rediscovery of Apocalyptic.* A polemical work on a neglected area of biblical studies and its damaging effects on theology and philosophy. (Studies in Biblical Theology, Second Series 22.) London 1972. (German original: Ratlos vor der Apokalyptik, Gütersloh 1970).

König, F., Zarathustras Jenseitsvorstellungen und das AT, Wien 1964.

- Der Glaube an die Auferstehung der Toten in den Gathas, *Vorderasiatische Studien für Viktor Christian.* Wien 1965, 69-73.

Koep, L., *Das himmlische Buch in Antike und Christentum.* Eine religionsgeschichtliche Untersuchung zur altchristlichen Bildersprache. (Theophaneia . . . 8.) Bonn 1952.

Kohl, H., Watzinger, C., *Antike Synagogen in Galilaea.* (29. Wissenschaftliche Veröffentlichung der deutschen Orient-Gesellschaft.) Leipzig 1916.

Kohler, K., The Pre-Talmudic Haggada. II.C.—The Apocalypse of Abraham and its Kindred, *JQR* 7 (1895) 581-606.

- (1897)—see *TestJob,* under *Texts.*

Kolenkow, A. C. B., *An Introduction to II Baruch 53, 56-74:* Structure and Substance. Unpublished diss. Harvard 1971.

Konovitz, I., *Beth Shammai—Beth Hillel.* Collected Sayings in Halakah and Aggadah in the Talmudic and Midrashic Literature. (Hebrew.) Jerusalem 1965.

Kopp, C., *Die heiligen Stätten der Evangelien.* Regensburg 1959.

Kraus, H.-J., Auferstehung III. In Israel, *RGG* I (3rd ed. 1957) 692-93.

- *Psalmen* I. (Biblischer Kommentar AT XV, 1.) Neukirchen 1960.

Krauss, S., Die Mischna . . . Sanhedrin-Makkot . . . Giessen 1933. Cf. *Mishnah,* under Texts.

Kuhn, H. W., *Enderwartung und gegenwärtiges Heil.* Untersuchungen zu den Gemeindeliedern von Qumran mit einem Anhang über Eschatologie und Gegenwart in der Verkündigung Jesu. (Studien z.Umwelt des NTs 4.) Göttingen 1966.

Kurfess, A., Das Mahngedicht des sogenannten Phokylides im zweiten Buch der Oracula Sibyllina, *ZNW* 38 (1939) 171-81.

- (1951)—see *OrSib*, under *Texts*.

Lampe, G. W. H., *A Patristic Greek Lexicon*. Oxford 1961.

Lanchester, H. C. O., The Sibylline Oracles, *Charles AP* II (1913) 368-406.

Laperoussaz, E.-M., Le Testament de Moise (Généralement appelé "Assomption de Moise"). Traduction . . ., Sem 19 (1970).

Laqueur, R., *Der jüdische Historiker Flavius Josephus*. Ein biographischer Versuch auf neuer quellenkritischer Grundlage. Giessen 1920.

Larcher, C., *Etudes sur le livre de la Sagesse*. (Etudes bibliques.) Paris 1969.

Lauer, S., Eusebes logismos in IV Macc, *JJS* 6 (1955) 170-71.

Laurin, R. B., The Question of Immortality in the Qumran "Hodayot", *JSS* 3 (1958) 344-55.

Lauterbach, J. Z., The Sadducees and Pharisees (1913), *Rabbinic Essays*. Cincinnati, 1951, 23-48.

- The Pharisees and their Teachings (1929), *ibid*. 87-159.

Lebram, J. C. H., Apokalyptik und Hellenismus im Buche Daniel. Bemerkungen und Gedanken zu Martin HENGELs Buch über "Judentum und Hellenismus", *VT* 20 (1970) 503-24.

Le Déaut, R., Les études targumiques. Etat de la recherche et perspectives pour l'exégese de l'AT, *EThL* 44 (1968) 5-34.

Leivestad, R., Er den apokalyptiske menneskesønn en moderne teologisk oppfinnelse? *NTT* 70 (1969) 221-35 = *NTS* 18, (1971/2) 243-67; also in *Annual of the Swedish Theological Institute* 6, 1968)

Le Moyne, J., *Les Sadducéens*. (Etudes Bibliques.) Paris 1972.

Léon-Dufour, X., Apparitions du Resusscité et Herméneutique, *La résurrection du Christ* et l'exégése moderne, ed. E.de Surgy, P. Grelot, M. Carrez, A. George, J. Delorme, X. Léon-Dufour. (Lectio Divina 50.) Paris 1969, 153-73.

- *Résurrection de Jésus et message pascal*. Paris 1971.

Lewis, C. T., Short, C., *A Latin Dictionary* . . . Oxford 1879 (new impr. London 1969.)

Liagre Böhl, F. M. T. de, Babylonien II, RGG I (3rd ed. 1957), 812-822.

Licht, J. (1957)—see *Essenica, Texts*.

- Taxo or the Apocalyptic Doctrine of Vengeance, *JJS* 12 (1961) 95-103.

- Abraham, Apocalypse of, *EncJud* III (1971) 125-27.

Liebermann, S., Some Aspects of After Life in Early Rabbinic Literature, *H. A. Wolfson Jubilee Volume*, English Section, II. (American Academy for Jewish Research.) Jerusalem 1966. (This was not available to me.)

Lifshitz, B., La vie de l'au-delà dans les conceptions juives. Inscriptions grecques de Beth-Shearim, *RB* 68 (1961) 401-11.

Lincke, K. F. A., *Samaria und seine Propheten*. Ein religionsgeschichtlicher Versuch mit einer Textbeilage: Die Weisheitslehre des Phokylides, Griechisch und deutsch. Tübingen, Leipzig 1903.

- Phokylides, Isokrates und der Dekalog, *Philologus* 70 (1911) 438-42.

Lindars, B., *NT Apologetic*. The doctrinal significance of the OT quotations. London 1961.

Lindblom, J., *Senjudiskt fromhetslif enligt Salomos Psaltare*. Diss. Uppsala 1909.

- *Das ewige Leben*. Eine Studie über die Entstehung der religiösen Lebensidee im NT. (Arbeten utgifna med understöd af Vilhelm Ekmans universitetsfond, Uppsala, 15.) Uppsala, Leipzig, 1914.

- *Jesaja-Apokalypse*. Jes 24-27. (Lunds Universitets Årsskrift, NF I: 34:3.) Lund, Leipzig 1938.

- *The Servant Songs in Deutero-Isaiah*. A New Attempt to Solve an Old Problem, (Lunds Universitets Årsskrift NF I: 47:5.) Lund 1951.

Lindner, H., *Die Geschichtsauffassung des Flavius Josephus* im Bellum Judaicum. Gleichzeitig ein Beitrag zur Quellenfrage. (Arbeiten zur Geschichte des antiken Judentums und des Urchristentums 12.) Leiden 1972.

Loewe, H., The Ideas of Pharisaism, *Judaism and Christianity* II . . . Essays by H. Loewe (ed.), W. L. Knox etc. London, New York 1937, 3-58.

Löwinger, A., Die Auferstehung in der jüdischen Tradition, *Jahrb.f.jüd.Volkskunde* 25 (1923) 23-122.

Lohse, E., Auferstehung, IV. Im Judentum, *RGG* I (3rd ed. 1957) 694 f.

- προσωπον *TWNT* VI (1959) 769-79.

- Michael I, *RGG* IV (1960) 932.

- Phokylides, *RGG* V (1961) 362.

- (1964)—see *Essenica*, under *Texts*.

- *Umwelt des NTs.* (Grundrisse zum NT . . . NT Deutsch, Ergänzungsreihe 1.) Göttingen 1971.

Ludwig, O., *Die Stadt in der Jesaja-Apokalypse*. Zur Datierung von Jes. 24-27. Diss. Bonn. Köln 1961.

Lueken, W., *Michael*. Eine Darstellung und Vergleichung der jüdischen und der morgenländisch—christlichen Tradition vom Erzengel Michael, Göttingen 1898.

Mach, R.,*Der Zaddik in Talmud und Midrasch*. Diss. Basel. Leiden 1957.

Macurdy, G. H., Platonic Orphism in the Testament of Abraham, *JBL* 61 (1942) 213-26.

Mai, A. (1833)—Gr. text of *TestJob*—see Kohler.

Maier, J., *Geschichte der jüdischen Religion* von der Zeit Alexander des Grossen bis zur Aufklärung mit einem Ausblick auf das 19./20. Jahrhundert. Berlin, New York 1972.

Maillot, A., Lelievre, A., *Les Psaumes*. Commentaire, I. Geneve 1961.

Manson, T. W., The Son of Man in Daniel, Enoch and the Gospels, *BJRL* 32 (1950) 171-93.

- the Bible and Personal Immortality, *Cong Quart* 32 (1954) 7-16.

Mansoor, M., Studies in the Hodajot IV, *JBL* 76 (1957) 139-48.

- (1961)—see *Essenica*, under *Texts*.

- Sadducees, *EncJud* XIV (1971) 619-22.

Marchel, W., De resurrectione et de retributione statim post mortem secundum 2 Mach. comparandum cum 4 Mach, *VD* 34 (1956) 327-341.

Marmorstein, A., The Doctrine of the Resurrection of the Dead in Rabbinical Theology, *AmJTh* 19 (1915) 577-91.

- Jüdische Archäologie und theologie, *ZNW* 32 (1933) 32-41.

Marrow, S. B., Resurrection of the Dead I. In the Bible, *NewCathEnc* XII (1968) 419-24.

Martin-Achard, R., De la mort à la résurrection d'aprés l'AT. (Bibliotheque théologique.) Neuchatel, Paris 1956.

Marxsen, W., Die Auferstehung Jesu als historisches und als theologisches Problem, *Die Bedeutung der Auferstehungsbotschaft für den Glauben an Jesus Christus*. (Schriftenreihe des Theologischen Ausschusses der Evangelischen Kirche der Union.) Ed. W. Marxsen, U. Wilckens, G. Delling, H.-G. Geyer. 3rd ed. Gütersloh 1966, 10-39.

Massingberd Ford, J., *A Trilogy on Wisdom and Celibacy*. (The Cardinal O'Hara Series.) Notre Dame, London 1967.

Masson, C., Immortalité de l'ame ou résurrection des morts?Reflexions critiques sur une étude récente, *RThPh* 8 (1958) 250-67.

Mauchline, J., *Samuel* 1 and 2. (New Century Bible.) London 1971.

Mayer, R., Reuss, J., *Die Qumranfunde und die Bibel*, Regensburg 1959.

Mayer, R., Der Auferstehungsglaube in der iranischen Religion, *Kairos* 7 (1965) 194-207.

Mays, J. L., *Hosea*. A Commentary. (OT Library.) London 1969.

McArthur, H. K., On the Third Day, *NTS* 18 (1971/2) 81-86.

McElwain, H. M., Theology of Resurrection of the Dead, *NewCathEnc* XII (1968) 424-27.

Mertens, A., *Das Buch Daniel im Lichte der Texte vom Toten Meer*. (Stuttgarter Biblische Monographien 12.) Würzburg 1971.

Metzger, B. M., *An Introduction to the Apocrypha*. New York 1957.

Meyer, R., *Hellenistisches in der rabbinischen Anthropologie*. Rabbinische Vorstellungen vom Werden des Menschen. (Beiträge z. Wissenschaft vom AuNT, IV:e folge, Hft 22; Der ganzen Sammlung Hft 73.) Stuttgart 1937.

- Abraham-Apokalypse, RGG I (3rd ed. 1957) 72.

- Abraham-Testament, RGG I (3rd ed. 1957) 73.

- *Das Gebet des Nabonid*. Eine in den Qumran-Handschriften wiederentdeckte Weisheitserzählung. (Sitzungsberichte der sächsischen Akademie der Wissenschaften zu Leipzig. Philologisch-historische Klasse. Band 107. Heft 3.) Berlin 1962.

- Σαδδουκαιος *TWNT* VII (1964) 35-54.

Meyer, W., see *VAE*, under *texts*.

Meyers, E. M., *Jewish ossuaries*. Reburial and rebirth. Secondary Burials in their Ancient Near Eastern setting. (Biblica et Orientalia 24.) Rome 1971.

Michel, O., *Der Brief an die Römer*. (Kritisch-exegetischer Kommentar über das NT . . .4.) 11th ed. Göttingen 1963.

Michel, O., Bauernfeind, O., Die beiden Eleazarreden in Jos. bell. 7, 323-336; 7, 341-88, *ZNW* 58 (1967) 267-272.

Michel, O., Bauernfeind, O., see *Josephus,* under *texts*.

Michl, J., Michael . . . Erzengel, LThK VII (1962).

- Engel VII (Michael), RAC V (1962) 243-51.

Milik, J. T., Le Testament de Levi en araméen. Fragment de la grotte 4 de Qumran. (Pl.IV.) *RB* 62 (1955) 398-406.

- Le travail d'édition des manuscrits de Qumran, *RB* 63 (1956) 49-67.

- "Priere de Nabonide" et autres écrits d'un cycle de Daniel. Fragments araméens de Qumran 4 (Pl.I), *RB* 63 (1956) 407-15.

- Hénoch au pays des aromates (ch.XXVII à XXXII). Fragments araméens de la grotte 4 de Qumran (Pl.I), *RB* 65 (1958) 70-77.

- Le couvercle de Bethphage, *Hommages à A.Dupont-Sommer*, Paris 1971, 75-94.

- Milki-sedeq et Milki-resa dans les anciens écrits juifs et chrétiens, *JJS* 23 (1972) 95-144.

- 4Q Visions de Amram et une citation d'Origene, *RB* 79 (1972) 77-97.

Molin, G., Entwicklung und Motive der Auferstehungshoffnung vom AT zur rabbinischen Zeit, *Jud* 9 (1953) 225-39.

Montgomery, J. A., A Critical and Exegetical Commentary on the Book of *Daniel*. (The International Critical Commentary.) Edinburgh 1927.

Moore, G. F., *Judaism* in the first centuries of the Christian Era, the Age of the Tannaim I-III. Cambridge Mass. 1927-30.

Morel, W., Eine Rede bei Josephus (Bell, Iud. VII 344 sqq.), *RheinMus* 75 (1926) 106-15.

Morgenstern, J., The Calendar of the Book of Jubilees. Its Origin and Its Character, *VT* 5 (1955) 34-76.

Morris, L. L., Resurrection, *New Bible Dictionary*, London 1962, 1086-89.

Mowinckel, S., *He That Cometh*. Oxford 1956.

- The Psalms in Israel's worship . . . I-II. Oxford 1963.

Mozley, J. H., The "Vita Adae", *JThS* 30 (1929) 121-49.

Müller, N., Bees, N. A., see *Jewish Inscriptions*, under *Texts*.

Muilenburg, J., The Son of Man in Daniel and the Ethiopic Apocalypse of Enoch, *JBL* 79 (1960) 197-209.

Murphy, R. E., To Know Your Might Is the Root of Immortality, *CBQ* 25 (1963) 88-93.

- Psalms, *JeBiCo* (1968) 569-602 (= *35*).

Mussner, F., ΖΩΗ. Die Anschauung vom "Leben" im vierten Evangelium unter Berucksichtigung der Johannesbriefe. Ein Beitrag zur biblischen Theologie. (Münchener Theologie I, 5.) München 1952.

- Jesu Lehre über das kommende Leben nach den Synoptikern, *Conc* 6 (1970).

Nagel, M., *La Vie grecque d'Adam et d'Eve* (Apocalypse de Moise). Diss. Strasbourg, Oberbronn 1972. (Not available to me.)

Nelis, J. T., Het gelof in de verrijzenis in het oude testament, *Tidjschr Theol* 10 (1970) 362-81.

Neusner, J., *Development of a Legend*. Studies on the Traditions concerning Yohanan ben Zakkai. (Studia Post-Biblica 16.) Leiden 1970.

- *The Rabbinic Traditions about the Pharisees before 70*, I-III. Leiden 1971.

- The Rabbinic Traditions about the Pharisees before 70 AD: The Problem of Oral Tradition, *Kairos* NF 14 (1972) 57-70.

- Josephus' Pharisees, *Ex Orbe Religionum*, Studies Geo Widengren Oblata I, *St H Rel* 21 (1972) 224-44.

Nickelsburg, G. W. E., *Resurrection, Immortality and Eternal Life in Intertestamental Judaism*. (Harvard theological Studies 26. Diss. Harvard.) Cambridge (Mass.), London 1972.

- Eschatology in the Testament of Abraham. A Study of the Judgment Scenes in the Two Recensions, *SCS* 2 (1972) 180-227.

- rev. of Stemberger (1972), *CBQ* 35 (1973) 555 f.

Nikiprowetzky, V., *La troisieme Sibylle*. (Etudes juives 9.) Paris 1970.

- La mort d'Eléazar fils de Jaire et les courants apologétiques dans le *De Bello Judaico* de Flavius Josephe, *Hommage à A. Dupont-Sommer*, Paris 1971, 461-90.

- L'exégese de Philon d'Alexandrie, *RHPR* 53 (1973) 309-29.

Nikolainen, A. T., *Der Auferstehungsglauben in der Bibel und ihrer Umwelt* I-II. (Annales Academiae Scientiarum Fennicae B XLIX, 3; LIX, 3.) Helsinki 1944-46.

Nilsson, M. P., *Geschichte der griechischen Religion* I-II. (Handbuch der Altertumswissenschaft 5.) 2nd ed. München 1955-61.

Noack, B., Fjerde Ezrabog, *De gammeltestamentlige pseudepigrafer* I (1953) 1-68.

- Sibyllinske Orakler, *De gammeltestamentlige pseudepigrafer* IV (1963) 441-508.

- De Sibyllinske oraklers baggrund, *SEÅ* 31 (1966) 64-79.

Nötscher, F., *Altorientalischer und alttestamentlicher Auferstehungsglaube*. Würzburg 1926.

- *Zur theologischen Terminologie der Qumransekte*. Bonn 1956.

- Hodajot (Psalmenrolle), *BZ* 2 (1958) 128-33.

Norden, E., *Die antike Kunstprosa* vom VI. Jahrh.v.Chr. bis in die Zeit der Renaissance I-II. Leipzig, Berlin 1923 (4th impression, 1st ed. 1898).

- *Agnostos Theos*. Untersuchungen zur Formengeschichte religiöser Rede. Leipzig, Berlin 1913.

North, C. R., *The Suffering Servant in Deutero-Isaiah*. An Historical and Critical Study. 2nd ed. Oxford, London 1956.

- *The Second Isaiah*. Introduction, Translation and Commentary to Chapters XL-LV. Oxford 1964.

North, M., *Das vierte Buch Mose*, Numeri, übersetzt und erklärt. (Das AT Deutsch 7.) Göttingen 1966.

Noy, C. ‏רחגבה‏ ‏חזרן‏, ‏נ אר ם‏ (Ez 36-37), *BM* 13, 35 (1968) 70-94.

Nyberg, H. S., *Die Religionen des alten Iran*. (Mitteilungen der vorderasiatisch-aegyptischen Gesellschaft e.V. 43.) Leipzig 1938.

- Smärtornas man. En studie till Jes 52.13-53.12, *SEÅ* 7 (1942) 5-82.

Odeberg, H., see *III En*, under *Texts*.

- *Pauli brev till Korintierna*. (Tolkning av NT 7.) Stockholm 1944.

O'Dell, J., The Religious Background of the Psalms of Solomon. (Re-evaluated in the Light of the Qumran Texts.) *RQ* 3 (1961/2) 241-57.

Oesterley, W. O. E., *Immortality and the Unseen World*. A Study in OT Religion. London, New York 1921.

Orlinsky, H. M., Studies in the LXX of Job, *HUCA* 28 (1957) 53-74.

Osten-Sacken, P.v.d., *Die Apokalyptik in ihrem Verhältnis zu Prophetie und Weisheit*. (Theologische Existenz heute 157.) München 1969.

Pannenberg, W., *Grundzüge der Christologie*. Gütersloh 1964.

Pedersen, J., *Israel*. Its Life and Culture, I-II. London, Copenhagen 1926.

Perler, O., Das vierte Makkabaeerbuch, Ignatius von Antiochien und die aeltesten Maertyrerberichte, *RivArchCrist* 25 (1949) 47-72.

Pernot, H., see DescMariae, under *Texts*.

Pesch, R., Heilszukunft und Zukunft des Heils. Eschatologie und Apokalyptik in den Evangelien und Briefen, *Gestalt und Anspruch des NTs*, ed. J. Schreiner, G. Dautzenberg. Würzburg 1969, 313-29.

Pfeiffer, R., *History of NT Times* With an Introduction to the Apocrypha. New York 1949.

Philon d'Alexandrie *Lyon* 11-15 Septembre 1966. (Colloques nationaux du centre national de la recherche scientifique.) Paris 1967.

Philonenko, M., Les interpolations chrétiennes des Testaments des Douze Patriarches et les Manuscrits de Qoumran, *RHPR* 38 (1958) 309-43.

- Le Testament de Job. Introduction, traduction et notes, *Sem* 18 (1968).

- (1968)—see *JA*, under *Texts*.

Pilcher, C. V., *The Hereafter in Jewish and Christian Thought*. London 1940.

Ploeg, J. v.d., L'immortalité de l'homme d'apres les textes de la Mer Morte, *VT* 2 (1952) 171-75.

- The Belief in Immortality in the Writings of Qumran, *BO* 18 (1961) 118-24.

- (1962)—see Le *Targum* de Job, under *Texts*.

Plöger, O., *Theokratie und Eschatologie*. (Wissenschaftliche Monographien z.AuNT 2.) Neukirchen 1959.

- Das Buch *Daniel* (Kommentar z.AT 18.) Gütersloh 1965.

Pope, M. H., *Job*. Introduction, Translation and Notes. (The Anchor Bible.) New York 1965.

Porteous, N. W., *Daniel*. A. Commentary. (OT Library.) London 1965.

Porter, F. C., The pre-existence of the Soul in the Book of Wisdom and in the Rabbinical Writings, *OT and Semitic Studies in memory of W. R. Harper* I, Chicago 1908, 205-69. Also in *AmJTh* 12 (1908) 53-115.

Preuss, H. D., *Jahweglaube und Zukunftserwartung*. (Beiträge zur Wissenschaft vom AuNT. Folge 5:7. Diss. Kiel 1965). Stuttgart 1968.

Procksch, O., Auferstehung im AT und Judentum, *RGG* I (2nd ed 1927.) 627-29.

- Jesaia. Erste Hälfte, Kapitel 1-39, übersetzt und erklärt. (Kommentar z.AT 9.) Leipzig 1930.

- ἅγιος *TWNT* I (1933) 87-97, 101-112.

Pryke, E. J., The Identity of the Qumran Sect: A Reconsideration, *NovTest* 10 (1968) 43-61.

- Some Aspects of Eschatology in the Dead Sea Scrolls, *StEv* 5 (1968, TU 103) 296-302.

Quick, O. C., *Doctrines of the Creed*. Their basis in Scripture and their meaning to-day. London 1938.

Quispel, G., Gnosticism and the NT, *VigChrist* 19 (1965) 65-85.

Rabin, C., (1954)—see *Essenica*, under *Texts*.

- *Qumran Studies*. (Scripta Judaica II.) London 1957.

Rad, G. v., *Das erste Buch Mose*, Genesis, übersetzt und erklärt, I-II. (Das AT Deutsch 2-4.) Göttingen 1949-53.

- *Theologie des ATs* I-II. München 1957 (1st ed.)—1962 (3rd ed.).

- *Das fünfte Buch Mose*, Deuteronomium, übersetzt und erklärt. (Das AT Deutsch.) Göttingen 1964.

Rademacher, L.—see *I En*, under *Texts*.

Rahlfs, A.,—see *LXX*, under *Texts*.

Rahnenführer, D., Das Testament des Hiob und das NT, *ZNW* 62 (1971) 68-93, (Diss. Halle 1967.)

Reese, J. M., *Hellenistic Influence on the Book of Wisdom* and Its Consequences. (Analecta Biblica 41.) Rome 1970.

Reider, J., The Book of *Wisdom*. An ET with Introduction and Commentary. (Jewish Apocryphal Literature.) New York 1957.

Rengstorf, K. H., Das NT und die nachapostolische Zeit, *Kirche und Synagoge.* I (1968) 23-83.

- *A Complete* Concordance to Flavius Josephus I, Leiden 1973.

Rese, M., Uberprüfung einiger Thesen von Joachim Jeremias, *ZThK* 60 (1963) 21-41.

Ridderbos, N. H., *De Psalmen* opnieuw uit de grondtekst vertaald en verklaard I. (Korte Verklaring der heilige Schrift met nieuwe vertaling.) Kampen 1962.

Riesenfeld, H., *Jésus transfiguré*. L'arriere-plan du récit évangélique de la transfiguration de Notre-Seigneur. (Acta Seminarii Neotestamentici Upsaliensis 16.) Diss. Uppsala. Lund, København 1947.

- *The Resurrection in Ezekiel XXXVII and in the Dura-Europos Paintings*. (Uppsala Universitets Årsskrift 1948: 11.) Also published in *No Graven Images*. Studies in Art and the Hebrew Bible, ed. J. Gutmann, New York 1971, 120-55.

- Daniel-Jesus-Paulus. Zwei Gastvorlesungen . . . *EuA* 47 (1971) 506-508.

Riessler, P.—see under *Texts, Collections*).

Rigaux, B., *Dieu l'a resusscité*. Exégese et théologie biblique. (Studii biblici franciscani analecta 4.) Gembloux 1973.

Ringgren, H., Apokalyptik I-II, *RGG* I (3rd ed. 1957) 463-66.

- *Psaltarens fromhet*. Stockholm 1957.

- *The Faith of Qumran*. Theology of the Dead Sea Scrolls. Philadelphia 1963. (ET of Swedish original, Tro och liv enligt Dödahavsrullarna, Stockholm 1961.)

Rist, M., Apocalypticism, *IDB* I (1962) 157-61.

Robert, J. et L., Bulletin épigraphique, *REG* 69 (1956) 104-91.

Robinson, H. W., The Hebrew Conception of Corporate Personality,*Beihefte ZAW* 66 (1936) 49-62.

- *The Cross in the OT*. London 1955.

Robinson, T. H., Die zwölf kleinen Propheten, *Hosea* bis Micha. (HAT I:14.) 2nd ed. Tübingen 1954.

Romaniuk, K., Die Eschatologie des Buches der Weisheit, *BiLe* 10 (1969) 198-211.

Rossbroich, M., *De Pseudo-Phocylideis*. Diss. Münster 1910.

Rost, L., Alttestamentliche Wurzeln der ersten Auferstehung, *In memoriam E. Lohmeyer*, ed. W. Schmauch. Stuttgart 1951.

Rowley, H. H., *Jewish Apocalyptic and the Dead Sea Scrolls*. (The Ethel M. Wood lecture.) London 1957.

- *Job*. (The Century Bible N.S.) London etc. 1970.

Rubinstein, A., Hebraisms in the Slavonic „Apocalypse of Abraham", *JJS* 4 (1953) 108-15; 5 (1954) 132-35.

- A Problematic Passage in the Apocalypse of Abraham, *JJS* 8 (1957) 45-50.

Rudolph, W., *Hosea*. (Kommentar z.AT 13:1.) Gütersloh 1966.

Rühle, O., (Edsman, C. M.,) Astralreligion, *RGG* I (3rd ed. 1957) 662-64.

Russell, D. S., *The Method and Message of Jewish Apocalyptic* 200 BC-AD 100. (The OT Library.) London 1964.

Ryssel, V., Die Apokalypsen des Baruch, *Kautzsch AP* II (1900) 402-57.

Sabourin, L., rev. of LAB, translated by M. R. James, *BTh* 2 (1972) 211-12.

Salomonsen, B., Om rabbinsk hermeneutik, *DTT* 36 (1973) 161-73.

Sambursky, S., *Das physikalische Welbild der Antike*. (Die Bibliothek der alten Welt.) Zürich, Stuttgart 1965.

Sandmel, S., *Philo's Place in Judaism*. A Study of Conceptions of Abraham in Jewish literature. Cincinnati 1956. (Augmented ed. New York 1971.)

Sawyer, J. F. A., Hebrew Words for the Resurrection of the Dead, *VT* 23 (1973) 218-34.

Schmaller, B., Josephos, *DkP* II (1967) 1440-44.

Schilling, O., *Der Jenseitsgedanke im AT*. Seine Entfaltung und deren Treibkräfte. Ein Beitrag zur Theologie des ATs. Mainz 1951.

Schlatter, A., *Die Theologie des Judentums nach dem Bericht des Josefus*. (Beitr. z.Förderung christlicher Theologie, II, 26.) Gütersloh 1932.

Schmid, H., Daniel, der Menschensohn, *Jud* 27 (1971) 192-220.

Schmid, J., Resurrection of the body, *SacrMundi* V (1970 ET) 333-40.

Schmid, W., *Wilhelm von Christs Geschichte der griechischen Literatur*. Sechste Auflage unter Mitwirkung von O. Stählin... (Handbuch der klassischen Altertumswissenschaft VII, 2:1.) München 1920.

Schmidt, F., *Le Testament d'Abraham*. Unpublished diss. Strasbourg 1971. (Not available to me.)

Schmidt, H. *Die Anthropologie Philons von Alexandreia*. Würzburg 1933, (Quoted after Hoffmann, 1966.)

Schmidt, J. M., *Die jüdische Apokalyptik*. Die Geschichte ihrer Erforschung von den Anfängen bis zu den Textfunden von Qumran. Neukirchen 1969.

Schmidt, K. L., διασπορα . *TWNT* II (1935) 98-104.

Schmidt, N., Bible Canon, *JewEnc* III (1903) 140-54.

Schmitt, E., *Leben* in den Weisheitsbüchern Job, Sprüche und Jesus Sirach. (Freiburger theologische Studien 66.) Freiburg 1954.

Schniewind, J., *Das Evangelium nach Matthäus*. (Das NT Deutsch 2.) 5th ed. Göttingen 1950.

Schreiner, J., *Alttestamentlich-jüdische Apokalyptik*. Eine Einführung. (Bibl.Handbibliothek, 6.) München 1969.

Schreiter, J., *Philo's Ideen über Unsterblichkeit, Auferstehung und Vergeltung*. 1813. (Not available to me.)

Schubert, K., *Die Religion des nachbiblischen Judentums*. Freiburg, Wien 1955.

- Das Problem der Auferstehungshoffnung in den Qumrantexten und in der frührabbinischen Literatur, *WZKM* 56 (1960) 154-67.

- Die Entwicklung der Auferstehungslehre von den nachexilischen bis zur frührabbinischen Zeit, *BZ* 6 (1962) 177-214.

- *Die jüdischen Religionsparteien* in neutestamentlicher Zeit. (Stuttgarter Bibelstudien 43.) Stuttgart 1970.

Schürer, E., *Geschichte des jüdischen Volkes im Zeitalter Jesu Christi* I-III. (3rd and) 4th ed. Leipzig 1901-09.

Schütz, R., *Les idées eschatologiques du livre de la Sagesse*. Strasbourg 1935.

Schwab, M., See *Talmud*, under *Texts*.

Schwabe, M., Greek inscriptions found at Beth-Shearim 1953, *IEJ* 4 (1954) 249-261.

Schwally, F., *Das Leben nach dem Tode* nach den Vorstellungen des alten Israel und des Judentums einschliesslich des Volksglaubens im Zeitalter Christi. Eine biblisch-theologische Untersuchung. Giessen 1892.

Schweizer, E., υἱός C I. 1b-3. Hellenistisches Judentum, Septuaginta (b-d); Josephus, Philo, *TWNT* 8 (1969) 355-57.

- Die Leiblichkeit des Menschen: Leib-Tod-Auferstehung, *EvTh* 29 (1969) 40-55; EvTh 29.

Schwyzer, E., *Griechische Grammatik* auf der Grundlage von Karl Brugmanns griechischer Grammatik I-III. (Handbuch der Altertumswissenschaft II, 1:1-3.) München 1939-53.

Sellin, E., Die alttestamentliche Hoffnung auf Auferstehung und Ewiges Leben, *NKZ* 30 (1919) 232-89.

- Das *Zwölfprophetenbuch* übersetzt und erklärt. (Kommentar z.AT 12.) Leipzig 1929.

Sharpe, J. L., The Second Adam in the Apocalypse of Moses, *CBQ* 35 (1973) 35-46.

Shires, H. M., *The Eschatology of Paul* in the Light of Modern Scholarship. Philadelphia 1966.

Siegel, S., see Boyarin, D.

Simon, M., Berakhoth, *The Babylonian Talmud* . . . (under *Texts*). London 1948.

Sjöberg, E., *Der Menschensohn im äthiopischen Henochbuch*. (Skrifter, Kungliga Humanistiska Vetenskapssamfundet, Lund, 41.) Lund 1946.

- *Der verborgene Menschensohn in den Evangelien*. (Skrifter, Kungliga Humanistiska Vetenskapssamfundet, Lund, 53.)

Smith, G. A., The Book of *Isaiah* I-II. New and rev.ed. London 1927.

Smith, M., The Description of the Essenes in Josephus and the Philosophumena, *HUCA* 29 (1958) 273-313.

Snaith, N. H., *Leviticus and Numbers*. (The Century Bible N.S.) London . . . 1967.

Sperber, A., see *The Bible in Aramaic*, under *Texts*.

Spira, S., *Die Eschatologie der Juden* nach Talmud und Midrasch. Diss. Halle 1889.

Staerk, W., *Soter*. Die biblische Erlösererwartung als religionsgeschichtliches Problem. Eine biblisch-theologische Untersuchung, I. (Beiträge z.Förderung christlicher Theologie II, 31.) Gütersloh 1933.

Stalker, D. M. G., *Ezekiel*. Introduction and Commentary. (Torch Bible Commentaries.) London 1968.

Starcky, J., Psaumes apocryphes de la Grotte 4 de Qumran (4Q Ps^{f}VII-X), *RB* 73 (1966) 353-371.

Stauffer, E., *New Testament Theology*. London 1955. (ET of 5th German ed., Die Theologie des NTs, Gütersloh 1948.)

Steiner, A., Warum lebten die Essener asketisch? *BZ* 15 (1971) 1-28.

Stemberger, G., *Der Leib der Auferstehung*. Studien zur Anthropologie und Eschatologie des palästinischen Judentums im neutestamentlichen Zeitalter (ca. 170 v.Chr.-100 n. Chr.). Rome 1972.

- Das Problem der Auferstehung im AT, *Kairos* NF 14 (1972) 273-90.

- Zur Auferstehungslehre in der rabbinischen Literatur, *Kairos* 15 (1973) 238-66.

Stendahl, K., see *Immortality and Resurrection*.

Stenning, see The *Targum* of *Isaiah*, under *Texts*.

Stoebe, H. J., *Das erste Buch Samuelis*. (Kommentar z.AT 8:1.) Gütersloh 1973.

Stola, R., Zu den Jenseitsvorstellungen im Alten Mesopotamien, *Kairos* 14 (1972) 258-72.

Storset, B., *Hesekiel*, Kommentar till en profetbok. (Swedish translation of Norwegian original.) Stockholm 1970.

Strack, H., *Einleitung in Talmud und Midrasch*. 5th ed. München 1920.

-, Billerbeck, P., *Kommentar zum NT aus Talmud und Midrasch* I-IV (VI). München 1922-28 (1959).

Strecker, G., The Passion and Resurrection Predictions in Mark's Gospel, *Interpr* 22 (1968) 421-442. (in German in *ZThK* 64, 1967, 16-39.)

Strobel, A., *Kerygma und Apokalyptik*. Ein religionsgeschichtlicher und theologischer Beitrag zur Christusfrage. Göttingen 1967.

Strugnell, J., Flavius Josephus and the Essenes, *JBL* 77 (1960) 106-115.

Suarez, P. L., Escatologia personal en los antiquos persos, XV *SemBiblEsp* 1954 (1955) 1-20.

Sutcliffe, E., *The OT and the Future Life*. London 1946.

Swete, H. B., see *LXX* under *Texts*.

Talmon, S., Double Readings in the Massoretic Text, *Textus* 1 (1960) 144-84.

Taylor, J. B., *Ezekiel*. An Introduction and Commentary. (Tyndale OT Commentaries.) London 1969.

Taylor, R. J., The Eschatological Meaning of Life and Death in the Book of Wisdom I-V, *EThL* 42 (1966) 72-137. (Part of diss. Louvain 1965.)

Tcherikover, V., *Hellenistic Civilization and the Jews*. Philadelphia, Jerusalem 1959. (2nd ed. 1961.)

Teichmann, E., *Die paulinischen Vorstellungen von Auferstehung und Gericht und ihre Beziehung zur jüdischen Apokalyptik*. Freiburg i.Br., Leipzig 1896.

Testuz, M., *Les idées religieuses du livre des Jubilés*. Geneve, Paris, 1960.

Thackeray, H. St. J. (1926), see *Josephus*, under *Texts*.

- *Josephus*. The Man and the Historian. (The Hilda Stich Stroock Lectures . . . at the Jewish Institute of Religion 2.) New York 1929).

Thoma, C., Die Weltanschauung des Josephus Flavius. Dargestellt anhand seiner Schilderung des jüdischen Aufstandes gegen Rom (66-73n. Chr.), *Kairos* 11 (1969) 39-52.

- Jüdische Apokalyptik am Ende des ersten nachchristlichen Jahrhunderts. Religionsgeschichtliche Bemerkungen zur syrischen Baruchapokalypse und zum Vierten Esrabuch, *Kairos* 11 (1969) 134-44.

Thomas, J., see Burchard, C., and others.

Tillich, P., *Systematic theology* I-III. Chicago, Welwyn, Toronto 1960-63.

Tischendorf, C.v., see *Collections* under *Texts*.

Tödt, H. E., *Der Menschensohn in der synoptischen Überlieferung*. Gütersloh 1959.

Torrey, C. C., *The Apocryphal Literature*. A brief introduction New Haven 1945.

Tournay, R., Relectures bibliques concernant la vie future et l'angélologie, *RB* 69 (1962) 481-505.

Towner, W. S., Form-Criticism of Rabbinic Literature, *JJS* 24 (1973) 101-118.

Townshend, R. B., 4 Maccabees, *Charles A P* II (1913) 653-85.

Tregelles, S. P., *Remarks on the Prophetic Visions of Daniel*. 7th ed. London 1965. (4th ed. 1852, 5th ed. 1864.)

Tromp, N. J., *Primitive Conceptions of Death and the Nether World in the OT*. (Biblica et Orientalia 21.) Rome 1969.

Turner, N., The "Testament of Abraham": Problems in Biblical Greek, *NTS* 1 (1954/5) 219-23.

Vaillant, A., see *II En*, under *Texts*.

Vaux, R. de, Esséniens ou Zélotes? A propos d'un livre récent, *RB* 73 (1966) 212-35.

Vawter, B., Intimations of Immortality and the OT, *JBL* 91 (1972) 158-71.

Vermes, G., Quelques traditions de la communauté de Qumran d'apres les manuscrits de l'Université Hébraique, *Cahiers Sioniens* 9 (1955) 25-58.

Vidler, A. R., *Christian Belief*. A course of open lectures delivered in the University of Cambridge. London 1950.

Vielhauer, P., Apokalypsen und Verwandtes, Einleitung, HS II (3rd ed. 1965).

- Gottesreich und Menschensohn in der Verkündigung Jesu, *Festschrift für G. Dehn.* Neukirchen 1957, 51-79.

Violet, B., see *IV Ezr,* under *Texts.*

Viteau, J., see *PsSol,* under *Texts.*

Vogt, E., Einige Werke über die Qumrantexte, *Bibl* 38 (1957) 461-69.

Volkmann, H., Hellenismus, *DkP* II (1967) 1009 f.

Volz, P., *Die Eschatologie der jüdischen Gemeinde* im neutestamentlichen Zeitalter nach den Quellen der rabbinischen, apokalyptischen und apokryphen Literatur. Tübingen 1934. (2nd ed. of *Jüdische Eschatologie von Daniel bis Akiba.*)

Wächter, L., Der Tod im AT. (Arbeiten zur Theologie, II, 8. Habil. Rostock 1964.) Stuttgart 1967.

Wahle, H., Die Lehren des rabbinischen Judentums über das Leben nach dem Tode, *Kairos* 14 (1973) 291-309.

Wallach, L., The Parable of the Blind and the Lame, *JBL* 62 (1943) 333-39.

Ward, J. M., *Hosea.* A Theological Commentary. New York 1966.

Weber, F., *Jüdische Theologie* auf Grund des Talmud und verwandter Schriften. 2nd ed. (F. Delitzsch, G. Schnedermann) Leipzig 1897.

Weber, W., Der Auferstehungsglaube im eschatologischen Buche der Weisheit Salomos, *ZWissTh* 54 (1912) 205-39.

Weiser, A., *Die Psalmen* I (1-60). (Das AT Deutsch 14/I.) Göttingen 1950.

Wells, L. S. A., The Books of Adam and Eve, *Charles AP* II (1913) 123-54.

Wendland, H. D., *Die Briefe an die Korinther.* (Das NT Deutsch 7.) 12th ed. Göttingen 1968.

Westermann, C., *Isaiah* 40-66. A Commentary. (The OT Library, ET of German ed. 1966.) London 1969.

Wevers, J. W., Septuaginta-Forschungen, *ThRu* 22 (1954) 85-138, 171-90.

- *Ezekiel.* (The Century Bible, NS.) London, New York 1969.

Whitaker, G. H., see *Philo,* under *Texts.*

Widengren, G., *Psalm 110* och det sakrala kungadömet i Israel. (Uppsala Universitets Årsskrift 1941: 7, 1.) Uppsala, Leipzig 1941.

- *The king and the tree of life* in ancient near eastern religions. (King and Saviour 4. Uppsala Universitets Årsskrift 1951:4.) Uppsala, Leipzig, Wiesbaden 1951.

- *Die Religionen Irans.* (Die Religionen der Menschheit 14.) Stuttgart 1965.

Wied, G., *Der Auferstehungsglaube des späten Israel* in seiner Bedeutung für das Verhältnis von Apokalyptik und Weisheit. Diss. Bonn 1965.

Wiencke, G., *Paulus über Jesu Tod.* Die Deutung des Todes Jesu bei Paulus und ihre Herkunft. (Beiträge zur Förderung christlicher Theologie.) Gütersloh 1939.

Wijngaards, J., Death and Resurrection in Covenantal Context (Hos. VI 2), *VT* 17 (1967) 226-39.

Wilcke, H. A., *Das Problem eines messianischen Zwischenreiches bei Paulus.* (Abhandlungen z. AuNT 51.) Zürich, Stuttgart 1967.

Wilckens, U., Die Uberlieferungsgeschichte der Auferstehung Jesu, *Die Bedeutung der Auferstehungsbotschaft für den Glauben an Jesus Christus,* see Marxsen. P. 41-63.

Williams, H. A., *True Resurrection.* London 1972.

Wirgin, W., The *Menorah* as Symbol of After-Life, *IEJ* 14 (1964) 102-04.

Wischnitzer-Bernstein, R., The Conception of the Resurrection in the Ezekiel Panel of the Dura Synagogue, *JBL* 60 (1941) 43-55.

Wolff, H. W., *Jesaja* 53 im Urchristentum. 3rd ed. Berlin 1952.

- Dodekapropheton I, *Hosea.* (Biblischer Kommentar AT XIV, 1.) Neukirchen 1961.

242

Wolfson, H. A., *Philo. Foundations of religious philosophy in Judaism, Christianity and Islam, I-II.* 3 rd ed. Cambridge, Mass. 1962.

Wood, J. F., Isaac Typology in the NT, *NTS* 14 (1967/8) 583-89.

Wright, A. G., *The Literary Genre Midrash.* Staten Island, N.Y. 1967.

Wright, R., The Psalms of Solomon, the Pharisees and the Essenes, *SCS* 2 (1972) 136-54.

Wünsche, A., *Bibliotheca Rabbinica.* Eine Sammlung alter Midraschim . . . I-Leipzig 1880-

Young, E. J., The Book of *Isaiah.* The English Text with Introduction, Exposition and Notes, II (19-39). Grand Rapids, Mich. 1969.

Zeitlin, S., The Account of the Essenes in Flavius Josephus and the Philosophoumena, *JQR* 49 (1958) 292-300.

Zeller, H., Corpora Sanctorum: Eine Studie zu Mt 27, 52-3, *ZkTh* 71 (1949) 385-465.

Ziegler, J., see *LXX,* under *Texts.*

Zimmerli, W., "Leben" und "Tod" im Buche des Propheten Ezechiel, *ThZ* 13 (1957) 494-508.

- *Ezechiel* II. (Biblischer Kommentar AT XIII, 2. Ez 25-48.) Neukirchen 1963.

-, Jeremias, J., *The Servant of God.* Rev.ed. London 1965.

- *Man and his hope in the OT.* (Studies in Biblical Theology, Series II, 20.) London 1971. (ET of *Der Mensch und seine Hoffnung im AT,* Göttingen 1968.)

Zimmermann, F., Book of Wisdom. Its Language and Character, *JQR* 57 (1966/7) 1-27, 101-35.

INDICES

I. Index of authors

Aalen, S., 3.2 n.25; 4.1.2; 4.4 n.4; 6.1
Abba, R., 7.4 n.1.
Adam, A., 3.6 nn.9.11(bis).
Ahlbrecht, A., 1 n.3.
Albeck, C., 5.n.20.
Alfrink, B., 2.2 n.15; 2.2 n.16.
Allegro, J.M., 3.5 n.43.
Anderson, G.W., 4.1 nn.22,24; 5.8.3.
Avigad, N., 3.14 n.11; 4.12 nn.11,12.

Bacher, W., 2.2 n.10; 5 n.32; 5.4.2 (bis); 5.4.3; 7.4 n.9.
Balz, H.R., 3.2. n.49.
Bardtke, H., 3.5 n.26.
Barr, J., 4.3 n.27.
Barrett, C.K., 2.1 n.24; 4.1 n.22.
Barth, C., 2.1.1; 2.1 nn.5,6,9,21 (bis); 3.5 n.35; 4.1 n.10; 5.8 n.21.
Barthelemy, D., 4.1 nn.25,33 (ter).
Batiffol, P., 4.9 nn.4,17.
Baudissin, W.v., 2.1 n.23; 5.8 n.19.
Bauernfeind, O., 4.6.3; 4.6 nn.8,9,10,11,12,17; 7.2 n.28
Becker, J., 3.3 (bis); 3.3.3; 3.3 nn.1,3,5,6 (bis),8,11,22 (bis),27.
Beek, M.A., 2.2 n.11; 4.1 n.24.
Bees, N.A., 4.12.5; 4.12 nn.2,9,17.
Beltrami, A., 4.8 nn.4,20 (bis).
Bentzen, A., 2.2 nn. 3,20,22.
Beresford, A.J., 1 n.23; 2.2 nn.11,17; 3.1 n.11; 3.5.4; 3.5 nn.3,31; 3.6 n.5; 3.7 n.14; 3.8 n.25; 4.1 nn.15,18,20,22,26,35; 4.4 nn.25,26,32; 5.8 n.19; 6; 6 nn.1 (bis),2,6,7,10,12.
Berger, K., 3.5 n.40.
Bernays, J., 4.8 nn.1,4,5,6,10,11,20,21.
Bertholet, A., 4.1 n.26.
Bertram, G., 4.1.3.
Bianchi, U., 3.6 n.17.
Bickerman, E.J., 4.3 n.4.
Bietenhard, H., 7.4 n.1.
Billerbeck, P., 1.1.4; 1 n.19; 4.12 n.16; 5; 5.5; 5.8.3; 5.8 n.8; 7.2.3.6; 7.2 n.9.
Birkeland, H., 2.1 n.25; 4.1 nn.22.26; 5.8 n.19.
Black, M., 3.2 nn.3,4,5; 3.5 n.2; 3.6.2; 3.6 n.5 (bis),11; 5.8 nn.16,17.
Blackman, P., 5.2; 5 nn.15,16.
Böhl, F.M.T., 7.2 n.20.
Böklen, E., 2.1 n.24.
Bogaert, P., 3.8 nn.3,4; 3.10 nn.1,4,5,11,12,21,27,22,27,30.
Bonner, C., 3.2 n.3; 3.13 n.3.
Bonnet, H., 2.1 n.22.
Bonsirven, J., 1.1.4; 5.8 n.15.
Bonwetsch, G.N., 3.11 n.12; 4.11 nn.3,5.
Bornkamm, G., 5 n.5.
Borsch, F.H., 3.2 n.49; 7.3 n.5.
Bousset, W., 1.1.4; 1 n.14; 2.2 n.14; 4.9 n.10.
Bowker, J., 5 n.35; 5.8.

245

Box, G.H., 3.9 n.18; 3.11.1; 3.11.2; 3.11 nn.1,2,3,5,6,10.
Boyarin, D., 5 n.14.
Braun, H., 3.5 n.3;
Brehier, E., 4.5 n.2.
Brock, S.P., 4.10 nn.6,9,10 (bis),11.
Brockington, L.H., 4.4 n.1.
Brooks, E.W., 4.9 nn.4,8,22.
Brownlee, W.H., 2.2 n.22.
Bruce, F.F., 2.2 nn.15,22; 3.5 nn.3,14; 4.6 n.6.
Brueggemann, W., 2.2 n.1.
Buber, S., 4.3 n.33.
Budde, K., 6 n.20.
Buchsei, F., 4.6 n.21.
Buckers, H., 4.2.1.2; 4.2 n.12; 4.4 nn.4,7,21,31,32; 6 n.20.
Buitkamp, J., 3.5 n.2.
Bultmann, R., 1 (bis); 1.1.1; 1 nn.3,6,7,; 3 n.6; 4.4 n.30; 4.5 n.7.
Burchard, C., 3.3 n.2 (bis); 4.9 (bis); 4.9 nn.2,3,5,6,8 (bis), 9,13.
Burkitt, F.C., 5.8 n.16.
Burns, J.B., 2.1 n.6.
Burrows, M., 3.5 n.1 (bis),3 (bis).

Campenhausen, H.v., 4.3 n.22.
Carmignac, J., 3.5 nn.4,31,33,37.
Causse, A., 2.1 n.24; 4.1 n.18.
Cavallin, H.C., 2.2 n.22; 3.3 n.28; 7.2 n.21.
Cazelles, H., 2.1 n.26; 3.1 n.5; 3.3 n.18; 3.5 n.3; 4.1 n.22; 7.2 n.20.
Ceriani, A.M., 3.7 n.1.
Charles, R.H., 1.1.4; 2.1 n.21; 2.2 nn.4,7; 3.1 nn.4,5,11; 3.2.4; 3.2.4.1 (ter); 3.2.4.2; 3.2.4.4; 3.2.4.5; 3.2.4.7; 3.2.5; 3.2.6.2; 3.2 nn.3,5,13,17,24,25,26,32,38; 3.3 nn.2 (ter),9,12,13,19, 20,21,25 (bis); 3.4 n.1; 3.10 nn.4,5,11,12,30; 4.1 nn.18,22,26; 5.8 n.19; 6 n.10 (bis),
Christ, F., 4.12 n.1.
Cohn, L., 3.8 nn.1,4,5.
Cohon, S.S., 2.1 nn.2,19,21.
Collins, J.J., 4.7 n.7; 7.4 n.1.
Colson, F.H., 4.5.1 (bis); 4.5.2 (bis); 4.5.3; 4.5.4; 4.5.6 (bis); 4.5 n.13.
Conzelmann, H., 3.10 n.16; 5.8 n.16.
Coppens, J., 2.1 n.21; 3.5 n.14; 4.1 n.9; 7.2 n.5.
Creed, J.M., 7.2 n.13.
Cullmann, O., 1.1; 1 nn.3,5.
Cumont, F., 7.2 n.3.

Dahood, M., 2.1 n.21 (bis); 4.1 n.9.
Dalbert, P., 4.7 n.17; 4.8 nn.1,3; 4.10 n.5.
Dalman, G., 2.2 n.22; 3.5.7; 3.14 n.6.
Danby, H., 5.2; 5 nn.15 (ter),17.
Daniel, C., 3.6 n.3.
Danielou, J., 4.11 n.3.
Davenport, G.L., 3.1.1 (bis); 3.1.2; 3.1 nn.5,6,7,9,13,16,17,18.
Davidson, H.R.E., 4.6 n.7.
Deissmann, A., 4.3 nn.1,4 (bis),5,6,8.
Delcor, M., 2.2 nn.2,3,7,22; 2.3 n.4; 3.5 n.36; 3.8 nn.1,4; 4.10 (bis); 4.10 n.4.
Delling, G., 4.12 nn.7,8,9,10,16.
Denis, A.M., 2.2 n.26; 3.2 nn.1,5,13; 3.3 nn.1 (bis),2; 3.4 nn.1,2,3; 3.7 nn.3,4,5; 3.9 nn.1 (bis),2 (bis),3; 3.10 nn.1,2; 3.11 n.1; 3.12 n.2; 3.13.2 (bis); 3.13 nn.2 (bis), 10; 4.7 nn. 1,2,3,4,5,6,7,8,9,10; 4.8 nn.1,3,4,5,6,7. 4.9 nn.1,5,6,7,13; 4.10 nn.3,4; 4.11 nn.1,2,3,6; 6 nn.4,9,11; 7.3 n.7.

Dhorme, E., 4.1 n.18.
Dibelius, M., 5 n.5.
Dieterich, A., 4.8 nn.1,3,6,23.
Doeve, J.W., 1 n.5.
Dornseiff, F., 4.8 n.1.
Driver, G.R., 3.5 n.1; 7.2 n.20.
Driver, S.R., 4.1 n.20.
Dubarle, A.M., 3.5 n.36.
Du Mesnil de Buisson, R., 4.1 n.29.
Dupont-Sommer, A., 3.5 n.36; 4.3.7; 4.3 nn.1,3,4,5,7,10,14,15,26,28,29,30,32; 4.4 n.17.

Easton, B.S., 4.8 nn.2,3,8,13,14,15.
Edelmann, R., 4.1 n.22.
Edsman, C.M., 3.0.2; 3 n.8.
Eichrodt, W., 2 n.1; 2.1 nn.5,25; 4.1 nn.8,26; 5.8 n.19.
Eissfeldt, O., 3.2 nn.1,6,7; 3.4 n.4; 3.7; 3.7 nn.3,5; 3.8 nn.3,4; 4.2 nn.6,7; 4.3 n.5; 4.4 n.1;
    4.11 n.3; 6 nn.2,3,4,5,7,8.10.
Ekenberg, A., 4.1 n.5.
Elbogen, I., 5.3.1; 5 nn.24,26.
Elmgren, H., 4.5 nn.2,6,13,15,28 (bis),29.
Engnell, I., 2.2 n.22; 7.2 n.20; 7.3 n.6 (bis).
Erlandsson, S., 7.2 n.7.
Etheridge, J.W., 5.8.1 (bis).
Evans, C.F., 3.5 n.3; 5.8 n.17.

Farina, A., 4.8 nn.3,10,16,23.
Farmer, W.R., 5 n.42.
Feldman, L., 3.6.1; 4.5.2.1; 4.5 n.2; 4.6.2 (ter).
Festugiere, A.J., 4.3 n.30; 4.4 n.22.
Feuillet, A., 2.2 n.22; 4.1 n.9.
Fichtner, J., 4.4 nn.1,7,12,16,17,26,28.
Finkelstein, L., 4.1 n.22.
Fisch, S., 4.1 n.26.
Flemming, J., 3.2 n.3.
Flusser, D., 3 nn.1,2; 3.12 nn.1,6.
Foerster, W., 7.2 n.16.
Fohrer, G., 2.1 n.21 (bis); 2.2 n.11; 4.1 nn.9,18 (bis),22,24,26; 4.4 n.17; 5.8 nn.3,19; 7.2 n.20.
Forbes, N., 4.11.1 (ter); 4.11.3 (bis); 4.11 nn.3,8,10.
Freedman, H., 5 n.1.
Frend, W.H.C., 4.3 n.22; 4.6 n.18.
Frey, J.B., 1.1.4; 1 n.20; 3.3 n.6; 4.12; 4.12 n.1.
Friedlander, G., 4.3 n.33.
Friedmann, M., 3.10 n.22.
Friedrich, G., 5.8 nn.11,13.
Frost, S.B., 2.1 n.11; 7.2 n.20.
Fruchtel, U., 3.2 n.23; 4.5 n.2.
Fuchs, H., 3.12 nn.1,6.

Gärtner, B., 4.9 n.23.
Gärtner, E., 4.4 n.26.
Galling, K., 4.1 n.26.
Geffcken, J., 4.7 nn.1,6,7,14.
Gehman, H.S., 4.4.3.4; 4.4 n.5.
Gerleman, G., 4.1 nn.1,13,15,16,17; 4.10 n.2.
Ginsberg, H.L., 2.2 n.9; 2.2 nn.16,22.

Ginzberg, L., 4.1 n.31.
Glasson, T.F., 1 n.12; 2.1 n.27; 3.2 nn.16,19. (bis), 20,24.
Gnilka, J., 1 n.3.
Goldin, J., 6 n.15.
Goodenough, E.R., 4.5 nn.1,2,9,18,19,21,22,26; 4.12 n.1.
Goodrick, A.T.S., 4.4 nn.10,12,14,15,18,27,28.
Grassi, J., 4.1 n.30 (passim).
Gray, G.B., 3.4 n.1; 5.8 n.4.
Gregg, J.A.F., 4.4 n.7.
Grelot, P., 1 nn.10,22; 3.2.2.1; 3.2.4; 3.2.4.1; 3.2.4.2; 3.2.6.1; 3.2 nn.12,13,18,19,20,25;
    3.4 n.3; 3.6 n.5; 3.9 n.17; 3.14 n.7; 4.4 n.26; 7.3 n.3.
Greshake, G., 1 n.13.
Gressmann, H., 1.1.4; 7.2 n.20.
Grossfeld, B., 5.8 n.26.
Grundmann, W., 7.2 n.13.
Grunwald, M., 3.11 n.11.
Guhrt, J., 4.3 n.27.
Guillaumont, A., 3.6 nn.13,15.
Gunkel, H., 3.10 nn.5,13.
Haag, E., 4.1 n.26.
Hadas, M., 4.3.1 (bis); 4.3.5; 4.3.10; 4.3 nn.1 (bis),3,7,8,14 (bis),17,18,19,22,24,25,26.
Haller, W., 1 n.23.
Hammershaimb, E., 3.2.4 (bis); 3.2.4.1 (bis); 3.2.4.2; 3.2 nn.4,5,7,8,9,10,24,25,26,27,50,52;
    6 n.11.
Hanhart, K., 1 nn.13,23.
Harnack, A.v., 4.9 n.12.
Harnisch, W., 3.9 nn.2,3,17; 3.10 nn.1,28.
Harrington, D.J., 3.8 nn.2,4.
Harris, J.R., 4.3 n.4.
Hartman, L., 3 n.3; 3.1; 4.4 n.20; 5.8 nn.10,11.
Hartman. L.F., 2.3 nn.1,4.
Hedegård, D., 5.3.1; 5.24bis.
Heinemann, J., 5.3.1; 5 n.24.
Heinisch, P., 4.4 nn.7,10,12,16,18,26,28,33.
Hengel, M., 1.2.1; 1 nn.4,24; 2.2 n.21; 3 nn.8,11; 3.2 nn.2,18; 4.2 nn.1,2,3,4,23; 4.10 n.5.
Henry, M.-L., 4.1 nn.23,24,26; 5.8 n.3.
Herr, M.D., 5.4.3; 5.7; 5 n.34.
Hindley, J.C., 3.2 n.6.
Hölscher, G., 4.1 n.18.
Hoffmann, P., 1.1.4; 1 nn.13,23; 2.1 nn.5,6; 3.1.3; 3.1 nn.11,13,14,15,16; 3.2 nn.19 (ter),39;
    3.4 n.4; 3.6 n.5; 3.8.5; 3.8.8; 3.8 nn.12 (ter),17,18,20,25,26; 3.9 n.9; 3.10 nn.29,30; 3
    nn.4,7; 4.2 n.23; 4.3 nn.2,9,15,30; 4.5 nn.3,5,6; 5.5; 5 n.1 (bis).
Hofius, O., 4.3 n.34; 4.6 n.20.
Holl, K., 3.13 n.2 (bis).
Holm-Nielsen, S., 3.5 nn.31,34,37.
Holtz, T., 4.9 nn.2,3,9,25.
Hruby,K., 5 n.3.
Hulsbosch, A., 4.4 n.4 (bis).
Hultgård, A., 3.3.3; 3.3 nn.1,2,4; 3.9 n.16.
Humbert, P., 4.1 n.23.
Hurwitz, M.S., 4.8 nn.2,4.
Hutton, D.D., 4.1 n.30.

Iersel, B.v., 1 nn.1,8.
Israelstam, J., 5.1.

250

251

Rabin, C., 3.5.4; 3.5 nn.2,18,19,26,29,32.
Rad, G.v., 2 n.1; 2.1 nn.13,15; 2.2 nn.11,23; 7.2 n.14.
Rademacher, L., 3.2 n.3.
Rahlfs, A., 4.1.2; 4.3 n.14.
Rahnenfuhrer, D., 4.10; 4.10 nn.2,5.
Reese, J.M., 4.4.10; 4.4 nn.1,2,23,26.
Reider, J., 4.4 nn.7,28.
Rengstorf, K.H., 4.6 n.22; 5 n.3.
Rese, M., 7.3 n.6.
Reuss, J., 3.5 n.4.
Ridderbos, N.H., 2.1 n.21.
Riesenfeld, H., 2.1 n.23; 2.2 n.22; 4.1 nn.17,18,22,26,29,30 (ter),31; 5.8 n.19; 7.2 n.20.
Riessler, R., 3.7; 3.10 n.5; 3.12 nn.1,3,4; 4.9 n.8; 4.10 n.2.
Rigaux, B., 1.2; 1 n.13; 2.1 nn.21,26; 2.2 n.12.
Ringgren, H., 2.1 n.17; 3 n.1; 3.5 nn.4,12,20; 3.6 nn.5,14.
Rist, M., 2.2 n.23.
Robert, J. and L., 4.12 n.3.
Robinson, H.W., 7.2 nn.20,25.
Robinson, T.H., 2.1 n.23; 5.8 n.19.
Romaniuk, K., 4.4; 4.4.3.2.
Rossbroich, M., 4.8 nn.3 (bis),5,8,10,11,12,13,14,16,19,20.
Rost, L., 4.1 n.26.
Rowley, H.H., 3.2 n.21; 3.5 n.4.
Rubinstein, A., 3.11 nn.1,2.
Rudolph, W., 5.8 n.18.
Ruhle, O., 4.1 nn.18,22.
Russell, D.S., 1 n.18; 2.2 nn.16,17,22,23; 3.0.1; 3.0.6; 3 nn.1,2,3,4,5,9; 3.2 n.53; 3.3 n.1
    (bis); 3.4 nn. 1,2; 3.5 n.4; 3.7; 3.7 nn.3,5; 3.9 nn.1,2; 3.10 n.1; 3.11 n.1; 4.1 n.22;
    4.4 n.1; 4.7 nn.4,5,6,7,8; 4.11; 6 n.10.
Ryssel, V., 3.10 nn.4,5,11.

Sabourin, L., 3.8 n.1.
Salomonsen, B., 3 nn.8,11.
Sambursky, S., 4.8 n.22.
Sandmel, S., 4.5 n.2.
Sawyer, J.F.A., 4.1.1; 4.1 nn.4,5.
Schaller, B., 4.6 nn.1,2.
Schilling, O., 2.1 nn.17,21 (bis),25; 2.3 n.4; 4.1 nn.9,18,22; 4.4 n.4; 5.8 n.19; 7.2 n.20.
Schmid, H., 2.2 nn.12,22; 7.2 n.14.
Schmid, W., 4.6 nn.5,17.
Schmidt, F., 3.12 nn.3,9.
Schmidt, H., 4.5 nn.3,5.
Schmidt, J.M., 4.1 n.24.
Schmidt, K.L., 5.8.3.
Schmidt, N., 2.1 n.3.
Schmitt, E., 4.1.3.
Schniewind, J., 7.2 n.9.
Schreiner, J., 3 n.1; 3.2 n.2; 7.2 n.22.
Schreiter, J.C., 4.5 n.15.
Schubert, K., 1.1.3; 1.1.4 (bis); 1 nn.17,21 (bis); 2.1 nn.6,22 (bis); 2.2 n.11; 3 n.12; 3.1
    nn.11,13; 3.2 nn.11,15,21,28; 3.3 n.16; 3.5 nn.1,2 (ter),26 (bis),30; 3.8 n.17; 3.9 n.10
    (bis); 4.1 n.22 (bis); 5 n.3; 6 n.13.
Schurer, E., 4.11 n.3; 5 n.3.
Schutz, R., 4.4 nn.1,4.
Schwab, M., 3.14 n.11.
Schwally, F., 1 n.23; 2.1 n.5.

252

Schweizer, E., 4.4 n.17.
Schwyzer, E., 4.4 n.11.
Sellin, E., 2.1 nn.18,21 (bis); 4.1 nn.9,23 (bis); 5.8 nn.18,19 (ter); 7.2 n.3.
Sharpe, J.L., 3.7 n.14.
Shires, H.M., 1 n.1; 3 n.6.
Short, C., 3.8 n.13.
Siegel, S., 5 n.14.
Simon, M., 5.3.2.
Sjöberg, E., 3.2 nn.7,49,50; 7.3 nn.5,6 (bis).
Smith, G.A., 7.2.1.1; 7.2 n.7.
Smith, M., 3.6 nn.5,8.
Snaith, N.H., 7.2 n.6.
Sperber, A., 5.8 n.26.
Spira, S., 1 n.23.
Staerk, W., 2.2 n.22.
Stalker, D.M.G., 4.1 n.26.
Starcky, J., 3.5 n.43.
Stauffer, E., 1 n.3.
Steiner, A., 3.6 nn.13,15.
Stemberger, G., 1.1.4; 1.2; 1.2.3; 1 nn.1,24 (bis),25; 2.1 n.17; 3.2.3.3; 3.2.3.6; 3.2 nn.12,18,
    24,25,26,31,34,39,42,43,44,53; 3.3; 3.3.1 (bis); 3.3.2; 3.3.3; 3.3.5; 3.3 nn.1,2,3,17,18; 3.4.1
    (bis); 3.4 nn.1,2,3,4,5; 3.8 nn.1,3,6,7,8,9,10,11,12 (bis); 3.9 nn.1,2,3,4,9,11; 3.10 nn.5,6,7,
    8,9,15,18,27,28; 3.13 n.1; 4.1 nn.9,18; 4.2.1.1; 4.2 nn.9,13,14,16,17,22 (bis),23; 4.7 n.16;
    5 nn.2,23,24 (bis),26,35; 5.4.2 (bis); 5.8; 5.8 nn.15,19,24.
Stenning, J.F., 5.8.3 (bis).
Stoebe, H.J., 2.1 n.15.
Stola, R., 2.1 n.22.
Storset, B., 4.1 n.26.
Strack, H., 3.14 n.4; 4.1.2; 5 nn.31,40; 5.4.1; 5.4.2; 5.4.3; 5.8 n.14.
Strecker, G., 5.8 n.16.
Strobel, A., 3 n.6; 3.2 n.49.
Strugnell, J., 3.6 n.5.
Suarez, P.L., 2.1 n.24.
Sutcliffe, E., 2.1 n.21; 2.2 nn.1,10,11; 3.3 n.15; 4.1.3; 4.1 nn.18,22,26; 5.8 n.3.
Swete, H.B., 4.3 n.14.

Talmon, S., 2.2 n.5.
Taylor, J.B., 4.1 n.26.
Taylor, R.J., 4.4 nn.4,26.
Tcherikover, V., 4.2 nn.1,3,5; 4.3 n.3.
Teichmann, E., 1 n.1.
Testuz, M., 3.1; 3.1.3; 3.1 nn.3,4,11; 3.6.1.
Thackeray, H.St.J., 3.6.1; 4.6.1; 4.6.2.1; 4.6.4.1; 4.6.5; 4.6 nn.1,2,3 (bis),7,13,17,18,19; 6 nn.
    25,26.
Thoma, C., 3.9 n.2; 3.10 n.2; 4.5 n.17.
Thomas, J., 3.3 n.2.
Tillich, P., 1 n.5.
Tischendorf, C.v., 3.7 n.1.
Tödt, H.E., 5.8 n.16.
Torrey, C.C., 4.10 n.2.
Tournay, R., 2.2 nn.9,22; 3.5 n.4; 4.1.3 (bis); 4.1 nn.1,4,7,16,19,22,33 (bis).
Towner, W.S., 3.8 nn.1,4.
Townshend, R.B., 4.3.6; 4.3 nn.4,5,6,14,25.
Tregelles, S.P., 2.2 n.15.

Tromp, N.J., 2.1 nn.5,6,7,15.
Turner, N., 3.12 nn.1,3,4,5.

Vaillant, A., 4.11.1 (quater); 4.11 nn.1,2,3,4,8,10.
Vaux, R.de, 3.5 n.1.
Vawter, B., 2.1 n.21; 4.1 n.10.
Vermes, G., 3.5 n.26.
Vidler, A.R., 1 n.5.
Vielhauer, P., 3 n.2; 3.2 n.6.
Violet, B., 3.8 n.3; 3.9 nn.6,7,8,11,13,14; 3.10 nn.5,27.
Viteau, J., 3.4 nn.1,2,3.
Vogt, E., 3.5 nn.4,31,37.
Volkmann, H., 3 n.10.
Volz, P., 1.1.4; 1.2.2; 2.2 n.13; 3.1.3; 3.1.5; 3.1 nn.5,6,11,12,15,16; 3.2.6.2; 3.2 n.49; 3.3 n.
    15; 3.4 nn.1,4; 3.7 n.9; 3.10 n.9; 3.11 n.5; 4.1.2; 4.1 nn.21,22; 4.3 n.4; 4.5 n.6; 4.10
    n.16; 6.10 (bis); 7.2 n.20.

Wächter, L., 2.1 nn.21,24; 4.1 nn.10.18.22: 7.2 n.20.
Wahle, H., 5.1.2.2; 5 nn.2,27,40.
Wallach, L., 3.13 n.2 (bis).
Ward, J.M., 5.8 nn.18,19.
Watzinger, C., 3.14 n.10.
Weber, F., 1 n.18.
Weber, W., 4.4 nn.4,7.
Weiser, A., 2.1 n.21.
Wells, L.S.A., 4.7 nn.3,4,5,10.
Wendland, H.D., 1 n.10; 5.8 n.16.
Westermann, C., 7.2 n.20.
Wevers, J.W., 4.1 nn.26,33.
Whitaker, G.H., 4.5.1; 4.5.2; 4.5.6 (bis).
Widengren, G., 2.1 n.22; 4.10 n.15; 7.2 n.5.
Wied, G., 1 n.23; 2.1 n.21; 2.2 nn.9,16; 2.3 n.4; 3.2 nn.12,25,26; 4.1.3; 4.1 n.18; 4.2 n.17; 5.
    8 nn.3,19; 6 n.1.
Wiencke, G., 2.2 n.22.
Wijngaards, J., 5.8 n.19.
Wilcke, H.A., 3.9 nn.15,17; 3.10 n.29.
Wilckens, U., 1.2; 1 nn.1,10; 2.1; 2.1 nn.19,25,26; 2.2 n.12; 3.1 n.13; 3.2 nn.16,18; 3.9 n.17;
    3.10 n.10.
Williams, H.A., 1 n.3.
Wischnitzer-Bernstein, R., 4.1 nn.26,29.
Wolff, H.W., 2.2 n.22; 4.1 n.22; 5.8 nn.18,19.
Wolfson, H.A., 4.5 n.2.
Wood, J.F., 4.3 n.34; 4.6 n.20; 5.8 n.16.
Wright, A.G., 3.8 n.1.
Wright, R., 3.4 n.4.

Young, E.J., 4.1 n.22; 5.8 n.4.

Zeitlin, S., 3.1 n.7; 3.6 n.5.
Zeller, H., 4.1 n.30.
Ziegler, J., 4.1 n.28.
Zimmerli, W., 4.1 nn.18,26; 5.8 n.19; 7.2 n.20.
Zimmermann, F., 4.4 n.1.

II. Index of passages

255

12:1	2.2 (bis); 2.2.4; 7.4.1.
12:2-3	*2.2* (bis).
12:2f.	3.0.7; 3 n.14; 3.2.3; 3.2 n.26; 3.3.2; 3.4.1; 4.5.8; 7.4.3.
12:2	*2.2;* 2.2.3 (bis); 2.2 nn.1,9 (bis),10 (quater),15; 2.3; 3 nn.13,14; 3.3.1; 3.3.2; 3.3.4; 3.3 nn.14,18; 3.4.1; 3.5.4; 3.5.6; 3.5.7; 3.5 nn.28,42; 3.8 n.22; 3.9.2; 3.10.3; 4.4 n.9; 4.10 n.6; *5.1.2;* 5.1.2.2 (ter); 5.3.1; 5 n.28; 7.1 nn.20,22.
12:2a.	*2.2;* 2.2 n.15.
12:3	*2.2;* 2.2.3 (ter); 2.2 nn.20,22; 2.3; 3 n.14; 3.2.3.6; 3.2 nn.30,41; 3.8 n.14; 3.9.3; 4.4.3.3; 4.4 n.16; 4.5.8; 4.11 nn.3,9; 4.12 n.1; 7.2.1 (bis); 7.2.1.2; 7.2.3; 7.2.3.5; 7.2 n.9; 7.3 n.2.
12:4-13	2.2
12:4	2.2 n.9.
12:6	2.2
12:7	2.2
12:13	*2.3;* 2.3 n.3; 3.5.7 (bis); 3.14.3; 5 n.28; 7.2.3; 7.2 n.16; 7.3 n.4.

I Chr (First book of Chronicles)

1:44f.	4.10 n.7.
29:28	2.1 n.10.

TARGUM

Gn

4:8	6 n.17.
25:29	6 n.18.
25:34	6 n.18.
30:22	5.8 n.15.

Ex

20:18	5.8.3; 5.8 n.12.

Nm

24:17	7.2 n.6.

Dt

32:39	*5.8.1.*

Tg Jon (Jonathan to the Prophets) 5.8.2 (bis); 5.8.3 (quater); 5.8.4.

Jg

5:31	7.2 n.9.

I Sm

2:6	*5.8.2.*
25:29	*5.8.2.*

Is

19:21	5.8.3.
25:8a	*5.8.3.*
26:14	4.1 n.24.
26:19	*5.8.3* (bis); 7.2.1.
27:12-13	2.2 n.25; *5.8.3* (bis)
27:12f.	3.2 n.11.
27:12	*5.8.3* (bis).
27:13	4.1 n.32; *5.8.3.*

Ez

37	5 n.7.
37:1-14	5.8 n.15.

Hos	
6:2	*5.8.4.*
Hagiographa	5.8 n.26.
Ps	
1:5	*5.8.5.*
22:30	*5.8.5.*
49:16	*5.8.5.*
65:9	*5.8.5.*
Job	
14:12-14	*5.8.6.*
19:25-26	*5.8.6.*
Prv	
12:28	4.1 n.4.

LXX (In the order of Rahlfs' ed.)
LXX	4; *4.1;* 4.3 n.27; 4.8 n.9; 4.9 n.12; 4.10 nn.2,14; 5.8.1; 5.8.3 (quater); 5.8.5 (ter); 5.8 n.3.
Gn	
2:7	4.8 n.17.
26:8	4.3 n.27.
Ex	
20:12	4.3 n.27.
Dt	
5:16	4.3 n.27.
32:39	*4.1.1* (bis); *4.1.7* (ter); 4.3.10.4.
33:3b.	*4.3.9.*
IV Ki (Fourth book of Kings)	
2:11	4.10 n.14.
Judith	6.1.
16:17	6 n.2.
Tob (Tobith)	6.1 (bis)

I Mcc (First book of Maccabees) 6.1 (bis); 6 nn.6,13.

II Mcc (Second book of Maccabees) *4.2;* 4.2.3 (bis); 4.3 (bis); 4.3 nn.3,4; 4.5.8; 7.1 n.1; 7.2.3.5; 7.3.3; 7.4.3 (passim).
2:23f.	4.2.
6-7	4.3.
6:18-31	4.2; 4.2.1.1.
6:26	*4.2.1.1.*
7	4.2; 4.2.1.2; 4.2 nn.2,13; 4.5.8; 7.1 n.8; 7.2.3.5; 7.3.1.
7:9	4.6.2.
7:9b-11	4.2.1.2.
7:96	*4.2.1.2.*
7:10-11	*4.2.1.2* (bis); 4.2 n.17.
7:11	3.10 n.12; *4.2.1.2;* 4.2.1.3.
7:14	*4.2.1.2* (bis); 4.3.2 (bis); 7.4 n.5.
7:22f.	*4.2.1.2* (bis).
7:22	*4.2.1.2;* 4.2.1.3.
7:36	*4.2.1.2* (bis).
7:37	4.3.6.
8:17	4.2 n.3.
12:43-45	4.2; 4.2.2.

12:43b-45	*4.2.2.*
14:37-46	4.2; 4.2.1.3.
14:46	3.10 n.13; *4.2.1.3;* 4.2 n.17; 7.1 n.8.
15:12-16	4.2; *4.2.3;* 7.2 n.24.

III Mcc (Third book of Maccabees)   6.1.

IV Mcc (Fourth book of Maccabees)   *4.3* (passim); 4.3.2; 4.3.4; 4.3.5 (bis); 4.3.6; 4.3.7; 4.3.10; 4.5.1; 4.5.8; 4.6 n.18; 7.1.8; 7.1 n.23; 7.2.3.3; 7.2.3.5 (bis); 7.2 n.23; 7.3.1; 7.3.3; 7.4.3; 7.4 nn.4,9.

1:1-3:18	4.3 n.1.
1:1	4.3; 4.3 n.21.
5-6	4.3.1.
6:17	4.3 n.21.
6:22	4.3 n.21.
7	4.3.1.
7:11f.	4.3 n.21.
7:18-19	*4.3.1.*
7:18f.	4.3.7.
7:19	4.3 n.21.
9:7-9	*4.3.1.*
9:9	7.4 n.6.
9:21f.	*4.3.6* (bis), 7.4.4.
9:21	4.3 n.21.
9:22	4.3.6 (ter); 7.2 n.l.
9:24	4.3.6.
10:11	4.3.2.
10:15	*4.3.2* (bis); 4.3.6; 7.4 n.5.
12:12	4.3.2.
13:14-17	7.1 n.17.
13:15	4.3.2.
13:16-17	4.3 n.21.
13:16	4.3.3.
13:17	*4.3.3;* 4.3.7; 7.2.3.4.
14:5-6	*4.3.4.*
14:7-8	4.3 n.29.
15:3	*4.3.2.*
16:3	4.3 n.21.
16:13	*4.3.4.*
16:16-23	4.3.1.
16:19-20	4.3 n.21.
16:20	4.3.7.
16:21	4.3 n.21.
16:25	*4.3.1;* 4.3.7; 4.3 n.21.
17:4-6	*4.3.7.*
17:4	*4.3.7;* 4.3 n.21.
17:5	*4.3.7;* 7.2.1.2.
17:6	*4.3.7;* 4.3 n.21.
17:12	*4.3.6.*
17:18f.	*4.3.9.*
17:18	*4.3.9;* 7.4.3.
18:1	4.3 n.21.
18:3	*4.3.8;* 4.8 n.10; 7.4.3.
18:11	4.3.7; 4.3 n.21.
18:12	4.3 n.21 (bis).

6:22-25	4.4.9.
7:1-8:16	4.4.9.
8:13	*4.4 n.24.*
8:17c.	*4.4.9.*
8:19-21a.	*4.4.9.*
8:19	4.3.5; *4.4.9.*
9:15	*4.4.10.*
10-12	4.4.11.
13-15	4.4.11.
13:11-19	3.11.5.
15:1-2	4.4.11.
15:3	*4.4.11;* 4.4 n.31.
15:8	4.4 n.11.
16	4.4.12.
16:12b-14	*4.4.12.*

Sir (Siracides, Ecclesiasticus)   6.1 (bis); 6 nn.1,13.

7:17	6 n.1.
17:30	4.3 n.16.
48:11	6 n.1.

Ps Sol (The psalms of Solomon) 3.4 (bis); 3.4.1; 3.4.5; 3.4 nn.4,5.

3	3.4.2.
3:10-12	2.2 n.10; *3.4.1;* 3.4.2; 3.4 n.5; 4.4 n.9.
3:10-12a.	7.4 n.5.
3:10	*3.4.1.*
3:11	*3.4.1* (bis); 4.4 n.5.
3:12	*3.4.1;* 4.11 n.9; 7.2 n.1; 7.3 n.1.
3:12b.	*3.4.1* (bis).
11:1f.	5.8 n.11.
13:9	3.4.3.
13:11	*3.4.3.*
13:11b.	3.4.3.
13:12	3.4.3.
14	3.4.4.
14:2	3.4 n.6.
14:3	*3.4.4.*
14:4	*3.4.4.*
14:5	*3.4.4.*
14:9	*3.4.4;* 7.4 n.7.
14:10	*3.4.4.*
15:1-3	3.4.2.
15:4-9	3.4.2.
15:4	3.4.2.
15:7	3.4.2.
15:10	*3.4.2.*
15:11	3.4.2.
15:12f.	4.4 n.9.
15:12	*3.4.2;* 7.1 nn.5,15.
15:13	3.4.3.
17:21ff.	3.9 n.16.
Hos	
6:1-3	4.1 n.33.
10:12	4.1 n.33.
Joel	
4:12	4.1 n.33.

Is
25:8a.   *5.8.3* (LXX, Theodotion, Pesh); 5.8 n.*5* (Aquila, Symmachus, Vulgate), *6* (Theodotion according to syro-hex.).
26:14   4.1 nn.24,25.
26:19   *4.1.5;* 4.1.7 (bis); 4.1 n.25; 7.1 n.8.
43:2   4.3.10; *4.3.10.1.*
53:11   2.2.3.

I Bar (Baruch, in LXX) 6.1; 6 n.5.
2:17   6 n.5.

Ep Jr (The Epistle of Jeremiah)
46   4.3 n.27

Ez
26:20   4.1 n.33
37   4.2 n.18.
37:1-14   *4.1.6;* 4.1.7. (quater); 4.1 nn.26,30; 7.1 n.8.
37:3   4.1.6.
37:6-8   4.1.6.
37:7   4.1.6; *4.1 n.30.*
37:10   4.1 n.30.
37:12-13   *4.1 n.30.*
37:14   4.1 n.30.

Dn
12:2 (LXX, Theodotion) 2.2 nn.4,6; 2.3 n.2; 3.3 n.14; 4.1.5; 4.1 n.30.
12:2b.   2.3 n.1.
12:3   2.3 n.1; 7.2 n.21.
12:13 (LXX, Theodotion) 2.3 nn.1,2; 4.3 n.31.

INDIVIDUAL WRITINGS - PSEUDEPIGRAPHA ETC.

Apc Abr (The Apocalypse of Abraham) 3.11; 3.11.1 (ter); 3.11.2; 3.11.4; 3.11.5; 3.11 n.5 (bis); 7.2 n.29.
1-8   3.11.5.
5   3.11.5.
13   *3.11.*
13-14   3.11.
20   3.11.
21   3.11.1; 3.11.3; 7.1 n.3.
22   3.11.
23   3.11.
29   3.11.
31   3.11.4.
31:1   5.8 n.11.

Apc Mos (The Apocalypse of Moses) 3.7 (bis)
10:2   3.7 nn.6,7; 7.1 n.5.
13:3b-6   *3.7.1.*
13:3b.   *3.7.1;* 3.7 nn.6,7; 7.1 n.5.
13:6   *3.7.1;* 3.7 n.8.
28   3.7 n.6.
32:4   *3.7.1;* 3.7 n.8; 7.2 n.17 (bis).
41:3   3.7 nn.6,7,8.
43:2   3.7.2; 3.7 nn.6,7; 7.1 n.5.

Apc Soph
4   4.9 n.10.

Ap Ez (Apocryphon Ezekiel) *3.13;* 3.13 n.2; 5.4.2; 7.1 n.23; 7.4 n.8.

Aristeas   6.1.

Asc Is   6.11 (bis).

Mart Is   6.1; 6 n.11.
2:9   6 n.11.
4:16f.   3.11 n.9.
8:14   3.11 n.9.
9:1-2,17f.,24-26 3.11 n.9.

Ass Mos (The Assumption of Moses) 6.1; 6 n.10 (ter).
6   6 n.10 (bis).
10:9   6 n.10.
10:10   6 n.10.
12:36   7.2 n.22.

II Bar (The Syriac Apocalypse of Baruch) 3.8; 3.8.1; 3.9 (ter); 3.9 n.2 (bis); *3.10;* 3.10.2.1.1
         (passim); 3.10 n.16; 4.7.3; 7.1 n.21; 7.2.3.5 (bis).
4:2-7   3.10 n.11.
6-10   3.10 n.2.
21:23f.   3.8 n.10.
21:23   3.10.1.1; *3.10 n.7;* 7.1 nn.2,13.
28-30   3.10 n.30.
28-29   3.9 n.16.
29-30   3.9.4.2; 7.1 n.19.
29   7.1 n.3.
29:1-8   3.10 n.30.
29:4-8   1 n.11; *3.10 n.26;* 7.4 n.11.
29:5   3.10.1 (bis); *3.10 n.26;* 4.5 n.16.
30   3.10.1.1; 3.10 n.8; 7.1 n.2.
30:1-5   *3.10.1.*
30:1   *3.10.1* (ter).
30:(1)2-5   3.10 n.30.
30:2-5   2.2 n.10.
30:2   3.8 n.17; *3.10.1;* 3.10.1.1; 3.10.3; 7.1 n.13.
30:4   *3.10.1;* 3.10 n.9; 7.4 n.5.
30:5   7.4 n.6.
42:7   3.8 n.10; *3.10.3;* 3.10 n.30 (bis); 7.3 n.1.
48-51   4.4 n.9.
48:47   3.10.2.3.
48:50   3.10.2.3.
49-52   3.10.2.3; 3.10.3; 3.10 n.30; 7.4 n.13.
49-51   *3.10.2;* 3.10.2.1.1; 3.10 n.8; 7.1 n.23.
49   3.10.2.1.1.
49:2   *3.10.2;* 3.10.2.3; 7.1 n.5.
49:3   *3.10.2;* 3.10 n.17.
49:3a   *3.10.2;* 3.10 n.17.
50-51   2.2 n.10; 3.10.1.1; 3.10.1.2; 3.10.1.3.
50   7.4 n.8.
50:2-4   1 n.11.
50:2-3   4.6 n.6; 7.4.2.
50:2   3.8 n.10; *3.10.2.*
50:3-4   3.10.2.1.
50:3f.   3.10.2.1.1.

L A B (PsPhilo, Liber Antiquitatum Biblicarum) 3.0.4; 3 n.9; *3.8;* 3.8.8; 3.8.10; 3.9; 3.10; 4.7.3; 7.1 n.1; 7.2 n.29.

3:10	*3.8.1;* 3.8 n.21; 4.4 n.9; 7.1 nn.6,11,15; 7.4 n.11.
4:11	3.8.2; 7.2.2.1.
10:5	7.2.1.1.
16:3	3.8.6.
19	3.8.9.
19:4	*3.8.9;* 4.11 n.9; 7.2 n.1.
19:6	3.8 n.4.
19:7	3.8.9.
19:10ff.	3.8 n.21.
19:12	*3.8.9;* 7.1 n.11.
19:13	*3.8.9.*
19:16	7.2.3.2.
22:10	3.8 n.25.
23:13	3.8 nn.12,17,25.
25:7	*3.8 n.25.*
28:3	3.8 n.12.
28:10	3.8 nn.21,*26.*
30:5	*3.8.4;* 7.2.2.1; 7.2 nn.10,18.
32:9	3.8.7; 3.8 n.14; 7.1 n.11; 7.2.2.1.
32:11	3.8.3.
32:13	3.8 nn.12,17,26.
33:2-9	7.4.3.
33:2ff.	3.8.5.
33:4	3.8 nn.12,15
33:5	*3.8.3;* 4.3 n.21; 7.2.1.1; 7.2.3.4.
40:3	3.8 n.26.
40:5-7	3.8.6.
40:5-7	3.8.6.
43:7	3.8 n.12.
44:10	3.8.8; 3.8 nn.12,26.
48:1	3.8.7; 3.8 n.20; 4.3 n.35; 7.2.3.1; 7.3.2.
51:5	3.8 nn.18,21,*26;* 7.2 n.1.
52:10	3.8 n.25.
54:6	3.8 ₁.12.
54:7	3.8 n.12
62:9	3.8.8; 3.8 nn.12,26.
62:9	*3.8.8;* 3.8 nn.12,26.
64:5-7	3.8 n.12.
64:6	3.8.8.

Mart Is (The Martyrdom of Isaiah) see Asc Is.

Od Sol

11:12	4.9 n.11.

Or Sib (The Sibylline Oracles) 4.7.2; 4.7.3 (bis); 4.7 n.17; 4.8 (bis); 4.10.

III	4.7 (bis); 4.7.2.
III, 66	4.7 n.17.
III, 663-697	4.7.2.
III, 663ff.	4.4 n.20.
III, 705ff.	4.7.2; 4.7 n.11.
III, 741-743	4.7.2.
III, 767-784	*4.7.2;* 4.7 n.11.
III, 767ff.	4.7 n.17; 7.1 n.3; *7.4.10.*

B 9	3.12.1.
B 11	3.12.3.
B 13	3.12.1.
B 14	3.12.2; 3.12.3; 7.2.2.3.

Test Job (The Testament of Job)   3.11.5; 4.10ff. (passim).

3:5	4.10.1.
4:9	*4.10.1;* 7.1 nn.6,11; 7.3 n.1.
33:2-9	4.10.2; *4.10.2.1;* 7.2.2.2.
39:12f.	*4.10.2;* 7.2.2.2.
39:12	4.10 n.11.
39:13	4.10 n.12.
40:3	*4.10.2;* 7.2.2.2; 7.2.2.3.
40:4	*4.10.1; 4.10 n.9.*
47:3	4.10.2.1.
52	4.10.2.1.
52:2ff.	*4.10.2;* 7.2.2.2.
52:2	*4.10.2;* 7.1 n.11.
52:9	*4.10.2* (bis); 4.10 n.14; 7.2.2.3.

Test XII Patr (The Testaments of the Twelve Patriarchs)   3.3; 3.3.5 (ter); 3.3 nn.1,2; 4.3.1; 7.3 n.7.

Sim	6:7	*3.3.1;* 4.4 n.9.
Levi		3.3 n.1.
	18	3.9 n.16
	18:3	7.2.1.1.
	18:9-14	3.3.3.
	18:10	3.3.3.
	18:11	3.3.3; 7.2.1.6.
	18:14	*3.3.3;* 7.2.1.6.
Jud	24-25	7.1 n.6.
	24:1-25:1	3.3.2.
	24	3.9 n.16.
	24:1	7.2.1.1.
	25:1	2.2 n.10; *3.3.1* (bis); 3.8.2; 4.4 n.9; 7.3 n.1.
	25:4	*3.3.2* (bis); 7.3 n.1 (bis).
Zeb	10:2	4.4 n.9.
	10:8	*3.3.1* (bis).
Dan	5:11ff.	*3.3.3;* 7.1 n.3.
	5:11f.	7.2.1.6.
	5:11	*3.3.3* (bis).
	5:12f.	3.3.3.
Napht		3.3 n.1.
Asher		3.3.4.
	2:7	3.3.5.
	6:5-6	*3.3.4* (bis); 3.5 n.10; 7.1 n.16.
	6:5	*3.3.4;* 7.4 n.6.
	6:6	*3.3.4;* 7.2 n.11; 7.3 n.1.
Benj	10:5-10	7.1 n.6.
	10:6-10	3.3 n.17.
	10:6f.	*3.3.1;* 3.8.2.
	10:6	3.8 n.14; 3.9.4.2; 4.4 n.9; 7.2.3.1.
	10:8	2.2 n.10; *3.3.2* (bis); 7.1 n.15; 7.3.2; 7.3 n.1 (bis); 7.4 n.8.

V A E (Vita Adae et Evae)   3.7 (bis); 3.7.2.

39:2	*3.7.2;* 3.7 n.10.

Posterit (De posteritate Caini)
39   4.5.2.1; 4.5 n.28.
43   4.5 nn.17,20.
122ff.   4.6 n.21.

Praem (De praemiis et poenis)
60   *4.5.2.1;* 7.1 n.16.
70   4.5 n.12; 7.1 n.10.
79-126   4.5 n.28.
110   4.5 n.28.

QGn (Quaestionum et solutionum in Genesim libri IV)
I,70   4.5 nn.12,28; 7.1 n.10.
I,75   4.5 nn.11,14bis,28; 7.1 n.10.
I,76   4.5 n.28.
I,85   4.5 nn.11,28.
I,86   4.5 nn.17,19,28.
II,8   4.5 nn.22,23.
III,11   4.5 nn.14bis,18.
III,27   4.5 n.28.
III,53-54   4.5 n.28.
IV,46   4.5 nn.12,14bis,28.
IV,66   4.5 nn.14bis,28.
IV,152f.   4.5 n.12; 7.1 n.10.
IV,152   4.5 n.14bis.
IV,153   4.5 n.11.
IV,164   4.5 nn.14bis,28.
IV,169   4.5 n.28.
IV,244   4.5 n.28.

QEx (Quaestionum et solutionum in Exodum libri II)
I,15   4.5 nn.14bis,28.
II,38   4.5 n.28.
II,39   4.5 n.28.
II,114   4.5 nn.22,23,28.

Sacr (De sacrificiis Abelis et Caini)
5   4.5.1; 4.5.6; 4.5 nn.6,28; 7.2.1.4; 7.2.3.
6f.   4.5 n.14bis.
6   4.5 n.18.
8   4.5 nn.19,28.
9   4.5 n.20.
129   4.5 nn.14bis,28.

Somn (De somniis)
I,151f.   4.5 n.13; 7.1 n.17.
I,164f.   4.5 n.20.
II,133   4.5.5.

SpecLeg (De specialibus legibus)
I,208   4.5 n.28.
I,303   4.5 n.28.
I,345   *4.5.1;* 4.5.2; 7.1 n.10.
II,262   4.5 n.28.

Virt (De virtutibus)
67f.   4.5 nn.19,20.
76   4.5 nn.19,20.

282

284

286

P R K
Achereth	5.8 n.8.
Wattha'mar Zion	2.3 n.3.

Seder Amram 5 n.24bis.

S Dt (Sifre on Dt)
§10 (to Dt 1:10)	4.12 n.1; 7.2 n.9.
§47 (to Dt 11:21)	7.2 n.9.
§306	5 n.7.

Shemone esre 5.3.1.
II	4.3 n.33; 4.9 n.11; 5.2.3; 5.8 n.24; 7.1.4; 7.1 n.11.
X	5.8.3; 5.8 n.11.

Shibbole ha-Leket
Buber 9b,18a.	4.3 n.33.

S Nm
§103	3.10 n.22.
§139	5 n.40; 5.8 n.2.

Tanch (Tanchuma)
Beresh 5	6.2.2.
Noah 10	5 n.8.
Wayyaza' 23B	5.8 n.15.
Wayyiqra' 12	3.13 n.1.
TanchB 3:8	3.12 n.1.

Tefillah (see Shemone esre)

INSCRIPTIONS

in Palestine	3.0.9; 3.14.
CIJ 476	*4.12.5;* 7.4 n.10.

For obvious space reasons this index does not contain other references to CIJ or Muller-Bees. They can almost all easily be found in 4.12 *supra.*

NEW TESTAMENT

Mt (The Gospel according to Matthew)   7.2 n.13.
2:2	7.2.1.1.
2:9f.	7.2.1.1.
2:20	4.3 n.11.
3:9	5.2.4; 7.2.3.6.
3:10	7.2 n.26.
5:3-10	4.11 n.4.
6:25	4.3 n.11.
7:13-14	3.12.1; 3.12 n.7.
8:11	4.3.3; 7.2 n.23.
10:39	4.3 n.11.
12:41	4.4 n.14.
13:43	3 n.14; 7.2 n.9.
16:25	4.3 n.11.
17:2	7.2.1.1.
19:28	4.6 n.21; 4.4 nn.8,14.
20:28	4.3 n.11.
22:16	6 n.15.
22:32	4.3.1.

23:8	6.2.2 (bis).
24:15	2.2 n.10; 3 n.14.
26:18	7.2 n.16.

Rm (Paul's letter to the Romans)

1:4	4.1 n.31.
4	3.11.5.
4:17	4.3 n.34; 4.6.4.1.
6:3-11	3.5 n.39.
7:23f.	3.10 n.17.
8:11	1 n.9; 4.1 n.31; 4.9 n.11.
8:17	4.3 n.21.
11:14	7.2. n.27.
11:16	7.2 n.28.
11:26	5.2.4; 7.2.3.6.
11:28	7.2.3.6.

I Cor (Paul's first letter to the Corinthians)   3.10.2.1.1; 3.10 n.16.

6:1-4	3.10 n.23.
6:2	4.4.8; 7.2 n.16.
6:14	1 n.9.
7:1ff.	3.6.3.
13:12	5.8 n.20.
15	1.1.2; 1.3.4; 1.3.4.1; 1.3.4.2; 1.3.4.4; 1 n.26; 2.2 n.18; 3.10.2.2.1 (bis); 3.10.2.2.1.1 (bis); 3.10.2.2.1.3; 3.10.2.2.1.4; 3.10.2.2.1.5; 3.10.2.2.2 (bis); 3.10 n.16; 4.2.2.1; 4.3.6; 5.4.4.
15:1-11	7.2.3.6.
15:4	*5.8.4.*
15:12-19	4.2.2.1.
15:20ff.	5 n.8.
15:20	3.10.4; 7.2 n.28.
15:22	4.9 n.11.
15:23ff.	3.3 n.17.
15:23	2.2 n.24; 7.2 n.28.
15:29	4.2.2.1; 4.2 n.21.
15:30-35	4.2.2.1.
15:35ff.	1.1.2; 1.3.4.3.
15:35	3.10.2.1.1.
15:36	3.2.4.5; 5.4.2.
15:37ff.	3.11 n.9.
15:40f.	7.2 n.9.
15:45b.	4.1 nn.30,31.
15:49	3.2.4.5; 3.10.4; 3.11 n.9.
15:50-54	4.3.6.
15:50	4.3.6; 4.3 n.21; 5 n.36.
15:51ff.	4.3 n.24.
15:51f.	3.10.2.1.1; 4.3.6.
15:51	3.3 n.19.
15:52	3.10.2.1.1; 4.3.6; 5.8 n.12.
15:53f.	3.2.4.5.
15:53	3.11 n.9.
15:54b.	5.8.3; 5.8 n.3.
15:58	4.2.2.1.

II Cor (Paul's second letter to the Corinthians)

3:6	4.1 n.31.
3:7-18	5.8 n.20.
4:14	1 n.9.

6:11	3.11 n.9.
7:9	3.11 n.9.
11:11	4.1 nn.30,31; 4.2 n.18.
11:13	4.1 nn.30,31.
13:8	4.9 n.10.
17:8	4.9 n.10.
20:3	3.9.4.2 (bis).
20:4	4.4 n.8.
20:12	4.9 n.10.
20:15	4.9 n.10.
21:4	5.8.3; 5.8 n.4 (bis).
21:27	4.9 n.10.
22:16	7.2.1.1.

NT APOCRYPHA

Desc Mariae (The descent of Mary into hell)
3	2.2 n.26; 5.8 n.12.

Ev Thom (The Gospel of Thomas)
22	3.6 n.17.
38	3.6 n.17.
51	4.9 n.23.
60	4.9 n.23.
79	3.6 n.17.
114	3.6 n.17.

THE APOSTOLIC FATHERS

Barn (The Epistle of Barnabas) 3.10.
11:9	3.10 n.2.
18-20	3.3 n.24.

Did (The Teaching, *didache,* of the Twelve Apostles)
1-6	3.3 n.24.
16:6	5.8 n.12.

Hermas, Mand (Mandates) 3.3.2.4.

Mart Pol (The Martyrdom of Polycarp)
15	*4.3.6* (bis).

OTHER EARLY CHRISTIAN WRITINGS

Clement of Alexandria, Strom (Stromateis)
III,47,3-48,1	3.6 n.17.

Exc ex Theod (Excerpta ex Theodoto)
65:2	4.9 n.23.

Hippolytus 3.6; 3.6.2.

Ref (Refutatio omnium haeresium, or Philosophoumena)
IX,18-28	3.6 n.11.
IX,18	3.6 n.12.
IX,27	*3.6.2; 3.6 n.9.*

Origen, Hom (Homilia) XXXV in Luc 3.5 n.40.

Synesius, Dio PG 66, 1120C   3.6 n.11.

Thomas of Celano, Dies irae v.3 5.8 n.12.

CLASSICAL AUTHORS

Aesopus   3.2 n.23.

Dio Chrysostomus   3.6 n.11.

Hesiod, Works 287-292   3.3 n.27.

Homer   4.8 n.9.

Inscr Gr (Inscriptiones Graecae) XII:7   4.3 n.30

Megasthenes, Indika   4.6 n.15.

P l a t o   7 n.1; 7.2.3.

Apology   4.6.4.

40 DE   4.6 n.14.

Gorgias
523A-527A   3.2 n.23.

Leg (Laws)
IX,873   4.6 n.10.

Phaedo   7.2.3.
60B   3.2 n.23.
61B   3.2 n.23.
81C   4.4 n.28.
87D   4.3 n.27.
105B-106E   7 n.1.
110B   4.3 n.12.
111E-114B   7 n.1.
113D-114B   4.3 n.12.
114D   4.3 n.12.

Phaedrus
237A   3.2 n.23.
247C-250C   4.5 n.10.

Republic
I,330D   3.2 n.23.
III,414B-415D   3.2 n.23.
X,608C-614A   4.4 n.2.

Symposium
211D-212A   4.5 n.10.

Pliny, Nat.Hist. (C.Plini Secvndi Naturalis Historiae libri XXXVII)
V,17   3.6 nn.11,12.

Xenophon, Mem (Memorabilia)
II,1:20-34   3.3 n.27.

III. Index of answers to questions (A) - (D) - background of table in 7.

Dn: *(A)*: 12:2f,13;
                 R: 12:13
                 RB: 12:2;
                 TH: 12:3;12:13?;
                 LD: 12:2f,13;
                 J: 12:2,

Jub: *(A)*: 23:30f;
                 IS: 23:30f;
                 Ri: 23:30f;
                 E: (23:27ff.);
                 LD: 23:30f;
                 J: 23:30f;

I En 83-90   *(A)*: 90:33;
                 R: 90:33;
                 LD: 90:33.

   1-36   *(A)*: 9+10+22+20:8;
                 R: 22+20:8;
                 IS: 22+9+10;
                 Int: 22;
                 Wic: 22+10;
                 LD: 22;
                 ADe: 9+10+22;
                 J: 9+10+22.

   91-104   *(A)*: 91+92+102+103; 100?
                 R: 91+92; 100?
                 IS: 102+103;
                 Wic: 103;
                 Ri: 102;
                 TH: 92+104;
                 Ass: 104;
                 LD: 91+92+100;
                 ADe: 103;
                 J: 91+103+104.

   37-71   *(A)*: 46+51+61;
                 R: 46;
                 RB: 51+61;
                 IS: 71?
                 Int: 51?
                 TE: 51;
                 TH: 51+68+62+71;
                 Ass: 71;
                 LD: 51+61+63;
                 ADe: 71?
                 J: 49-51+63.

   108   see table in 7.

Test XII Patr: *(A):* Sim 6+Zeb 10+Benj 10+Jud 25+Asher 6+Levi 18+Dan 5;
                      R: Sim 6+Zeb 10+Benj 10+Jud 25;
                      IS: Asher 6;
                      Wic: Asher 6;
                      TE: Dan 5;
                      T: Benj 10;
                      Ex: Benj 10;
                      LD: Sim 6+Benj 10+Jud 25+Levi 18+Dan 5;
                      ADe: Asher 6;
                      J: Zeb 10+Benj 10+Asher 6.

Ps Sol: *(A):* 3;
                      R: 3;
                      TH: 3;
                      LD: 3+14+15;
                      J: 3+13+14+15.

Q: *(A):* 4QPsDn+4Q181; 4QAmram?
                      Real: 1QS XI+1QH III+XI;
                      R: 4QpsDn+4Q181; 4QAmram?
                      E: 1QS IV+4QPsDn;
                      TH: 1QS IV+1QS XI+1QSb III+1QH XI+4Q181;
                      Ex: 1QH XI;
                      LD: 1QS IV; 1QH VI?
                      J: 1QS IV+4QPsDn+4QAmram+4Q181.

Essenes in   *(A):* BJ II,154ff.+Ant XVIII,18;
Josephus: *IS:* BJ II,154ff.+Ant XVIII,18;
                      Wic: BJ II,154ff;
                      InQ: BJ II,154ff.+Ant XVIII,18;
                      ADe: BJ II,154;
                      J: BJ II,154ff.

Essenes in   *(A):* Ref IX,27;
Hippolytus: *RB:* Ref IX,27;
                      IS: Ref IX,27;
                      InQ: Ref IX,27;

VAE+Apc Mos: *(A):* ApcMos 13+32+10+28+43+VAE 39+43+51;
                      R: ApcMos 13+10+28+43+VAE 51:2;
                      RB: ApcMos 13;
                      IS: ApcMos 13+32+41?
                      Int: ApcMos 13+32+41?
                      Ri: ApcMos 43;
                      T: ApcMos 13;
                      TH: VAE 39;
                      Enth: VAE 39;
                      LD: ApcMos 13+41+10+43;
                      ADe: ApcMos 13+32:4+43:2?

LAB: *(A):* 3+4+19+23+32+33+48+62;
                      Real: (30:5);
                      R: 3+19;
                      RB: 3?
                      IS: 23+32+62; 44+48?

	Co: 62;
	Ri: 23+32;
	TH: 19+33;
	H: 19;
	Ex: 4;
	Ass: 30;
	LD: 3+19;
	Ade: 19+62; 44?
	J: 19.

IV Ezr: *(A):* 7+4+14;
                R: 4+14;
                RB: 7;
                IS: 4+7;
                Int: 7+4;
                Co: 4+7;
                Wi: 7;
                Ri: 4;
                TH: 7+8;
                LD: 4+7;
                ADe: 4+7;
                J: 7+14.

II Bar: *(A):* 30+49-51+42+21;
                R: 21+30;
                *RB:*49-51+42;
                IS: 21+30;
                Int: 21+30;
                E: (29+73-74);
                TH: 51;
                Ex: 51;
                LD: 30+51+73+21+42;
                ADe: 21+30;
                J: 51+30+42.

ApcAbr: *(A):* 13; 21?
                RB: 13?
                E: 21;
                TH: 13;
                LD: 31;
                J: 13+31.

TestAbr: *(A):* A 1//B 4+A 7//B 13+*B* 14+A 11-13//B 8-11;
                IS: A 1//B 4+A 7//B 13+B 14÷A 11-13//B 8-11;
                Ass: B 14;
                ADe: A 1//B 4+A 7//B 13+B 14+A 11-13//B 8-11;
                J: A 11-13//B 8-11.

ApEz: One fragment - see table in 7.

InscrPal: *(A):* CIJ 964+874+875+965+966+972+892+900+988+143 ?? 13?
                    according to n.9; (CIJ 981+2 according to n.11); Bethphage cover?
                R: (CIJ 981+2 according to n.11); Bethphage cover?

LXX: *(A):* Job 14+19+42+Is 26+Ez 37; Dt 32+Ps 1+21(22)+48(49)+65(66)+Prv 9?
           R: Job 14+42; Dt 32+Ps 1+65?
           RB: Job 19+Is 26+Ez 37;
           IS: Ps 21+48?
           E: Ez 37;
           Ass: Ps 48;
           LD: Job 42+Is 26+Ez 37;Ps 1?
           ADe: Ps 21+48?
           J: Is 26+Ps 1+Prv 9+10+12+15.

II Mcc: *(A):* 6+7+12+14+15;
           R: 12;
           RB: 7+14;
           IS: 15?
           Co: 15;
           Ri: 15;
           ADe: 15;
           J: 6+12?

IV Mcc: *(A):* 7+16+9+10+12+13+15+13+14+18+17;
           IS: 18;
           Ri: 18;
           TH: 9+17+18;
           H: 9+18;
           Ass: 17;
           ADe: 7+16+13+14+18+9+17;
           J: 9+10+12+13.

Wi: *(A):* 3+4+5;
           IS: 3+4;
           Ri: 1+2+3+4+5+15;
           TH: 3+5;
           Ass: 4;
           LD: 3+5; 4?
           ADe: 3+5+4;
           J: 2+3+4+5.

Philo: *(A):* Opif 77+135+152+165+Praem 60+Gig 14+61+Vita cont 13+Sacr 5+
               LA I,105-108+II,57+III,41-44+Det 159+Heres 68-74+85+276+QGn I,
               85+IV,153;
           Real: Congr 57+SpecLeg I,345+Vita cont 13+LA I,107f+Praem 70+Legatio
               91+QGn I,70,75+IV,46+l52f;
           IS: Opif 77+135+152+165+LA I,105-108+II,57+III,41-44+Det 159+Gig 13-
               14+61+Heres 68-74+85+276+QGn I,85+IV,153+Vita cont 13+Sacr 5;
           Wic: Praem 60+Exsecr 152+Cher 2+Somn I, 151f+II,133; Opif 135+Insid 90;
           Ri: SpecLeg I,345+Opif 77+Gig 14+61;
           TH: Gig 14;
           InQ: 61+Sacr 5;
           Ass: Gig 61;
           LD: Exsecr 158f;
           ADe: Vita cont 13+Gig 14+61+Opif 152+LA I,108+II,57+III,44+Sacr 6f+
               129+Det 75+141+159+Legatio 91+QGn I,75+III,11+IV,46+66+152+
               164+QEx I,15;
           J: Praem 60+Exsecr 152+Cher 2+Somn I,151f+II,133.

Josephus: *(A):* BJ II,163+Ant XVIII,14+BJ I,648ff+III,362-382+Ant I,231+CAp 218f;
                   (BJ VI,46-48+VII,341ff);
                   R: Ant XVIII,14+CAp 218f;
                   RB: BJ II,163+III,374f;
                   IS: BJ II,163+Ant XVIII,14+BJ I,648+*III,372*,374f+Ant I,231; (BJ VI,46-48+
                   VII,341ff);
                   Int: BJ II,163+III 374f; Ant XVIII,14?
                   Co: BJ III,374f?
                   Wic: BJ II,163+Ant XVIII,14+BJ III,374f;
                   InQ: BJ II,163+Ant XVIII,14+BJ III,372; (BJ VII,341ff);
                   Ri: BJ I,648; CAp 218f; (BJ VI,46-48);
                   TH: (BJ VI,46-48+BJ VII,341ff);
                   H: BJ III,374f+Ant I,231;
                   LD: BJ III,374f+CAp 218f;
                   ADe: BJ II,163+Ant XVIII,14+BJ I,652+III,372ff+Ant I,231+CAp 218f;
                   (BJ VI,46-48+III,341ff);
                   J: BJ II,163+Ant XVIII,14+BJ III,374f.

OrSib   *(A):* IV,171ff; III,767ff?
                   RB: IV,171ff;
                   IS: III,771;
                   E: IV,171ff+III,767ff;
                   LD: IV,171ff+III,767ff;
                   J: IV,171ff+III,663-697, 741-743.

PsPhoc: *(A):* 103-108+115;
                   RB: 103;
                   IS: 105-108+115;
                   TH: 104,108;
                   LD: 103;
                   ADe: 105-108+115.

JA: *Real:* 8:10f+15+16+18+27;
                   R: 8+15+16+27;
                   RB: 16;
                   IS: 27;
                   Ri: 8;
                   TH: 18.

TestJob: *(A):* 4+39+52+33; 3+40?
                   R: 4; 40?
                   IS: 52; 3?
                   TH: 33;
                   Ass: 39+52;
                   Enth: 40 - *cf.*33;
                   LD: 4;
                   ADe: 33+52.

II En: *(A):* 8-10+42+61+65; (58);
                   R: 65?
                   IS: (58);
                   Wic: 61?
                   TH: 65+66;
                   LD: 61+65+66;
                   ADe: 8-10;
                   J: 8-10+58+66.

InscrDiasp: *(A):* CIJ 1510+1536; CIJ 1513+the inscriptions enumerated in nn.2,4,5,6?
              (CIJ 476);
              R: (CIJ 476); CIJ 1513?
              IS: CIJ *1510*+1536;
              E: (CIJ 476);
              LD: CIJ 1513?   (CIJ 476);
              ADe: CIJ 1510+1536;
              J: (CIJ 476?)

Rabbinica: *(A):* GnR 14:5//LvR 14:9+TSanh 13:3//RH 16b-17a+MSanh 10+Shemone
(Exc.Tg)   esre II+Ber 60b+Sanh 90b (two pericopes)+Sanh 90b-91a+Sanh 91a+
                Shab 152b; (Ber 28b);
              R: TSanh 13:3//RH 16b-17a+MSanh 10+Shemone esre II+Sanh 90b (two)+
                Sanh 91a;
              RB: GnR 14:5//LvR 14:9+Ber 60b+Sanh 90b-91a;
              IS: Shab 152b; (Ber 28b);
              Wic. Shab 152b; (Ber 28b);
              H: Shab 152b; (Ber 28b);
              LD: GnR 14:5//LvR 14:9+Shemone esre II+Ber 60b; (RH 16b);
              ADe: Shab 152b; (Ber 28b);
              J: TSanh 13:3//RH 16b-17a+MSanh 10+Shab 152b; (Ber 28b).

Tg: *(A):* Dt 32:39+I Sam 2:6+I Sm 25:29+Is 25:8+Is 26:19+Is 27:12f+
                Hos 6:2+Ps 22:30+Job 19:25f;
              R: Dt 32:39+I Sm 2:6+Is 27:12f+Hos 6:2+Ps 22:30;
              RB: Is 26:19;
              IS: I Sm 25:29+Ps 49:16+Ps 65:9;
              Int: I Sm 25:29;
              H: Hos 6:2;
              LD: Dt 32:39+Is 25:8+Is 26:19+Is 27:12f+Hos 6:2+Ps 1:5+Ps 65:9;
              ADe: I Sm 25:29;
              J: Is 26:19+I Sm 25:29+Ps 1:5+49:16.

IV. Index of persons

Aaron, 4.3 n.21.
Abbahu, 2.3 n.3.
Abel 3.12.1; 4.3.10 (bis).4.3 n.21.
Abraham, 3.0.1; 3.3.1 (bis); 3.11 (bis); 3.11.1 (bis); 3.11.2; 3.11.3 (bis); 3.11.5 (quater); 3.11
    nn.6,11; 3.12; 3.12.1 (bis); 3.12.2 (bis); 3.12.3; 4.3.1; 4.3.5 (quater); 4.3.6;
    4.3.7 (quinquies); 4.3 nn.21 (passim),33; 4.5.5; 4.5.6; 4.5 n.6; 4.6.4.1 (passim);
    4.10; 5.2.4; 7.2.1.4; 7.2.2.1; 7.2.3; 7.2.3.2; 7.2.3.3 (bis); 7.2.3.4; 7.2.3.5; 7.2.3.
    6; 7.3.3; 7.4.3; 7.4 n.3.
Adam, 3.7; 3.7.1 (bis); 3.7.2 (bis); 3.7 nn.6,8; 7.2.3.2.
Akiba, 3.14 n.4; 5.4.2; 5.8 n.12.
Alexander, 2.2; 3.0.5.
Alexander Jannaeus, 6 n.24.
Ammi, 5.4.3.
Amram, 3.5.5; 3.5 n.40 (passim).
Ananias, 4.3.10.
Antigonus of Soko, 6 n.15.
Antiochus III, 2.2
Antiochus IV Epiphanes, 2.1.5; 2.2 (bis).
Antoninus, 3.13; 3.13 n.3; 5.4.2.
Arsinoe, 4.12.3 (bis); 7.2.3.4.
Asenath, 3.11.5 (bis); 4.9 (ter); 4.9.1; 4.9.2 (quater); 4.9.3 (ter); 4.9.4 (bis); 4.9 nn.8 (bis),15;
    4.10; 7.2 n.22.
Ashi, 2.3 n.3; 5 n.28.
Azariah, 2.3 n.3 (bis).
Azarias, 4.3.10.
Azazel, 3.11 (bis); 3.11.2 (bis); 3.11 nn.5,6 (bis).
Benjamin, 4.9.3.
Boethus, 6 n.15 (bis).
Cain, 4.3.10; 4.3 n.21; 6.2.3.
Chiyya b.Abba, 5.1; 5 n.28.
Chiyya b.Joseph, 5.4.2.
Christ, 5 n.9; 7.2 n.28.
Cleopatra, 5.4.2 (passim); 5.4.3.
Dan, 4.9.3.
Daniel, 2.3 (ter); 2.3 n.3; 3.0.1; 4.3.10; 4.3 n.21 (bis); 7.2.3.
Deborah, 3.8.3; 3.8.4; 3.8.5 (bis); 7.2.1.1.
Dinah, 4.9.
Dokiel, 3.12.1.
Eleazar, 4.2.1.1 (bis); 4.3; 4.3.1.
Eleazar of Masada, 4.6.2.1; 4.6.4 (passim); 4.6.6 (bis); 4.6 n.14; 5 n.42; 7.1.6.
Eliezer, 5 n.40 (bis).
Eliezer b.Hyrkanus, 5.4.1; 5.4.2; 5.6 (passim); 5 nn.40,41; 5.8 n.1.
Eliezer b.R.Jose, 5.4.1; 5 n.40; 5.8 n.2.
Elijah, 2.1.2; 4.4.12; 4.10.2; 5 n.9; 7.2.2 (bis); 7.2.3; 7.3.2 (ter).
Elisha, 2.1.2; 4.4.12; 5 n.9; 6 n.19; 7.2 n.19.
Enoch, 2.1.2; 3.0.1; 3.2; 3.2.5; 3.2.6; 4.4.5; 4.5.5; 4.11.1 (ter); 7.2.2; 7.2.2.1 (bis); 7.2.3; 7.2.3.
    1; 7.3.2 (passim); 7.3.3; 7.4.3; 7.4 n.4.
Epiphanius, 3.13 n.3.
Epitomist, the, 4.2 (bis).
Esau, 6.2.3.
Eve, 3.7.1; 3.7.2; 3.7 n.6.
Ezekiel, 3.13; 5.1 (bis); 5.1.1; 5 nn.8,35; 5.8 n.1.
Gad, 4.9.3.

94